SMOKEY BEAR 20252
A BIOGRAPHY

D0743340

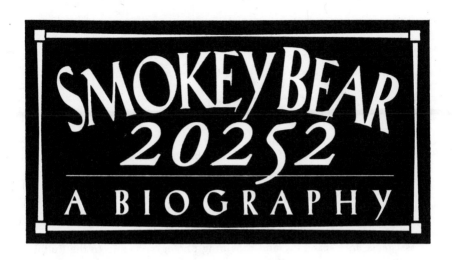

WILLIAM CLIFFORD LAWTER JR.

LINDSAY SMITH PUBLISHERS

Lindsay Smith Publishers
P.O. Box 30312
Alexandria, VA 22310-8312

FIRST CLOTH AND PAPER EDITIONS 1994
First printing 1994

Special thanks to Jean Pablo, Ph.D., curator of the 1994 Smokey Bear Exhibit, for her assistance in researching and providing photographs and to the Rudolph Wendelin Foundation for its support.

Manufactured in the United States of America.
Printed on recyled paper.

A portion of the proceeds from the sale of this book go toward furthering Smokey Bear's forest fire prevention efforts.

Library of Congress Cataloging-in-Publication Data

Lawter, William Clifford.
  Smokey Bear 20252: a biography / by William Clifford Lawter Jr.;
  [many photographs researched and provded by Jean Pablo]. — 1st
  cloth and paper eds.
       p.   cm.
  Includes bibliographical references and index.
   ISBN 0-9640017-0-5 (cloth). — ISBN 0-9640017-1-3 (paper)
   1. Advertising—Forest fire prevention. 2. Smokey Bear.
   I. Title. II. Title: Smokey Bear.
   HF6161.F618L38   1994
      634.9'618—dc20   94-5997
                                                          CIP

To Susan and Allison

CONTENTS

PREFACE

This book is a biography of a bear—perhaps the most famous bear in the world, and certainly the only bear in America with his own ZIP code.

Preliminary research began in 1990 when I wrote about the 1950 rescue of a tiny, burned bear cub from the Capitan Gap forest fire in New Mexico's Lincoln National Forest. After my story appeared in newspapers in several states, I received a letter from a Forest Service employee who said that several veterans of the fire were interested in talking with me.

A few phone calls later, my interest in Smokey Bear—both the origina lposter bear and its living symbol rescued from Capitan Gap—had been aroused. But when I sought more information about the critter, I discovered that although Smokey had been patrolling America's forests for almost 50 years, no comprehensive study of his life and times had ever been published. Unable to contain my curiosity, I began researching Smokey's background.

I soon learned that as a public persona, Smokey Bear has become the darling of three generations of American children. But I also found that under his broad-brimmed campaign hat, Smokey is a triumphant creation of America's advertising industry, the U.S. Forest Service and the National Association of State Foresters. Smokey's leadership in preventing forest fires has been artfully designed, carefully nurtured and skillfully executed by thousands of talented American men and women doing their daily jobs with determination, dedication and competence. So by one standard, Smokey is nothing more than a wildly-successful figment of the collective imagination of 260 million Americans.

Nevertheless, over many years Smokey Bear has assumed his own personality—a personality that reflects the compassion and persistence of the people who created him. Thus, to record and portray Smokey's 50-year history, I believe a writer must tell about the people who put Smokey into our hearts and minds and made him part of the great American folklore. I reasoned that Smokey's engaging story demanded a look behind the scenes at the real human drama that sometimes occurred. This, then, is a "people" book—a book about our innovative fellow Americans who created and then propagated Smokey for the past half century.

Through three years of research, my objectives were simple: (1) identify individual motivation as reflected in the social environment of the times, (2) weave events into reasonable chronological order and (3) through extensive use of quotations, let the people who led Smokey to his lofty preeminence tell his story.

I began research with no preconceived notions of heroes or events, no position to support, no ax to grind and no idea of my eventual destination. Initially, I had no idea where to turn or what questions to ask, but eventually I talked with nearly 150 people and combed through almost a thousand letters, reports, speeches, log books, diaries, manuscripts, newspaper articles, magazine stories, books and essays. The Library of Congress, the National Archives and the Smithsonian Institution all graciously cooperated with my efforts. I was escorted on field trips and welcomed into many homes where I helped sift through file cabinets, scrapbooks, closets and memories as the story of Smokey Bear gradually began to unfold. After preliminary interviews, participants frequently called or wrote with additional information. Others learned of my research and volunteered assistance. Invariably, I was treated with patience, kindness and support.

Many people contributed significantly to the development of Smokey Bear, and many more claimed credit for doing so; perhaps they all advanced his cause. Certainly, it sometimes was difficult to determine the exact sequence of events or even to identify actual participants. With the passage of 50 years, honest disagreements sometimes arose between well-meaning people who remembered events a little differently. Those varying perceptions of past incidents sometimes were frustrating, but in my efforts to capture historic events for posterity, I tried to address those differences as fairly as possible.

But notwithstanding the considerable lapse of time since Smokey's creation and the fact that many of the events represented herein occurred before my birth, I believe that this book accurately and honestly illustrates the presentation of Smokey Bear and his forest fire prevention message to the American public. To the best of my knowledge, all dialogue and conversations reconstructed, all events recaptured, all descriptive details and all conclusions (except where indicated) are factual, as are the physical settings, moods and feelings depicted.

For each chapter, I consulted the most knowledgeable people and authoritative chronicles available, but it is possible that some important documents or contributors to Smokey's development were overlooked; certainly, hundreds of people who played relatively minor roles were omitted from this edition. So to those people and their families, I apologize.

Although I believe all events and background facts are correct as portrayed, I sometimes took literary liberties to represent events—by using composite overviews to illustrate developments, by merging interviews to add meaning and enhance understanding, or by blending interviews, speeches and documents to add chronological order.

I wanted participants to tell Smokey's story in their own words, so I relied heavily on creditable, primary sources—especially personal interviews and personal writings. I corroborated material when I could because primary sources sometimes disagreed and secondary sources often were inaccurate. Finally, I asked for criticism from almost two dozen people who read drafts that touched on their knowledge of events; I always corrected factual errors, but sometimes ignored recommendations when my interpretations were challenged. Thus, any remaining oversight or error is entirely mine.

Smokey Bear 20252 is my way of saying "thanks" to those thousands of Americans who get up every morning and go out and save our forests. This is their story. I hope it reflects the enormous admiration I hold for them.

Bill Lawter
January 1994

Acknowledgments

I will be forever indebted to those individuals who helped me record this small piece of American history by contributing their knowledge of Smokey Bear and the people portrayed herein. Almost everyone I encountered proved eager to help, but a few people were indispensable to the effort.

In Virginia, Rudy Wendelin, a fellow Kansan and the most acclaimed of the great Smokey Bear artists, taught me the role of art in forest fire prevention. Rudy painted the wonderful cover for this book and drew the 24 chapter illustrations. Also in Virginia, Don Hansen helped piece together much of the information regarding the Smokey Bear program's later years.

In Maryland, Bill Bergoffen, the "man who put the pants on Smokey," enlightened me on the early Smokey communications effort, and James Cassidy greatly expedited my research at the National Archives.

In Washington, D.C., Terry West supplied extensive historical perspective and background, Gladys Daines directed me to critical historical files and Jean Pablo helped research and collect photographs and artwork.

In New Mexico, Ray Bell, the state's "flying game warden," spent more than a week guiding me around the state, and Dorothy Guck eagerly shared her early research and writings. Ken Bowman initiated my fire control education by insisting that I visit the Forest Service's Southwestern Region fire control center, and then escorted me to meet with Mescalero Apache firefighters, while Sam Servis filled in the technical holes.

Also in New Mexico, Bill Chapel saved me considerable travel by arranging a gathering of many knowledgeable people, Joyce Pankey provided key documents relating to the Capitan Gap fire and Teresa Engelking allowed complete access to documents housed by the Smokey Bear Museum.

In California, Jack Foster patiently explained the process of developing Smokey advertising materials, and Jim Felton shared his extensive knowledge of early Foote, Cone & Belding advertising and challenged—sometimes vigorously—my thinking and direction.

In New York, Brad Lynch provided Advertising Council background and the invaluable 1952 manuscript by Harold Thomas, and I would have been unable to effectively portray Smokey's advertising effort without John O'Toole's fine book, *From One Person to Another.*

Acknowledgments

In Idaho, Kay Flock contributed important personal background, and in Washington, Mal Hardy supplied several hundred pages of detailed reports and analysis. In Georgia, Harry Rossoll donated essential file material on the program's early personalities, and James Sorenson uncovered information from the Smokey Bear workshops and other sources. In Texas, Jeanne Knapp shared her research on Don Belding, and in Oklahoma, Phyllis Larson edited many of my initial drafts and helped me develop the book's structure.

When I thought I faced bureaucratic barriers, Jimmie Hickman of the Forest Service's regional office in Albuquerque; Ray Gallegos, New Mexico State Forester in Santa Fe; Roger Davis, Oklahoma State Forester in Oklahoma City; and Dick Klaxon, Utah State Forester in Salt Lake City, went to bat for me.

Finally, I want to thank: the Library of Congress, the Smithsonian Institution and the National Zoological Park in Washington, D.C.; the National Archives in Suitland, Maryland; the Mescalero Apache tribe in Mescalero, New Mexico; all the people of Capitan, New Mexico; Forest Service offices in Albuquerque, Capitan, Alamogordo, Boise, Atlanta, South Lake Tahoe and Washington, D.C.; Foote, Cone & Belding in Los Angeles; the Advertising Council in New York; Jennifer Smith in Virginia for believing in this book; Phil Brewster in Georgia who started this project with his letter; and more than 100 other fine folks identified in the bibliography.

1

AN AMERICAN HERITAGE

"Fire control began as a crusade for the first generation of Forest Service employees. During fire season, when the weather is dry and the east winds blow, we all sniff the air for smoke."

— Terry West

Mark Twain lived before America had Smokey Bear, so Mark Twain never saw a Smokey Bear poster or watched a Smokey Bear commercial. Mark Twain never shook hands with a costumed Smokey Bear or sang the Smokey Bear song. Mark Twain never cuddled a Smokey Bear doll or heard Smokey Bear's slogan. Maybe that's why Mark Twain set fire to one of America's forests.

While on an extended Western visit, Twain camped on the north shore of scenic Lake Tahoe in 1862 or 1863. As his friend Johnny unloaded provisions, Twain lit a cooking fire next to a tree, then returned to his boat for a frying pan. But Twain would have no supper that night.

"I heard a shout from Johnny," Twain recorded in his book *Roughing It*, "and looking up I saw that my fire was galloping all over the premises." Encircled by flames, Twain and Johnny saved their lives by fleeing to their

1

boat and rowing out onto Lake Tahoe. By Twain's account, only 90 seconds were required for the cool, damp forest to explode into an inferno. He watched, spellbound, from his boat. "Within half an hour all before us was a tossing, blinding tempest of flame," he recorded.

Twain's fire roared up ridges, momentarily disappeared, then emerged to relentlessly devour hilltops and canyons as far as his eyes could see. By 11:00 that night, after four hours in their boat, Twain and Johnny were able to return to land. "Hunger asserted itself now," Twain wrote, "but there was nothing to eat. We were homeless wanderers again, without any property."

The zealous decimation of American forests began not with Mark Twain, but with the 1607 arrival of English colonists in Jamestown, where settlers found seemingly endless forests extending almost a thousand miles inland along the entire Atlantic seaboard. More than a billion acres of forest stretched across the present-day United States, and pioneers eagerly felled trees for fuel, fences, cabins and cropland.

It didn't take long for the devastation to show. "By 1800, a wood shortage developed near large East Coast cities," Terry West, Forest Service historian, explained. "By the 1830s, so many trees had been razed that commercial lumbering began shifting to the Great Lakes region of Michigan, Wisconsin and Minnesota. Those forests were depleted by 1880, and lumbermen turned to the southern pines in the 1890s, and then to the last virgin forests on the Pacific Coast in 1920."

But 95 percent of the populace lived on the land for much of America's first three centuries, so agriculture claimed the most forests. Between 1850 and 1910, farmers cleared an average 13.5 square miles of forest each day; Ohio—a typical midwestern state—saw forested areas reduced from 96 percent of its land to 25 percent. By the mid-1800s, America had 3.2 million miles of wooden fences, and wood provided almost all its energy, with steamboats alone burning almost a million cords of fuel wood annually. Railroad tracks—350,000 miles of them by 1900—required more than 15 million acres of forestland just to replace crossties. And prospectors took millions of board feet to reinforce mine tunnel ceilings.

By 1918, America's forests reached their nadir of 740 million acres: almost one-third of the nation's forests had fallen. Americans had denuded 300 million acres of land, leaving much of it so eroded that almost 100 million acres was useless for crops.

Worse, Americans seemed determined to incinerate their forests before they could harvest them. "Indians burned forests to flush game and create

2

meadows for forage, game habitats and crops," conceded West, an Oregon native with a B.S. in anthropology from the University of Oregon in Eugene, and a Ph.D. in anthropology from the New School for Social Research in New York City. "But the number and scope of wildfires exploded with the spread of European settlers. Hunters, travelers, teamsters and miners all started forest fires."

Incredibly, some forest visitors set fires as entertainment. In nineteenth-century Oregon, it was great sport to see who could start the largest fire in the Cascades. In the 1890s, tourists near Washington's Mount Rainier enjoyed igniting fir trees and watching their spectacular explosions. Then fires became weapons in battles between landowners: southerners set fires to keep Civilian Conservation Corps workers out of their way; cattlemen set retaliatory fires to protest government land rules; union members lit fires on timber company lands in the Northwest. And entrepreneurs set fires in hopes of being paid to fight them.

Although the concept of conservation initially was rejected as ludicrous, and Americans had no way to understand the role of trees as the Earth's factories of life, people slowly became aware of declining wildlife populations, the possibility that forests were not inexhaustible and the fact that future timber supplies could be threatened. But it was the growing recognition that forests were important for watershed protection that finally focused public attention on the national disgrace. As easterners began to appreciate that forests could ensure secure supplies of drinking water and protect against floods, and westerners grew concerned about irrigation, watershed protection became a national issue.

Spurred by writings such as those of George Perkins Marsh in 1864 and Frederic Starr in 1865, many citizens suddenly developed an interest in conservation, and forestry issues soon appeared on the nation's political agenda. "Between 1868 and 1872," West explained, "seven states enacted laws offering bounties or tax breaks to encourage tree planting. Wisconsin began studying forests in 1867. Maine followed suit in 1869, and Minnesota created the first state forestry association in 1876. California established a state forestry board by 1885, and three years later, its legislature asked Congress to stop selling public lands and, instead, to protect state watersheds by creating forest reserves."

With public opinion leaders finally aware of the problem, forestry conservation activities began in earnest by 1872. The first Arbor Day was celebrated in Nebraska to encourage tree planting, New York appointed a commission to study a possible forest preserve in the Adirondack Mountains, and Congress reserved 2 million acres for Yellowstone National

Park. Infused with energy, the conservation movement grew and broadened its appeal by working to protect timber and wildlife as well as water resources.

"In many respects," West emphasized, "women, through state and national federations of women's clubs, popularized the conservation crusade. Men led in the scientific, legal, policy and political arenas, but women were critically important as educators, advocates and lobbyists."

Mary Eno Pinchot headed the Daughters of the American Revolution conservation committee that directed conservation education toward schoolchildren. Lydia Phillips exercised strong influence as chair of the General Federation of Women's Clubs forestry committee. Mabel Rosalie Edge campaigned for conservation in New York, while Mrs. Lovell White helped save redwoods in California.

D. Priscilla Edgerton, a Forest Service employee, authored a forest handbook for teachers. On speaking tours, Forest Service educator Margaret March-Mount advocated tree planting so effectively that she is credited with motivating the DAR to promote the planting of 5 million seedlings in thirty-six states. March-Mount also developed a "penny pines" Children's Conservation Crusade to fund planting pine trees in national forests. Other women leaders started sanctuaries, helped found the Save the Redwoods League and promoted forestry schools.

Feeling pressure, federal legislators introduced two hundred land policy bills between 1871 and 1897, and Congress responded with a plethora of legislation. The Timber Culture Act, passed in 1873, donated 160 acres of public land to anyone who planted 40 acres. In 1891, the Forest Reserve Act changed public policy from disposal to retention and authorized the president to create timber reserves that eventually would be administered by the Forest Service.

The U.S. Forest Service seems to have sprouted from seeds sown in a research effort. Although Congress apparently had planned to delegate forestry matters to the Department of the Interior, that effort failed in 1874. But in 1876, a rider to an appropriations bill named Dr. Franklin B. Hough as the first federal forestry agent, assigned him to the Department of Agriculture and provided $2,000 to study the conditions of American forests.

Hough, a fifty-four-year-old physician from Martinsburg, New York, recommended in his multivolume *Report on Forestry* (1878-1884) that the United States actively manage federal timberlands, create forest experimental centers, plant trees and educate the populace about the value of forest conservation. So Hough was named chief of the Department of Agriculture's new Division of Forestry in 1881.

Bernhard Fernow, who replaced Hough in 1886, encouraged research on forest use that led to ideas such as an 1887 suggestion that railroad crossties and trestles be treated with preservatives to increase durability and reduce waste. It was, however, the strong-willed Gifford Pinchot who led American forest management out of the wilderness.

In many respects, America's early conservation battles often were dominated by two intriguing men. In the West, John Muir argued for pure preservation as well as conservation. A gangling Scottish-born mountaineer with flowing beard, Muir offered simple logic: "Any fool can destroy trees. They cannot run away." Among other efforts, Muir labored for the creation of Yosemite National Park and formed the Sierra Club with twenty-six California friends.

In the East, Gifford Pinchot, Muir's sometime antagonist, preached conservation-for-use. Perceived as a puritanical patrician, but respected as perhaps America's first professional forester, Pinchot carved his niche as an ardent conservationist. A lanky woodsman from Yale, Pinchot had studied forestry in Germany and had managed forests on the Vanderbilts' Biltmore estate in North Carolina. Pinchot viewed trees as a crop to be tended, harvested and replanted, but he insisted that the waste of America's forests be stopped.

In 1898, Pinchot replaced Fernow as chief of the Division of Forestry, which grew to a 179-member organization within the next three years. Because trained foresters were rare, Pinchot formed the core of his future workforce by recruiting college students to map timber and conduct surveys on federal forest reserves.

But Pinchot suddenly wielded power far beyond that normally available to the head of a minor government program. "In 1887," Terry West observed, "Theodore Roosevelt helped establish the Boone and Crockett Club to encourage conservation of big game habitat. Although the club had only one hundred core members, its powerful membership included many influential opinion leaders. As the newly elected governor of New York, Roosevelt met Pinchot in 1899, when Pinchot conducted a private forest inspection in the Empire State. Impressed with Pinchot and his views, Roosevelt nominated his new friend for membership in the Boone and Crockett Club, and the two men became close comrades."

In some respects, the Boone and Crockett Club could be viewed as a northeastern elitist movement with selfish motives—an intent to preserve elk, bear and other big game for the club's members to hunt. But the club's recognition that game habitat had to be preserved contributed to the nationwide campaign to save the nation's wildlife.

A year after he met Pinchot, Roosevelt was elected vice president, and he assumed the presidency when William McKinley was assassinated. Quite willing to encourage government to manage natural resources for the public good, Roosevelt eagerly sought Pinchot's advice on conservation policy and allocated favors in return. "Two of the things that made Pinchot so effective," West acknowledged, "were his wealth and social ties that allowed him to meet Roosevelt on equal terms."

In the Transfer Act of 1905, Congress moved administration of federal forest reserves from the Interior Department to the Department of Agriculture; on March 3, 1905, the Bureau of Forestry became the Forest Service, with Pinchot appointed its first chief forester. Pinchot aggressively supported the legislation for a simple reason: he believed that Interior was plagued with political appointees, but his Forest Service boasted professional foresters.

"Although conservationists urged professional management of forests," West shrugged, "there were no schools at first, so early advocates of forest conservation were self-taught naturalists. However, Cornell, Biltmore [then a private school] and Yale soon offered degrees in forestry, and between 1903 and 1914, another twenty-one schools, such as Michigan State, Iowa State and Minnesota, added similar programs."

Although 40 million acres of woodlands already had been designated as federal forest reserves by 1897, the roots of America's national forest system actually stem from the Forest Management Act of 1897, when the use of timber and water resources was brought under government supervision. By 1905, 63 million acres of forests were under federal management, the Forest Service was flourishing with Pinchot's leadership, and his staff had grown to five hundred. And with Roosevelt's fervent support, Pinchot established an ambitious goal: bring another 100 million acres of forests under government control.

But as Pinchot neared his target, a displeased Congress rebelled against the Pinchot/Roosevelt land grab and passed a bill to abolish Roosevelt's power to create new "national forests" (thus named in 1907) in seven western states. After the legislation hit Roosevelt's desk on February 25, 1907, Pinchot's staff worked day and night to nominate new reserves for Roosevelt's signature before the deadline. When Roosevelt finally found a pen to sign the bill itself on March 4, 16 million acres of new national forests had appeared. And by the time the superbly confident—but sometimes haughty—Pinchot was fired by President William Howard Taft in 1910, national forest reserves totaled almost 200 million acres.

"Pinchot strongly supported sustained yield, multiple-use of the national forests and protection of local communities," West explained. "So the Forest Service mission gradually included recreation, range, timber, watershed protection, wildlife and wilderness." But not everyone supported Pinchot.

"Accustomed to taking timber and forage from public lands at will, many users were not receptive to national forests under government stewardship," West continued. "Prospectors opposed national forests because of possible restrictions on mining. Ranchers used to open range resisted Pinchot's implementation of grazing fees and regulations. An exploding population demanded access to forest resources, leading to conflicts over forest use. When the Forest Service could not allocate larger and larger shares to satisfy increasing demand, the service itself was attacked."

The early job of winning cooperation from forest users fell to Pinchot's district forest rangers. Hired for about $1,000 a year, rangers paid for their own horses, guns and clothing before heading out to patrol hundreds of thousands of acres. As policemen, game wardens, rescuers and peacemakers, rangers were expected to organize and lead fire-fighting crews, build roads, negotiate grazing fees and timber sales contracts, direct reforestation and disease control projects and run surveys. They often relied on their spouses for unpaid logistical, communications and clerical assistance.

Pinchot delegated responsibility to his rangers, and most became adept woodsmen and armchair scientists, engineers, economists, accountants and public relations experts. In turn, they did their jobs well and developed an intense loyalty to the Forest Service. To emulate that success, the states began recruiting professional foresters.

But state forestry efforts often began only after state forests already had been devastated. "Furthermore," West pointed out, "state forestry efforts regularly faded because of inadequate funding or a lack of state forests to administer." When Congress passed the Weeks Act of 1911 to encourage formation of state forestry agencies, the primary role in assisting the states fell to the Forest Service.

Because states needed Forest Service help to conserve wildlife, Pinchot's staff worked closely with game wardens to enforce laws protecting fish and game. But the Forest Service also contributed money and technical advice to support state efforts at fire control, forest management, forest growth and tree planting. By insisting that the Forest Service respect states' rights, Pinchot set it onto a successful track that usually avoided political scandals. And many years later, a *Newsweek* cover story attributed Forest Service success to two Pinchot policies: decentralization and cooperation with anyone who would cooperate.

Decentralization reportedly started in 1908, when, with a staff of 1,500, Pinchot told his headquarters professionals to "get out into the woods or get out of the service." That plan became policy; half a century later, only two percent of Forest Service staffers were assigned to Washington, D.C.

The Forest Service accepted help from almost anyone, but it received its greatest infrastructure construction boost when President Franklin Roosevelt signed an executive order to establish the Civilian Conservation Corps in 1933. Soon, the Forest Service was swamped with workers, as hundreds of thousands of unemployed young men clamored for the $30-a-month jobs.

"Most of the 1,300 CCC camps were located in national forests, where the men worked on projects supervised by state and federal foresters," Terry West explained. "By the time the CCC was terminated in 1942, 2.5 million youths in 'Roosevelt's Forest Army' had planted two billion trees, built 122,000 miles of road, constructed six million erosion check dams, erected thousands of fire towers and office buildings, and laid out hundreds of campgrounds and thousands of miles of hiking trails." In the Prairie States Forestry Project alone, the Forest Service supervised the planting of 217 million trees on more than 30,000 ranches and farms from North Dakota to Texas.

Fire is a natural element of forest life, and many fires are caused by lightning or other acts of nature. Early American explorers wrote of traveling for days in sight of smoke from forest fires presumably begun by natural causes. And without question, fire can be good.

Most plants adapt to the effects of fire as it prepares land for seeding, reduces potentially hazardous accumulations of ground fuel, helps maintain healthy grasslands and chaparral and initiates changes in the life cycles of forest communities. The growth rings of some California redwoods indicate that natural fires occurred about every twenty-five years for several centuries. While fires burn off ground cover and other debris, they sometimes destroy few trees—some of which are dependent on fire for regeneration.

Certain pines release seeds from their cones only when fire heats them to at least 150 degrees; then, those seeds grow only when fire provides bare soil and full sunlight by clearing a forest floor of its cumulative layers of needles that exude an oil deadly to pine seedlings.

Aspens, too, regenerate themselves through fire. As they age, aspens become highly flammable and easily fall to fire, but then new shoots spring from dead tree roots. Fire assists redwoods by helping deposit minerals into the ground for seedlings, but usually spares mature trees, which develop an almost fireproof bark. Fire helps protect forests against disease, as when smoke from burning pine needles reduces tree rust and mold. But forests must be protected against too many fires.

Fire is not always friendly; it is a feared environmental enemy that Pinchot called the "dragon devastation." Fire threatens forests simply because its violence can destroy everything in its path. A relatively small 1,000-acre mountainside fire can multiply many times within a day. A forest fire can travel more than eight miles an hour, stretch dozens of miles in length and claim a perimeter of 100 miles. Such an inferno can generate heat and winds so intense that it creates its own weather patterns. As it pulls in air to feed its flames, a forest fire's winds can reach tornado force and uproot trees, while intense heat bursts granite boulders and causes some trees to explode like giant dynamite sticks. Every two minutes, it has been estimated, a firestorm can generate energy equivalent to the 20-kiloton atomic bomb dropped over Hiroshima.

Eventually, of course, nature repairs the ruin of a forest fire, but the rehabilitation process is slow. Nature may have taken hundreds of years to create the forest, and it may take hundreds of years to heal the damage.

Apparently, surprisingly few states took early legislative action to address forest fires. Massachusetts Bay Colony enacted a law in 1631 to regulate fire practices, and Texas made deliberate range burning a felony in 1884. New York and Yellowstone National Park established fire patrols with the U.S. Army. But neither states nor private landowners could provide effective fire protection, so the nation looked to the Forest Service for leadership.

As would be expected, fire protection always was a principal objective of professional foresters. In 1899, Gifford Pinchot claimed that fire was the primary enemy of America's forests, and he demanded that rangers protect them against fires. By 1905, forest fire protection became a national priority by which the Forest Service was measured, so fire control became a crusade and an internal rite of passage for Pinchot's staff.

"Public opinion gradually began to support the Forest Service after a series of massive western fires in 1910, when Idaho and Montana fires burned more than three million acres and killed eighty firefighters," Terry

West stressed. Then, because 20 million to 50 million acres burned each year, it became apparent that fire was the greatest single cause of forest depletion, and Congress passed the Clarke-McNary Act in 1924 to provide for forest fire control.

Meanwhile, Forest Service fire-suppression technology continued to improve. The first aerial forest fire patrol was developed in 1919, the portable two-way radio for fire control use followed in the late 1920s and smoke jumping was first used in 1940. With modernized technology, foresters contained most wildfires within a few acres, and by 1935 the Forest Service adopted its self-imposed "10:00 a.m." rule, whereby every forest fire was supposed to be controlled by 10:00 a.m. on the day after it started.

Because fire initially feeds on a forest's floor of leaves, branches and other decaying debris, the primary effort in suppressing a forest fire is aimed at removing that fuel from its path. So foresters learned to use "prescribed" or "controlled" burns to eliminate accumulations of ground fuel; by igniting small fires in forest debris, fuel for potentially larger fires is reduced. Results can be impressive: a prescribed burn can reduce the likelihood of wildfire for as long as twenty years. Further, foresters know that controlled fires minimize tree and soil damage, but kill insect pests and unwanted seedlings. Fighting fire with fire thus serves as a tool to help protect healthy forests.

But far too many accidental, unnecessary fires are started, and some are truly horrendous. "The same day as the Great Chicago Fire of 1871," West explained, "the Peshtigo Fire [named after a local river] swept rural Wisconsin. It is still regarded by many as the worst fire in the history of the United States—more than 1,200 people died and 2,400 square miles of forest were burned. The fire was started by careless burning to clear farmland."

Of course, not only people suffer from forest fires. Animals, too, lose their food, water, cover and lives. So perhaps it's appropriate that the Forest Service recruited a bear to educate Americans about carelessness in their forests.

2

A BEAR MARKET FOR ADVERTISING

"Not advertising your product makes as much sense as winking at a pretty girl in a dark room."
— John O'Toole

Erato, Muse of poetry, surely looked with favor upon America's advertising industry in the early 1940s, for seldom has a business under such strong attack responded so effectively to its tormenters. Blessed with leaders of vision, advertising learned to channel its immense creative talents to benefit the nation, but the process wasn't easy.

With full employment and an avalanche of consumer goods, America thrived on its post-World War I economic growth. As if on a prolonged shopping spree, Americans spent and spent and spent. Supported by credit, and confident that prosperity had no limits, they eagerly looked to advertising to guide their buying binge.

By 1929, however, America and its businesses were in trouble. As the economic crisis deepened, advertising fought to protect itself and other industries by urging Americans to spend their way out of their problems. Advertisements grew bolder, more forceful and more demanding, but it didn't work. People were broke.

As unemployment grew, paid advertising volume dropped from $3.4 billion in 1929 to $1.3 billion in 1932. As advertising, too, slashed its payrolls, confidence deteriorated and a consumer movement gathered strength. With their faith in business and government shaken, angry Americans rebelled against exhortations to keep spending. As ads focused on materialism and insulted the poor, Americans began to lose faith in businesses supported by advertising. Disgusted with the ceaseless hard sell, opinion leaders insisted that advertising was part of the problem.

Advertising, critics reasoned, drove up costs with expensive marketing and brightly colored packages. Advertising promised everything but added no value or improved quality. Brand names promoted monopolies instead of ensuring quality. Advertising exaggerated. Advertising was a fraud. Advertising was irrelevant. Advertising must be abolished or controlled by government.

Sensing vulnerability, elected officials, college professors and the media pointed their accusing fingers. Writers attacked advertising with "insider revelations," as President Franklin Roosevelt's administration, his congressional supporters, the League of Women Voters, office workers, schoolteachers and labor unions joined the fray. And in 1939, *Business Week* identified twenty national consumer groups preaching from a stack of four dozen books demanding honesty in advertising.

To advertising executives, it seemed that the attacks threatened to replace baseball as a national pastime, and the onslaught became a major concern as it gathered momentum. Industry leaders knew that if government could limit advertising, it could destroy advertising and other businesses.

Madison Avenue, of course, viewed its product not as consumer exploitation but as a constitutional guarantee. Advertising believed—or at least argued—that it was an issue of freedom of speech and freedom of the press. Certainly, some advertising leaders vigorously defended those freedoms.

Don Belding, executive vice president of the Lord & Thomas advertising agency in Los Angeles, California, refused to buckle under the assault. Willing to fight for his fundamental beliefs, Belding became president of the Pacific Coast Advertising Clubs in 1940 and initiated a counterattack on his industry's critics. Advertising, Belding insisted, enabled a free press to achieve the solvency that ensured its freedom. Without a free press, America could not continue as a free nation, so advertising must be the most important pillar in America's political and business structure. The issue, he claimed, was the very survival of American democracy.

Belding believed that Americans should preserve the free enterprise system that had produced the world's highest standard of living. With advertising, Belding maintained, businesses could grow and absorb advertising costs through increased sales. Although conceding that advertising had its share of shaky practices, Belding rejected a wholesale indictment of his profession and argued for reform through cooperation with civic organizations and government.

Belding supported creation of a public education program and urged the formation of legislative committees and business associations. Belding's group offered speakers, published newspaper and magazine advertisements, reached opinion leaders with direct mail, broadcast their positions on radio and dotted the countryside with outdoor advertising. And, convinced that some consumer groups took guidance from communists, Belding challenged communism so ardently that at times he seemed obsessed with the search. It was communists, Belding insisted as he accused forty-four consumer groups of having communist connections, that wanted to abolish advertising.

While communists may not have been hiding behind every billboard, Belding sometimes found evidence to support his accusations. After one hundred University of California professors petitioned Congress to abolish wartime advertising, Belding and his association discredited that effort by revealing that two men who circulated the petition had communist connections.

But Belding's efforts seemed lost in the din. Proclamations of free speech rang on deaf ears, and amorphous promises of self-regulation convinced no one of advertising's repentance. Belding and his colleagues could neither halt the criticism nor develop a national response to their attackers. Advertising was badly outgunned, and the industry knew it.

Harold B. Thomas, writing in a research manuscript, "The Background and Beginning of the Advertising Council," the council that he helped found, observed 1941's dire situation: "Times were bad indeed. Not only was there not a chicken in every pot, but often there wasn't even a pot. There wasn't a car in every garage. Those who were fortunate enough to be able to meet the last installment on the partial payment plan that they had started in the 20s, found themselves possessed of an old jalopy held together with [baling] wire and had to save up to buy a quarter's worth of gas."

Noting that reforms often occur only in bad times, Thomas concluded that the call for change was understandable. If people view everything as wrong, he reasoned, then new gods arise and new creeds are expounded and people insist on change—sometimes simply for the sake of change itself.

"Business was attacked from all sides," Thomas wrote, "because business wasn't producing—wasn't making money—wasn't providing jobs. Quite naturally advertising, as the business practice most prominently in the eye and ear of the public, came in for a large share of criticism and condemnation. This voice of business, advertising, seemed at that time to take on a raucous, jangling, irritating note as it urged the public to buy when the public had no money. The people didn't want goods. They wanted jobs. Business was attacked through advertising and advertising per se was attacked as though it were something tangible."

So despite its public bravado, advertising began an internal self-examination as the tidal wave of criticism undermined its very existence. Would consumers drain the lifeblood from magazines, newspapers, billboards and radio? Were Roosevelt's supporters serious in their talk of government control of advertising? Had advertising misled itself with its own propaganda? Was the advertising industry guilty as charged?

In the summer of 1941, Paul West, president of the Association of National Advertisers (ANA), and Chester LaRoche, chairman of Young & Rubicam, initiated the first coordinated industry self-examination. West envisioned a joint meeting with the American Association of Advertising Agencies (AAAA) and the media to discuss problems facing advertising, and LaRoche made the meeting successful.

Demanding action, West suggested on August 28 that three elements were critical: a united front, accurate facts and a forceful presentation of those facts. West opined first on the need for unity: "This would seem so obvious that there would be little need to mention it, except for the fact that the lack of it has been painfully evident. The common cause . . . is survival." Then West identified key groups with vested interests: as buyers, advertisers held the purse strings and should ensure that advertising was not destroyed as a marketing tool; the existence of advertising agencies depended upon their ability to practice their skills; media freedom depended upon a revenue stream from advertising. "But the first essential requirement," West asserted, "is that we all sink our petty differences."

Responding to West's entreaty, a twelve-member planning committee of the AAAA and ANA called a meeting at the Homestead Resort in Hot Springs, Virginia, on November 13-15, 1941. The assemblage would focus on the looming threats to advertising, develop facts about its economic effects, solicit testimonials to prove the indispensability of advertising and create an action plan.

The meeting started poorly with ineffective diatribe offering innocuous concepts of "planning," "enlightenment" and "building goodwill." If the gathering had ended with that hot air, the Hot Springs session might have faded into anonymity. But James Webb Young, former professor at the University of Chicago and former executive of the J. Walter Thompson agency, single-handedly salvaged the meeting when he offered a solution to advertising's image problem.

"We are in an era of soul searching," Young conceded in one of the major speeches in advertising history. "We have a demand to justify advertising now as a social force. What a nuisance! But let us make no mistake about it. The demand is insistent and in volume. It runs with the current of the times. If we do not meet it, we will be damaged."

Young issued his challenge: "We have within our hands the greatest aggregate means of mass education and persuasion the world has ever seen, namely, the channels of advertising communication. We have the masters of the techniques of using these channels. We have power. Why do we not use it? Use it to confound the critics of advertising with the greatest demonstration of its power they have ever seen."

Then Young outlined his concept of public service advertising: "Advertising is the most modern, streamlined, high-speed means of communications plus persuasion yet invented by man. It ought to be used extensively by governments . . . by political parties . . . by labor unions . . . by farm organizations . . . by churches and by universities. It ought to be used for open propaganda in international relations . . . to wipe out such diseases of ignorance as child-bed fever . . . to do the nutritional job this country needs to have done. It ought to be the servant of music, of art, of literature and of all the forces of righteousness."

Young's advocacy struck a responsive chord in the assembly, sowing seeds for the great American Advertising Council and generating an immediate pledge of support from many of his colleagues. The Hot Springs meeting finally had a focused direction, but it still needed a unifying cause.

At the closing luncheon, William Batt, director of the Materials Division of the Office of Production Management, insisted that that cause was national defense. First praising advertising for facing its problems, Batt then chastised the attendees for failing to recognize that advertising's problems should play a secondary role to the vital issues facing their nation. "This profession has an obligation," Batt charged. "It certainly has an opportunity. I suggest that you find out what your clients ought to be doing to help save paper, or to save cardboard, or to save anything of which we are short for defense purposes."

Stung by Batt's speech, Chester LaRoche called a second meeting to develop an action plan. And on November 27, LaRoche, West, Frederic Gamble, Miller McClintock, Harold Thomas, Lee Bristol, Arthur Kudner and Thomas Ryan met at the Cloud Club in New York to consider a plan to raise $100,000 each year for five years to fund a new organization.

Gamble's notes from that meeting indicate that the name was recorded as "the new Advertising Council or whatever it is to be called." Paul West agreed to study the government's defense needs and explore opportunities to assist with advertising, and he left for Washington on December 7, 1941, not knowing that the value of his fledgling Advertising Council soon would mushroom far beyond anything he had ever imagined—thanks to a Japanese naval fleet lurking 6,000 miles away in the vast dark expanse of the Pacific Ocean.

America soon would be at war with a formidable enemy—a capable, determined and highly focused nation that didn't fit the smug Western stereotype of small, meek, incompetent people with buckteeth and thick glasses. And advertising men would be called on to show how their talents could help fortify their nation for the long struggle it faced.

3

THE ADVERTISING COUNCIL

*"Americans are not going to be guarded by piles of material
stacked on somebody's desk in Washington."*
— Frederic Gamble

Japan's bombing of Pearl Harbor altered the direction of the fledgling
Advertising Council. As darkness claimed the eastern seaboard on the night
of December 7, 1941, the council's founders had no way to know that their
industry soon would be waging the longest, most challenging advertising
campaign in history. But their concept would develop far beyond
expectations because competent people would perform brilliantly. America
never again would legitimately question the value of advertising to the
nation's welfare.

The complete legacy of the Ad Council's farsighted founders cannot be
measured, but conservative estimates are staggering. By the end of World
War II, the Wartime Advertising Council (as it was called until 1945) pushed
advertisers and media to contribute more than $1 billion—about $1 million
each day—in war-related advertising to motivate the American public.

Advertising sold 800 million war bonds valued at $30 billion.
Advertising salvaged tons of strategic tin, steel, rubber and waste fats.

Advertising recruited soldiers, inspired blood donors, conserved gasoline and persuaded 60,000 nurses to join the Cadet Nurse Corps. Advertising generated 50 million victory gardens that produced a billion gallons (8 million tons) of canned food—40 percent of the canned vegetables consumed—put up by 25 million households. The armed forces initially resisted the Ad Council's overtures, but in only one year, advertising helped Women's Army Corps recruiting increase 400 percent and coaxed 2 million women into war-related jobs, and the army and navy responded by bringing new issues to the council almost monthly.

By 1945, more than 200,000 Ad Council messages for almost 100 different advertising campaigns had appeared in the nation's daily and weekly newspapers. Business, farm, religious and general-interest magazines echoed the wartime cry for help. In one campaign, more than 1,300 magazines contributed almost 1,900 advertisements; despite paper shortages, more than 2,000 magazine covers were devoted to the war bond campaign alone. Reminder jingles and songs were broadcast again and again on hundreds of radio stations. Still, there was more. "No one could ever count the editorial paragraphs or the hints in news stories or the small ads about pianos that carried a short message for the government or the front page boxes and the editorial page boxes and the sport page streamers in the newspapers," John Carlyle explained in *Nation's Business*.

Certainly, some advertisers used war campaigns more for their own benefit than for the public good. But the Ad Council's enthusiasm, commitment and constant prodding helped confine advertiser attempts to tie unrelated products to the government's war themes. And with better integration of the advertising industry, individual companies were able to offer stronger support for the nation's cause.

Operating with such impressive efficiency that some experts estimated it would have cost the government $1 billion per year to replicate, the Ad Council incessantly hammered on its industry by explaining war themes and urging "A War Message in Every Ad!"

And this effort didn't cost American taxpayers a cent. The creative talent, planning, space, airtime, distribution and coordination were donated or paid for by corporate and private contributions. Advertising helped America win a war, and the industry's performance routed its most formidable critics when Secretary of the Treasury Henry Morgenthau praised the advertising effort and President Roosevelt admitted his preference to see the Ad Council continue its work in peacetime.

"So advertising, voice of American industry, foolishly denounced by some as wasteful, sometimes despised as frivolous and actually marked for destruction by extremists in various governmental agencies, has modestly accomplished tasks essential to the United States and to a free world," *Collier's* summarized in 1944. "In the process, advertising has been sifted and improved. It has risen to a great opportunity and given itself a new importance and a new dignity."

By its fiftieth anniversary in 1992, the Ad Council would create 20,000 different advertisements. Media and advertiser contributions of space and time would be valued at $20 billion. The American public's understanding of national issues would be enhanced, their lives would be saved by seat belts, charitable contributions would swell and opportunities for handicapped and minority Americans would be created—all because of the Ad Council.

Even with inflation, it still wouldn't cost taxpayers a nickel. Businesses, individuals, media, advertisers, agencies, artists, writers and everyone associated with American advertising would contribute to the public good. The industry's focus on public service advertising would generate a legacy of achievement perhaps unmatched in the nation's business history. But in the beginning, of course, nobody guessed that a bear would be the star of advertising's show.

Paul West's mission changed after the Japanese attack, and his concerns shifted from his industry to his country. But advertising's leadership had been mobilized, and Donald Nelson, executive director of the Supply, Priorities and Allocation Board, voiced support for the concept and called advertising executives to Washington, D.C., on December 9, 1941.

Writing from his office in the Social Security Building, to Paul West in Room 1700 of 330 West 42nd Street in New York, Nelson insisted: "One of the pressing requirements of the Government is to have the help of the established organizations representing the creative ability of advertising and the channels of communication reaching the public. There are, and will be, many campaigns having to do with public education, morale, problems of conservation, use of alternative materials in place of those now urgently needed for war purposes. In short, we must have the means of quickly and effectively disseminating facts to the American people. It is therefore our patriotic duty to explore the possibilities of establishing a working relationship between the Division of Information and the Advertising Council."

On December 15, West, Chester LaRoche and Harold Thomas met with Nelson and Drew Dudley, an advertising veteran on loan to the government from the Wrigley Company. Dudley acknowledged that the government's needs were almost beyond comprehension, but he identified areas where the Ad Council could help: conservation, health and welfare, civilian defense and accelerating production.

It wouldn't be easy, as difficult hurdles stood ready to frustrate the advertising industry. When Frederic Gamble visited Washington to analyze the opportunities, he recorded instead a litany of problems in his notes of December 19. "Use of paid advertising by Government is a much more difficult problem . . . than advertising people can possibly imagine," Gamble opined, focusing first on government strong-arm tactics. "Washington newspaper publishers told me that the Treasury has recently negotiated department store rates for Defense Bond advertising, to be contributed by retail stores or anyone else. Representatives of the Treasury persuaded one publisher to give the department store rate and the others resentfully followed suit."

Second, Gamble noted an inclination to avoid paid advertising because of a fear (at least in the Treasury Department) that such advertising would increase government control over media. His third worry was the issue of media and advertising agencies profiting from government advertising—especially during a war. A fourth problem was the inability to convince government of the effectiveness of advertising; confusion, ignorance, red tape and lack of interest seemed to prevail instead.

Gamble's fifth concern perhaps was the most surprising: "Mrs. Roosevelt . . . seems to be having friends of hers produce material, the details of which are not known to others in Civilian Defense, supposedly in charge. They give as example a film on handling incendiary bombs, made in Hollywood. For some reason, a 16mm film was made, whereas 35mm is needed in theaters and there is great technical difficulty in changing. The agency men . . . were told that Mrs. Roosevelt was passing on the advertising. They finally decided to take some of their material to Mrs. Roosevelt. She looked at the advertising and told them that she would have to take it up with the Board of Child Psychologists."

Sixth, Gamble fretted over a lack of technical expertise: "The Civilian Defense office includes some Civil Service artists, who seem to know nothing whatever about layouts, according to the agency men. For example, one of the agency men wanted a headline larger and suggested that the type be blown up. The Civil Service artist said, 'Oh, you can't blow up type.'"

Finally, Gamble summarized his feelings: "The agencies which have tried it feel that it can't be done by the voluntary services of agencies which go to Washington. They are completely baffled and return having accomplished not much of anything. They point out that Americans are not going to be guarded by piles of material stacked on somebody's desk in Washington for months."

While chaos temporarily reigned in Washington, the advertising men evaluated their potential contributions. They certainly knew the government never could unearth enough money. Americans routinely snapped up government savings bonds as safe investments, but an America at war needed more money than the government had ever requested from its citizens. Further, the government had no machinery to sell a massive volume of bonds to a nervous public.

Advertising also understood that America needed military men and women and fighting equipment. John Carlyle assessed the situation facing the advertisers: "Compared to the millions in the German and Japanese armies our Army resembled the dollar-a-head warriors who used to circle Oscar Hammerstein's back-drops. Our flying arm consisted mostly of pious plans. Our Navy had been pretty good but it had been scattered, starved and sunk."

To produce war materials and feed its people, conservation of American resources would require huge efforts. Motorists could be encouraged by billboards to donate blood, and magazine readers could be urged to save waste fats. But, as Carlyle explained, the government had no artists, writers, distribution networks or advertising's widespread infrastructure, and it had neither time nor money to create the machinery to procure them. Moreover, huge blocks of advertising time and space would be required. If government paid for all its advertising, scarce funds would be diverted from arms manufacture; if government didn't pay, cooperating media would lose revenue required to stay in business. Yet, 135 million Americans had to be taught the rules of war—that dramatic, immediate action was required.

Americans could learn the nation's needs through advertising, but the public couldn't be enlightened until the Ad Council dealt with two problems identified by Gamble: overcoming government dependence on press releases and conquering government prejudices against the advertising industry.

For more than a hundred years the federal government relied primarily on press releases to educate and communicate with its citizens. Not only did government ignore advertising, it had no faith in advertising's products and didn't trust the industry. Government simply couldn't picture itself as an advertiser trying to sell ideas and products. So advertising had to demonstrate that the Ad Council could be the solution.

Further, in advertising's view, government was plagued with multiple branches, overlapping efforts, internal competition, dozens of subordinate components and a record of separate dealings with each element of media and advertisers. Advertising had to offer a single source for contact and would have to persuade government to work with their designated entity.

The Ad Council believed that it could offer experience, continuity, effectiveness and better timing, but it first had to corral hundreds of highly competitive groups into an effective fighting team. Although the council planned to recruit large advertisers to participate in the program, many advertisers disagreed about wartime advertising; some planned to eliminate it, while others insisted on highlighting their contributions to the war effort. Already, oil and rubber companies had started their own conservation campaigns, and other industries had opted for generic institutional advertising.

Certainly its ambitious plans would challenge the Ad Council, but as Carlyle explained, it had to be done: "Every phase of the war effort [would have to be] brought before the public again and again—shouted, sung and danced until the 135 million of us worked as a team." But advertising had a clear objective. A nation called, and like millions of their fellow Americans, the Ad Council founders' only focus was on contributing to the nation's defense. That dedicated group didn't know exactly what to do or how to finance it, but America needed advertising talent and the Ad Council was determined to deliver. Their industry could do a better job than the government of conveying a message of sacrifice and conservation to the public. American advertising would showcase its skills. American advertising was going to war.

As meetings continued in Washington, organizational work continued in New York, and on January 5, 1942, the Ad Council began to crystallize. Chester LaRoche was chosen temporary chairman, Frederic Gamble as his assistant and Paul West as secretary. Proceedings never were officially recorded, but Harold Thomas felt they had passed a milestone: "It would appear . . . that that date might well be considered the birthday of the Council." But Thomas offered a word of caution for putative historians: "It might be noted that to those most closely concerned, the Council didn't actually have a birthday. It just came into existence in the rush of events of December 1941."

Five days later, a memo attached to a letter from LaRoche summarized the council's goal: "This nation must be converted from peace-time habits and customs . . . to an all-out war basis. The organized machinery of *advertising* is essential in getting this job done and the government has asked our cooperation toward that end." Finally, the memo reminded members of James Young's charge: "We have power. Why not use it?"

Then LaRoche wired Donald Nelson: "The Advertising Council has been formed and is ready to report. We await your orders."

Soon, the Ad Council developed a three-part approach: serve government as a single point of contact with the advertising industry, coordinate all advertising efforts with the federal government, and raise funds for a full-time administrator to conduct its business. The council would not advertise or stand in for existing organizations; the council would deal with government, serve as a clearinghouse for assignments and try to avoid duplication of efforts. Further, public service advertising would rely on three equal partners: (1) national advertisers, to direct the process and provide funding, (2) advertising agencies, to create campaign materials and (3) the media, to disseminate the messages.

Ad Council efforts would be directed only toward nonprofit, nonpartisan and nonpolitical causes selected by the federal government. Except for wartime activities, the council would restrict the number of campaigns it would sponsor, and eligible projects would be those for which the government was incapable of providing publicity and that needed the power of commercial advertising. Industry donations and assessments on sponsors would support the council; no government subsidies or public funding would be accepted. Further, no public officials would be permitted on the board of directors or key committees.

Procedurally, the council agreed to choose a coordinator from among business advertisers for each project. In turn, the coordinator would select an advertising agency from among the 446 that quickly volunteered. With guidance from the national coordinator, each agency would create a comprehensive advertising campaign and ship completed campaign materials to its government client. When appropriate, the council would solicit commercial sponsors from business, but if no sponsor could be found, agencies would provide their services free and would minimize the costs of artists, writers and creative personnel. If a commercial business sponsored a project, the sponsor would pay for film, tapes, printing and supplies, and agency services would be provided free. Agencies could bill commissions, but they would be encouraged to return at least part of those commissions to the council. To avoid any appearance of self-interest, no agency represented on the executive committee would be allowed to accept a sponsored campaign.

Council members were confident that their nascent system would be attractive to government because their coordinated efforts would be far more successful than asking agencies to respond to individual requests from the government's maze of bureaus. The collective judgment of advertising would be available to direct the best resources for each project and integrate the industry's efforts into packaged campaigns.

Advertising, too, would benefit from the arrangement. Not only would the industry be positioned to present a strong united front, but as LaRoche explained, "It provides a substantial opportunity for advertising to demonstrate what a potent force it is . . . and to demonstrate by accomplishment that we deserve a place at the council tables in the great task of reconstruction after the war."

There were risks. Public service advertising could only offer facts or plead for support of a cause; each person would decide to accept or ignore those requests. But Americans had learned to rely on advertising to decide how to spend their money, so the council believed that people would accept similar guidance in conserving resources. If it worked, the advertising industry could show the power of mass communications—that it could generate change by focusing public attention on the war effort.

The Ad Council met again on January 14, and to enlarge its base of support, considered geographical expansion to avoid perception as a "New York organization." After members agreed to add the heads of leading advertising-related organizations to the council's advisory board, the American Association of Advertising Agencies and the Association of National Advertisers offered to lend funds to help the council meet organizational expenses.

On January 19, the council agreed to expand further by adding representatives—including Don Belding—of advertising agencies, newspapers, magazines, radio and advertisers. Seeking even more support, LaRoche and West wrote to every organization affiliated with advertising to request their cooperation with the council's activities. At its February 2 meeting, the council focused expansion efforts on industrial advertisers, agreed to raise $100,000 for the first year's operation, and concluded that Dr. Miller McClintock, a former teacher at Harvard and Yale, should be named executive director.

On February 3, the AAAA contributed the first $25,000 to the council, and the council committed to McClintock, who would prove to be a powerful influence in Washington. "The choice of McClintock for this key spot obviously was based on his background as an organizer," said an admiring *Business Week.*

On February 11, the council recommended that Raymond Rubicam be appointed advertising manager for the government, and legal counsel George Link prepared a certificate of incorporation for filing with the Secretary of State in New York. Office space was selected at 60 East 42nd Street in New York and at 1010 Vermont Avenue in Washington, D.C. And most important, a plan for financial sponsorship was adopted: both the AAAA and ANA would contribute $20,000; magazines, newspapers, outdoor and radio each would donate $15,000.

On March 4, the council's first officers were elected for one-year terms. Chester LaRoche (of Young & Rubicam) was elected chairman; Harold Thomas (The Centaur Company), vice-chairman; Paul West (ANA), secretary; Frederic Gamble (AAAA), treasurer; and Miller McClintock was formally appointed executive director. LaRoche and his fellow officers would serve without pay, while McClintock and his staff of eight executives in New York and Washington accepted reductions in their normal income to work for the council.

Chosen as council members were William Chandler (Scripps-Howard Newspapers) representing newspapers; Albert Winger (Crowell-Collier Publishing) representing magazines; Paul Keston (Columbia Broadcasting System) representing radio; and Kerwin Fulton (Outdoor Advertising, Inc.); H. W. Roden (Harold Clapp, Inc); A. O. Buckingham (Cluett Peabody & Company); Arthur Kudner (Arthur Kudner), James Young (J. Walter Thompson Company), Don Belding (Lord & Thomas); Leo Burnett (Leo Burnett Co.); Neil McElroy, (Procter & Gamble Co.); Charles Mortimer Jr. (General Foods Sales Co.); Linwood Noyes (Ironwood [Mich.] Daily Globe); Fred Bohen (Meredith Publishing Co.); John Elmer (WCBM, Baltimore); Paul Garrett (General Motors); and James Palmer (Marshall Field).

Harold Thomas spoke like a proud papa: "This date of March 4, 1942, and the council meeting on that day clearly marks the formal, official beginning of the council. Perhaps it could be said that the Advertising Council was born on January 5 and christened on March 4. In any event, by the latter date it was a going concern."

All four major advertising branches—magazines, newspapers, outdoor and radio—immediately pledged support. All faced barriers such as long-term contracts, erratic schedules, manpower and newsprint shortages, but only a negligible percentage failed to cooperate. And the council grew and grew, welcoming groups from advertising agencies, advertisers, typographers, direct mail, lithographers, editing and agriculture. Soon,

490 magazines with a circulation of more than 90 million were contributing a page each month. Newspapers in 170 major markets participated, and almost 20,000 outlets for print, broadcast, outdoor and transit advertising, bill stuffers and even bread packages offered their help.

The Advertising Council was open for business.

4

BIRTH OF A BEAR

*"I certainly hope they develop and use the bear character as a
continuing, full-time actor instead of the squirrel. The squirrel
is a nuisance and just a damn rodent."*

— Jim Richardson

Most Americans in 1942 knew that trees played a role in their everyday
lives. Trees were the raw material to build—and sometimes heat—homes.
Trees provided wood for tools, toys, bridges and furniture. And some folks
understood that their Sears catalogue, morning newspaper and bathroom
toilet tissue all came from trees.

But most Americans didn't realize that the War Department placed
lumber almost on a par with ammunition as a combat necessity. They didn't
know that a battleship required 300,000 board feet of flooring for each deck,
that the "mosquito" bombers soon to fly over Germany were made mostly
of wood, and that pontoons alone would require 23 million board feet of
lumber each year. They didn't know that the army would drop supplies
with paper parachutes, that a 75-foot-long PT boat was made almost entirely
of wood, that a single tree could provide cellulose for 7,500 rifle cartridges

or that wood was essential for rifles, gliders, barracks, bomb crates and hundreds of other military uses.

Nor did Americans realize that each year 210,000 forest and range fires, 575 each day, raged throughout the 48 United States, claiming timber that could have built 215,000 five-room frame houses, enough to house the entire population of Washington, D.C.

Americans didn't understand that a million man-hours of labor— enough to build 800 fighter planes—were required each year to fight the nation's forest fires. Americans could not comprehend the number of trucks, bulldozers, tools and other equipment tied up fighting fires. They could not measure the gallons of fuel needed to power those vehicles, or the cost of that fuel and of the labor, food or tools needed to fight fires.

Most important, Americans didn't understand that their own carelessness started 90 percent of those wildly destructive forest fires.

By any standard, forest fires were an American disgrace. Drab fire prevention posters printed as early as 1902 led a meager effort to call public attention to the problem, and as late as 1939, a poster by James Montgomery Flagg featured a forest ranger (resembling Uncle Sam) pointing to a raging forest fire with the accusation "Your forest—your fault."

But World War II offered an opportunity to focus attention on the problem and create a long-term solution. If Americans started forest fires, they had to be alerted to their forest responsibility. Americans had to understand that they were destroying valuable war materials and diverting manpower needed for war.

The urgency to address forest fires rose from an unexpected threat by an unlikely predator—the Japanese Navy. On February 23, 1942, a Japanese submarine attempting to destroy fuel tanks shelled a Goleta Valley oil field at Ellwood Beach seven miles north of Santa Barbara, California. Nobukiyo Nambu, a lieutenant on the 384-foot submarine, later explained that Ellwood Beach had been picked by accident.

Trailing a U.S. Navy task force from the Marshall Islands, the sub and its crew of seventy men arrived off San Diego on February 20. With orders to attack a coastal target and divert American warships northward, the sub headed to San Francisco. Shooting into that city wasn't practical, so the submarine swung south and surfaced about a mile off Ellwood Beach just after 7 p.m. on February 23. Five nervous sailors scrambled on deck and fired a quick volley of almost two dozen five-inch shells. Bright flashes briefly lit the dusk as whistling shells interrupted nearby families listening to President Roosevelt's fireside chat.

No injuries were incurred, and losses barely reached $500 for a damaged shed and catwalk owned by the Barnsdall-Rio Grande Oil Co. But the shelling's psychological impact unnerved Californians, who suddenly felt vulnerable. The attack proved that Japan could bring its war to America's mainland.

The shelling occurred near the Los Padres National Forest, and military authorities quickly recognized that coastal forest fires could be started by saboteurs among Los Angeles's large Japanese population. But the attack also spotlighted the potential damage to America's war effort from accidental fires caused by careless citizens.

Because Southern California hosted four national forests, William V. Mendenhall, Forest Service supervisor of the Angeles National Forest, was appointed forest defense coordinator for the area. Mendenhall and his fire prevention officer—Arnold B. Larson, a former newspaperman—wanted to educate the public about its role in forest fires. So Larson developed a simple plan: ask advertising agencies to encourage clients to incorporate forest fire prevention messages into advertising or to donate posters for the effort.

Neither Larson nor Mendenhall knew of the efforts in New York and Washington to allow the Advertising Council to deal with issues such as that identified by Larson, so they didn't pursue their idea through official channels. Moreover, if Mendenhall had ever considered the quality of prewar fire prevention materials, he might have seen that the government's efforts lacked professional management. But Mendenhall air-mailed his letter on April 28, 1942, to advertising agencies across the nation. "We need your help in arousing the public to join us, as never before, in protecting America's 160 national forests," Mendenhall wrote. "It's a big part of the job of defeating the Axis."

When Young & Rubicam president Sigurd Larmon, in New York, recognized the issue's potential, he immediately telegraphed his support to Mendenhall: "Your request of April 28th has been turned over to Dr. Miller McClintock, managing director of the Advertising Council. It is our considered judgment that your cause can be served more promptly and completely through this organization than through individual agencies."

Anxious to help, McClintock reasoned that the Pacific Coast had the greatest immediate need for forest fire prevention and the deepest resources to respond. As head of the Los Angeles office of Lord & Thomas, president of the Pacific Coast Advertising Clubs and an Ad Council founder, Don Belding was the logical choice to assume responsibility for the project, and he eagerly accepted his assignment when McClintock called. Bolstered by the Ad Council's Los Angeles talent pool of twenty copywriters, artists, producers, and public relations experts, Belding could generate a fast, creative effort to protect California's forests.

With his typical quick response, Belding talked with Mendenhall. "You gotta do something, Don," Mendenhall urged. "They [the Japanese] can illuminate the whole West Coast by setting our forests on fire." Belding agreed the need was urgent, and he called a meeting of his volunteers for May 6 at the Biltmore Hotel in Los Angeles.

"Lord & Thomas was, by far, the major buyer of art and the instigator of many public and civic activities in Los Angeles," freelance artist Ren Wicks explained, "and Don Belding always was the promoter. Lord & Thomas was one of the few agencies in the world that was loyal to its cadre of contractors." So when Don Belding called, professionals such as Wicks quickly responded.

"There was quite a gathering in the 'Bowl' [a major Biltmore ballroom]," Wicks recalled. "Lord & Thomas executives, art directors, contractors and supporters were there with Department of Defense people. There was a war atmosphere—a patriotic fervor. The flag was waving and I was anxious to do my part."

For an hour and a half at that morning session, the group listened intently to a parade of speakers stressing the need for immediate action. Then Mendenhall briefed the assembly on the threat to forests, and Belding issued work assignments for posters, radio scripts, newspaper ads and bookmarks. Wicks agreed to draw a menacing Japanese soldier for a poster, while John Gudel, producer of the *Art Linkletter Show*, took the lead on radio scripts. "Everyone had offices within a few blocks of the agency [Lord & Thomas]," Wicks explained. "We were not averse to working all night."

Just three days later, a complete kit of campaign materials, with written literature and radio programs, was delivered to Los Angeles airport by Belding and Larson and sent by air express to the Ad Council's offices in Washington, D.C. The day before, however, someone had realized that Forest Service headquarters in Washington, D.C., knew nothing of the proposed campaign, so a call was placed to Dr. John Shea, Forest Service fire psychologist, who agreed to notify acting chief Earle Clapp. Then, at a May 12 meeting of the Los Angeles County Conservation Association, Belding announced that Lord & Thomas would lead the effort to develop a national campaign to prevent forest fires.

By May 16, the Forest Service was on board, but Belding had to abandon preliminary plans to let Kiwanis International sponsor the program. "Big companies all over the country," the Forest Service reasoned, "will not come in on any sporadic local campaign."

On May 18, the Ad Council presented Belding's materials to Secretary of Agriculture Claude Wickard, and in a May 26 letter to Miller McClintock, Wickard officially accepted the council's offer of cooperation. On June 3 the Forest Service completed its budget plans and, on June 11, announced that Richard F. Hammatt of its Washington office had accepted a full-time job as director of the "Wartime Forest Fire Prevention Campaign."

Born sometime around 1885, Richard Fox Hammatt, a native of Hyde Park, Massachusetts, was a 1906 honors graduate of Harvard University's first forestry class. After serving the Forest Service in Oregon and California, Hammatt resigned to become executive officer of the California Redwood Association. Returning to the Forest Service eleven years later, Hammatt transferred to Washington, D.C., in 1933 to help President Roosevelt organize the Civilian Conservation Corps.

Wallace I. Hutchinson, brought in from San Francisco to direct the forest fire prevention campaign, had turned it down. "He didn't want the job of running it," Hammatt wrote. "I did, and got it largely because of my ten years developing direct-mail campaigns [in California] and working with agencies on a national advertising campaign for the California Redwood Association, of which I was Secretary-Manager for 1921-31."

The Ad Council outlined its plans for a continuing campaign on June 25 and asked for help from the Association of State Foresters, the American Forestry Association and the National Lumber Manufacturers Association. Perry Merrill, state forester of Vermont, and Joe Kaylor, director of conservation for Maryland, immediately pledged the support of the Association of State Foresters, and state foresters agreed to coordinate the program.

This cooperation added a new element to the forest fire prevention effort. Previously, states and communities wrestled with fire prevention individually, without the benefits of consistency, continuity and economies of scale. But through the coordination offered by the Ad Council, fire prevention materials could be created nationally and adopted locally. So a pleased Secretary Wickard announced the nation's new forest fire prevention program on CBS's radio network show *Report to the Nation*.

By July 22, finished campaign materials began arriving in every corner of the nation. More than 10 million envelope stuffers, 5 million air raid warden leaflets, 2 million bookmarks, 1 million red denim cigarette "fag bags," 20,000 car cards for trolleys and buses, 10,000 posters for service stations, 5,000 "24-sheet" billboard posters (for which Lord & Thomas later won an advertising award of distinction), a series of radio spots and a motion picture trailer were distributed. The Forest Service spent $43,000 for the materials and estimated that an equal value in time and talent had been contributed by Lord & Thomas and the Ad Council.

The Ad Council had done its job well, usually through Ralph Allum, assistant to Miller McClintock in New York. "He was a peach," Hammatt wrote, "really enthusiastic, thoroughly sold, and went way beyond what he was supposed to do in order to get the campaign going under those trying first- and late-year conditions. He certainly deserves recognition." The Ad Council had created a workable forest fire prevention vehicle.

Don Belding seems to have been both architect and driver behind that first campaign as he demonstrated the speed, talent and professionalism that private enterprise could contribute to solving a "government" problem. Belding generated the energy behind the effort and, apparently, personally directed most of the advertising coordination. But partly because of Belding's aggressiveness and partly because the Ad Council was still developing, the parties had overlooked one of the council's fundamental principles: advertisers—and not advertising agencies—were required to coordinate all Ad Council campaigns.

So on September 1, the Ad Council ruled that Don Belding had to step down from his role as campaign coordinator. Ever cooperative, Belding recommended three people to fill his vacated slot—Wilmot Rogers of Del Monte in San Francisco, Roderic Olzendam of Weyerhauser Timber in Tacoma, and Belding's client, Russell Z. Eller, advertising manager of Sunkist in Los Angeles, whom Belding preferred because of his proximity to Lord & Thomas. When the Association of National Advertisers concurred, Eller was appointed volunteer coordinator—a post he would hold for twenty-three years.

Thus, a five-part foundation was established for forest fire prevention. The federal government would provide leadership through the Forest Service; the advertising industry would develop materials through the Los Angeles office of Lord & Thomas; the Ad Council would ensure national distribution of materials; state governments would guarantee state and local distribution through the Association of State Foresters; and private enterprise would sponsor campaigns and coordinate the entire effort through Russell Eller of Sunkist Growers. Except for a name change, that combination would remain until 1965.

The name change occurred when Albert Lasker, owner of Lord & Thomas, sold the agency's assets in late 1942 to Emerson Foote, Fairfax Cone and Don Belding. Lord & Thomas ceased to exist on December 31,

1942, but awoke the next morning as Foote, Cone & Belding, with the new owners directing their respective operations in New York, Chicago and Los Angeles. Sunkist Growers elected to continue with FCB as its advertising agency, and Russell Eller opted to continue as volunteer coordinator for the forest fire campaign.

On September 12, 1942, Dick Hammatt wrote to Belding that a few problems had surfaced. "There are many owners of stumpage and manufacturers of lumber who are very suspicious that the Forest Service will use this Wartime Forest Fire Prevention campaign as a vehicle through which to preach public control of cutting practices on privately owned forest land, and there are members of the Forest Service who believe some of those owners and manufacturers might be glad to throw a spike or two in the wheel of a forest fire prevention campaign undertaken in any large way by the Forest Service."

Further, the 1942 poster reflected a wartime emphasis. Ren Wicks's threatening rendition featured a grinning Japanese soldier holding a flaming match under the caption "Careless Matches Aid the Axis. Prevent Forest Fires." In truth, Wicks's grim poster may have reflected more of an anti-Axis propaganda effort than a true attempt to prevent forest fires.

But reports of pesky Japanese assaults reminded Hammatt of their mission's urgency. A Japanese submarine fired at the Oregon coast; a Japanese pilot bombed Oregon forests; a Japanese balloon bomb exploded in the Northwest. Damage was slight or the reports false, but the message was there, and a questionnaire developed by Allum and Hammatt collected ideas for the 1943 campaign. Not surprisingly, South Carolina suggested a different poster: "While the Jap face was an excellent symbol, it must be remembered that the Japs are somewhat far away to the people in the South while the Nazis are much closer. Pictures and mats possibly using a combination of the Nazi and the Jap would be more effective."

So 1943's poster showed Hitler and Tojo leering malevolently, and everywhere Americans turned on subways, buses, offices or highways they faced broadsides of the fiendishly grinning duo reminding Americans that "our carelessness" was their "secret weapon." And an incredible 36 million copies of forest fire prevention materials were distributed nationwide in that second year.

But the campaign seemed flawed as officials began to understand that the program wasn't as successful as had been hoped—partly because of intimidating posters. "There was a lot of debate about the posters the first few years," Jim Felton, the program's second national coordinator, explained. "They weren't well received and the schools didn't want to put them up." So midway through 1943, the Wartime Advertising Council, Foote, Cone & Belding and the Forest Service agreed to drop the scare tactics for 1944.

"Someone got the idea of asking Walt Disney to donate a poster," Felton recalled. "*Bambi* the movie was a big hit, so Disney did a Bambi poster and donated it to the campaign." In addition to the four dozen people in its Los Angeles office in 1943, FCB staffed a Hollywood office and motion picture unit with another twelve to fifteen people. Because the Hollywood office helped develop advertising support for radio programs originating in Hollywood, and had close ties with the Disney studios, it is likely that FCB's Hollywood staff, rather than its Los Angeles personnel, arranged with the public-spirited Disney to use Bambi in the 1944 campaign.

So of the eight forest fire prevention posters prepared for the 1944 campaign, the year's most memorable carried a plea from Bambi—the star of Disney's hit cartoon movie. With Thumper the rabbit and Flower the skunk, Bambi offered his message: "Please Mister, Don't Be Careless." Suddenly, forest fire prevention took a major step forward when enthusiastic children wanted to take the Bambi poster home from school.

With only two full years under its belt by the summer of 1944, the new forest fire prevention effort couldn't yet claim success. However, the program had captured the attention of business leaders and the idea of forest fire prevention had caught on with the American public—particularly on the West Coast. As a state close to the Pacific theater, and a possible target of another Japanese attack, California's forest fire prevention efforts were widespread by July 1944, only a month before the official birth of Smokey Bear.

Standard Oil, Shell, Atlantic-Richfield and other oil companies displayed thousands of posters at their service stations and promoted the issue in company magazines, on company premises and on radio. Elevator riders in Shell buildings faced the "Grim Specter"—a sketch of a burned forest. American Box, Marin, Pacific Telephone, 247 post offices and 134 military stations displayed fire safety posters. J. C. Penney created fire prevention window displays, logging camps and sawmills exhibited posters and the California State Automobile Association reproduced campaign material in its literature.

National and regional foresters solicited companies to sponsor fire prevention messages on billboards. The Office of Wartime Information in San Francisco distributed fire prevention radio platters, and San Bernadino National Forest employees wrote, produced and aired a series of noon broadcasts on station KFXM. Cartoons were provided to newspapers that also carried announcements of 1944 campaign efforts.

"Bambi" and other posters were sent to a thousand California libraries that requested 80,000 bookmarks. More than 4,000 posters were distributed to Los Angeles-area primary schools, and secondary schools took thousands more.

Among the talented people who participated in the creation of Smokey Bear, one man—Bill Bergoffen—survived long after his colleagues had passed away. With an aptitude for critical observation, a keen memory and a penchant for accurate accreditation, Bergoffen typifies the Forest Service people who contributed to the birth of the world's most famous bear.

William Wolf Bergoffen came into the world in New York City in 1908. By "Wolf's" fourth birthday, his family had moved to the sleepy mountainside village of Monticello, in upstate New York's borscht belt. While his Polish father toiled as town tailor and his Hungarian mother took in boarders, Wolf ran barefoot, caught squirrels, rabbits and yellow perch, and learned to love the forest.

After moving to Newark at age twelve, a determined Wolf focused on getting to a summer forestry camp in the Hudson River country. "I worked like hell in a cardboard tube factory so I could pay my way," Bergoffen recalled. And at camp he learned forestry skills that led him to a degree in 1931 from Syracuse University, after studies at the New York State College of Forestry.

Then the Civilian Conservation Corps program needed forestry leaders for its work groups. "Military men ran the camps and had responsibility for food, discipline and quarters," Bergoffen, now going by the name "Bill," recalled. "But state or federal people [such as Bergoffen] were the work foremen. Many CCC enrollees came from New York and other metropolitan centers and didn't know anything about forests, so the world opened up to any forester." Hired by the Forest Service, Bergoffen learned his forests as trainee and foreman and in a series of assistant forest ranger jobs. Bergoffen learned about forest fires in Georgia, Tennessee, Alabama and Mississippi, but he focused on writing as a district forest ranger in Blue Ridge, Georgia.

"Part of my duty was to publicize the newly established Chattahooche National Forest and offer some good preachments, especially about preventing woods fires," Bergoffen grinned. "So I started a column in several weekly newspapers. We called it the 'Ranger's Corner,' and I like to think it helped accent the need to keep the forest most productive and useful to the people in the surrounding communities."

At the DeSoto National Forest in Mississippi, Bergoffen parlayed his writing into a daily column entitled "Ranger Bill Says," and he added a Sunday morning radio program, where he told stories about ranger work. Soon, CCC enrollees competed to provide musical background for Ranger Bill's stories. "We had spirituals, work songs and even jail songs," Bergoffen remembered. "That was a pretty effective program, and we attracted some attention."

When word of the imaginative "writing ranger" reached Forest Service headquarters in 1940, Bergoffen transferred to Washington, D.C., to serve in the Division of Information and Education (I&E). There Bergoffen wrote forestry material for nationwide use and authored scripts for a weekly 15-minute radio segment, "Uncle Sam's Forest Rangers," broadcast on NBC network's *National Farm and Home Hour*.

In August 1944, Bergoffen had the good fortune to be part of a group of folks from the Forest Service and the Office of War Information who began planning supplemental material for the mass-media items produced by Foote, Cone & Belding for 1945's forest fire prevention campaign. But before acting, the group carefully assessed their progress.

"First, they had tried scare tactics with grinning Japanese and German terrorists," Bergoffen summarized. "The result: the United States actually had *more* fires by arsonists. The arsonists thought they had good reasons— to kill boll weevils and to green-up grass. Many of those people were resentful of the posters. They thought they were accused of being the enemy. So those posters did more harm than good in some states. But Bambi did get a positive reaction—especially from kids who started sending in letters. Our sole objective was to find a way to tell the forest fire prevention story most effectively. Many advertisers felt that children and animals were the two best attention getters, and animals and forests certainly were a natural combination.

"We learned very quickly that animals were effective in getting people— especially the young—to react," Bergoffen emphasized. "People go for animals as a visual image. That was especially important because we thought we wanted to try to educate the youngsters. It was the kids who started writing in, plus older folks had not been doing a very good job. It was the adults who started a lot of roadside woods and brush fires—they just tossed lighted matches and cigarettes away. But we thought—or hoped—children could influence their adults. We were just groping, feeling our way, and trying to provide angles and ideas to FCB."

In fact, the Forest Service had searched for some time to develop a consistent symbol for forest fire prevention, and two of those attempts are documented.

By 1944, Frank Sweeley, in the Stanislaus National Forest abutting Yosemite National Park in California, had created "Little Willie," "Sapling Sam," "Ranger Bill," "Ranger Jim" and other fictional crusaders for fire prevention. "Fables about Willie," published weekly by area newspapers, documented Willie's difficulties in making his thoughtless father more fire conscious. Although Forest Service headquarters in Washington knew of Sweeley's efforts, no attempt appears to have been made to adopt Sweeley's characters nationally.

A more concerted attempt developed in the Forest Service's regional office in Atlanta, Georgia. "From 1938 through 1940 foresters and conservationists were worried about all the fires in the southeast," Forest Service artist Harry Rossoll explained. "So in 1942, Clint Davis [I&E officer in Atlanta] said, 'Harry, get your creative juices going and come up with a symbol to help.' I read and thought about it and generated about a hundred ideas, but with just rough sketches. My first idea was 'Ranger Jim.'"

Stalwart Ranger Jim, bedecked in Forest Service uniform, dark tie, pipe, and ranger hat, boasted a profile bearing an uncanny resemblance to the as yet unknown General Dwight Eisenhower. Rossoll's heading over each portrayal included "Ranger Jim Says:" with appropriate captions to trail each drawing. But Ranger Jim never saw a forest. "Ranger Jim was a big flop," Rossoll admitted. "The average person hated the government because of the depression."

"Then I tried a 'fire devil' that had a wooden head, a wooden body and a pitchfork," Rossoll continued. "He would be the epitome of a firefighter. He was wooden, so he hated forest fires. That was a complete flop too. Then we tried a flat-tailed beaver. This beaver could put out fires; we figured he could flap them out with his tail. Flap, flap, flap, flap, flap. But that would have gotten monotonous to go around flapping out fires all the time." So Rossoll faced another flap . . . er, flop.

"In 1943," Rossoll continued, "H. F. Sears, a fire guy in Atlanta, said, 'How about a bear?' So I said, 'Let's try it,' and I made a bear—a fuzzy bear with dungarees. He was a terrible-looking bear. It had a bulb nose and a World War I campaign hat with a chin strap. The bear didn't have a name. We produced a few sketches and drawings to try it out." But Rossoll's bear never saw a forest either.

"I was about to be drafted. Later I thought that after I left, my idea might have made it to Washington because they hadn't developed their bear yet. I always thought they might have seen my sketches." But Rossoll enlisted in the navy and headed to an artist's training center on Treasure Island in San Francisco. "I forgot all about the Forest Service," Rossoll explained. "I didn't know if I would ever be back."

Ranger Jim Says:

"There is more tree cutting than there is tree planting."

Artist Harry Rossoll created "Ranger Jim" in 1942 as a possible forest fire prevention symbol. *(Courtesy of Harry Rossoll.)*

When the 1944 Washington task force decided to focus on a forest animal, some staffers thought that Bambi would make an attractive permanent symbol for the campaign. "But there were a number of copyright problems and other complications in continuing the use of Bambi," Bill Bergoffen recalled. "Disney would *loan* Bambi, but wouldn't release the deer." In any event, FCB didn't believe that Bambi was the answer. Although Americans could sympathize with an animal victim of a forest fire, they couldn't associate a deer with the hard work of preventing forest fires. A new symbol was needed.

38

Several animals were suggested, and a squirrel seemed to be an early favorite, so a draft poster of a squirrel was produced by New York artist Albert Staehle. The squirrel finally was rejected, however, because it had the same problem as a deer: it is difficult to conceptualize a squirrel fighting a forest fire. As other animals were rejected, thoughts even turned to consideration of whether Montgomery Flagg's "Uncle Sam" would have an appeal.

Finally, the task force agreed that a large animal might be best— especially one that could stand upright, fight a forest fire and perhaps be humanized. As the team wrestled, it became apparent that a bear might be the answer. A bear was strong. A bear could be humanized. A bear was the toughest animal in the forest and, because might makes right, could be a powerful force for fire prevention. Who would argue with a bear?

And so, on August 9, 1944, Smokey Bear was born* at 14th and Independence on the third floor of the Department of Agriculture Building in Washington, D.C., when program director Richard Hammatt issued these instructions:

August 9, 1944

Special Art for Wartime Forest Fire Prevention Campaign Through OWI Art Pool

For use on:
  (1) Kraft paper book cover (6 x 9").
  (2) Bookmark, 2 1/2 x 6 1/4" (bristolboard).
  (3) Poster, 14 1/4 x 20" (120 lb. coated paper).

Subject: Characterization (Disney manner?) of a (cub?) bear in a green (unburned) pine forest setting.

> *Nose short (Panda type), color black or brown; expression appealing, knowledgeable, quizzical; perhaps wearing a campaign (or Boy Scout) hat that typifies the outdoors and the woods.*
>
> *A bear that walks on his hind legs; that can be shown putting out a warming fire with a bucket of water; dropping by parachute*

Technically, in this writer's judgment, Smokey Bear was *conceived* on August 9, 1944, and truly *born* about eight months later in the spring of 1945 when his image first appeared publicly on posters throughout the United States. However, in 1954 and at periodic intervals thereafter, the Forest Service has celebrated Smokey's birthday as August 9, 1944. Putative revisionists can't expect to overturn fifty years of fine tradition.

> *to a fire; reporting a fire by phone from a lookout; plowing a fire-*
> *line around a new-made clearing; building a campfire in the right*
> *place and way; carrying a rifle like G.I. Joes, etc.*

Note: Do not simulate bears drawn by Cliff Berryman of the Washington Star
(Teddy bears); used in Boy Scout publications; used by Piper Cub (airplane); the
bear that symbolizes Russia; the bears on attached Forest Service bookmark.

Message: PREVENT FOREST FIRES.
Tag line: To be determined later.

Preliminary art not later than September 4; final art within 30 days of approval of
preliminary; payment not to exceed $300 on acceptance of final art.

Exactly who created Smokey Bear? Nobody seems to know. Richard Hammatt, as campaign leader, generally (and, apparently, appropriately) is given most of the credit. But the decision to focus on a bear seems to have been a collective effort. No documentation credits any single individual with the idea, and no record suggests that anyone in Washington, D.C., ever saw Harry Rossoll's early Atlanta drawings. The foresters, OWI staffers and, perhaps, Ad Council representatives seem to have been concerned more with their wartime responsibilities than with allocating recognition. Bill Bergoffen, the only living participant fifty years later, could not identify a single person to be credited with the original idea or anyone who aggressively promoted it. "A lot of people threw a lot of ideas into the stew pot," Bergoffen shrugged. And some people insist that Smokey wasn't even developed in Washington, D.C.

Russell Daigle, retired from the Forest Service, is one of those uncorroborated (so far) challengers. Daigle credits Wallace Hutchinson, a native of New Brunswick, Canada, and an early 1900s graduate of the Yale School of Forestry, for inspiring Smokey. According to Daigle, "'Hutch' was an impressive writer, public speaker, and creator of national forest map folders, pamphlets and signs. His speciality, actually a passion, was the cause of preventing man-caused fires in forest lands." With Hutchinson's okay, a Miss Ziegler, of Shell Oil Company's California public relations office, tried to help the cause. "Along in 1941," Daigle continued, "she presented us with a free-lance artist's rendition of a cub bear in a forest setting. Wallace Hutchinson immediately named the spunky little fellow 'Smokey.'"

One Washington newspaper later reported that more than six hundred people eventually claimed to have been the father of Smokey Bear. Maybe they were, because by all accounts the achievement seems to have been the product of a true team effort.

In any event, the Forest Service has for many years officially (and, given extant evidence, perhaps gracefully) credited Foote, Cone & Belding and the Ad Council with generating the idea for America's fire-preventing bear. However, some evidence indicates that, as of mid-August 1944, FCB knew nothing about the pending bear symbol. An August 14, 1944, letter from Ford Sibley of FCB in Los Angeles to Richard Hammatt talks of an "American Enemy" trailer, Disney and other 1945 material, but makes no mention of a bear or suggests any involvement with the Washington team behind the bear.

Sibley's letter, mailed from FCB's offices at 601 West Fifth Street in Los Angeles, was received in Forest Service headquarters in Washington on August 17, 1944. Given the pivotal role played by FCB in the forest fire prevention program from its inception, it seems surprising that the agency may not have been involved in the actual creation of Smokey Bear. But FCB alumni with knowledge of 1944's events didn't seem bothered by their apparent exclusion from a key decision by their client. "That was their privilege," Bill Belsey, a former FCB executive, explained without even a hint of irritation or abandonment.

"FCB served as the agency for production of the material and implementation of the theme," Jim Felton agreed, "but there was never any question who the client was. The antiwar posters were not going over with schoolkids, and Ford Sibley also was calling in other art directors from agencies in Los Angeles to see if they had ideas. But we needed posters with appeal, and [Albert] Staehle's direction was not to draw only a bear, but other animals too. Staehle came back with seven or eight posters—an owl, a squirrel, a chipmunk and a mangy-looking bear; out of this, the committee selected a bear." (They also adopted Staehle's squirrel poster.)

"FCB was involved to the point they knew they were in the process of getting away from the hard-sell antiwar philosophy," Felton continued. "FCB was aware that they were going to have a change; to what extent, they did not know. The most important graphic was a poster for schools— not a visual for television. Kits for schoolkids always focused around a central theme demonstrated in the poster, and the Staehle bear would be the poster."

Jacques Dunlany of OWI, who is credited with choosing Staehle, officially asked the artist to create the bear outlined by Hammatt. Staehle,

41

who was born in Munich, Germany, in 1899, and emigrated to the United States at age fourteen, was one of the nation's best-known animal artists. A freelancer recognized for his flop-eared cocker spaniel "Butch" on *Saturday Evening Post* covers, Staehle earned his reputation at age nineteen by entering a poster of a cow and a calf in a 1918 art contest. His work captured attention from the Borden milk company, which developed Staehle's poster into its corporate symbol, Elsie the Cow. Staehle worked fast, and Smokey made his debut in September at Forest Service headquarters.

Staehle's rough art ignited a controversy, however, as curious crowds, including Forest Service chief Lyle Watts, gathered to view the drawing. Staehle had interpreted the new fire prevention symbol as a cute bear with floppy ears, big eyes, a humped neck and natural-looking paws pouring a bucket of water on a campfire.

"The consensus was that the bear didn't have the appeal of Bambi, who was a national hero," Bill Bergoffen remembered. "Staehle had drawn a naked animal; it wasn't enough; it was lacking. The baby was born, but most people were a little taken aback at the idea of a naked bear throwing water on a fire."

Still, the bear appeared to be favored over Staehle's other characters, although his squirrel had strong support, as evidenced in a September 5 memo from Jim Richardson to Chief Watts: "I certainly hope they develop and use the Bear character as a continuing, full-time actor instead of the Squirrel—my conviction is that the Squirrel does not have nearly the human interest plus art possibilities that the Bear, whose human-like antics appeal to, amuse and instruct all ages in all localities urban and rural, while the Squirrel is a nuisance and just a damn rodent to farmers and rural people in many localities."

So early one September afternoon, Richard Hammatt called Dana Parkinson (director of I&E), Fred Schoder and Bill Bergoffen into his office to solve the issue of Staehle's naked bear. Although not a forester, Schoder was viewed as a good publications chief whom Hammatt called "the guy who gets things done—and I *mean* done." Bergoffen, too, held pleasant memories of the man born in Denver, Colorado, in 1904: "Fred was a very active, vibrant individual who became as involved as anyone else with Smokey. Fred really took that bear to heart."

Knowledgeable, likable and a good administrator, Hammatt was determined to fix their problem. Hammatt was too intense a worker to notice the drabness of his small, third-floor office overlooking Independence Avenue. Usually only Hammatt's wooden desk and two visitor chairs filled the sand-colored room with high white ceiling, plain linoleum floor and forest scenes adorning the walls. But that day an easel supported the drawing of Staehle's bear.

Bergoffen, with his usual open-collared shirt, contrasted with the white shirt and tie worn by the more formal Hammatt, but Bergoffen remembered the meeting as relaxed and informal. The four men felt neither a sense of mission nor urgency. They simply had to decide what to do with their new product.

"Staehle had drawn a bare bear," Bergoffen laughed, "and Hammatt decided it had to be humanized. That feeling stemmed from a general reaction that the bear simply lacked an emotional appeal. The poster had the action and the message, but it didn't have the impact Hammatt wanted. We did not consider changing animals; the question was to see what we could do with what we had."

And so a debate waged for two hours until Hammatt broke the stalemate. Insisting that the bear needed a name, Hammatt himself apparently suggested "Smokey"—or at least Bill Bergoffen thinks he did. Like the actual idea for the creation of the bear, the person to be credited for naming the bruin "Smokey" seems never to have been conclusively determined. Bergoffen isn't absolutely certain that Hammatt came up with the suggestion (it may have been Schoder), but to the best of Bergoffen's memory, it was Hammatt.

Almost all later reports credited Hammatt (or whomever) for taking inspiration from the exploits of "Smokey Joe" Martin, a deceased assistant chief of New York City's fire department. Newspaper articles, however, sometimes referred to "Smokey Joe Ryan" or "Smokey Joe Wood" as the genesis; others suggested the name was created independently of New York's Smokey Joe. It cannot be stated with certainty that Hammatt suggested the name or that Smokey Joe Martin was a factor. But a review of Martin's career suggests he would have been a wonderful inspiration for America's fire preventin' bear. If that isn't the way it was, perhaps that's the way it should have been.

Joseph B. Martin and Smokey Bear shared more than a name—they each grew into living legends, and both seem to have been destined for greatness as firefighters. America's great Civil War still raged when Martin was born in New York City, apparently in 1863. Almost from birth, Martin sought no greater calling, no greater honor and no greater thrill than being a fireman for more than forty-six years. Raised on East 13th Street in Manhattan, the little boy was capitivated by Engine Company 5's firehouse. There, bewhiskered firemen soon had an eager Martin running errands.

Ignoring parental pleas, Martin dropped out of City College after two years and proudly donned a fireman's hat for Franklin Street's Engine Company 27 on January 18, 1884. A fast learner, Martin was promoted to lieutenant in 1889, to captain in 1892, to battalion chief in 1908 and to assistant chief of the New York City Fire Department in 1912. Whether commanding an engine company or a hook-and-ladder outfit, fighting a fire or dealing with his men, Martin relished life as a firefighter.

Although dedicated to the safety of the men under his command, Martin frequently pushed himself to the limits of human tolerance, and his reputation for gallantry grew to phenomenal heights. Even as age advanced, Martin wouldn't walk away from a fire. He fought thousands of fires, made numerous rescues, repeatedly risked his life for others, was seriously injured twenty times and cited for bravery six times.

While fighting with Engine Company 31 in 1898 to save a burning building at 71 Walker Street, Martin kicked down the door of a fourth-floor, smoke-filled room and charged in to control the blaze. But Martin badly underestimated the fire, and as the fourth floor collapsed, Martin fell with accumulating flaming debris through the fourth, third, second and first floors, finally collapsing into the basement amidst burning wreckage.

Martin's men raced in, pulled away flaming rubble to save his corpse from burning, and delivered his charred, mangled body to a local hospital. Left unattended throughout the night, the supposed cadaver suddenly shouted for a drink of water at dawn the next morning and cursed an immigrant Italian orderly who couldn't believe Martin's bloodied body was indeed alive. Astonished doctors treated the irascible firefighter for extensive burns, several sprains and various internal injuries and then sewed nineteen stitches into his stubborn head. Three months later, a very-much-alive Martin walked out of the hospital.

The next year, Martin acquired the nickname by which he would be remembered for more than one hundred years. Joseph A. Lawler, a lieutenant in Engine Company 69, wrote about Martin in 1948 in *WNYF*—a fire department magazine:

> Let us recall . . . a cold winter night in 1899, when Chief Edward F. Croker was in command of a warehouse fire at West and Hubert Streets. It was a terrible night and a terrible fire with the basement clogged with thick, strangling smoke. Someone had to enter that basement with a hoseline and fight the fire, and Captain Martin, who

44

was in command of Engine Company 31, led his men down the stairs. The smoke forced them back.

The crew of Engine 31 finally gave up and reeled up the stairs to gasp mouthfuls of fresh air, all except Captain Martin. He stuck with the hose in the basement. They were about to give him up for dead when Croker himself went charging in, feeling for the hose and crawling across the basement on all fours. He found the Captain at the nozzle still fighting the flames. Croker ordered him out and the Captain followed his Chief. The latter escorted the grimy, smoke-stained figure up to a group of reporters and gasped, "Gentlemen, this is 'Smokey-Joe' Martin. By the Gods, he certainly does love it."

At age sixty-eight, Martin collapsed of exhaustion during a three-alarm blaze on 33rd Street and, with a nudge from the department's medical board, finally hung up his beloved fireman's hat. On November 1, 1930, the firefighting career of Smokey Joe Martin ended. But the medical board couldn't drain the firefighting blood from Martin's veins, and until his death at 12:37 a.m. on October 25, 1941, Smokey Joe responded to major alarms throughout the city.

"After Hammatt suggested the name, it all began to come together," Bergoffen remembered. "Hammatt really gave the bear a personality with that name. Schoder proposed a hat—a ranger hat or a World War I campaign hat." Then Bergoffen recommended dungarees. "Well, we sure couldn't put him in a suit or civies," Bergoffen shrugged. "Dungarees were just perfect for the outdoors. It was a natural. The bear wouldn't have looked good in anything else."

As the meeting broke up, none of the participants knew they had just made a major contribution to the forest fire prevention effort. Bergoffen brushed aside their achievement: "There was no special sense of elation or feeling of accomplishment. The meeting was routine; it was part of our job. We just went back to work. We didn't realize we had passed a milestone." But Staehle's bear wasn't the only one to pick up a tag line that afternoon. When word of the meeting spread throughout the Forest Service, Bill Bergoffen became known thereafter as "the man who put the pants on Smokey."

BILL BERGOFFEN...

... the man who put the pants on Smokey

In 1967, artist Rudy Wendelin commemorated Bill Bergoffen as "the man who put the pants on Smokey" in 1944. *(Courtesy of W. W. Bergoffen and USDA Forest Service.)*

The naked bear was returned to Staehle with a request to dress his animal in dungarees, toss on a hat and name him Smokey. And in a September 13 meeting with Dunlany and Jackson (of OWI), Hammatt gave the green light for final art on Smokey, to be delivered by October 10 with layouts for a poster, bookmark and book cover.

So Staehle dressed his chocolate-brown bear in a hat akin to a World War I campaign hat held on by a leather band. Sky-blue, cuffed and baggy dungarees held up by a narrow belt completed his attire. A large left ear snaked around Smokey's hat, a black pupil peered from a white eyeball and a long snout completed the bear's head. A blue sky and green silhouette forest provided background for the bare-torsoed, intelligent-looking Smokey. Shoulder, back and arm muscles rippled under a bright sun to illustrate strength as he poured water from a pail onto a campfire in a grassy clearing. At the bottom, a green-and-orange tag line insisted: "Smokey Says—Care *will* prevent 9 out of 10 forest fires."

In a November 4 letter to Staehle at his art studio at 551 Fifth Avenue in New York City, Chief Watts expressed his pleasure with Staehle's work: "This note is to tell you how much all of us like 'Smokey'—which is the name of the bear you've just done for us at the request of Jacques Dunlany of OWI. He has a right engaging personality, this Smokey of yours. And he'll appear widely—on posters and bookmarks—in public libraries and public schools during 1945. We're hoping, however, that he'll be so versatile and popular that he'll play an even more important role, as time goes on, in the nationwide forest fire prevention program that Federal and State agencies are carrying on, now, at the request of the Armed Forces as part of the war effort. Thanks again for your help. We in the Forest Service appreciate it, and so do the State Foresters."

The jury was out. Hammatt, Parkinson, Schoder, Bergoffen and their colleagues had to await the verdict of the American public.

5

SMOKEY'S EARLY YEARS

"Within the next year or two it became apparent that we had hit the jackpot with Smokey Bear."

— Bill Bergoffen

"I want to save the forests. Whatever the Forest Service wants, you guys get it for them."

— Don Belding

Judgment was quick and overwhelmingly positive. Virtually everyone associated with the new caricature decreed Albert Staehle's Smokey Bear poster to be an initial success. Like his colleagues, Bill Bergoffen marveled at the public's swift reaction: "The forest fire prevention campaign really came alive when Smokey Bear was released. Almost overnight Smokey became a popular character, especially in contrast to other materials the campaign had used. Letters started flowing in from kids, and we got a strong, positive media reaction. Suddenly we had a large demand for Smokey Bear materials. Naturally, everyone in the campaign approved of the concept—the Forest Service, Foote, Cone & Belding, the Ad Council and the state foresters. That bear really cemented state and federal relationships in forest fire prevention; he strengthened their attitude about working together."

With the effort officially named the Cooperative Forest Fire Prevention campaign, the CFFP began developing its 1946 strategy. Smokey had not yet demonstrated his staying power, but the bear offered more attractive marketing possibilities than his companion squirrel, so on FCB's recommendation, Staehle was commissioned to draw another Smokey poster. When Richard Hammatt reported objections that Smokey's hat did not meet uniform specifications, a series of heated discussions followed, but the CFFP stayed with the concept.

"It was clear that Smokey was a 'go,' at least for the next year," Bergoffen explained. "But at that time I don't think anyone envisioned or even would have believed what lay ahead for Smokey Bear."

Although not readily apparent in 1945, Smokey Bear was destined for stardom. His career as a symbol of forest fire prevention had been launched. Over the next fifty years proud Americans would learn to love their bear, and millions of people around the world would be able to identify Smokey's image and his message. Trailing only Santa Claus (or the Coca-Cola logo or the Bell Telephone symbol, depending upon your source), Smokey Bear would become the second most-recognized symbol in America. And Smokey Joe Martin, the fearless New York firefighter, would be immortalized by the poster bear carrying his name.

When 1946 news ads used Smokey's caricature in a variety of costumes and situations, FCB and the CFFP began to appreciate Smokey's attention-getting potential. Caricature made the human situations in which Smokey appeared more believable and reflected a trend to humanize animal figures and let them communicate as they entertained. But despite that initial success, neither the CFFP nor the advertising people were completely comfortable with their newborn creation. Without deciding to permanently employ Smokey, the CFFP elected to try a third campaign with their new bear, and in 1947 another interpretation of Smokey appeared in a poster illustrated by Russ Wetzel.

Wetzel's interpretation proved popular, but concern developed that a humorous appearance would detract from Smokey's serious message. So Smokey's appearance changed again in the 1948 "praying bear" campaign poster by James Hansen, a noted illustrator who portrayed a human-looking Smokey on his knees, asking that people be more careful.

Over the next few years dozens of leaders and organizations across the nation encouraged public acceptance of Smokey as a unifying symbol in America's battle to prevent people-caused forest fires. Solid effort, careful planning, a willingness to learn from mistakes and blind luck all played a role in Smokey's development, but Smokey's sparkling success certainly wasn't an accident.

Bill Bergoffen (middle), Rudy Wendelin (right) and a technician check an early Smokey Bear poster. *(Courtesy W. W. Bergoffen.)*

While Foote, Cone & Belding in Los Angeles nurtured Smokey's growth and development from a rookie firefighter to a symbol of international prominence, Forest Service headquarters in Washington, D.C., cleared the way politically and engineered support from federal and state governments. Among the many contributors to the program throughout those early years, two men—Don Belding and Clint Davis—played pivotal roles. If these two pillars had contributed nothing but their personalities and leadership, the campaign might have achieved success on that basis alone.

Clint Davis, a former outdoor writer and army photographer, replaced Richard Hammatt as director of the CFFP program in 1946. Don Belding, who rose from desperate poverty to ownership of one of the world's largest advertising agencies, hammered home the advertising principles that made the national media so receptive to Smokey Bear. The backgrounds of both men illustrate the caliber of the people who helped Smokey emerge as an effective force for forest fire prevention.

Davis's good friend Mike Frome reported in *American Forests* that "Clinton Leon" apparently was born in 1910 in Unadilla, Georgia, where, as a growing boy, he favored the great outdoors over schoolrooms. Leon attended the University of Georgia Extension School in Atlanta but didn't receive a degree—largely because of his preference for fishing, hunting and hiking through Georgia's forests. But Leon turned his love of the outdoors into a paying career, first during a three-year stint as public relations director for Georgia's Department of Game and Fish. There, Leon learned the value of partnership efforts as he helped develop the nation's first federal-state cooperative wildlife management area.

Then in 1933, introducing himself as "Clint Davis," the young man convinced the *Atlanta Constitution* that its readership would love an outdoor sports column. So young Davis/Leon began a brief career as an outdoor writer and photographer. In 1937 the stocky, six-foot-three Davis became an administrative assistant in the Forest Service's Atlanta regional office, but soon moved up to information director for the region's eleven states, where he helped develop a cooperative tree-planting program with several states and private landowners.

Traditionally, the Forest Service promoted from within, and accountants, foresters and rangers were transformed into "Information and Education" people. But Davis was the first outsider hired directly into I&E, and it proved to be a good marriage. With a well-honed nose for publicity, Davis learned forestry so quickly that no one cared that he had not risen through the ranks. And because he understood the public relations potential of relatively minor events, Davis didn't take long to establish his value.

Frome summarized Davis as "expansive"—large in size and in his appetite for both food and ideas. Apparently only a few men could compete with Davis in the gastronomic delights. Davis enjoyed loitering over breakfast and lunch and liked to finish dinner late at night. A fan of red-eye gravy and hickory-cooked steaks, Davis liked his own cooking best, and campers claimed they never had a better-supplied companion on the trail. Davis loved people and spread good cheer as effectively as Johnny Appleseed spread his fruit.

During World War II, Davis developed skills as a motion picture technician and producer in the Army Signal Corps and, after the war, transferred to Forest Service headquarters in Washington, D.C., to oversee the CFFP program. Because of Davis's thirst for ideas and his willingness to delegate, he attracted highly creative people who delivered the quality work Davis expected. Over time, Davis left routine work to his staff while he traveled widely to promote Smokey Bear. But Davis's primary contribution to the campaign was his guidance of the development of fire prevention policy through the Forest Service, state foresters, the Ad Council and FCB.

"Clint Davis was, instinctively, a terrific promoter—one of the best," Bill Bergoffen insisted. "Clint had an assistant director and a secretary; that was his only real staff. But Clint had access to Forest Service help— people such as Fred Schoder, Rudy Wendelin, me and other writers. We were Forest Service personnel but, technically, not a special part of the Smokey Bear staff."

By 1946 it became apparent that posters, newspapers and magazines weren't the only mass-media vehicles that could communicate Smokey's message. The Ad Council and FCB recognized the potential of radio and television to help promote Smokey, and Davis, armed with skills he learned in the army, jumped into the lead with his usual enthusiasm. Although FCB eventually produced almost all of Smokey's TV and radio commercials, that wasn't the case initially—largely because Smokey still was only a supplement to the primary campaign in 1946. And Davis ensured that Washington contributed its share of work to the cause.

Because radio and television fit within Bill Bergoffen's primary responsibilities, Bergoffen assumed the task of exploring the benefits of increased Smokey exposure over the airwaves. Although Bergoffen eventually headed the Forest Service audiovisual program, in Smokey's early years Bergoffen devoted only part of his time to fire prevention. "I was just a regular, all-around staff guy in I&E," Bergoffen recalled. "Three or four of us did editorial work, printing, exhibits and things like that." But Smokey flashed his charm, and whoever fell in with that engaging character soon became enamored with him and proud to be a member of the Smokey Bear team.

"I spent about 50 percent of my time on the Smokey program," Bergoffen explained. "My other work required producing more routine, day-to-day Forest Service materials." But in his spare time, Bergoffen recruited help for the CFFP's unofficial family of supporters. Apparently, both FCB and the CFFP agreed that Smokey could be a more effective spokesbear if he communicated directly with his intended audience, so in 1947 Bergoffen put some life into Smokey's posters.

"We felt we needed a voice," Bergoffen grinned. "The message had always been there, but we had never done a program with Smokey Bear talking. Jackson Weaver—a radio broadcaster—was well known as a man of several voices. He was an impressionist and had been doing some work for the Department of Agriculture. He was best known around the office as the voice of Bessie the Cow."

He had never met Weaver, but Bergoffen simply called the radio star. "I told Jackson that we were looking for a voice of Smokey Bear and that we were impressed with the work he had done. I guess I praised him a little. Then I asked, 'Can you be a gruff old bear?' and Jackson immediately gave me several renditions. They all sounded good, so I made an appointment to meet in a radio studio." When Weaver tested well, Bergoffen arranged for Weaver to be Smokey's official voice.

"Back then we cut 'platters'—the old 33 1/3 rpm records," Bergoffen recalled. "We cut records of 'spots'—20 seconds; 30 seconds; one minute. If you goofed halfway into the recording, you had to do it all over again, so we spent a lot of time cutting records." That process could be laborious as the Forest Service produced a thirteen-week series of spots, with at least one new series each year.

Because Bergoffen wanted year-to-year familiarity with the bear, Weaver and Bergoffen devoted considerable time to developing a solid Smokey voice. Just as Smokey's posters had more impact with a consistent rendering of his character image, so too would a consistent voice prove more effective. "We wanted to humanize him and we wanted him to have a deep voice," Bergoffen said, "but we certainly didn't want a gruff voice. The bear simply had to be friendly, so we wanted to be careful that he wasn't intimidating. We didn't want Smokey to be a threat; we wanted him to sound as if he were making a request."

To achieve the right timbre in the voice, Weaver and Bergoffen first put their heads together and then stuck Weaver's head into a bucket. So there was Jackson Weaver, a polished radio man, spewing out fire prevention messages from a bucket. Eventually, Weaver created his characterization without the bucket, and the voice of Smokey Bear spread across America's radio and television airwaves. And although Bergoffen didn't realize it, he had recruited a man who would become so famous in his own right that the very mention of his name recalled the image of Smokey Bear. Over and over and over again, Jackson Weaver would generate publicity for Smokey Bear.

Born in 1920 in Buffalo, New York, where he began his broadcasting career, Weaver worked in Erie, Pennsylvania, and Manitowoc, Wisconsin, before moving to the Washington, D.C., area in 1942 to begin a fifty-year

Bill Bergoffen (standing, left) and a technican watch as Jackson Weaver (seated), the "voice of Smokey Bear," records at radio station WMAL in Washington, D.C. *(Courtesy of W. W. Bergoffen.)*

career with station WMAL. Although primarily a radio announcer, Weaver provided both radio and TV coverage for almost every type of news program, including White House press conferences. By the early 1950s, Weaver was announcer of *The Navy Hour*, a nationwide radio program, but when he teamed with Frank Harden for a morning radio show in 1960, its time demands led Weaver to surrender his television activities.

A short, rotund figure who sported a walrus mustache in later years, Weaver reportedly couldn't read a piece of copy straight, so he stopped trying and invented his own array of imaginary characters—a medical doctor, a band leader, a U.S. Senator, a roving special events reporter—all with special accents. Impossibly straight in real life, however, Weaver often missed the point when his associates teased him, and someone usually had to explain "dirty" jokes to him. Weaver loved people, and everyone loved Weaver, who never seemed to be in a bad mood.

Weaver's partnership with Frank Harden blossomed into a thirty-two-year success story and helped lift WMAL from the ranks of an also-ran to a major media influence in Washington. As one of the world's highest-paid radio stars, Weaver reportedly earned $250,000 annually and his morning show commanded advertising fees as high as $800 per minute.

Everywhere, Jackson Weaver was associated with Smokey Bear. When newspapers talked about Harden and Weaver's one million public service announcements, they mentioned the voice of Smokey Bear. When Weaver took his annual trip overseas, the press mentioned the voice of Smokey Bear. When Weaver was praised for the millions of dollars he raised for charity, they told the story of the voice of Smokey Bear. When Weaver spoke at public functions or emceed major events, he was introduced as the voice of Smokey Bear. When Weaver donated money to community causes, he was honored as the voice of Smokey Bear.

And when Weaver died in late 1992, the face of Smokey Bear appeared on network television screens across the nation, and a familiar deep, sonorous voice boomed out to millions of viewers as Jackson Weaver delivered his final words to the American public: "Remember, only you can prevent forest fires."

Like most of his colleagues, Bergoffen helped protect Smokey's image, right down to his dungarees. When Bil Keane, nationally known artist of the syndicated cartoon "Channel Chuckles" drew Smokey wearing "bib" overalls, Bergoffen wrote Keane to thank him for publicizing Smokey but pointed out the "bib" slip. "I guess we were a bit sticky," Bergoffen admitted. But Keane didn't think so. With a note of appreciation, he sent Bergoffen his original art with the bib erased.

Bergoffen could be more flexible when he wasn't protecting the bear's physical image. Before FCB created all major radio commercials, Bergoffen wrote scripts for forest fire prevention radio messages featuring such figures as Hopalong Cassidy and Jelly Elliott and the three Knotheads. There he let nature take its course.

Ed Kerr, writing in *Forests and People*, reported that Jelly Elliott, a native of Louisiana's Franklin Parish, learned to play the fiddle long before his feet reached the floor from his bandstand chair. Well known in Louisiana for his singing and back-country humor, the affable radio star loved to hunt and fish in the "sportsman's paradise." But folks were surprised one day to see a different side of Elliott.

After a routine radio show, Elliott drove fifty miles to a favorite hunting area and found that the forest had been badly burned in a fire the previous day. Incensed at the waste, a grim-faced Elliott launched into a tirade on his next broadcast, berating anyone who would burn Louisiana's woodlands.

Sensing an ally, Louisiana forestry officials appeared at Elliott's studio with a simple request: Would Elliott make six radio programs about forest fire prevention, free of charge? Elliott agreed, and Smokey Bear had another supporter.

Elliott's six programs were such a hit that the following year he agreed to a series of recordings that were distributed to 700 southern radio stations. Soon, the series expanded to 1,000 stations across the nation and then rose to 1,500, winning awards from the Radio-Television Institute for Education and attention from *Life* magazine, which sent a writing and photography crew to tail the "Washington boys" on their annual trip to Monroe.

Each November in the late 1940s and early 1950s, the Washington boys— Clint Davis, Bill Bergoffen and H. G. Eberly—ventured into Monroe with Winn Adams, an engineer for the U.S. Recording Company. There, in the music building of Northeast State College, Jelly Elliott cut loose with his whooped-up "cattle call" to begin recording fifteen platter programs—five for southern audiences and ten for nationwide use.

Although ostensibly responsible for writing Elliott's scripts, Bergoffen unabashedly admitted to actually writing very little material for Elliott, preferring to work out appropriate themes and let the personable star express his thoughts in his own words. As Elliott churned out phrases like "Friends, I wanta tell you about the woods" or "Well, well. There's old Herman sitting over there like a tree fulla hoot owl," or "Hey, wait, there's something going on in front of my back," Bergoffen refused to interrupt Elliott's audience rapport. But at the end of each raucous day, Bergoffen and the Washington boys worked in their hotel until two or three in the morning, reviewing hour-long rough tapes, looking for mistakes, snipping objectionable material and splicing until they had their fourteen-minute programs.

While Clint Davis and his Washington boys were promoting Smokey from Forest Service headquarters, the Los Angeles office of Foote, Cone & Belding produced some of the most powerful and effective advertising ever seen in America. Virtually invisible to the American public, this silent force behind the nation's favorite bear welcomed its responsibility to plan the explosive popular growth of Smokey Bear. A blue-chip firm with impeccable pedigree, FCB took its lead from the remarkable Don Belding.

When New Englanders Daniel M. Lord and Ambrose L. Thomas opened their Chicago advertising firm in 1881, neither man expected Lord & Thomas to become the world's giant. Specializing in advertising Christian periodicals, their largest accounts by the turn of the century were Anheuser-Busch and Cascarets—a laxative owned primarily by Thomas.

Lord & Thomas's destiny was sealed in 1898 when the legendary Albert Lasker—perhaps America's greatest single advertising personality—arrived from Galveston, Texas. Lasker, whose success in both business and Republican politics earned him the title "uncrowned king of Chicago," began his career at Lord & Thomas by sweeping floors and emptying spittoons for ten bucks a week. Stunningly creative, Lasker moved fast, and when Lord retired in 1904, the twenty-four-year-old bought one-fourth of the firm. By 1912, Lasker was sole owner of Lord & Thomas—then the largest advertising agency in the world.

The agency's primary account—Sunkist (the California Fruit Growers Exchange)—was acquired in 1907. Partly to help service the Sunkist account, Lord & Thomas opened its Los Angeles office in 1914, and it was here that Don Belding—perhaps Smokey Bear's greatest supporter—arrived.

Jeanne Knapp, Belding's biographer, penned her basic observation in the simple terms that Belding would have appreciated: "There is no real reason why a boy from Grants Pass, Oregon, should attain the greatness Don Belding gained in his lifetime." Certainly for much of his life, it seemed the world conspired against him.

Born into poverty in 1897, life turned worse for young Belding when first his father, and then his older brother, deserted the family home on Sixth Street. Emotionally wounded, Belding developed a severe stutter that he could never fully conquer, even though he tried to shake the impediment by entering speech contests. It seemed to make no difference, however, because Knapp reported that Belding made such an impressive nomination speech for a high school classmate that he in turn was elected class president by acclamation.

Despite his problems, Belding excelled in academics, and a job with Western Union generated funds for the University of Oregon. Although a social misfit, Belding ran track and cross-country and joined the Oregon National Guard where, Knapp reported, he earned supply sergeant's stripes by the time World War I interrupted his education.

Don Belding, the driving force behind Smokey's early national advertising campaigns. *(Courtesy Don Belding Jr.)*

Belding loved the military, but it did not reciprocate. In a training accident in Virginia, Belding was struck in the left eye and earned a permanent and visible impairment that kept him from an officer's commission. In another accident in Saumur, France, Belding was gassed during maneuvers.

Returning to the University of Oregon, Belding graduated with honors in 1919 with a B.S. in commerce. But despite managing the Klamath Falls Western Union office for $100 per month (where his emphasis on customer service increased revenues sixfold) and running the *Klamath Falls Record* until the local economy collapsed, Belding could not improve his financial status.

Broke and tired, Belding was admitted to Camp Kearney Hospital in 1922 with pulmonary tuberculosis caused by the gas in France. He was given four months to live, but a year later the determined young man left the hospital and the army with a full disability rating. Then, backed by veteran's pay of $155 a month, Belding presented himself to the Los Angeles office of Lord & Thomas. He wanted to be an advertising man.

Armed only with incredible courage and self-confidence, Belding sat, according to Knapp, for two full days, hat and hands in his lap, patiently awaiting an opportunity to plead his case. One has to wonder how Belding, almost destitute, visibly disfigured and unable to speak without stuttering, planned to create a favorable first impression. What hopes did he harbor? What did he think he could offer to that prestigious advertising agency?

Perhaps those two days says it all about Don Belding: bulldog tenacity and a single-minded focus. The young man refused to accept or even recognize barriers, and finally, as in so many other aspects of his life, Belding succeeded.

With no salary, Belding first worked as office boy, ghostwriter and assistant space buyer. Then on April 1, 1924, after six months with neither desk nor remuneration, Belding joined the payroll for $60 a month as a probationary space buyer. A few months later Belding earned a permanent position, at $250 a month, as space buyer and research manager.

Enamored with advertising, Belding became a devoted student of the business, learning from colleagues when he could but relying primarily on hard work and his creative skills. Knapp reported that Belding soon developed a recognizable writing style. Ken Thurston, a long-time Belding associate, explained in a brief biography that Belding focused on stark, methodical simplicity: "You agree with his first sentence, and it invites you to the next. You go from one agreement to another, by easy steps until you feel obliged to give yourself good reason if you don't agree to buy. The words are short and plain in meaning. The sentences are short and straightforward. You are aware of what is said, never aware of how it is said. It is the best of copy and it is the hardest to write."

There in the 1920s, perhaps, the ground was laid for the Smokey Bear campaign. Would any campaign ever be more simple, more agreeable, shorter, plainer in meaning or more straightforward? Would Americans ever be able to find a good reason not to agree? Perhaps that is why Americans would not forget Smokey Bear even after fifty years.

Named a junior account executive in 1927 and assigned the Union Oil account, Belding worked with Bob Philippi to produce Union's famous "76" logo. Assigned the Sunkist account in 1933, Belding was elected vice president and manager of the Los Angeles office in 1938, named one of three executive vice presidents in 1941, and on January 1, 1943, became one of the three new owners of the firm renamed Foote, Cone & Belding.

Continuing to stutter throughout his professional life, Belding never appeared to let it affect him—especially as he achieved success—and because of his strong personality, Belding's colleagues seemed not to notice his eye disfigurement. "Don became a dominant figure in public life," Jim Felton, a colleague, shrugged, "and once you're on top, those things go away." Belding's conservative, dark office—guarded by his secretary Helen Gurley (Brown)—sported three walls covered with photographs of the great moments in his life—posing with Dwight Eisenhower, Howard Hughes, movie stars and advertising colleagues. But physically fit because he labored on his Pauma Valley ranch, Belding was respected most for his solid work ethic.

"Don just outworked most people," Felton explained. "It was sheer delight to watch him attack problems. He would say, 'Here are the facts; go home and think about it; come in with a creative idea tomorrow.' So we'd all go home and come up with an idea and then go to bed, but Don would stay up all night thinking and come back with a hundred ideas. Many would be atrocious, but some would ring a bell. If his batting average was only fifteen percent, he had us out-thought fifteen to one."

Belding worked not only hard, but extraordinarily fast, concentrating so intently that he frequently didn't even exchange pleasantries. "Don Belding was a very intense man," Felton recalled. "He had a one-track mind: succeed in advertising. Don always charged like a bull. He never walked. He never strolled. He charged. If Don invited you to lunch, you knew you either were going to get promoted or fired, and his routine never varied. He always took people across the street to a little lunch counter in a drugstore, and he always ordered the same thing: a bowl of soup, a cheese sandwich and a piece of apple pie. But before you unfolded your napkin, he would be through eating and ready to go back to work."

Belding embraced public service advertising because he felt obligated to contribute toward improving his profession, and he relentlessly pushed FCB to a total commitment to forest fire prevention. "Nothing could stand in his way," Felton explained. "Don would stand up at meetings and say, 'I want to save the forests. Whatever the Forest Service wants, you guys get it for them.'"

Few American advertising agencies in the late 1940s were fortified with the confidence of Foote, Cone & Belding. Bolstered by Lasker's reputation, FCB enjoyed a preeminent status in its industry. More books had been written about and from FCB than any other agency, and many alumni had established their own firms. Above all, FCB was supremely confident of its creative abilities.

Unfortunately, FCB didn't have to look far to identify potential obstacles to a successful fire prevention advertising effort. But FCB was far better positioned to address those issues than its client at Forest Service headquarters in Washington, D.C.

First, FCB recognized that the advertising industry perhaps never would fully recover from the assaults of the 1930s. Many Americans still were hostile to advertising, and with the war won, the public's inclination to respond to public service advertising could be expected to wane.

Second, FCB understood that many Americans simply didn't like advertising unless they happened to be interested in a particular product at a particular time. Arguably, forest fire prevention was an unlikely candidate to attract a typical American. To force an interest, FCB had to respond to age-old questions: "What's in it for me? What benefit do I get for paying attention to your ad?" FCB had to divert attention from pressing matters in consumers' lives if they wanted to save the forests.

Third, the inherent nature of forest fire prevention made it difficult for the public to understand the product. Most products were directed to specific audiences who easily understood their value, but public service advertising had to address every American.

Fourth, because of postwar emphasis on consumerism and the explosion of ads, consumers would be hard-pressed to associate with any particular campaign.

FCB's challenge was to convince the American public that they had a stake in preventing forest fires. Except in the war years, public service advertising had never been used on a mass scale in the United States. Like political, institutional and advocacy advertising, public service advertising promoted only a *concept*. FCB would have to provide facts, interpretations and suggestions so the public could draw proper conclusions.

Fairfax Cone, head of FCB's Chicago office, insisted there is no such thing as a "mass mind," that advertising aimed at the masses rarely moves anyone. A mass audience, Cone argued, consists of *individuals* and good advertising addresses those individuals. Thus, a forest fire prevention message had to be personalized so that people could be taught to care about forests. But why should someone surrounded by pavement in New York City care about preventing forest fires? Well, FCB reasoned, because that person may want to visit a forest some day, and therein lay the key: *every* American had a stake in America's forests.

FCB felt confident that a successful campaign could be conducted even without a unifying war, because FCB recognized that ads could make individuals feel that someone was speaking personally. If ads could evoke a personal reaction, then emotional currents could be tapped and a one-on-one relationship could be established. And perhaps never in the history of advertising was this principle of talking to *a person* more brilliantly applied than in 1947.

One of FCB's most talented account executives was Ervin Grant, a native of Taft, California, who grew up in Pasadena within walking distance of the Rose Bowl. While playing football at a Pasadena high school, the accommodating Grant picked up his musical instrument at half-time and played in his school band.

A popular figure at FCB, Grant sported a round face, blond hair and a constant smile. As a trim five-foot-ten 170-pound athlete, Grant was viewed by his colleagues as the prototype all-American boy. A respected copywriter and account executive, Grant was assigned the fire prevention account in 1943 and helped produce some of the campaign's early posters. With quiet manners, an engaging personality, high creativity and reputation as all-around good guy, Grant's primary responsibility was selling oranges for Sunkist. But Grant worked so hard on forest fire prevention that his associates began to identify him with Smokey. "Erv *was* the Smokey Bear campaign as far as we were concerned," Ken Thurston conceded.

And in 1947 Ervin Grant apparently coined one of the most famous, effective and continued-use tag lines in history: "Remember, only you can prevent forest fires." Following form with other aspects of Smokey's history, apparently no written documentation of Grant's creation exists. However, at least two of Grant's colleagues are comfortable ascribing credit to Grant for the noted line.

"Erv came up with it—I'm almost absolutely certain," insisted Jim Felton, a close cooperative with Grant at FCB, who, as the second national coordinator for the forest fire prevention campaign, researched the matter in the 1960s. "Erv was a very laid-back individual. He would not claim credit for anything; that is probably why no one remembered him creating the phrase. But it was the kind of a line that would be obvious once you began to look at the figures about who caused forest fires. Most were caused by humans—a tractor, a campfire or a cigarette thrown out of a window. With those statistics it was a logical thing: people cause them; only people can prevent them."

George W. (Bill) Belsey Jr., a senior executive with FCB in Los Angeles, agreed with Felton's assessment that Grant penned the famous line. "Erv was handling the account and I think he wrote that line," Belsey recalled. "I'm as sure as I can be. Within the agency, every campaign went to a plans board—senior fellows who reviewed material before it was submitted to a client. Bill Pringle, Don Belding, Nelson Carter, Ford Sibley and I were on the plans board and we had a debate because we didn't understand the

Erv Grant (left, hoisting his catch offshore California) wrote Smokey's famous slogan: "Remember, only you can prevent forest fires." Dick Stow stands to the left. *(Courtesy Betty Stow. Photo by John Meredith.)*

line. I remember that Erv had to explain it—that man-made fires was what he was after."

Grant's creation certainly had staying power and eventually became one of the world's best-known phrases. Decades later, surveys showed that more than three-fourths of American adults, when shown the phrase "Remember, only you . . . " could complete the slogan.

Smokey's slogan, perhaps as well known as any single line in advertising history, helped generate the phenomenal impact of Smokey's message. Extraordinarily appropriate, Smokey's personalized message aimed at the heart of a national problem and ensured the bear's place in American folklore. For the first time, the responsibility for forest fire prevention was placed on a personal basis—a basic principle of effective advertising. Each individual was urged by a powerful bear to help prevent

An early Rudy Wendelin-designed cover for a platter with nine Smokey Bear radio commercials. *(Courtesy USDA Forest Service.)*

forest fires. Smokey Bear suddenly seemed to represent a benefit to people's lives. He diluted a natural human inclination to distrust ads, and his simple slogan triggered an emotional response to let people sell themselves on forest fire prevention. Through Smokey's slogan, FCB made each ad personal, as if it were speaking to each individual person. FCB successfully used that approach in campaigns such as Clairol's "Does She or Doesn't

By 1948 , dozens of corporations rushed to Smokey's Cause. *(Courtesy USDA Forest Service.)*

She?" and "Is It True Blondes Have More Fun?" Neither of those questions promoted products; they simply initiated conversations with consumers.

Smokey Bear could initiate those conversations. Through FCB, Smokey Bear could help Americans identify how forest fire prevention could play a meaningful role in their lives. Smokey Bear could make fire prevention ads understandable. Smokey Bear could create an enormous advantage for the forest fire prevention campaign by adding the dimension of continuity. And Smokey Bear's familiar face could substitute for the personal presence of a salesman.

As use of the bear shifted from supporting role to leading player, FCB assumed more and more control until it finally developed the superstar caricature Americans loved. Although Bill Bergoffen and his Washington colleagues continued for a few years to develop supporting radio commercials and other advertising independently of FCB, the Los Angeles agency, relying heavily on its Hollywood relationships, proved so skillful, so adept and so effective that it was only a matter of time before the entire advertising effort moved to FCB.

Driven by Don Belding, FCB labored to promote its bear. Staffers joked about their "unbillable account"—hundred of hours of work (at an estimated cumulative value by 1951 of almost half a million dollars) with not a cent in compensation—but never produced anything less than a first-class product for the CFFP program. Belding insisted that the agency's fire prevention account deserved the same internal attention and critical review it gave to commercial accounts.

By 1950, FCB's effort had been so intense and prolonged that the Ad Council, recognizing FCB's extraordinary commitment, tactfully offered to reassign the CFFP account to another agency. But Belding refused to surrender the account and fired back a one-paragraph letter to Ted Repplier, president of the Ad Council, insisting that FCB was in for the long haul; FCB would stay on as long as the foresters were satisfied. Case closed.

Supporting the creative talent at FCB stood the enormous resources of the Advertising Council—an organization dedicated to its public service campaigns. With far more thoroughness, speed and efficiency than its Forest Service friends could ever hope to match, the Ad Council continued to place Smokey's fire prevention materials in mass communications systems across the country, at no cost to the CFFP for either airtime or publishing space. By cajoling, pleading with and begging the nation's media and advertisers for support, the Ad Council generated staggering support for forest fire prevention. In a 1951 article for *American Forests*, Clint Davis insisted that the numbers for 1950 alone told the story.

That year Gillette Safety Razor Company sponsored fire prevention on World Series TV and radio broadcasts, American Tobacco Company plugged fire prevention on five weekly shows including the "Jack Benny Show" and "The Hit Parade," and more than one hundred other major sponsors of network programs donated time for fire prevention messages.

On the publishing side, companies such as Caterpillar Tractor, Aetna Insurance, International Nickel Company of America and other large corporations sponsored forest fire ads in magazines such as *Newsweek, Time*

TWO MEN OF DISTINCTION (BETWEEN FIRES)

Smokey takes a break with Russell Eller, the Advertising Council's first national Smokey Bear campaign coordinator. *(Courtesy USDA Forest Service.)*

and the *Saturday Evening Post.* Banks, department stores, grocery chains and other businesses paid for more than 11,000 Smokey newspaper ads. The National Comic Group carried full-page forest fire prevention ads in 10 million copies of 33 different comics. Almost 100,000 "car cards" presented fire messages to an estimated 50 million riders on streetcars and buses in 400 cities. Railroad passengers saw Smokey posters in cars, railroad stations and on timetable inserts.

The Cooperative Forest Fire Prevention campaign's first three directors: Richard Hammatt (left), Clint Davis (center) and William Huber. *(Courtesy Rudy Wendelin and USDA Forest Service.)*

That massive effort was both successful and necessary. Although the Wartime Advertising Council conducted more than one hundred campaigns, the postwar Ad Council (with the word "War" dropped) was needed more than ever in the forests. Few people visited forests in the early 1940s, when millions of American men were overseas and public travel was limited by a shortage of automobiles, tires, gas and time. The real test began after the war.

Based on National Park and Forest registrations, sales of hunting and fishing licenses and sales of recreational vehicles, it was apparent that public use of the outdoors had broken all records by 1950 with a 40 percent increase over the peak year of 1941. Those increased visits translated into more opportunities for people to start fires, which, in theory, should have risen by at least 40 percent and, perhaps, much more because millions of acres of privately held land had been added to state fire control.

But instead of the expected growth from 210,000 fires in 1940 to 300,000 by 1950, the number of fires actually decreased. From 1946 through 1950, man-caused forest fires were held to 190,000 per year—a reduction of 20,000 despite vastly increased use of forests.

It was difficult to identify each element that deserved credit for the reduction. Schoolteachers, the Keep Green Program sponsored by American Forest Products Industries, Girl Scouts, Boy Scouts and the American Red Cross sent out foot soldiers. The federal government supported the effort through the Post Office and the Departments of Agriculture and Interior, and virtually every state backed the program.

But one fact stood out: by 1950, because of the Ad Council, the American public knew more about the need for preventing forest fires than ever before in history. This massive advertising altered public attitudes and established a rallying point for individuals, organizations and governments battling to protect the nation's forests. And widespread cooperation generated other dividends: state legislatures passed fire laws, the judicial system convicted almost 95 percent of fire law violators brought into court, forest fire protection spread to new areas and state foresters won additional financing.

The passage of time also revealed that the Ad Council's campaigns accomplished more than just saving forests or selling savings bonds. Nonpolitical and nonpartisan, the Ad Council endowed four other benefits: public service advertising was raised to unexpectedly high standards; industry-government relationships reached new levels of trust and respect and laid the groundwork for future cooperation; increased involvement in social issues helped American businesses recognize the impact they could have in resolving national problems; and the advertising industry had resolutely entrenched itself as an indispensable tool for public service.

6

FOREST FIRE IN CAPITAN GAP

"May 4th in 1950 was the beginning of a forest fire known to the whole Nation, not because of its size or spectacular losses, but because a tiny five- pound black bear cub named Smokey was rescued from it."

— Dorothy Guck

At an altitude of 6,400 feet, Capitan, New Mexico, seldom numbered more than 1,000 hardy souls after its founding near the end of the nineteenth century. With the discovery of coal in sprawling Lincoln County, Capitan grew rapidly through 1897, but it was Capitan Mountain that first fueled Capitan's growth and then provided a niche in history for the tiny mountain village.

Ringed by flat country on three sides, Capitan Mountain thrust itself up into the middle of an arid plain unsuitable for farming. Somehow, a stubborn portion of the Lincoln National Forest grew there, surrounded by prairie speckled with sparse ground cover and intermittent juniper or piñon. Only a few determined cattle and sheep grazed on the spotty vegetation.

Resembling two giant loaves of French bread, Capitan Mountain offers a geological oddity by running east and west instead of along the traditional

71

Rocky Mountain north and south axis. Each mountain sector peaks at more than 10,000 feet and covers a width of about three miles at its base. "West Mountain" rises from a high plain nine miles northeast of Capitan, angles toward its crest, runs due east for four miles, dips down 2,000 feet into the Capitan Gap, climbs back onto "East Mountain," and continues another fourteen miles.

With thick forests offering a ready supply of crossties, Capitan Mountain lured the El Paso and Northeastern Railway when it built lines to area coal mines. By 1903, Capitan flourished as a lumber center, but when the coal fields played out and the railway left, Capitan settled into near obscurity, overshadowed by nearby Lincoln, focal point of the exploits of Billy the Kid.

Like 90 percent of forest fires in the United States, the devastation that produced a living symbol for America's forest fire prevention program was triggered by basic human carelessness. The first of two fires began on a dry, windy Thursday, May 4, 1950, at a logging camp operated by Willis Ivory Whitcamp. There, on the north side of Capitan Mountain, a cabin cookstove, only 75 feet from the Whitcamp home, simply overheated. Sparks escaped from a stovepipe about 2:15 p.m. and, on that blistering hot day, blew into nearby debris. Tinder erupted in flame and, pushed by the unforgiving wind, spread into nearby brush and trees. Whitcamp and five loggers battled the fire until they recognized their inability to contain it, so Whitcamp drove four miles along a base road to the Lon Merchant ranch, telephoned the Forest Service in Capitan, and asked for help. But Forest Service ranger Dean Earl already was moving toward the smoke.

Only minutes before, Ray Bell, chief law enforcement officer for New Mexico's Game and Fish Department, winged his way into the area on a trip from Santa Fe to Roswell. As Bell reached Capitan Mountain, he flew into a sandstorm so dense he struggled to see the ground only a few hundred feet below. Old-timers claimed that the 1950 sandstorms were as dense as any in memory, probably because of a particularly dry spring when barely a quarter-inch of moisture fell from January through May. Winds gusting as high as 70 miles per hour blew relentlessly. Grass turned brown, underbrush turned brittle, dried pine needles almost snapped under their own weight, and Forest Service staffer Sam Servis offered a technical assessment of the stifling air: "Basically, it was drier than a popcorn fart." And as fire danger reached a critical level, the Forest Service knew Capitan Mountain's green forests were ripe for disaster.

As Bell skirted the storm hiding the mountain and turned back to Santa Fe, an alert Bob Lathum, Forest Service fire spotter and former cowpuncher, vigilantly studied his terrain from the "Block lookout"—a Forest Service tower on the Block ranch north of East Mountain. As the storm's winds shifted, Lathum spotted a wisp of smoke slowly swirling into the sky. Lathum phoned Dean Earl in Capitan, explained that with the dust and wind he couldn't see clearly, but he believed he could smell smoke and proffered a guess on its approximate location.

Dorothy Gray Guck, Associated Press stringer at the 1950 Capitan Gap forest fire. *(Courtesy Dorothy Guck.)*

Both Earl and his 1948 green Ford pickup stood ready for action. With a .45-caliber pistol in the pickup's glove compartment, one side box for korticks, ropes and tools and another side box for bed roll and personal effects, Earl was always prepared to mend tents, repair roads and phone lines, nab poachers or fight fires. Earl knew what to do and, with the proper staff, was the right man to do it. So by the time Whitcamp's call arrived at Capitan's ranger station—a typical New Mexico adobe building adorned only by a single tree and a few scrub bushes—Dean Earl was in action. Roy Morgan, a Forest Service "blade man," had just parked his road grader along a dirt road near Nogal after a tough, dusty shift when Dean Earl roared up with two men in his truck. "We have a fire in the mountains," Earl explained to Morgan's dismay.

As a boy in his native Hutchinson, Kansas, Dean Martin Earl listened intently each time his fourth-grade teacher read letters to her class from a son in the Forest Service. Enraptured, young Earl decided forestry offered a life of adventure and challenge, and despite insistence from Earl's physician grandfather to study medicine, forestry won out.

Working his way through college during the Depression, Earl survived by holding two jobs, and he struggled through one winter eating only a single meal each day. But Earl won a degree in civil engineering from Kansas State University and a degree in forestry from Utah State University a year later. Hired by the Forest Service and assigned to the north rim of the Grand Canyon, Earl and his new wife, Della, soon learned that ranger's wives were part of the team. "Much of the business took place in my kitchen," Della Earl confirmed. "The Forest Service didn't have radios at first, but we had telephones. So it was my responsibility to help with the phones because I was home with the children."

With a slight authoritative air, the forty-four-year-old perfectionist Earl sometimes could be hard to work for, but as an experienced firefighter, Earl had accumulated a solid knowledge of fire behavior and had been a strong advocate of using new techniques. He was a reliable man to have running a fire, and because the fire had broken out in his ranger district, Earl was responsible for directing fire suppression efforts.

But poor visibility, winding mountain dirt roads and the hazardous sandstorm slowed Earl down. By the time Earl arrived, the fire had destroyed the logging camp and, courtesy of the high winds, was almost out of control. Nevertheless, Forest Service and logging men battled the inferno until they lost track of time and, perhaps, even their own location.

As nightfall approached and the sandstorm continued unabated, Forest Service lookouts still were unable to determine the fire's size. In tiny Capitan, dust was so thick that hazy air made it difficult even to see across Main Street. From the cramped twelve-foot-square, peaked-roof Block lookout station midway along East Mountain, fire spotters had only one report: smoke was thick and getting thicker. As the Mon Jeau lookout tower tried unsuccessfully to pinpoint the fire's location by the use of triangulation, no further reports came in from the Merchant ranch and no messengers reported back. So Bob Earl—Dean Earl's sixteen-year-old son—took over the radio at Capitan's ranger station, where the three adobe buildings housed living quarters, ranger offices and equipment.

"We were waiting for Dad's call," Bob Earl explained, "because a Forest Service family had to fill in when a ranger was out. Everything was ready to go, because the Forest Service had caches set up for five-, ten- and twenty-five-man crews. All the gear—axes, shovels and korticks—were in the packages. The caches had written instructions for food too, explaining how much bread and other supplies to order. We also had a truck to haul gasoline to service vehicles in the field. It was a pretty extensive network."

Ed Guck, Forest Service ranger in the neighboring Ruidoso District, stationed himself by his phones and radio to act as backup. A native New Yorker and graduate of Cornell University, the lanky Milton Edmond Guck was one of the most respected men in the Forest Service's Southwestern Region. Armed with a degree in forestry and an engaging personality, Guck was a good choice for fire dispatcher: his voice carried well on both radio and telephone and he handled people with his sense of humor. As tempers got short in the heat of battle, firefighters sometimes needed a peacemaker, and Guck was their man.

At daylight on Friday morning, an exhausted Dean Earl radioed in and instructed Bob Earl to issue a general call for help. "Dad said to go set off the fire alarm in the town hall in Capitan," Bob Earl remembered with a grin. "It was exciting to drive the pickup into town to set off the alarm. The Jehovah's Witnesses were meeting in the town hall, but I didn't see them until after I pulled the alarm. They were upset with me because they thought I was pulling a prank. I was petrified. They had Bibles; they called me a devil; they said I was going to hell."

Meanwhile, Dean Earl called Lincoln National Forest supervisor Earl Moore at his headquarters in Alamogordo and asked him to call Fort Bliss. With Moore's okay, Earl also called the Apache "Red Hats" at their nearby reservation in Mescalero, and then told his son to direct the army toward the fire.

When the Forest Service issued a call for help, some folks certainly looked the other way. But little prompting was needed in Capitan, and a fire camp grew as crews arrived and pitched in on the "Los Tablos fire" roaring in Los Tablos Canyon. Ranchers and cowboys reported in to fight alongside insurance salesmen and car dealers.

One of the first volunteers was thirty-seven-year-old Capitan native Fred "Peg" Pfingsten, a strapping hulk of no-nonsense rancher. Raised on horseback, the congenial Pfingsten was at his best a few feet off the ground. "We rode horses before we had cars," Pfingsten explained. "As kids, we started by getting bucked off every two or three days. If you weren't pretty tough, you didn't make it." Both tough and good, Pfingsten was a desirable addition to any fire crew—especially with the rugged terrain on Capitan Mountain.

"My family has been associated with that forest for a long time," Pfingsten added. "We've had forest-use cattle permits in the area since 1894. We have 22,000 acres in the family, plus rights to 6,000 acres on the north side plus forest permits for 6,000 acres. One time we had eighteen sections more in the White Mountains. I've been over all of it on horseback and know the mountain."

Capitan Gap firefighters Fred "Peg" Pfingsten (left) and Ray Bell. *(Courtesy William Clifford Lawter Jr.)*

Pfingsten accepted his responsibility. "We all were raised that whenever they had a forest fire, go help put it out," he stated simply. "We used the land, so we helped protect it. We had a vested interest in the forest and always went to all the fires. We'd take whatever crew was around—me, Dad, brother Bert and anyone else. People grabbed whatever they had—animals, pickaxes, shovels and tools. We took ranch horses to the fire—good, solid, stable horses that we could depend on. My favorite was 'Schick,' a sorrel. Dean Earl was a good ranger, and he knew people and would trust those that he had experience with. I'd been on fires long enough so that I usually was assigned to do something important. The people running that fire—Dean Earl, Orville Luttrell, Ray Bell—they knew what they were doing."

New Mexico state game warden Elliott Barker had instructed all Game and Fish Department employees to rush to any nearby forest fires. So by dawn Friday, Ray Bell was back on the scene, his landing guided by Lincoln County Sheriff Sally Ortiz's police car radio tuned to the same frequency as the state police radio in Bell's plane. Bell was ready to help in any way Dean Earl, his good friend and hunting partner, requested.

As expected, Earl asked Bell to take him aloft for a look at the Los Tablos Canyon inferno. New Mexico's Department of Game and Fish owned Bell's pride and joy—the first airplane bought by the state of New Mexico, and Bell used the modified Piper 115-horsepower PA-12 Supercruiser to run game surveys, assist posses and track fires. Because the Forest Service had no planes in eastern New Mexico, Bell had helped with mapping on several fires.

At Bell's request, Piper had installed a special controllable pitch prop on the red- and cream-colored vehicle. The fixed-wheel plane could land at low speeds on runways as short as seventy-five feet, and could climb quickly after taking off from as little as forty feet of runway. "That allowed me to get in and out of some pretty tight places," Bell explained. "I could pull it to a high rpm for take-off and climb out of narrow, steep places in the mountains."

Cramped seating allowed room for a pilot in front with two passengers on a rear seat, but Bell normally carried only a first aid kit, fire rations, a Handy-Talky and a water canteen for companionship. Two wing tanks each carried eighteen gallons of aviation fuel—enough for the thrifty engine to fly almost five hours. With a special waiver for low flying, Bell typically cruised at 75 miles per hour at 500-feet altitude to watch game—experience that helped enormously when flying at treetop levels to map forest fires. "When you have to gain altitude to get over telephone lines, you know you're flying kinda low," Bell admitted.

And Bell had his admirers, including Sam Servis. "A lot of people were bothered flying close to the ground," Servis confirmed. "They got scared pea green. But I never thought Ray did anything he shouldn't do. He was extremely careful in the mountains, where air currents come up the sides of ridges. I rate Ray pretty damn high as a pilot. I landed with him about a hundred times; he never scared me in any way."

The spartan equipment in Bell's aircraft included only a compass, an oil gauge, a fuel gauge and an altimeter. Bell had flown the plane for two years and felt comfortable with it, although the tiny vehicle had its drawbacks. There were no flaps, it didn't carry enough fuel to satisfy Bell, and he believed it was underpowered. But the small plane fit Bell's everyday needs.

Wearing trifocals to read his instrument panel, Bell took off from an open pasture, and Dean Earl began mapping from the rear seat. Bell tried to maintain an altitude of 400 to 500 feet, flying at an angle from the fire to allow Earl to map the fire in relation to fire lines, rock slides, hills, water and arroyos. Aerial mapping was the only way Earl could pinpoint the fire's location and accurately determine its breadth and direction. And from his airborne perch, Earl could spot fuel in the fire's path and assess the possibilities of cutting it off.

An experienced crew could map a good-size fire in about half an hour. With a talented mapper such as Earl or Servis, who was also adept at reading terrain, Bell had to fly the fire only once, thus spending less time on that dangerous duty over the fire and its gusting winds.

But Earl kept busy in that half hour. Forest fires react to changes in fuel, weather, heat and slope of the land. If those factors change, the speed and direction of the fire can change too. Earl first checked prevailing wind currents that provided oxygen and blew heat and flames toward unburned fuel. He knew that winds could quickly spread a fire into unburned areas, sometimes carrying embers two or three miles to ignite new fires.

Air temperatures, too, had to be measured because fires spread easily on hot days and less quickly on cooler days or at night. Earl also studied the terrain abutting the fire to estimate speed and direction in which the fire was likely to spread. He knew that steep slopes drew fire upward by convection, with heat rising to warm air above the fire, preheating overhanging branches or timber and kindling fuel on the upper slopes of a canyon. By contrast, Earl knew the fire would travel more slowly on flat terrain, although radiant heat could transfer heat from a burning fire to nearby ground fuel.

After his aerial survey, Dean Earl radioed Earl Moore in Alamogordo and asked for more help. Moore, a transplanted Pennsylvanian, agreed to send Earl whatever he needed and also volunteered the services of Sam Servis, Charlie Sutton and Lee Beall.

"Whispering Sam" Servis and his booming voice received an eager embrace from Dean Earl. Servis made friends easily and had firefighting experience as a sector boss and crew boss. Servis grew up where he was born in 1913—in Geneseo, New York, on a 250-acre farm abutting the Genesee River, and matriculated to the New York State College of Forestry at Syracuse University. Small but fiery, Servis joined the wrestling team and, as a senior captain, went undefeated and won the Eastern Intercollegiate 140-pound championship in 1935. "The coach wanted me to stay on, get my master's and try out for the 1936 Olympic team," Servis chuckled. "That was a bunch of horse wash. I had no money, my ears hurt like hell, and I was tired. Instead, I graduated in June and took the offer of the Forest Service in Albuquerque, New Mexico."

In 1948, Servis transferred to Alamogordo and, by 1950, had acquired so much experience fighting fires that his diary during the Capitan Gap fire reflected only a simple notation: "On fire all day."

No one fooled with Whispering Sam on a fire. Never a slave to protocol, the outspoken Servis could be counted on to assess a situation and take quick action. Servis told people what to do and expected them to do it quickly and get on with fire fighting. His mapping skills were so highly developed that he could map a fire in only a few minutes. "I had been trained in aerophotography at school," Servis shrugged. "I couldn't see fiddling around."

Charlie Sutton, an amiable forester in charge of construction and maintenance for the Lincoln National Forest, was welcome in any fire camp. Born in St. Louis, Missouri, in 1898, Sutton quit high school to join the army. He served in World War I as a private with the Second Division in France and Germany, but emerged from World War II as a colonel with battle experience on Iwo Jima and other South Pacific hot spots.

Although talented and hardworking, Sutton enjoyed life's lighter side. "Charlie never was serious," news reporter Dorothy Guck grinned, "but the fellows all liked him. Charlie always had a bunch of jokes that ladies weren't allowed to listen to. He was probably the most competent man they had to set up a camp. He would get a call, and two hours later he would be serving a hot meal at a fire."

Lee Beall, a lanky Texas cowboy, was assistant supervisor and fire control officer on the Lincoln National Forest. Often quiet, Beall could tell a good story wrapped around his dry wit. Quite thin, Beall probably was too sick and a little old to be fighting fire by 1950. "Lee was not well," Servis confirmed. "He had tularemia from skinning a rabbit in the twenties and nearly died. He was tall—six feet plus—and a walking skeleton."

Earl rounded out his camp staff with his son Bob. Born in Moab, Utah, Bob Earl and his sister lived with their parents the previous eight years in Luna, New Mexico, before Dean Earl was transferred to Capitan in December 1949. If the living symbol of Smokey Bear hadn't been rescued from the Capitan Gap fire, 1950 would have been remembered as the year that electricity came to Capitan—a thrill for the young Earl. "Capitan was exciting because we had electricity," Bob Earl explained without apology.

"They needed every available hand," Bob Earl added. "My role was radio operator, cook's helper and timekeeper. Our radio was so primitive that during the heat of the day we could hardly get any contact. It was an 'SPF' set—a big, gray boxlike thing. No one wanted to fiddle with the radio, but Dad taught me to run a radio when I was a small boy."

Bob Earl threw a tarp over a cluster of six-foot-high pine trees to create a communications tent and arranged his radio—call number SPF 890—under that crude cover. "The Forest Service communications system was hardly better than a wax string and coffee cans," Earl recalled. "New Mexico Game and Fish had a better network." When his radio was working, Earl kept busy talking with the Block lookout, Forest Service offices in Silver City, the Capitan ranger station and the Mon Jeau tower near Ruidoso. "I stayed by the radio day and night, ordering supplies and personnel, and talking to the towers looking for outbreaks of other fires," Earl explained. "I passed messages to the fire lines on their Handy-Talkies, and told them where to pick up or dispatch crews."

Servis, Sutton and Beall arrived Saturday morning just as the night shift—led by Ray Bell—came off the fire line, so Dean Earl now had the staff he needed to handle the Los Tablos fire. "Dean Earl was fire boss," Servis explained. "Charlie Sutton was camp boss, Ed Guck was service chief, and I wound up as plans chief." So as Sutton set up camp deep in a timbered area, Earl asked Servis to supervise the day shift while he turned his attention to planning strategy to contain the fire.

At first, Earl's luck held as his 150 men whipped the Los Tablos fire. When the windstorm finally quieted down after burning about 1,000 acres, Earl declared the fire under control at 2:30 on Saturday afternoon, May 6. Relieved, Earl instructed Ray Bell and Lee Beall to oversee the fire camp breakup, and then began walking the fire line, ordering some men to organize into mop-up crews of three men each and sending others home.

Unfortunately, the battle was far from finished. Just as Beall began striking camp, someone looked east and saw smoke a half-mile away outside established fire lines. Wind blew hard as Lee Beall yelled to the men. "We all grabbed some kind of a fire tool, jumped in trucks, and raced about a mile over a very rough road to the smoke," Ray Bell remembered. "We arrived to find a fire about fifty to sixty feet across in an oak thicket jammed with a thick cushion of leaves. Roy Morgan was working as fast as he could with a kortick trying to build a line around the burning spot."

The first group of six men pitched in building the fire line. Expecting no problems, they nevertheless spared no effort because they understood that anything could happen in a forest fire. "Give it everything you've got," Lee Beall insisted, "because if a wind hits it we're in trouble." Beall's mistrust was well placed; when the fire was almost completely surrounded, a narrow whirlwind darted into the oak thicket, picked up burning grass and brush, and set it down across the dirt road. Immediately, the fire took off up the mountain, roaring through the Capitan Gap, from which the new fire derived its name.

Although nobody documented the actual start of the Capitan Gap fire, most participants believed the blaze was man-caused. In 1950, a single dirt road cut through the 8,000-foot-high gap between the two mountain sections before winding down into New Mexico's high flatlands. For motorists heading south, this popular shortcut was the only good way off the mountain. So when the second fire started next to the Capitan Gap road, most Lincoln County residents assumed that either a careless tourist returning from a look at the Los Tablos fire or a firefighter going home tossed a match or cigarette from a car. Some suspected arson, believing that the fire was set by a disgruntled firefighter dismissed by the occasionally short-tempered Dean Earl. Others believed it might have been started by two drunk, unhappy job seekers who had been denied work at the fire camp.

Regardless of cause, wind swept fire through dense stands of Ponderosa pine, spruce, fir, oak thickets and quaking aspen. The new fire soon spread out of control, offering a far more difficult set of problems than the Los Tablos fire. Heavy rocks strewn throughout the thick timber made it much harder to build fire lines. Steepness prevented bulldozers and road graders from reaching the battle area. And dense timber loaded with crackling dry underbrush provided hundreds of tons of fuel and ideal conditions for the roaring fire.

Winds fanned the flames roaring up Capitan Gap's steep ridges, and the small crew's valiant efforts proved futile. Because of heat and the speed with which a fire moves uphill, firefighters can't battle a ridge fire from above. But loose boulders and burning firebrands roll downhill with frightfully deadly force, and men can't fight from below. Even with reinforcements, Lee Beall and his crew couldn't control the spreading fire.

Acting as a giant air-conditioning vent, the Capitan Gap brought in fresh air to feed the rapidly growing fire. Smoke hid firefighters and blazing trees; eyes burned despite painful squinting; flaming underbrush popped; burning pine needles whistled in the crackling flames. From time to time, turpentine in a dry spruce or Ponderosa pine tree got so hot that trees exploded in a dynamite-like blast, sending flaming needles and limbs flying around Capitan Mountain. As fire leaped from bush to bush, flames raced through Capitan Gap. Unstoppable, the hungry fire raced up the mountain. The sky blazed in fury; the earth trembled. Lee Beall's battle was lost.

Gray and white smoke signaled the disaster for more than a hundred miles as it billowed high into the blue sky, enshrouding rugged Capitan Mountain and rendering it invisible except for momentary glimpses when the heavy smoke parted. "In a short eight or ten hours," Bob Earl recalled, "the whole side of the mountain burned off. The fire burned so hot that the sun was blood red. After we got into the flatlands, one of the most beautiful sights I ever saw in my life was that mountain; it just looked like a huge city lit up on the side of a mountain."

7

Fire Camp

"Stew. Stew every meal. Stew any time. That was a real good feed. Put everything you got in there and a little bit more. We built a good stew."

— Ray Taylor

Smoke obscured the Capitan Gap, but the Forest Service didn't have to issue a second call for local help. "Everyone for miles around could see what had happened," Bob Earl explained. Merchants, clerks and railroad crews reported into fire camp, and by nightfall, fresh crews manned the spreading fire lines.

Coordination of much of the recruiting was left to thirty-four-year-old Lincoln County Sheriff Salvador Martin "Sally" Ortiz. Born in Arizona, Ortiz moved to New Mexico while still a child. Somewhere he learned to love donuts—cook 'em, eat 'em or just talk about 'em—it didn't matter. "Donuts was the first thing I did after the army," Ortiz explained with delight. "I bought a donut machine and ran short orders and donuts. Yes sir, people are happy when they're eating hot donuts. Ice them in chocolate and vanilla and you've got a friend."

Donuts filled his gullet but not his wallet, so Ortiz bought a Chevron gas station and hauled his own gasoline out of El Paso and Artesia. Then Carrizozo's postmaster approached Ortiz in 1948 about running for sheriff against an entrenched incumbent. "I hadn't planned on a law enforcement career," Ortiz recalled, "but I was fortunate to be elected."

With deputy Clyde Atwood, jailor Happy Jutierrez and a black Chevy Fleetline topped with a single red light, Ortiz, later voted New Mexico's outstanding peace officer by his peers, began his on-the-job training and turned to New Mexico's game wardens for help.

"I had a lot to learn," Ortiz acknowledged. "The game wardens helped me on criminal investigations. They helped find evidence and investigate poaching, illegal spotlighting and illegal trapping. If I needed extra help, I just called on Ray Bell or Orville Luttrell. But I had to have help from the people, too. My theory is that you have to have the people in the community behind you or you ain't worth fifteen cents in Mexican money."

Then Ortiz learned to fight fires. "The Forest Service called me in," Ortiz explained. "I was expected to help handle communications, probably because, at first, I had the only two-way radio that could communicate with Forest headquarters in Alamogordo. After we got communications going, I was supposed to recruit help from nearby military bases. I'd get people to serve under the supervision of the Forest Service. We contacted Holloman Air Force Base, Walker Air Force Base, the Merchant Marine Hospital at Fort Stanton and several other volunteer organizations. All the men on the Los Tablos fire were called back, and we helped coordinate recruitment of townspeople from Capitan. We rang Lydia Hall, the telephone operator in Capitan, told her we needed so many men, and she got them."

As the fire spread and more volunteers arrived, Ed Guck transferred into Capitan (with his companion bucket to nurse tobacco spittle) to man the base radio at the Capitan ranger station, and Della Earl helped operate the district's telephone. High school boys were excused from classes to work on the fire; if eighteen or older, they were allowed on the fire lines; if younger, they helped the camp cooks.

Charlie Sutton had established his Los Tablos fire camp in the forest at the intersection of the Capitan Gap road and the north frontage road. But when the Capitan Gap fire broke out, Sutton's camp was doomed. On Sunday morning, Dean Earl ordered an evacuation to a flat (and safer) treeless area on the broad plains abutting the north side of East Mountain. "Dad called me with Ray Bell's radio," Bob Earl remembered. "He told me we had less than an hour to evacuate the whole camp. There were about fifty men in camp. Shortly thereafter smoke from the fire was pretty obvious and it started blocking the sun, which looked blood red." Calm but persuasive, Dean Earl ordered his men to load up what they could, leave the rest, and get out.

"We moved everything except one pickup—a 'thirty-eight Ford—that had a steering column locked," Peg Pfingsten added. "Charlie had a new light plant generator, so I got my jeep and towed it out. We also moved a supply tent and, of course, the stew. The cooks [Earnest McDaniels and Leroy McKnight] had fixed a big pot of fresh stew and the men weren't about to throw it away."

No one expected hungry firefighters to pass up good stew, and that batch tasted so good that villagers still talked about it forty years later. "They had a big kettle of stew cooking over an open fire," Dorothy Guck reported. "They got that stew into the truck and never spilled a drop. They were proud that they were able to save the stew."

Evacuation proved more harrowing than expected because the firefighters had to drive through the fire to reach the flatlands below. "Smoke was everywhere," Bob Earl explained. "Trees were falling across the road, and the road into the gap was rocky and littered with tree limbs and debris." And within two hours, the fire burned through Sutton's old camp.

Undaunted, Sutton reorganized his Capitan Gap fire camp near the intersection of the gap's dirt road and a winding gravel road from Capitan (later designated New Mexico Highway 246, and named Highway 48 today). Given the area's terrain, Sutton's choice perfectly met the needs of the hundreds of men, dozens of trucks and tons of supplies arrayed against Capitan Gap's horrible fire.

From the center of Capitan, 246 led through grassy flatlands offering an excellent view of the unburned south side of Capitan Mountain. "It was just a country road—not even a state highway then," explained Tom Guck, son of Ed and Dorothy Guck, and later a career man with the Forest Service. "You could drive twenty miles an hour—maybe thirty in places." About four miles from town, 246 began to twist, pitch and roll through low hills broken by arroyos strewn with scrub brush and dotted with piñon and juniper trees. Flat again, 246 paralleled Capitan Mountain to the gap road, 14.5 miles from Capitan.

On that vast, treeless plain almost 7,000 feet high, Charlie Sutton's 200-yard-wide camp blossomed as men looked up at the raging fire. Sutton ran a good fire camp, and this one grew rapidly into a small city. Within hours Sutton hosted more than 500 firefighters, including 300 soldiers, 125 local volunteers and 100 government personnel. The main camp rose on the east side of the gap road, while the army claimed the road's west side. In a frenzy of activity, men and women rushed through camp on foot, on horseback and in pickup trucks. A Red Cross first aid station sprouted, and administrative tents grew like mushrooms.

Pup tents dotted the camp's perimeter, but relief crews unfolded sleeping bags wherever they wished under open skies. Latrines were dug and covered with tents. Water wagons, scattered hay bales and white tents littered the camp. Soldiers lolled around in fatigues and battle helmets. Forest Service and military vehicles parked near large supply boxes, piles of blankets, tethered horses, saddles and water cans. Not a single tree offered shade.

Sutton set up his light plant—an engine and generator on two wheels— and ordered his cooks to start work. But except for the lone pot of salvaged stew, all Sutton could provide were sandwiches delivered from Capitan housewives, and he soon would have to feed three meals a day to hundreds of exhausted men.

Word reached Ray Taylor and Leo Joyner, veteran fire camp cooks. Taylor, who claimed to have been "raised in Texas like everybody else," moved to Lincoln County in 1933 and loved the Southwest and its history. "I like good westerns," Taylor admitted, "especially about them Oklahoma outlaws that came to New Mexico to shoot it out."

Now an oil well drilling contractor at age thirty-seven, Taylor was helping a friend take the 1950 U.S. census. They drove along 246 toward the smoke billowing over Capitan Mountain and, as hoped, stumbled across the fire camp. Unlike most volunteers, Taylor was compensated for his labors: "I got paid $1.40 an hour to cook," he explained, "but I lost a hundred bucks a day on my rig. Charlie Sutton and Dean Earl were good men, but everyone was running around like crazy."

Peg Pfingsten explained the haste: "When setting up a fire camp, if you weren't oriented before dark, you weren't any good."

Capitan housewives continued to send in sandwiches, but surging firefighters overwhelmed them. "The sandwiches weren't a drop in the bucket," Taylor snorted. "It was a big fire, but they hadn't brought much stuff in yet so we didn't have much to cook. We had a little coffee, but if you got two pieces of bread with an Oklahoma T-bone [bologna] in between, you were lucky to have a meal. Charlie Sutton told us to start dinner, but how were we supposed to feed people with nothing to cook? The Forest Service was always broke. So Charlie said to send a truck to Capitan and get anything we wanted."

Finally, cooking gear began to arrive. "The truck came in from the Forest Service warehouse in Alamogordo with the stoves," Taylor remembered. "They were little sheet iron ground stoves that had been stored in that warehouse for a thousand years, maybe a little bit less. They were brand new so we broke them in—got four of them going all the time—but they were low to the ground. We had some serving tables set up, but we didn't have any working tables. The fire camp was out in the middle of nowhere, and we had to work on the ground like Indians. We would have been uptown if we had had tables."

Then food poured in by the truckload: hind quarters of beef, cases of oranges and apples, candy bars, steaks, canned vegetables and fruits, eggs, ham, peas, beans, potatoes, jams and white bread. Many supplies came from Murphy's and Titsworth's stores in Capitan. "We didn't have enough room to cook because there were too many people around," Taylor offered. "You couldn't walk from the stove to the shack without running over four or five people. We roped off a cooking area to keep people away so we could have room to work. We had Tom Guck and about ten high school boys helping. Two or three boys handled the coffee pot and served it by the gallons; some chopped wood or carried water."

Peg Pfingsten was pleased. "They had started in with army cooks who didn't think a bunch of firefighters would eat like that," Pfingsten laughed. "Those boys ate everything the army had. Charlie Sutton sure was looking out for the army personnel; that was free labor so he figured to keep them happy. We always were fed pretty well at a fire after they got organized, but the first day or two you were lucky if you got anything to eat."

And hungry men lined up. "Biggest thing on a fire is to have good food and plenty of it," Taylor insisted. "Instead of the expected two hundred for dinner, three hundred would show up. They kept a'comin. I was busier than a cranberry merchant. For breakfast, we had eggs on big platters; over easy, eyes open; limit two. Some would take a half dozen if we let them, but the line was a hundred yards long. We had bacon, hashed browns, grits and plenty of coffee that we made in a big stew pot. We baked biscuits in those little ovens. One of them pans would hold a hundred and fifty biscuits, and each man got two with lots of jam and jelly. Those California boys said we had the best meals they ever had on a forest fire."

Firefighters ate lunch on the fire line. "We fixed a lot of sack lunches," remembered Taylor. "The high school boys put two roast beef sandwiches, an orange and a bar of candy in each bag. We threw those sack lunches out by the hundreds."

But Taylor staked his reputation on the "evening" meal. His secret? "Stew," Taylor beamed. "We brought stew pans that held at least twenty gallons, and cut up potatoes and a quarter of a beef into a kettle for stew. Those boys came off the mountain without food; they deserved a hot meal. Stew. Stew every meal. Stew any time. That was a real good feed—put everything you got in there and a little bit more. We built a good stew—put a lot of beef in it with taters, tomatoes, corn, peas, onions and garlic. Cook it up, let it simmer down with lots of good thick juice in it. Boy, it was tasty. A plate of that stew and some white bread would fill up most guys.

We had ham, too," Taylor continued. "Lots of ham. Cooked lots of fresh frijole beans. We bought potatoes by the hundred pounds. We tried to give them enough for a pretty good meal. Uncle Sam was sitting there gritting his teeth, afraid we would break the government if we spent some money. We were so busy, we didn't have time to sleep. I sure didn't need that bed roll."

Despite the frenetic work pace, Bob Earl remembered a few humorous moments. "One morning we got a load of supplies that included some canned corn with swelling ends. Cookie said to throw it away, so we tossed it into a fire burning in the garbage dump. But it was pretty cold and two firefighters were by the fire keeping warm. I told them the corn could blow up, but they squatted down like cowboys do and one guy told me I was full of bologna. At that moment, one of the cans of corn cut loose and exploded creamed corn all over his face. Another morning Cookie was breaking frozen eggs two at a time when a baby chick fell out of one eggshell. Cookie just picked it up and threw it on the ground, but a firefighter who was standing there turned around and barfed."

As time passed, the fire camp became organized. At first, Dean Earl had survived with local volunteers and a few professionals. But camp activities changed rapidly after trained firemen arrived to relieve the gallant local citizenry. State troopers established a communications network by placing three patrol cars with their powerful radios around Capitan Mountain. Blankets arrived with the grocery deliveries. Capitan High School placed its shower rooms at the disposal of exhausted firefighters.

Sheriff Ortiz kept recruiting by badgering recalcitrants at Pearl's Cafe (now the Smokey Bear Cafe) in Capitan and other Lincoln County gathering spots. Each morning Ortiz added to the horde when he charged up in a flatbed Ford truck laden with five or six handpicked men from his Lincoln County jail in nearby Carrizozo. Most of Ortiz's "volunteers" had been arrested the night before for drunkenness or vagrancy. "They were local alcoholics," Ortiz admitted. "But we needed help, and they were sober in the morning, so why not?" Dean Earl wouldn't trust Ortiz's sober recruits on the fire lines, but if they passed Charlie Sutton's scrutiny, they were allowed to help the cooks.

When the driving wind eased that evening, Dean Earl asked Ray Bell to fly the fire so they could look at the holocaust. "Early morning and late evening are the best times to observe a fire from the sky," Bell explained. "Air is more stable, greater lift is available at that altitude, fewer air pockets of heat threaten an aircraft and fewer gusts of wind make it less dangerous to fly."

Again, Earl didn't like what he saw. The Capitan Gap fire was alternately slowing up, then breaking out with the wind. Fire lines were being lost and crews were scattered. Logical fighting areas were inaccessible because of rugged terrain. Deep canyons couldn't be defended without risking lives. Heavy equipment couldn't reach high ridges. Roads, rivers and other natural barriers were limited. Flying embers were igniting dozens of new fires.

Earl needed more help, and by early the next morning, it seemed that every available man in Lincoln County was on the fire, and it still wasn't enough, so Ed Guck called Albuquerque. Several fires, however, had broken out in New Mexico, and Guck found it difficult to bring in experienced fire bosses. Rangeland was burning in northeastern New Mexico, 550 men were fighting a 15,000-acre fire in the Carson National Forest in the north central part of the state, and another large fire was developing eight miles southeast of Chama.

But eight Forest Service men arrived from California and five came in from Arizona to help with administration and supervision. Orville Luttrell and other game wardens arrived with men from across New Mexico, and the Southern Pacific pipeline sent in a crew. Boy Scouts of Capitan Troop 55 were excused from school to deliver supplies, and Dick Cox, an eighth-grade student in Capitan, was among those called. Although not old enough for a driver's license, Cox made a delivery to Sutton's camp. "We could see the fire from our house in Fort Stanton," Cox recalled. "Dad was a baker, so I took a load of bread and groceries to the fire camp. It was thrilling because of the smoke. The fire camp was kind of grim, but you could really see the fire."

Luckily for Smokey Bear fans, the Capitan Gap fire had its own private reporter on the scene. As a debater, orator and vice president of the class of

1931 at South High School in Grand Rapids, Michigan, Dorothy Gray won the silver cup traditionally awarded to the outstanding girl achiever. A companion award for outstanding boy achiever was presented to her friend and classmate Gerald R. Ford. "It's funny," Dorothy Gray Guck laughed. "For years, I kept my silver cup in the basement . . . until Gerry became Vice President."

At the University of Wisconsin, Gray created a series of radio programs depicting children's nature tales and wrote fictionalized stories of animals and birds that were broadcast to schools throughout Wisconsin. In 1934, Gray traveled by bus to New Mexico to visit her brother, a forestry foreman in a CCC camp. There, Gray met her brother's friend Ed Guck, and New Mexico's crisp air catalyzed their chemistry. Within a week Ed proposed, Dorothy accepted, and the pair soon were married.

As Ed Guck transferred around New Mexico and Arizona, Dorothy Gray Guck took up pen and paper and began writing, and when the young couple moved to Mesa, New Mexico, Dorothy found a demand for her writing skills. "I sent a few items to the *Lincoln County News*," she remembered, "and right away, I was asked to do write-ups for local communities. Then I was asked to write a regular column for the *Nogal-Mesa News*. The Associated Press learned I was doing the local articles and they called and asked me to be a stringer. The Associated Press wanted articles about travel, the Forest Service and camp meetings. But they were primarily interested in fires, so in 1949 I was assigned to follow the Red Hats."

Although Guck's articles appeared in several newspapers and magazines, she didn't earn enough money to celebrate too late into the night: "My writing was all volunteer; I wasn't paid a cent. Well, one time I got sixty-three cents for a travel article. I called in most of the articles and someone else wrote them, so I wasn't given credit for a lot of the Associated Press articles."

So Dorothy Guck, the only reporter at the Los Tablos and Capitan Gap fires, called in her articles to the *Lincoln County News* in Carrizozo. The *News*, in turn, placed the stories with the AP, which distributed them over the wires. "I called in five or six stories as things happened on the fire," Guck recalled. "It was more or less a daily report. The story I called in about Speed's men getting trapped probably was the biggest."

8

APACHE FIREFIGHTERS

*"White man and Indian fight together in World War I, lick the
Kaiser. White man and Indian fight side by side in World War
II, beat Hitler and Hirohito. What the hell, white man and
Indian fight together, lick a little forest fire!"*

— unidentified Mescalero Apache to Dorothy Guck

Fighting forest fires in 1950 involved two basic steps: building fire lines to
contain spreading ground fires, and mopping up to actually extinguish fires.
In the first step, men and bulldozers created barriers in front of advancing
fires simply by clearing fuel from the fire's path. Everything flammable—
trees, stumps, branches, pine needles, leaves—was cleared down to soil or
a rocky surface. When possible, natural barriers such as roads, rivers, lakes
or rocky outcroppings were used. Relatively narrow man-made fire lines—
often only two feet wide—could be widened by "backfiring," where a fire
deliberately was set in front of an advancing fire to widen a barrier.

When a fire raged among steep slopes, deep ravines and giant boulders,
machines couldn't help. Then, huge supplies of manpower were needed
to build miles of fire line by hand, usually with rakes, shovels or a "kortick,"

the favorite fire tool of most forest fire fighters. An ideal weapon for digging fire lines, the heavy, short-handled kortick usually was ten inches wide with six rake-type tines on one side and a hoe blade on the other. Building a fire line was—and is—backbreaking work, especially when compounded by the 7,000- to 10,000-foot altitude at Capitan Gap. Crews of twelve to fifty men were assigned to various sections of fire lines and, while they typically worked eight- to ten-hour shifts, men sometimes toiled for up to eighteen hours at a stretch.

Theoretically, building fire lines is both simple and effective, but forest fires don't always cooperate. With changes in wind, humidity and air pressure, forest fires unpredictably can change direction, speed and intensity. Wind carries burning embers across fire lines, falling trees carry sparks across natural and man-made barriers, and ground fires erupt into indefensible crown fires racing through treetops.

When firefighters finally corral a fire, the mopping-up operation can take weeks as every burning stump and brush pile is extinguished so that gusting winds cannot carry fire outside a contained area. Bulldozers help where they can, but most of the work falls to hand labor with a "pulaski," which has a five-inch hoe blade on one side and an ax on the other.

If the Capitan Gap fire had broken out in a flat area, Dean Earl probably would have had sufficient equipment to contain the fire in its early stages. Nolan and Willis Loveless brought in a tractor from Corona, unloaded their D-7 Caterpillar bulldozer, and cleared a landing strip for Ray Bell's plane. A landing site was available one mile north of the Block lookout, but Bell already had landed in the pasture near the new fire camp. "The guys with bulldozers just followed my tracks," Bell explained. "They flew themselves, so those boys knew what to do."

Rancher Ambros Guest trucked in two D-7 "Cats," Lincoln County contributed two road graders and one bulldozer, and the army arrived with a D-6 Cat. But because of Capitan Mountain's steep terrain and countless rock slides, those heavy machines, for the most part useless, were destined to be relegated to the less dramatic role of digging out fire roads to permit access into the fire area.

Even a tenderfoot could have understood Dean Earl's problem. As Earl surveyed the battlefield from his new fire camp, a casual glance told him all he needed to know. Just behind the Lon Merchant ranch to Earl's right, a single ridge climbed almost a thousand feet straight up into West Mountain. Across the gap on East Mountain, 200- and 300-foot cliffs ran like folds in drapes, creating giant canyons. The first three canyons to Earl's left—Koprian Canyon, Dry Canyon and Shoemaker Canyon—housed massive rock slides deposited thousands of years earlier. Covered with stones ranging from pebbles to teetering boulders the size of Volkswagens, the rock slides were slippery and dangerous, but perhaps easier to traverse than surrounding brush. Packed into the crowded timber, oak thickets reached ten to twelve feet high, growing so dense that men sometimes couldn't walk through them. Earl knew that stopping the fire on East Mountain would be a nightmare.

So perhaps it was the dozens of smaller trucks that were most important, for as they roared into camp with clouds of dust, they brought men, supplies and fire equipment—korticks, rakes, pulaskis, hand saws and a few chain saws. Virtually all the fire fighting at Capitan Gap would be by hand; crews simply couldn't get heavy machinery where it was needed.

Earl appointed two experienced men to serve as line bosses—one for each side of the fire—and another eight veterans to act as sector bosses over designated areas. Earl relied on men he could trust, ignoring rank, age or employer, picking as he saw fit from the Forest Service, the military and New Mexico's game wardens. "The game wardens could do it all, so Dean Earl assigned them to many different jobs," Dorothy Guck confirmed. Working with his line and sector bosses, Earl selected another twenty reliable men as crew bosses and assigned them twenty-five-man crews for various sectors. The fire had to be attacked by hand, and perhaps the very best at that tough job were two dozen Mescalero Apaches.

Apache. For hundreds of years the very name struck terror into the hearts of anyone nearing Apache territory. Before Europeans arrived, Apaches moved from America's central plains into an area 500 miles square, covering much of today's West Texas, New Mexico, Arizona and northern Mexico. Apaches moved in as conquerors, living as nomadic hunters with little interest in farming. They called themselves "Indee," meaning "the people," but neighboring Zunis had a different word—"Apachu"—which meant "enemy." The term was well deserved: fierce Apache warriors neither gave nor expected mercy.

Apaches divided their 250,000-square-mile territory among a loose-knit alliance of perhaps ten autonomous bands that usually went their separate ways, but sometimes engaged in internecine warfare among themselves. The Chiricahua band, that produced Cochise and Geronimo, became the best known and perhaps the most formidable.

Some U.S. military personnel believed Apache land, with its scarcity of water, to be the harshest terrain in North America. Marked by dry flatlands and steep mountain ranges, it seemed that only cactus, thorny scrub brush and rattlesnakes populated that wasteland. But Apaches mastered their land and knew where it hid water, so they flourished in a desert where white men would have died. But by the time the United States acquired most Apache territory from Mexico through the Treaty of Guadalupe Hidalgo in 1846 and the Gadsden Purchase of 1853, only 7,000 Apaches roamed the Southwest.

Unlike most American Indian tribes, Apaches never developed a dependence upon horses for the same reason they didn't farm—their barren mountains, deep arroyos and sandy plains could barely support people, much less their animals. Horses might have been useful to purchase a bride or fill a stewpot, but they generally were not favored by Apache warriors. And as Apaches learned to survive in their difficult terrain, they seldom advertised their presence with bright war paint and found that while their colorful foes revealed themselves on horseback, Apaches could easily conceal themselves on foot.

Reliance on their feet probably contributed to Apache successes on the battlefield, and Apache warriors were widely known as perhaps the most fierce, vicious, tireless fighters in the Southwest. One nineteenth-century admirer called Apaches "one of the toughest human organisms the world has ever seen." Certainly, warriors drilled from boyhood, stayed awake for days to learn to cope with exhaustion, went long periods without food or water and trained for long-distance running. In their desolate terrain, an experienced, agile Apache warrior could traverse at least seventy miles a day on foot—far more than a white man could negotiate on horseback. Apaches could jog up mountains, run through cacti with their roll-up boots and leave a trail so faint that only another Apache could follow. Because it seemed that only an Apache could catch another Apache, the Apaches were one of the last tribes to be subdued by the "white eyes."

Occupying an area south of Capitan, one of the Apache bands became known as the "Mescaleros," probably because of their periodic harvests of the agave plant. Mescaleros roasted the sweet fleshy base of the agave, made thread from its fibers and used its sap to make beverages such as *mescal,* from which the Mescaleros were named.

By the spring of 1950, about 1,100 Mescalero Apaches lived on their 400,000 acres of tribal land. Vast stands of yellow pine, Ponderosa pine and Douglas fir—perhaps 250,000 acres—stretched across rugged mountains at an altitude more than a mile high. Here the Mescaleros thrived in their scenic desert oasis. Some lived in modern houses, some in tepees. Some were loggers, cowboys, mechanics or artists; others managed timber or roads. But it does not take much imagination to believe that the bloodlines that made nineteenth-century Apache warriors so feared also allowed 1950-era Apaches to stand out as firefighters. The Mescaleros had laid down their forefathers' war clubs, but they gathered new weapons—picks, shovels, korticks and pulaskis—and earned a nationwide reputation for fierceness in forest fire fighting.

To protect their New Mexico homeland, the Mescaleros devoted considerable effort to fighting fires on their heavily wooded reservation. Fire fighting became a way of life for most men of the tribe, and every able-bodied male was expected to battle fires on Apache land. Many Mescalero children began their fire training at age ten. "At that time, age made no difference," Mason Guydelkon, a veteran firefighter, explained. "When you are an Indian, you start manual labor at age twelve. Old men would be out there too. If you didn't want to go to a fire, they threatened you with jail. I don't know if anyone ever went to jail, but everyone had to fight local fires on the reservation."

The Apaches' world began to change when New Mexico's wilderness was opened by Civilian Conservation Corps programs in the 1930s and '40s. Then, with World War II's gas rationing gone, more and more tourists drove into the area—sometimes encouraged by the Mescaleros, who collected fees for fishing the reservation's trout-filled streams. But when the area suffered from a prolonged drought, Mescalero forests became exposed to an increasing threat from careless tourists.

Although historical documents conflict as to exact dates, Bureau of Indian Affairs forest supervisor Reino Sarlin apparently suggested in early 1948 that a top-notch fire crew be created to lead the Apaches' response to reservation fires. A group called the "Red Hats" eventually was formed, with responsibility falling on Bert Shields to create a first-class firefighting team under the auspices of the BIA and the Mescalero Apache tribe. Shields, a former Forest Service employee, served as timber supervisor and fire chief on the reservation for thirty years. An Anglo, Shields was congenial and well respected by the Apaches.

Shields was assisted by Rufus Lester, a husky, barrel-chested forty-eight-year-old part Frenchman and part Apache given to faded denims, thick logger boots and a short haircut. Talkative, jolly and well liked by his colleagues, Lester coordinated Red Hat affairs while Shields directed their training.

Prophetically, Bert Shields explained his intentions in an April 19, 1949, letter to his Apache friends: "Memorandum to men who have indicated their willingness to join the Red Hats or the crack fire fighting squad on the Mescalero Indian Reservation. Will it be possible for you to meet with us on Saturday night, April 23, 1949, at the office at 6:30 p.m.? I greatly appreciate your willingness to cooperate in such an important job and I hope to help you fellows organize yourselves into a group who will make history in the Southwest. Bring along some other sucker who you think has what it takes to be a red hatted fire eater."

Only nineteen men, mostly veterans of World War II, showed up at the first meeting. After considerable discussion, one man rose to support the proposal. "Fighting forest fires is one thing the white man does that makes sense," he reasoned. Then an unidentified tribal elder rose to agree. "White man and Indian fight together in World War I, lick the Kaiser. White man and Indian fight side by side in World War II, beat Hitler and Hirohito. What the hell, white man and Indian fight together, lick a little forest fire!" he declared.

And so began the official recorded history of the Mescalero Apache Red Hats. That small group would grow to more than two hundred highly trained Mescaleros that, with the exception of full-time professionals, became the first organized firefighting group in the American West. They showed that Apaches loved excitement and welcomed physical challenges shunned by most people. With volunteers from seventeen to fifty years old, and bolstered by a series of magazine stories written by Dorothy Guck, the Red Hats would become famous fighting fires throughout the western United States and would spawn dozens of imitator Indian and Hispanic teams. Eventually the Red Hats traveled so extensively that a paraphrased slogan attracted new members: Join the Red Hats and see the world.

Curiously, the tradition of actually wearing red hats on the fire line wasn't implemented until 1953, when red tin hats were ceremoniously awarded to new members upon completion of their rigorous training program. Before 1953, in fact, Red Hats wore gray tin hats, although the tribe apparently got the idea for their name from Ed Wynn, a nationally known radio and television comedian who frequently acted out skits wearing a red fireman's hat. Whatever their hat color, these tough Apaches became noted for their discipline, fire camp manners and outstanding firefighting efforts.

An original Red Hat, Aloysius Mendez later became fire control agent for the Mescalero reservation, responsible for running the sprawling reservation's entire fire control program and its 350 miles of telephone wires between lookout towers. Quick to smile and with an easy laugh, Mendez— a full-blooded Apache blend of the Mescalero, Lipan and Chiricahua tribes— was born in 1920. After growing up on the reservation, he showed his grit during World War II, winning superior performance awards with the army transportation corps in Australia, New Guinea and the Admiralty Islands.

But after the war, except for fire prevention and fire fighting, there wasn't much paying work available back on the reservation. Each winter Mendez worked part-time on construction or road building on government-sponsored projects. "But sometimes we spent time at the agency just because we had nothing to do," Mendez explained. "We'd wait around for a fire call—it was a way to survive, one of the few ways to earn money."

Born in 1931, Mason Guydelkon, another full-blooded Apache, remembered his own recruitment: "The Forest Service and BIA people asked if we wanted to make some money. People were kind of poor then. I was about fifteen or sixteen, so it was exciting when I first got into it. The Forest Service recruited all the help they could get. The group was already called the Red Hats, and all my uncles had fought on the reservation."

So the Red Hats of fame—a final original group of sixty-four tough Mescalero Apaches—began their training under Bert Shields. "First, we learned the tools—ax, shovel and rakes," Guydelkon explained. "We started with garden rakes, then they introduced the kortick rake and, later, the pulaski. Then we learned three versions of the 'bump-up system.'"

Because Ray Bell was district game warden in nearby Capitan, Shields asked Bell to help with training exercises. "The Apaches were very good," an admiring Bell beamed. "They could work long hours and were good firefighters. They were good students, too."

"We learned by training," Guydelkon emphasized. "People told us what to do and the crew boss kept us in line. They placed an emphasis on personal safety, but the Red Hats got to be good because we never said no. We just went and did it. As we took on the tough jobs, we got the experience, and I felt we had good leadership. I never felt like we were misled. We usually had two leaders—one Apache and one government man—so we never had any problems with cultural differences."

The Red Hats trained arduously for almost a year, focused as if they were warriors of old. Each week men met to practice line building and experiment with firefighting tools, sometimes studying them as closely as they studied their traditional tribal dances. As they trained, their Apache attributes of physical stamina, agility in rough terrain and ability to work long hours in intense heat with little water or food emerged. Physically hardened through lives of manual labor, the Mescaleros began to understand fires, to read signs in the winds and canyons and to learn to sense danger.

Training was not without an occasional setback. Despite modern dress and literacy, ancestral superstitions sometimes surfaced. Dorothy Guck visited to write about their exploits, but the Red Hats would not allow a woman to take their photos. Bert Shields had to explain the logic of backfiring to skeptical Apaches who believed the gods would be mystified by fools starting fires when their objective was to put one out. And once—but only once—a crew panicked and ran in the face of an as-yet-unseen but howling and rapidly advancing fire.

In time, response procedures were finalized. When a fire call was issued, Red Hats formed crews from the first men reporting to the dispatch point. Phones were scarce, so reservation fire and recreation guards rounded up men by car or messenger. With typical Apache ingenuity, the guards occasionally relied on a traditional communication—smoke signals—to reach men working in remote rangeland.

As Red Hats arrived in answer to a call, they boarded a red fire truck equipped with two long bench seats and a complete case of firefighting tools. Wearing heavy shoes or boots, jeans, a cotton shirt, gloves and a neckerchief, each man loaded a sleeping bag and a small pack holding a change of clothes, perhaps an old jacket, a toothbrush and personal effects. Arriving at a fire, the Red Hats hopped off their truck in systematic order, dumped personal gear at the fire camp, donned tin hats, buckled water canteens to their waists, and headed straight for the fire.

Even after the Red Hats established themselves, training continued with annual refresher courses. "We had firefighting school in April each year," Aloysius Mendez recalled. "We built a mock fire camp and trained for at least a whole day. We built fire lines, studied first aid and learned to take care of our tools. We kept knapsacks with extra clothes and stuff in the Mescalero forestry warehouse. Everything was ready in the locker."

Finally, the Red Hats became so skilled at defending their own homeland that they began to assist their white neighbors by "boundary busting" at fire calls. When fighting alongside untrained volunteer help, the Red Hats soon learned they had the stamina to work in areas from which white men would flee, so the Red Hats took pride in their ability to work longer and harder than anyone else. They kept in top physical condition, and it showed. "They can stand low humidity and high temperatures," an observer noted. "They never drink water. They go forever. They are like camels. They know their limits, and are willing to go to their limits."

"We could get by on just the bare essentials," Guydelkon pointed out. "We lived off the land; we think that way." And Mendez explained another element in the Apaches' success: "Prayer is powerful."

Although Red Hat historical records indicate that Capitan Gap was only the second major fire they fought outside their reservation, Dean Earl instinctively respected them. Their first foray had been at Bonita Lake in Ed Guck's ranger district, and Guck, too, had been impressed with their skills and attitude. The Red Hats were good; they were committed; they were Earl's kind of men. The Red Hats would serve as Earl's shock troops in the battle to save Capitan Mountain.

Although he fought many forest fires, Guydelkon couldn't participate in the Capitan Gap fire. While that fire raged, Guydelkon was battling an international fire with the U. S. Navy, pushing fighter planes around an aircraft carrier—the USS *Kersarge*—off the coast of Korea.

But Mendez rode in the first of two vehicles that carried the Red Hats to the fire that produced America's most famous bear. Because Ray Bell knew both the Red Hats and the Capitan Mountain area, Dean Earl appointed Bell to serve as the Red Hats' crew boss at the Los Tablos fire and assigned the Apaches to one of the worst areas on the fire line.

From the outset, the Apaches showed their toughness, skill and determination. As "line locator," Bell walked ahead of the fire's path, looking for favorable contours in the rugged terrain where firefighters could tie their line into rocky spots. Bell plotted the best course to prevent the fire's spread and tried to identify the easiest areas to clear by keeping his men out of areas with brush too heavy to clean. Like bird dogs, the tenacious Mescaleros followed behind, so closely that Bell had difficulty keeping ahead and didn't need to mark the line with hatchet marks on trees. The Apaches, using Shields's "one-chop" system, worked almost as fast as Bell could walk. "By golly, if you got a bunch of those rascals on your tail, you had to hustle. They built a line as fast as I could lead out," Bell recalled.

The nationwide fame of this group of Red Hats was no accident; these men earned their reputation step by step, chop by chop, and sweat drop by sweat drop. With the one-chop system, the lead man took a single swipe with his kortick, raking away ground fuel for a length of two to three feet, stepped over two paces—about ten feet—and took another swipe. Each man then took a single swipe against his predecessor's mark. Chop, four steps; chop, four steps; chop. This production line technique built a fire line rapidly while allowing workers to straighten their backs with brief rests between each chop; usually, that two-to-three-foot-wide fire line could stop a ground fire.

In thick underbrush, men armed with pulaskis followed the advance guard, chopping limbs and hauling away cut branches and logs. Other men with hoes and brush hooks stripped the fire line of anything flammable.

In heavy fuels, sawers mixed with rakers as men rotated responsibilities to ease aching muscles. Always, crews kept alert for their biggest threat— red-hot boulders crashing down from one of the area's many rock slides or outcroppings. While Red Hats usually couldn't see the fire, they certainly could hear its roar.

Rufus Lester told of the Capitan Gap fire: "We started work on the line about 9 a.m. No food, no rest until 2 p.m. the next day. Then a big army captain came up to relieve us with his soldiers." According to Lester, neither the captain nor his men had ever seen a forest fire and had no idea what to do, so somewhat bemused, the tired Red Hats gave the soldiers a brief, one-hour lesson in firefighting.

Eventually, the Apaches began to play a game, dog-trotting up the mountain and falling to work the minute they hit the fire. Chagrined white crews, exhausted by the time they reached the fire line, couldn't work until they caught their breath. Some whites reportedly were embarrassed at how many times they had to stop and breathe while the Red Hats kept chopping. To Mendez, the difference was cultural: "White man travels on his stomach, looks at what he takes in and takes pride in that. Indian takes pride in the grease he rubs on his knees."

But altruism wasn't the Apaches' only incentive. Entrepreneurs emerge even on reservations, so fortune—but, interestingly, not fame—proved to be a motivating force for the Apaches. "Money was the best thing," Guydelkon grinned. "We were paid less than five dollars an hour, but that was pretty good money then. We could buy a lot of food and clothing and treat the whole family when we came back. We were not particularly aware of our reputation, but we were always in front at a fire; we always climbed the hill first."

Mendez agreed on several counts. "Money was the most fun, but we never realized we were famous," he explained. "We just did our job on the fire line and then went home. We didn't realize what we were starting. We just felt we were doing something great for the nation and our people. It was a good feeling to put out a tough fire."

Although no Red Hats were in the immediate vicinity when the famous little bear cub was rescued, most approved of the idea. "It was great to save that bear," Mendez confirmed. "Bears are symbols of the forest in Apache culture. I think it was okay to put clothes on the poster Smokey Bear, too, because it helps stop forest fires."

So as Mendez and his colleagues proved so many times, huge boulders, steep ravines and towering cliffs could stop a bulldozer, but they couldn't stop the Apache Red Hats. But five hundred men were battling Capitan Gap's raging fire and the worst was yet to come.

9

BEARLY ALIVE

"Speed Simmons saved a lot of lives that day. Mine was one of them."

— Harry Collins

New Mexico's thirteen district game wardens were about as tough a lot as you could find in 1950s America. Bronc-busters, trappers and outdoorsmen, they lived with and off the land they loved. They spoke a little Spanish and a few phrases of Native American tongues; they knew and respected terrain, weather, people and animals; and they handled firearms with deadly accuracy. Charged with conserving New Mexico's wildlife through enforcement of game and fish laws, those rugged men pursued their prey in trucks, on horseback, from the air and on foot. Few game violators could outdistance, outshoot or outsmart those determined law enforcement officers.

Given a choice, the game wardens preferred to focus on land and wildlife conservation. They conducted game surveys, treated injured animals, reported on water and fishing conditions and developed game and stream programs to benefit future generations. Perhaps most important, they watched for fires, because wildlife conservation required forests for a habitat. If called to a fire, game wardens subordinated themselves to the Forest Service, but because of extensive experience, physical conditioning and leadership skills, the game wardens often were assigned important responsibilities.

Orville Luttrell, district game warden in Alamogordo, arrived at Dean Earl's fire on Saturday, May 6. Born in Capitan in 1915, Luttrell joined the army air corps after high school and spent World War II as a tech sergeant in Australia and the South Pacific, finally island-hopping to the Philippines before leaving the service in 1946. As a Lincoln County deputy sheriff, Luttrell took flying lessons and met Ray Bell, who convinced Luttrell to join him in the Game and Fish Department. Luttrell began patrol work in 1947 as a firefighter, pilot and antelope trapper until appointed game warden in early 1950.

Rugged, tough and independent, with a cowboy hat over his chiseled face, the deep-voiced Luttrell was a good officer, a good shot, a good bronco rider, a good carpenter and a good pilot. "The son-of-a-gun can do anything," Bell asserted. And Dean Earl wanted Luttrell at Capitan Gap.

After completing his battle plan early Sunday evening, May 7, Earl assigned Luttrell and George Hightower, a game trapper, to lead a crew of Fort Bliss soldiers. Their mission: build a fire line up the fire's west perimeter on Capitan Mountain. Plunging into action, Luttrell walked ahead of his men, laying out a fire line as Hightower supervised the clearing work of twenty soldiers. With vigorous effort, the crew toiled through the night to take advantage of the fire's tendency to lie dormant in the darkness. They understood that although fires become violent during daylight hours as winds increase and temperatures rise, they cool at night—especially at high altitude—to allow close-in work.

As daylight emerged about 5:15 a.m., the exhausted crew tapered off work to await a relief squad. Aching muscles needed rest, but several ears perked up as the men heard an eerie whining riding the soft breeze from the south. At first faint and distant, the whining grew louder as it approached, and curious soldiers turned toward the sound. Luttrell and Hightower, recognizing the intermittent cry of a bear cub, just smiled.

Finally a tiny chocolate-colored black bear cub poked through dense underbrush, picking his way down the steep hill, about forty feet from the perimeter of the slow-moving ground fire. Even when the bear noticed the firefighters only thirty feet away, his loud wailing continued as if he were a sobbing child. Hesitating a few seconds, the noisy cub, too young to be afraid of the grinning humans, scaled a fallen tree, walked out on a limb and sat down. "The bear was uninjured," Luttrell remembered. "It was neither burned nor panicky; it was just lost and trying to stay out of the line of the spreading fire."

As fascinated soldiers cautiously inspected the ursine intruder, his howling stopped when he turned his attention to the dirty men. The cub sat passively, seemingly content to enjoy the soldiers' company. Luttrell and Hightower, aware of the dangers of fooling with a bear cub, cautioned that a mother bear could pose a formidable threat in a bear-knuckles bout. But Mama didn't show, and the crew watched the wailing cub for twenty minutes until relieved by game warden Speed Simmons, who followed the fire line to Luttrell's position.

After Luttrell left, the new crew watched the cub until Simmons ordered them to work. The cub briefly trailed the firefighters, but then wandered off. A pleased Simmons, who expected Mama Bear to appear, preferred to be nowhere near when the reunion occurred.

At age fourteen, Lee William Simmons graduated from his eighth-grade class in a one-room schoolhouse, left his stepfather on their central Pennsylvania farm, and headed west to be a cowboy. Simmons became a top hand on ranches in Kansas, Wyoming, Montana and New Mexico and, after joining the Game and Fish Department as a patrolman in 1937, accepted a district game warden's post at Artesia in 1946. Known to be fast in a foot race and exceptionally quick with a pistol, the aptly named "Speed" was respected by his colleagues as an unusually good law enforcement officer known for his strict adherence to the law.

A woodsman at heart, Simmons loved wildlife and conservation. He taught his children to track game and showed them how to distinguish young from old, male from female, by looking at the shape and depth of tracks. At six feet two inches, Simmons was a stern taskmaster. Issues were black or white, right or wrong. If Simmons had to do a job, he found a way to deal with every obstacle. He pushed his men hard and himself harder, thinking he had to give more than anyone else. Although hot-tempered, Simmons spoke slowly and deliberately; he expected people to understand him the first time; it was inefficient to repeat or explain. Simmons wasn't an easy man. Perhaps that's why he became a hero.

When Simmons was in the wilderness, he seemed obsessed with anticipating every eventuality. Simmons's friends believed he lay awake at night plotting every contingency, but when an emergency occurred, Simmons had thought it through and would be reacting while others were trying to decide what to do. At age forty-six and in his prime as an officer, the self-reliant Simmons soon would use his vast experience to save twenty-five lives.

At 7:30 on Sunday night, May 7, Simmons received a phone call at his home in Artesia from a game warden in Roswell, who explained the fire on

L. W. "Speed" Simmons, hero of the Capitan Gap forest fire. *(Courtesy Joyce Pankey.)*

Capitan Mountain was out of control and experienced firefighters were needed. Simmons, who had just returned from patrol, was asked to report for fire duty as soon as possible.

"I used some unlady-like language," Speed's wife, Marcelle, explained. "Speed always came in from work late. The family had eaten about six o'clock because I had to feed the kids. But I started dinner all over again—bacon, eggs and toast—and we had just sat down to eat when the call came from Roswell. Speed didn't like the Capitan area because it was a bad area for a fire. He said: 'Oh hell, if that one's out of control, it's a bad one.' So I said: 'I suppose you have to go.' I wasn't surprised; that was part of his job."

So Simmons wolfed down his supper, loaded fire gear into his patrol car and set out on the eighty-five-mile drive. Simmons had seen smoke climbing into the eastern skies and had begun his mental preparation, thinking about his firefighting experiences in Montana and New Mexico as he drove the winding mountain roads to Capitan. Simmons arrived at the fire camp near midnight and reported to Dean Earl, who told his welcome recruit to roll out his bedroll and sleep until 4:00 a.m.

During the night, Earl reviewed reports coming in by Handy-Talky radio from Orville Luttrell, high on Capitan Mountain. Luttrell didn't like what he saw—elements favoring a possible holocaust were in place: steep terrain, dense underbrush, preheating pine trees and widespread rocky outcroppings. Although he felt firefighters could handle the blaze if it stayed on the ground, Luttrell was afraid his fire lines could not contain a crown fire. In the event of a "blowup," Luttrell wasn't certain that men should even be in the area.

Earl studied Luttrell's comments and consulted weather forecasts that offered a grim warning: high temperatures, low humidity, increasing winds. But Earl's maps disclosed no other logical place to make a stand, and he knew that blowups usually didn't occur until 2 or 3 p.m.—the hottest part of the day. With a good crew and a good leader, perhaps the fire could be contained. Dean Earl needed Speed Simmons.

Arising promptly at 4:00 a.m., Simmons munched breakfast as he listened to Earl's briefing. Earl explained his concerns about the potential hot spots reported by Luttrell and advised Simmons to beware of wind gusts that could carry the blaze over the fire lines. "Prediction is for a forty-mile wind later today, and the blaze might jump the barrier," Earl noted, "but with your experience and this crew I think you can handle it." It was the type of challenge on which Simmons thrived.

Edwin Harrison "Harry" Collins was one of the Forest Service staffers assigned to Simmons. Born in Fruitville, Florida, the twenty-eight-year-old Collins grew interested in forestry during a summer job in Grants Pass, Oregon. Following a World War II stint as an armorer with the army air corps in a B-26 outfit in England and a B-47 group in Germany, Collins won a degree in forestry from the University of Florida in 1948. After one year in Arizona, Collins transferred to Alamogordo in 1949 to manage timber sales for the Lincoln Forest.

There, Sam Servis took Collins under his wing, determined to give the rookie solid fire experience. And learning that Simmons was taking a crew up the mountain, Servis arranged for Collins to join the group. "I was a green young forester," Collins confessed, "but Sam was looking out for me.

I reported to the fire and was assigned as crew boss for some soldiers from Fort Bliss—an artillery outfit. Speed was the leader; I was green as green."

Before daylight Simmons and his men rode trucks to the end of a dirt road, then hiked a mile and a half to Luttrell's location, each man carrying tools and a canteen of water on his belt. Men were left at intervals along the fire line with instructions to improve and patrol it, but Simmons took twenty-nine men with him to the head of the fire.

Relieving Luttrell, Simmons's men began their backbreaking task with shovels, axes and saws, cutting fire lines, scraping brush and hauling limbs from the fire's path to cut a line up a tree-filled ridge around the right flank of the fire to stop its spread in that direction. Collins, wearing dark green, long-sleeve Forest Service-issue cotton work clothes, a white hard hat and gloves, worked with his shovel alongside the soldiers clad in fatigues and hard hats. Peg Pfingsten rode on horseback between the groups, serving as messenger.

Simmons, meanwhile, turned his thoughts to safety. Part of any crew leader's job was to protect his men; their safety was paramount, and Simmons was concerned about fire conditions and the coming weather that would make fire fighting not only difficult, but perhaps dangerous. The fire had stayed on the ground, but Simmons decided to take precautions.

By 11 a.m. winds grew stronger, raising the odds for a crown fire. Alarmed, Simmons scurried to find shelters but had few options in the heavily timbered slopes halfway up steep Capitan Mountain. Simmons finally identified two possible havens. A large open rock slide flowed near the top of the mountain, but it was about a half-mile away across a deep canyon; closer to the head of the fire, Simmons found a small rock slide almost a hundred yards in diameter and, in places, as much as four feet deep. That scouting trip saved his life.

Cresting a ridge a few minutes later, Simmons saw ominous fresh dark smoke billowing up two miles west of his men. There was only one conclusion: the fire had jumped the line to their rear, cutting them off, and was roaring up the mountain, rushing toward firefighters directly in its path. A blowup had occurred, and the fire was leaping from treetop to treetop. Simmons knew the forest could not be saved that day. He also knew he was in trouble.

A forest fire blowup is like dumping gasoline on a bonfire. Pine tree resins heat up and release explosive gas pockets, which when triggered by flames can hurl fire more than two miles from one ridge to another. Trees explode with enough force to fly across canyons like giant darts, boulders break open from intense heat and roaring noise resembles bulldozers charging through the forest. Anyone downwind from such a fire is in a desperate predicament, but anyone trapped in fuel on a slope above the fire faces circumstances virtually impossible to handle. Men have no control over a blowup, and firefighters have more sense than to fight it. Orville Luttrell summarized the options: "All you can do is get the hell out of the way."

Without the luxury of pausing even an instant to think through his problem, Simmons ordered Peg Pfingsten to pass the word to every man on the fire line to rush away from the fire. "We had to get out of there, but quick, or get fried," Simmons wrote. Pfingsten rode down to the trailing squads to lead them as they ran for their lives to the side of the fire, but Simmons and the men near him had no escape.

Within seconds, Ross Flatley and four crewmen ran up the fire line. Believing Flatley had time to reach the larger slide area, Simmons ordered the five men to dash across the canyon to the rocky opening on the opposite hillside.

Minutes later the final twenty-four men arrived—mostly soldiers, but also including Harry Collins, Roy Morgan and Joe Phillips, a Capitan High School student. As rolling smoke engulfed him, Simmons realized his crew could not outrace the fire to the large rock slide. Refuge in the nearer, smaller rock slide—in a draw only a hundred yards long and seventy yards wide— was their only chance for survival. "Simmons didn't yell," Collins recalled. "He told us what to do and he expected us to obey." And as his twenty-four charges piled into the rocky draw, Simmons noted that it was precisely 11:50 a.m. He ordered everyone to wet their handkerchiefs with water from canteens, hoping they could breathe through the wet cloths and avoid smothering from inhalation of black smoke. Simmons insisted the men burrow facedown into the rocks and squeeze together, facing each other, with an arm over the back of the man next to them.

As the morning sky darkened with black clouds and the roar intensified, everyone obeyed, knowing it would be difficult to breath through the thick smoke being pushed in their direction. Simmons shouted for the soldiers to watch each other's backs and crush out sparks as soon as they landed on clothing. As a final warning to those who thought they could outrun the fury, Simmons promised to hit any man in the head with a shovel if they tried to leave the group. Concerned that if one man panicked, they all would panic, Simmons gave strict orders: "If your buddy gets up, you better get him before I have to get him."

"I am very fortunate that Speed Simmons was there, because he had the experience," Collins confirmed. "Simmons was quiet, very firm, and very much in control. We had no great fear and did not worry because Speed told us what to expect. He gave us a feeling of confidence and he acted confident. We formed a circle just before the brush ignited."

"We beat the flames by about two minutes," Simmons wrote, "and I suggested that these two minutes might well be spent in silent prayer for our survival."

Then one of the men asked, "Do we have a chance here?" Simmons, unsure of the odds of survival, responded curtly, "Talk to the Man above."

"Speed had a deep religious streak," Marcelle Simmons explained. "He had strong feelings about a higher power, but he had no illusions. He knew it would be a miracle if they got out of there alive."

Then the terrible crown fire engulfed the twenty-five men, roaring over them through the treetops as waves of scorching heat numbed the senses of its trapped prey. Dense smoke stifled breathing as men struggled for air while intense heat and embers falling like hail caused patches of clothing to burst into flame. In raging fury, a jet stream swept flames so hot that treetops on the opposite side of the slide at once caught fire. Time and again clothes caught fire; time and again, blistered hands beat out the blazes.

"It was hot as an oven and it seemed we would be roasted alive," Simmons reported. "Breathing even through our handkerchiefs was a problem." To save precious oxygen, Simmons ordered no talking and insisted that heads be kept down except to glance sideways now and then to see if a buddy's clothes were on fire.

It was neither the time nor the place to panic, and they didn't. They waited—desperately, intently, hugging rocks and earth, blinded and choking on smoke. Some of the soldiers, hardened veterans of World War II, had survived Anzio Beach, D-Day and other major battles. As trees exploded around them, some soldiers had flashbacks of their experiences many years before, the roar of the fire eerily reminiscent of Anzio's beachhead bombardment. "I thought I heard a five-hundred-pound bomb blowing up underneath us," Collins admitted.

The fury intensified. Death stalked uncomfortably close. Smoke grew so dense that Simmons couldn't see his wristwatch. Men coughed as breathing became almost impossible. Sheets of flame swept close to the marooned men as the fire claimed towering trees and devoured dry underbrush. Firebrands and ashes swirled by, thickening already dense smoke.

Burning limbs hurtled past men clawing deeper into their protective depression only three or four feet below surrounding terrain. "It was so hot it would have seared your head off if you had stood up," Simmons reported. As flames roared over them, the pinned-down men tried to wedge under rocks as they battled heroically to save themselves and their partners. They emptied canteens over clothes and swatted flaming sparks from each other's backs. Eyes swelled shut and throats were parched raw from the searing heat. Preheated fir, spruce and pine trees released so much gas in front of the blaze that a tree standing one second would be replaced with a flash of flame and a puff of smoke.

"It was hot, but the air through the rocks was cool and fresh," Joe Phillips recalled. "Because of our leadership, I didn't feel my life was threatened. Roy Morgan, my crew boss, told me what to do."

Because of strong westerly winds, East Mountain absorbed the brunt of the fire's attack over an area nine miles long and more than two miles wide, but the blaze again jumped Capitan Gap to burn part of West Mountain. On the plains below, the raging fire moved with long fingers from the mountain's base, but bulldozers saved the Lon Merchant ranch. As the blaze neared the 10,000-foot-high summit of East Mountain, smoke climbing high into New Mexico's sky could be seen in Portales, almost two hundred miles northeast of the burning mountain. And people closest to the thundering holocaust were amazed at the devastation they witnessed.

Sheriff Sally Ortiz gaped in stunned disbelief at the awesome sight evolving before his eyes. "That place was an inferno," Ortiz remembered. "The fire was jumping from canyon to canyon. In one sense it was beautiful—no, you can't call it that. It was a bad thing to see, but it was there anyway, maybe a mile and a half from camp. The floor of the forest was spectacular. With dark skies above and the light flowing down from the crown fire, it looked like a football field lit up. And windy; good Lord, it was windy. We drove down little country roads blowing sirens and horns, trying to alert people to get out of the forest. Limbs were cracking and falling off trees onto cars. No question, it was impressive."

"The side of the mountain looked like a city," Peg Pfingsten agreed. "Five or six miles of the mountain were burning from high up to clear down in the foothills." Riding his horse along a ridge, Pfingsten caught glimpses of the men trapped in the rock slide below, but he could only watch and wait, hoping for their survival. "I was worried," Pfingsten conceded, "but they had four or five guys there that could survive if there was any way to do it. The trapped men kept pulling rocks out of the slide to dig deeper. I knew that cold air came out of rock slides, so if the smoke hugged the ground it would probably flow over. I was about a quarter of a mile away and between clouds of smoke I could see those boys working to stay in the hole. I couldn't get to them because the fire was heavy between us."

And how safe was Pfingsten and his horse? "It was hot even where I was sitting," Pfingsten confirmed. "Shick's legs were singed and his tail was getting pretty short," Pfingsten added with a straight face.

Three friends and Capitan Gap firefighters: Ray Bell (left), Sam Servis (center) and Orville Luttrell. *(Courtesy William Clifford Lawter Jr.)*

If they had thought about it, most onlookers would have realized that Simmons and his crew weren't the only creatures trapped in that blowup. No one ever knew how many animals were caught in the exploding forest, but somewhere in that inferno, a tiny, frightened bear cub was experiencing the same trauma as Simmons. Certainly, the small cub handed off from Orville Luttrell's crew a few hours earlier couldn't have traveled too far from the time Luttrell left it. The small bear probably stumbled into a rock slide that saved his life.

Bear cubs are taught to climb trees in times of danger, and "Smokey" eventually was found clinging to a burned tree stump, so newspapers later speculated that Smokey survived by climbing a tree. That conclusion cannot be accurate. If the bear had been in a tree as the fire passed, he most likely would have been "fried" (as Simmons so graphically described his own situation) and the hoopla over a living symbol of Smokey Bear might never have materialized. Most likely the bear survived the same way his human counterparts survived—by burrowing into the protective coolness and fresh air in a rock slide. Later, when rock surfaces were hotter than the charred tree, the tiny cub probably returned to his natural safety zone.

Also, many newspapers and magazines concluded that because the cub's mother wasn't found in the immediate area, she must have been killed in the fire. That conclusion, too, seems likely to be incorrect. The fact that Luttrell earlier had seen the bear without its mother suggests that mother and cub had parted ways at least several hours before the blowup. Because adult bears are known to range as far as one hundred miles, the cub's mother might not have been anywhere nearby if she thought she was permanently separated from her cub. Moreover, if the tiny cub was in fact the runt of a litter of triplets as the game wardens believed, he simply may not have been able to keep up as his family fled the raging fire.

Further, the National Park Service began tagging Yellowstone's grizzly bear population with radio transmitters several years later and, during the great Yellowstone National Park fires in 1988, tracked twenty-one radio-collared grizzlies. Park Service data showed that thirteen bears moved into the burn area after the fire passed, three survived by taking refuge inside the fire lines, and three stayed outside the burn areas by sidestepping onrushing fires. Only two bears were unaccounted for and presumed killed. If New Mexico's black bears share the survival instincts of Wyoming's grizzlies, simple extrapolation suggests that Smokey's mother had a less than 10 percent chance of being killed in the Capitan Gap fire.

A full hour elapsed before the red tide passed. Gradually, the inferno's heat eased slightly as visibility improved to a few feet, then to a few yards. Badly shaken, with charred clothing, minor burns and a few blisters, all twenty-five men survived.

But no one at the fire camp knew what had happened to the trapped men, and Dorothy Guck filed her report: 250 firefighters had been on the mountain at the time of the blowup, but thirty men had not reached safety. And eighty-five miles away, Marcelle Simmons heard Guck's story on Artesia's radio station. "The radio said the fire was terribly out of control and that a game warden with a group of men didn't get out of the fire and down the mountain and that no one knew what had happened to them," Simmons explained. "I spent the rest of the night wondering What do I do now? That has to be Speed. If we are lucky, he will get out."

Although the fire continued to burn surrounding timber, wind blew black smoke away from the firefighters, who at last could take a decent breath. After four hours, the westerly winds subsided, smoke began to clear, heat gradually faded and burning embers no longer blew into the rock slide. Finally, the men were able to rise.

Ross Flatley and his crew trekked back across the canyon, gingerly picking their way through cooler areas in the hot, charred forest to rejoin Simmons. As they left for the fire camp at precisely 4 p.m., walking through open places and sometimes stepping on rocky ridges where the heat was less intense, the shaken men worked their way through the burned forest toward the fire road. Pfingsten, still on horseback, led the men downhill.

"They were all black-faced," Dorothy Guck recalled. "We took one of the boys back to Capitan. He showed us the soles of his shoes that had curled from the heat. The back of his hair was singed, part of his arms were as if they had been sunburned, and he had little places on his shirt where the sparks had hit. Tears were running down his cheeks and he was shaking. Because of the smoke we couldn't see the mountain from the camp, so the men almost reached camp before they were seen."

Simmons, grateful that his men had come out alive, later said it was the worst experience he ever had in a fire. "Had it not been for the fact that the men were so well trained in following instructions and looked out for each other's welfare so well, I feel that none of us could have survived," Simmons reported.

But Simmons's soldiers had another view: under a less competent foreman they would have burned to death. Harry Collins, suffering only slightly from smoke inhalation, offered his own assessment: "Speed Simmons saved a lot of lives that day. Mine was one of them."

10

A BEAR CUB'S RESCUE

"I should have knocked that damn bear in the head right after I got it."

— Ross Flatley

The events of the actual rescue of America's living symbol of Smokey Bear never were convincingly documented. At first, perhaps only one man appreciated the possible significance of the tiny cub, but that man was in the fire camp two thousand feet below the site of the rescue.

No apologies are needed, of course. Hundreds of exhausted men struggled through long days to fight an intense battle. Amid fire, smoke, dust and frenetic activity, they were weary from lack of sleep. And the fire camp topic on Tuesday, May 9, 1950, was the survival of Speed Simmons's crew. Nobody cared too much about a wild animal. Some men, still stunned by their frightfully close brush with death, may not even have realized they had participated in the rescue. Certainly no one understood that they had just contributed to America's history.

Over time, participants died and memories faded, so only two "facts" are more or less certain today. The first is that several men in camp talked about a bear cub repeatedly spotted halfway up Capitan Mountain, where

Orville Luttrell saw it at dawn on May 8. Soldiers had resisted temptation to adopt the cub—probably because the game wardens leading them enforced the rule that wild animals be left where they are found. Nature takes its course; young animals usually find their mothers.

The second is that Orville Luttrell told Ray Bell about the lost bear, and despite official rules, Bell asked Luttrell to bring the bear to camp if he saw it again. Like many foresters and game wardens, Bell often took injured animals home to nurse back to health. And perhaps because he was chief law enforcement officer of Game and Fish, Bell figured he could bend a rule from time to time.

For reasons he couldn't identify even in his own mind, Bell simply "felt there may be something there" but admitted he wasn't exactly sure what that "something" could be. So acting on instinct, Bell asked Luttrell and Simmons to watch for the bear. Many years later, both Luttrell and Bell remembered discussing the bear in the fire camp on Monday, May 8, and then glaring at each other in stony silence. Bell was irritated at Luttrell for not bringing the bear in when he had the chance.

"Orville came in off the fire line and we were standing in front of the cook shack talking," Bell remembered. "Orville said he had seen the bear but would not let the soldiers bring it in. I said, 'Orville, you should have brought it in because the mother is probably burned up.' Orville kind of took it to heart; I didn't reprimand him, but he took it seriously. It just seemed it would have been good judgment to bring the bear down.

"But Orville was going according to policy, and the policy was to not pick up baby animals," Bell admitted. "He was right. Mother bears will go off and prowl around, maybe hunt for food, but usually come back. But the old bear could have been cut off or killed. Orville is a real good man. I didn't intend to chew him out; it was just my opinion. Orville did what he was trained to do, but when Orville told us the cub was up there, it just hit me: a lost bear; a forest fire; it just all fit."

So Bell issued another order to Luttrell. "If you go back up there and if you see it again," Bell demanded, "bring it down."

Bell also discussed the bear with Speed Simmons, and before Monday's fire blowup, may have reminded Simmons by radio to watch for the bear. "I distinctly remember talking to Speed and telling him what Orville had said about the bear," Bell recalled. And after Simmons returned with his charred crew, cleaned up, rested and ate dinner, Bell again raised the issue of the wandering cub. "I explained that the little bear could be too young to live without help," Bell said, "and I asked Speed to bring the critter into camp if it reappeared."

Simmons's lack of concern is understandable in view of his harrowing flirtation with the Grim Reaper. And although Luttrell acknowledged that Bell asked him to bring the little bear into camp, some observers think Luttrell didn't believe Bell actually wanted him to bring in an uninjured animal. As chief field warden, Bell enjoyed considerable freedom in directing statewide law enforcement through the thirteen district rangers (including Simmons and Luttrell) and seven patrolmen under his supervision. But the sometimes authoritative Bell had been their boss only since January, so other observers believe that Luttrell, as notoriously independent as any of the self-sufficient game wardens, simply ignored Bell and substituted his own judgment. But America has a better story because Luttrell didn't bring in the bear on May 8.

The best-documented version of the rescue indicates that Simmons rose at 4:00 on Tuesday morning and thirty minutes later received handwritten instructions from Dean Earl: "Place: Fire Camp. Hour 4:30 A.M. Date 5/9. Sector #3. Speed Simmons w/radio. 50 soldiers. Keep constant patrol of line and extend it as far as possible but still hold."

Subsequent events are related in a June 21, 1950, report from Simmons to State Game Warden Elliott Barker: "I was sent out in charge of my same crew of soldiers to the same sector to improve the new fire line which had been cut during the night and to extend it as far as possible around the head of the fire. One of the night men told me that he had seen a small cub bear scurrying around the edge of the fire during the night. As we went up the trail dropping off a small detail of men along the fire line to improve it we found a tiny bear cub weighing about five pounds, his hair singed and feet severely burned, clinging to a small tree at the edge of the fire chewing on the bark, apparently trying to get some food and moisture.

"As we walked up the little fellow stared down at us with a bewildered look in his beady little eyes, too young to fear man but in a very unhappy predicament, apparently having lost his mother in the fire and wanting to go back to her. One of the boys of this mop-up detail captured the little fellow and cradling him in his arms, fed and watered him while the rest of us went on cutting a new line around this sector of the fire.

"Later in the day the Major in charge of the detail trudged up the fire line with some extra canteens of water and doctored the little bear's feet with his first aid kit. He overtook us and reported on the condition of the little cub. Upon our return to the road that night to be picked up by the trucks, the little cub was cuddled up quite contentedly on the shoulder of the soldier who had rescued him. However, whenever anyone else held out a friendly hand toward him he immediately snapped at it with his sharp little teeth. Naturally there were many outstretched hands as the little fellow had been trapped in the same fire with us and a strong bond of friendship was created by this experience.

"They wanted to adopt him and take him back to Fort Bliss. However, as this was not practical, nor in the best interest of the little bear, the boys kept him at their camp overnight where he was given every care."

In view of his reputation for accuracy and truthfulness, Simmons's report should have laid the matter to rest. However, the report left many questions unanswered.

First, Simmons failed to name either the soldier who picked the bear off its snag or the major who treated the bear. "Speed talked a lot about the event," Marcelle Simmons recalled. "He said that a fairly young soldier got the bear and didn't want to give it up. The soldier was very, very upset, and Speed told them to go ahead and take it out."

Second, Simmons's report, although written close to the actual event, was not extemporaneous. Almost six weeks passed from the rescue—a period when Simmons had been sick and in which events may have been juxtaposed in his mind.

Third, Simmons added a curious closing to his written report to Barker: "NOTE: My reading time on this is 8 minutes. The conclusion of the bear story after arriving in Santa Fe and proper warning regarding fire prevention should be written by Mr. Barker to make up the 10 minute story." This comment suggests Simmons was writing the text for an oral presentation, a radio program or some other public relations purpose—perhaps the home movie produced just before Smokey's flight to Washington, D.C., on June 27. If so, it is possible that Simmons could have taken the story in a different direction than if the report had been filed extemporaneously. Simmons's cover letter of June 21 to Elliott Barker could support that possibility, because it clearly stated that Simmons prepared the report as ordered: "In accordance with your request of June 20 I am enclosing a report on the crew of men who were trapped in the crown fire on the north side of Capitan Mountain on May 8, also the finding of Smokey, alias Hot Foot Teddy and his early history until he arrived in Santa Fe."

Fourth, Simmons incorrectly reported the bear's first night in captivity. A number of witnesses agreed the young soldier didn't want to surrender the bear until a game warden—reportedly Simmons—had "quite a session" with the soldier. Marcelle Simmons recalled her husband's comments: "Speed explained that they couldn't make a pet out of this little animal that was so badly hurt. They wanted to take the bear back with them, but Speed said it was impossible. There was a lot of emotion because the soldiers figured the bear was lucky to be alive and they felt he was part of them."

Of course, Simmons's report may be accurate. Most Forest Service and Game and Fish veterans with personal knowledge of the event who were contacted in the research for this book support Simmons's claim that his crew rescued the bear.

From another viewpoint, an uncorroborated oral report suggests that Harlow Yaeger, a Forest Service timber management aide on the Elden Ranger District of the Coconino National Forest in Arizona, played a memorable role.

Born in Flagstaff, Arizona, in 1921, Yaeger attended the University of Arizona while working as a fire guard for the Forest Service. "But I didn't save any money to go to school," Yaeger explained, "so I got patriotic and joined the army. I tried to enlist in the horse cavalry, but repeatedly was put off. Finally, they told me: 'You wanted horses, so we got you a place at Fort Sill, Oklahoma, with the horse-drawn artillery.' Then they sent me to Corregidor in the Philippines, which was about as far from a horse as you could get."

Working as a corporal with a four-man artillery crew on a .50-caliber antiaircraft gun, Yaeger was captured when U.S. forces surrendered Corregidor to the Japanese. Shipped by freighter to Korea, he finished the war working in a forging shop in Mukden, Manchuria. Back in the States, Yaeger spent six months in a hospital, where he suffered through two operations for a head tumor caused by the rifle butt of a Japanese guard.

Then the forests called. "I went to work in 1948 for the Forest Service as a 'timber beast'—marking trees for cutting and scaling logs near Flagstaff," Yaeger explained. He learned to fight fires, too, and by 1950 had been assigned to more than eighty forest fires in California, Arizona and New Mexico.

When the call for help came on Sunday evening, Yaeger and four colleagues drove all night from Flagstaff and arrived in Capitan on Monday morning. "The wind blew so much sand into our bedrolls that we couldn't sleep," Yaeger recalled. "Then we worked the night shift and they made us squad bosses. That fire was a mess, and I never felt sorrier for a man in my life than I did for Dean Earl. I was assigned a flock of soldiers—I think from Fort Bliss—and a radio operator. He wore a uniform and had a Game and Fish radio, so I figured he was a Game and Fish man."

Yaeger detailed the ensuing events: "We built fire line all night—until at about 3:30 a.m. we ran our line into a large burned-over rock slide where no fire could ever burn again. There was no sense in building line any further because that huge rock slide had stopped any lateral or forward spread of the fire. I spread the soldiers back down the line that we had built and told their squad bosses just to patrol the line and work on hot spots until they were relieved. The fire wasn't doing much that night. The fire line came almost to the slide and the fire was only 30 feet away, but it was dormant."

Then Yaeger and his radio operator sat down on the edge of the rock slide, facing east on a level section of ground. "We were just sitting there, kind of numb because we had been out all night," Yaeger continued. "Soldiers were chattering and we could hear the popping and cracking of the fire. Then we heard squealing. It was loud, so I asked the radio guy: 'What is that? Some kind of bird making that noise?' The fire was okay, so I decided to walk down there—about fifty yards. I had nothing else to do. It was hard walking because the rocks were hot, but not hot enough to burn a pair of logger boots. Finally, I spied a snag only nine feet high and something was hanging on the side—about chest high—squalling its fool head off. By then it was light and as I got closer I could see that it was a bear. It was scared and hurt. I was wearing gloves and a leather jacket. I ran my hand down his back, but he still squalled. I wasn't stupid enough to get my head by him, but then I said what the hell and put my arm under his belly and picked him off. His hair and pads were singed and his butt was burned, too, so he must have sat on the rocks."

But Yaeger wasn't sure what to do. "I thought: Now that I have him, what am I going to do with him? Then the radio squelched—I could hear the chatter clearly across the slide. The bear wanted to grab onto anything— maybe his mother, maybe a tree, maybe me—so I put him back on the tree and walked back to the radio. Another crew was coming to relieve us but it would be a while, and I had to wait to brief the relief crew. So I told the radio guy that there was a bear down there and that I wanted to take it back to camp. He said, 'It would not be a very good idea. This is a game refuge and it's a $300 fine to take him out of here.'"

The money caused Yaeger to reconsider. "I was a GS-5 and $300 was about half my annual salary," Yaeger winced. "That kind of made me mad," he later wrote. "Then I saw this yardbird soldier that had been giving me fits all night. He stood out because he was not doing anything; he was all mouth and no work. I don't remember his rank; he could have been a corporal because they never work. If it was illegal, that soldier was going to do it. So I told him that a little old bear was up there and that he would pull out before me. I suggested he grab that bear and get him back to camp any way he could. That was the last I saw of the bear. I got back to camp later and heard the bear was already there. Some people in camp told me they heard I had found a bear, but all I wanted was food and the sack."

As with Simmons's account, Yaeger's rendition is not conclusive. First, like Simmons, Yaeger didn't know the names of his fellow participants. Second, a number of people questioned why Yaeger's role never emerged until many years after the 1950 rescue. Also, Yaeger was unable to reconcile his memories with Simmons's report.

"There may have been another bear; I don't know," Yaeger shrugged. "I told the other guys in the car while we were driving back to Arizona, but I never talked about the bear otherwise. I was low down on the ladder; I didn't even know it [the tie-in to the Smokey Bear poster] was growing until Coconino Forest supervisor Ken Keeney showed up in my office with a glossy photo one day. He said, 'I got this from Lyle Watts [Chief, U.S. Forest Service]; he mailed it to me to be given to you for finding Smokey Bear.'"

Then a plaque of tooled leather in the shape of a shield with the Forest Service emblem and an engraving of Smokey Bear was mailed to Yaeger after his retirement. With a border outlined in gold, its inscription reads: "Harlow Yaeger, Coconino N.F. 6/8/40-3/1/53, Prescott N.F. 3/5/61-1/16/81, Found Smokey Bear May, 1950, Lincoln N.F. Fire."

Some critics challenged the plaque as an improper attempt by the federal government to claim credit for what was, at that point, an effort of New Mexico's Game and Fish Department. Several Capitan Gap veterans remembered that after the cub's rescue became national news, Dean Earl was criticized for letting a New Mexico game warden, rather than a Forest Service employee, head up the group that rescued the bear.

"Dean knew Speed personally, and he put a Game Department man in charge of that fire crew," Ray Bell offered. "It was in the normal spirit of cooperation. Dean was criticized about it, but he told them to go to hell. Dean said, 'When I am in charge of a fire, I am going to put the best men in the best places.'"

Another uncorroborated report suggests that Army Air Corps Sergeant David Leroy Fish of Oklahoma City, Oklahoma, rescued the bear. Fish, born in Waurika, Oklahoma, in 1923, served as a combat medic and surgical technician with the Army's 75th Division in France and Germany, seeing action in battles of the Bulge, Rhineland and the Ardennes. Fish left the service in 1946 but reenlisted in 1947. Eventually he was stationed at Holloman Air Force Base in New Mexico and assigned to an emergency crew at White Sands Missile Range.

Sent to set up an aid station at Capitan Gap, Fish reportedly was walking with another soldier on May 9 when they heard a noise and saw a bear cub clinging to a snag. Fish reportedly took the bear to the aid station, applied ointment to its burns and asked a game warden if he could take it back to the base as a mascot. When told no, Fish gave the animal to a game warden.

Several Capitan Gap survivors neither confirmed nor refuted the report of Fish's participation. While the basic story fits their memories of events, some inconsistencies can't be resolved. Assuming that Yaeger's role was as represented, then Yaeger's remembrance of the soldier is important. Yaeger did not recollect the soldier being a sergeant, but he *did* remember the soldier as a contrary character who would do whatever he was asked *not* to do.

Marcelle Simmons recalled Speed Simmons's observations: "Speed said that he felt the soldier who carried out the bear needed a cause to continue, so he assigned responsibility for the bear to the recalcitrant soldier, told him to put him under his coat and take him out." Others have supported that personality assessment, with the soldier being referred to as "a wild-eyed fool," "bossy," "loud-mouthed" and "generally contrary"; he is remembered as "probably short and stocky—but not necessarily" and "probably a sergeant—but not necessarily." Sergeant Fish, however, was tall and thin and is remembered by his family as quiet, thoughtful and agreeable.

In another story, Praceso Salcido of Hondo, New Mexico, insists the bear was taken from a tree by Diego Ulibarri. Salcido recalled that he and Ulibarri left the fire camp with Bert Pfingsten, driving a truck along the foot of East Mountain. Near the eastern gap, about 11 a.m., they saw soldiers gathered around a charred ten-foot-high juniper tree three hundred yards from the base road. Leaving the truck, Salcido, Ulibarri and Pfingsten saw that the soldiers were looking up at a brownish-colored bear cub with a burned bottom and legs. According to Salcido, Ulibarri, deaf and unable to speak except by sign language, climbed the tree, rescued the bear and handed it down to a soldier. "The bear was burned, he was squealing and he bit the soldier," Salcido recalled. "That was the last we saw of the cub."

The fifth version maintains that Lincoln County Sheriff Sally Ortiz took the cub from a tree with the help of a game warden.

A sixth story highlights Major Bob Cooper, from Fort Bliss. Various reports assigned Cooper to an important role, but with different timing. The first report is that Cooper went to see the site of the crew's previous day's ordeal; the bear already had been rescued and Cooper treated the cub from a firstaid kit. The second report is that Cooper came to the fire camp late in the day, bandaged the cub's tiny paws and treated his burns with medication.

Of course, all these stories could be accurate, because it isn't difficult to construct a fitting scenario. Assume that Yaeger first found the cub at dawn, but that his yardbird soldier, ignoring Yaeger's suggestion, did not take the bear down the hill. Assume next that Simmons's crew relieved Yaeger's crew (a likely possibility), and Simmons's men took the bear from the charred snag. Both stories, then, would be accurate. Assume further that the cub bit his rescuers (a solid probability) so many times that they finally put the bear down and he scampered up another charred tree. If this action were repeated several times, then the stories about David Fish, Diego Ulibarri, Sheriff Ortiz and Major Cooper could all be factual.

Richard Bitter, then a tech sergeant at Walker Air Force Base in Roswell, New Mexico, was one of the volunteer firefighters present at the rescue. "The whole area was covered with people," Bitter explained. "I don't recall who actually picked him up. A group of people working through the woods found him. I just have vague recollections, but I would say that about a half-dozen people handled him. I think it is likely he was passed around even more."

So stories abound. With the passage of time, perhaps even more and more men witnessed the rescue or saved the bear. Meanwhile, the questions also abound. Did Simmons direct the rescue of the bear or did he oppose it, only to find the bear smuggled to camp under a soldier's jacket? Were there two bears, as some claimed? If so, did Simmons direct that an unharmed bear be left on the charred mountainside and agree to the injured bear's rescue? Did Simmons "officially" refuse to let his crew return the injured bear, but then close his eyes to what he knew was a certain rescue? Did Simmons believe the bear would die anyway? Was Simmons even aware of all the activities of the men under his command?

Absent convincing proof, the guess here is that Simmons sanctioned the rescue and detailed two men to care for the little fellow while he and the rest of his crew went about their business of fire fighting. Simmons was a known animal lover and may have been willing to let his crew have a little fun. Because of his irritation at Simmons the next morning, Ray Bell had a clear memory of their brief discussion. "The only thing that Speed said was 'I told the soldiers they could bring him in, which they did.'"

Harry Collins concurred: "They found the bear in a tree as they were coming down a canyon. Speed gave approval to take it in."

By mid-afternoon on May 9, Ray Bell's physical limitations had been reached. Exhausted from long shifts on the fire, and having worked twenty-four hours straight as a radio dispatcher, Bell had all he could handle. About 3 p.m., he walked to the edge of camp, where he found a sleeping spot next to a state police car. Bell dug holes for his hips and shoulders, laid down a white tarp for ground cover, stretched his white bedroll on the ground, tossed down his small pillow and collapsed into a deep, peaceful sleep. Within two hours, the soldiers arrived with their bear.

Not surprisingly, there is some disagreement over the events that transpired after the cub arrived in camp. Although reports of the timing of the bear's arrival range from midmorning to almost dusk, Speed Simmons's report to Elliott Barker, which indicates approximate arrival just after 5 p.m., may be the most factual.

All accounts agreed that a soldier arrived at the fire camp with the tiny animal cradled in his arms. Some reports indicate the soldier stopped first at the army encampment a hundred yards away, and a group of soldiers followed the soldier with his little bundle. As many as seventy-five people may have gathered to fuss over the whimpering cub, but when someone tried to pet him, the bear lashed out at everyone but the soldier carrying him.

Many reports indicated that the squalling cub was hungry, and Sam Servis produced a can of Pet condensed milk from Charlie Sutton's kitchen tent. Servis poked two holes in the can's top and handed it to the sergeant, who waved it under the bear's nose; the bear promptly grabbed the can and as the sergeant tipped it up the bear gobbled down the entire can. Another firefighter reportedly brought out a jar of grape jam; when the bear sniffed it, he stuck his burned paw into the jar and slowly but deliberately licked off the jam. Then the men agreed the animal had had enough and should not be overfed.

Another report focused on camp cook Ray Taylor. "Some military guys brought that little bear down to the camp," Taylor recalled. "There were a lot of people outside the roped-off area—maybe twenty to thirty if I had to guess. So an air corps guy turned the bear over to me—just handed him over the rope. They didn't know what to do with him; I didn't either. His feet were singed and hurt and he was fussing because he wanted food. I hadn't fed no bear before; how did I know what he ate? Charlie Sutton had milk in camp—in a half-gallon carton—because he had ulcers. I gave the bear a little milk on a spoon, and it bit the spoon. So I fed him some small pieces of beef, then I put ointment on his feet. But I was busy and I wanted to get rid of the bear. Ross Flatley said he would take the bear, so I turned the bear over to Ross."

Others observed the little bear's fighting spirit. "The state police were there with their German shepherd dogs," Bob Earl explained. "The first time I saw Smokey, I saw this little bear cub on an army blanket on the ground and here came a shepherd—I think it was Sally's [Sheriff Ortiz's]. The dog sniffed the bear, and the bear raised up on his hind feet and took a swat at the dog. The bear was burned on his tummy, pads and rear end. They tried to give the bear candy and peanuts. He didn't go for any food at all, but he drank a little water. Some of the state policemen may have tried to feed him, and I think Sally tried to feed him a candy bar."

"I saw the bear after dark, in the artificial light from a campfire," Harry Collins added. "The bear was badly singed, and he was nipping and biting people—biting everything he could. The soldier used gloves to keep from getting bitten. The sergeant wasn't feeding the bear, he was just being kind—just holding him and trying to keep him calm. The sergeant was short and stocky—about five-foot-eight; I am five-foot-ten, and the soldier was a little shorter than me. The soldiers weren't allowed to keep the bear in their camp, so they eventually turned the cub over to the locals milling around the campsite. Little by little, the curiosity wore off and even the locals straggled off to sleep or back to the fire line for their tour of duty."

Not everyone was enamored with the cub. "I saw the bear at the fire camp around the kitchen area, but I didn't pay much attention," Peg Pfingsten confessed. "Bert had had a pet bear and I knew you could damn sure get bit."

Eventually, someone found an empty canned food box for the little cub, who promptly curled up in it and dozed off, ignoring the men eating dinner nearby.

Before Capitan rancher Ross Flatley drove home for the night, he reportedly told Speed Simmons that he would keep the bear at his place until its paws healed, and then turn the little guy loose on the mountain. Simmons, dead tired and again forgetting or ignoring his orders from Bell, reportedly agreed.

So Flatley, a part-time Forest Service employee, left camp with the injured bear, driving past the dreaming Ray Bell, who didn't even roll over in his sleeping bag. But Flatley's wife, Patricia, apparently wasn't pleased with her husband's gesture. "You can take that bear right back to camp," she reportedly said. "I'm not going to have him in this house. He smells too bad."

And as darkness claimed five hundred weary firefighters, at least three truths emerged from the day's confusion.

First, the Capitan Gap fire would be contained within twenty-four hours, thanks in part to natural elements—a dense, misty fog already settling over Capitan Mountain that would allow Dean Earl to bring the massive fire under control. "Clouds came up," Sam Servis explained. "Earl Moore called Alamogordo, and the air force from Roswell seeded the clouds twice with silver iodide. The next morning, we had a big fog that slowed everything [the fire] down."

But 17,000 acres of timber were destroyed, and burned trees marked the entire north face of the mountain. No grass remained to feed game or protect soil from heavy rains or attract campers and sportsmen. And more than four hundred years would pass before the mountain would look as it had just five days earlier.

Second, Speed Simmons, recognized as a hero, had proved his mettle. Perhaps his personality and mental preparation over forty-six years had prepared Simmons to be the right man in the right place at the right time. Dean Earl's faith in Simmons had been rewarded. Without Simmons, the tragedy of the Capitan Gap fire—devastating as it was—would have been catastrophic if the fire had claimed the lives of twenty-five firefighters. When the Fort Bliss soldiers left the fire scene two days later, filing past a teary-eyed Simmons, they respectfully saluted the tall game warden, silently thanking him for their lives. The admiration was mutual; for the rest of his own life Simmons preached about the bravery of the volunteer soldiers. At least one soldier offered his thoughts: "The army has passed in review for a lot of men that didn't deserve it, but Speed Simmons deserved it. He saved their lives."

Although Simmons didn't know it, his beloved field career was nearing an end. Smoke inhalation had damaged his lungs and heart so badly that within days he would be suffering from pneumonia. Simmons would be unable to stand the rigor and physical strain of a game warden's work and, in 1951, would be transferred to a desk job in Santa Fe.

"Speed was asked to make a lot of speeches," Marcelle Simmons recalled, "and it started just after he had come home and was sick as a dog. Elliott Barker called Speed to tell him about a TV show that had a report of the bear; they wanted to know if the person responsible could go to New York and make a speech. But Speed was too sick; he just said, 'The hell with that.'"

Third, no creature within earshot of the Flatley ranch would sleep that night. Although Patricia Flatley separated her new charge from the family's

German shepherd, the loud cub helped determine his own fate as the painfully long night crept along. Hungry, burned and lonesome, the terrified bear wailed with all its might for hour upon hour. Supported by powerful lungs, the bear spewed forth a cacophony of sounds as Flatley's shepherd, annoyed but curious about the wee intruder, eagerly joined in the serenade.

As the moon climbed into New Mexico's eastern skies, their ear-piercing chorus rose with it, echoing off nearby foothills, trailing crescendo after crescendo, each member of the dueling duet determined to outlast his partner. Usually good-natured, Ross Flatley summed up his feelings: "I should have knocked that damn bear in the head right after I got it."

11

A BEAR IN THE AIR

*"It wasn't an accident the bear was named Smokey. We had it
in mind at the fire camp and we carried through with it."*
— Ray Bell

Just before dawn on Wednesday, May 10, Ray Bell woke, stretched, sniffed
the air and slowly rolled out of his sleeping bag. Standing up, he stretched
once more and sniffed again—this time in search of coffee. Following his
nose toward the cook tent, Bell glanced south at the looming mountain to
see the orange glow of the smoldering fire. Irritated at the fire's persistence,
Bell still was as grouchy as, well, a bear.

Wandering into Charlie Sutton's kitchen area, Bell found his first sign
of morning life—Dean Earl, now in his sixth day with virtually no sleep,
pouring hot coffee. "Well, they found your bear, Ray," Earl casually
remarked. "Brought him in last night after you sacked out. Too bad you
missed him."

Annoyed, Bell listened impatiently as Sutton confirmed Earl's comment:
"A bunch of soldiers brought him in. We had no place to keep it so Ross
Flatley took the bear to his place." Then Flatley, who had just returned
from his ranch, filled in the details.

"I was pretty upset about it when I found that Speed had brought the bear in and didn't keep him," Bell recalled. "Speed didn't pay any attention to me, but Speed was kind of like Orville—he did what he thought was proper. But the more I thought about it, the more I wanted the bear. I told Ross I'd like to get the bear if he didn't mind. Ross said, 'I wish you would. The damn thing is sick, and he cried all night. He's just going to die. You can have him.'"

"I want that bear and I'm going after it," Bell replied. Because Bell had arrived by plane, he needed transportation to reach Flatley's ranch, and Flatley, leaping at the chance to rid himself of the bear, offered to loan his car to Bell.

Before Flatley could change his mind, Bell hopped in the aged black two-door Chevrolet coupe and aimed it southwest along Route 246. Ten miles from camp, Bell turned west onto the Flatley ranch cutoff, leaving a rooster tail of dust trailing his course through flat, sparsely vegetated land that finally merged into forest. Carefully picking his way the last mile over a heavily rutted, winding road hemmed by trees, Bell crossed a small bridge into a clearing where Ross and Patricia Flatley's ranch nestled against Tucson Mountain.

On Bell's right, a single-story, rectangular white house with dark red trim faced southeast; across the wide yard Flatley's complex of dark red barns faced northeast. A windmill, a gully behind the house, rattlesnakes under the back porch and a series of small cattle pens behind the barns filled out the dusty spread.

Even before Bell slid to a stop, Patricia Flatley, wearing a dark housedress, opened the front door and came out to meet her visitor—a normal custom in those parts. Flatley, a tall, slender woman, at once recognized Bell, clad in blue Levi's and black high-heeled cowboy boots with a wide silver Navajo handmade watchband on his left wrist. But Bell's trademark white Stetson cowboy hat was missing; he wore instead his long-billed khaki "flying" cap.

"Morning," Flatley said, as Bell, exchanging only brief pleasantries, asked Flatley if she still had the bear cub. "Yes," she growled, "but I'm going to leave here if the damn bear doesn't go first." So when Bell explained that he wanted the cub, Flatley finally smiled. "Well, I'm glad you've come after him because he cried all night and he's going to die," she insisted.

Flatley walked back inside her home and quickly returned with the tiny animal curled up in an open-top pasteboard box. With no premonition of the aggravation that critter would cause him in the next two months, Bell first looked at his future foe, then reached to pick up the bear for a cursory examination. Almost weightless, the animal was nothing but a ball of fur. His belly growled as he rolled listlessly, occasionally moaning. And for one of the few times in his life, the bear did not resist Bell's attentions; the cub simply was too ill to care.

Bell had handled dozens of sick animals; many had been injured, but none burned like that tiny bear. Bell had treated deer, beaver, birds, colts, calves and even bears—but never one quite this small. "The cub had badly burned paws, singed hair, and a little tail that looked like a skinned rabbit," Bell remembered.

Bell thanked Flatley, wished her good morning, and hopped back into the Chevy, stowing the quiet little bear beside him on the single bench seat. But when Bell hit his first bump, the bear, jolted out of its lethargy, began a high-pitched screech that lasted the entire thirty minutes back to camp.

Pulling to a stop, Bell carried the bear into the cook tent, helped himself to a handful of cowboy salve (bacon grease), and smeared it on the cub's paws and rear end. The soothing grease seemed to help, but despite his efforts to be careful, Bell's handling of the cub jarred it even more than Lincoln County's roads. So as he raised the volume of his cries, the bear again attracted attention. Dean Earl, trooper Al Hathaway, Sally Ortiz, Sam Servis and others gathered around with coffee, looking at both the bear and Bell.

Finally, Dean Earl broached the question shared by all the men, but which no one wanted to ask of the stone-faced, sober-minded Bell. The moment of truth had come. "Ray," Earl asked, "why were you so anxious to get your hands on this fool bear?"

As Bell pondered his answer, respectful silence unintentionally added drama to the moment. But the men waited patiently. Bell had a reputation for thinking before he spoke or acted.

"Well," Bell replied at last, shrugging his shoulders as if confessing, "I've been thinking. You know that poster bear—the one the Forest Service plasters all over the woods? Well, maybe there could be a live bear to go with the poster. You never know; maybe there's something there if we can save this cub." Suddenly self-conscious, afraid he had bared his soul, Bell shut up, uncertain of the response from his friends. After all, even good men had stupid ideas once in a while.

But nobody laughed. Nobody talked. Nobody shuffled their feet. They just stood there, occasionally looking at the squalling bear, but mostly thinking. They looked at Bell, then back at the bear.

Finally turning to Dean Earl, Bell himself broke the silence. "Dean, what's the name of that bear on the poster? I don't even know his name," Bell admitted.

"I think it's Smokey," Servis interjected. "They've been using him for several years. I think you may have something." And to Bell's surprise, he found a chorus of support. There were no dissenters. It seemed the idea was solid. Bell was pleased; he believed it must be right if people like Dean Earl and Sam Servis supported the concept. So prodded by Earl, Bell explained his plan to fly the screaming cub to a veterinarian he knew in Santa Fe. If the vet could save the bear, then maybe there was a possibility they could find a way to tie him to the poster bear.

"It wasn't an accident the bear was named Smokey," Bell emphasized years later. "We had it in mind at the fire camp and we carried through with it. We discussed possibilities, but the idea of the National Zoo didn't arise. We just hadn't gotten that far along. That came later; we didn't even know there was a zoo in Washington. We only agreed that we might have the bear that could be the living symbol of Smokey. We were just talking possibilities, but Dean and Sam agreed it was a natural, that something should be done and we could do it together. It was their fire and my bear. No, it was a Forest Service fire and a Game Department bear, but that made a bind and a tie.

"About ten or fifteen people were standing around looking at the little bear as the discussion went on," Bell continued. "It was just an idea; nothing had happened; we had a long way to go. I didn't know whether it would go over or not. I was afraid the bear was going to die, and I thought he needed some help. Dean and Sam both agreed the proper thing to do was to take the bear to Santa Fe, but I had pretty well made up my mind to do that when I went to the Flatley ranch. Altogether, we talked about an hour at the fire camp, but the first thing was to see if he would die."

The decision made, Bell asked for a box. "I brought the bear from Flatley's without a box," Bell explained. "But I didn't want to get the plane greasy from the cowboy salve." Servis dug around the tent until he found a brown pasteboard box slightly larger than a shoe box, and gently lifted the squawking bear into his new baggage cart. Because the box had held groceries, the bear stopped hollering while he sniffed. Finally he lay down, not seeming to care where he was.

Then Servis produced a length of heavy cord to tie around the box and grabbed a black Forest Service-issue mechanical pencil and poked holes in the box, pushing away Bell and his pocketknife before Bell could inadvertently poke a hole in the bear.

132

But Dean Earl, recognizing his priorities, knew the fire still had to be contained, so he asked Bell to fly Servis over the fire before leaving for Santa Fe. Bell placed the boxed bear in Flatley's car, road with Servis in Earl's truck the quarter-mile to the grass landing strip and then flew the fire. This time, Servis liked what he saw, correctly assessing that the huge fire was almost under control, so Bell felt comfortable leaving for Santa Fe.

Then, to a hearty farewell, Sheriff Ortiz escorted Bell and the bear back to his plane. Because everyone else had direct responsibilities to fight the fire, Bell would fly alone to Santa Fe. But it was Bell's prerogative to do what he did and no one thought to question him. So Bell carefully laid the box with its precious cargo on the right side of the back seat and strapped it down with a seat belt. After completing a safety check, Bell gave a thumbs-up to Ortiz, who snapped the prop of the little cruiser. With a gentle breeze on his nose, Bell's take-off took less than a hundred yards before he lifted smoothly into the morning sky shortly after 7 a.m.

Bell leveled off after reaching his preferred cruising altitude of only three hundred feet. "It was force of habit," Bell explained. "I liked to fly low so I could see animals and I treated that flight as a routine patrol. I had a waiver for low flying from the FAA." As Bell aimed northwest, he corrected slightly for a mild western crosswind, and settled back for the fifty-minute flight to Santa Fe. Finally, he pushed up his cap, looked out at the beautiful morning and smiled for the first time in three days.

Soaring above New Mexico's high flatlands, Bell once again was in his element—the sky he so dearly loved. Like a cowboy on his horse, Bell was most comfortable in the single-engine Supercruiser that had replaced the horses on which he had been raised.

Born in Frederick, Oklahoma, in 1911, Bell was only a month old when his Canadian-born Scotch father, a horse breeder, relocated the family to Yeso, New Mexico. There Bell grew up with a rope in his hand, a horse between his legs and Blue, his female greyhound and close companion from the time they both could walk.

Although his family moved to Arkansas, Nebraska and then North Dakota, Bell couldn't shake his affection for New Mexico, where he returned in 1929 to work as a cowboy. Before long Bell was wooing Ruth Wilson— the boss's daughter—and soon they were herding cattle together as husband and wife. Bell followed the seasonal rodeo trail for five years through Arizona, New Mexico, Utah and Idaho, sometimes harvesting potatoes to send money home. "But it was kind of stupid," Bell admitted. "I got hold of some pretty tough Brahmas and decided I would never get to be an old man doing that."

So Bell hired on as a range rider with the Soil Conservation Service and United Pueblos Indian Service, working, doctoring and vaccinating horses, cattle, sheep and goats. Fishing and hunting became his passions. A crack shot with pistol, rifle or shotgun, Bell amassed dozens of trophies in competitive pistol shooting. He hunted deer, elk, pheasant, quail, rabbits, ducks, geese, boar, javalina, moose (his favorite meal) and antelope, and reeled in bass, trout, pike and walleye in New Mexico, Texas, North Dakota, Alaska and Canada.

In 1941, Elliott Barker hired Bell as a Game and Fish Department patrolman in the Pecos District. But when he could, Bell stashed away spare change from Ruth's household fund and slipped off for a flying lesson every time he amassed three dollars. An Aronica, a Taylorcraft and a J-3 Piper became his new mistresses, and he soloed just before he found himself drafted into the army in 1942. With pride, Bell flashed his logbook and new student pilot's license and was promptly assigned to the army air corps—but not as a pilot. After intensive training in Denver, Bell was detailed to work on remote control turrets on B-29 bombers.

Shipped to India with the 20th Air Force, 40th Bombardment Group, Bell flew numerous hops "over the hump," crossing the Himalayas into China to work on problem B-29s. Bell remembered only one reprimand while in India: after boasting of his riding prowess, he roped a Brahma bull, hopped aboard and rode it through camp until he dismounted just before the terrified beast disappeared with a collection of clotheslines into a jungle. Bell completed his military career on Tinian Island in the Pacific Ocean, where in July 1945, when the 509th B-29 Squadron arrived, Bell was assigned to help remove turrets from a plane named the *Enola Gay* to lighten its weight.

After the war, Bell returned to the Game and Fish Department as game warden in Capitan, but was promoted and transferred to Santa Fe in April 1950. And when Elliott Barker spent $3,000 for the first State airplane, Bell became known as New Mexico's "flying game warden." Serious, polite and patient, Bell was a man of vision and ideas.

Although he enjoyed reminiscing, Bell found himself jarred from his daydream as the tiny bear let out a piercing shriek. Jolted back to contemplating his situation, Bell began to consider his boss, Elliott Barker. "I was concerned about Mr. Barker's reaction," Bell confessed. "I was flying all the way to Santa Fe with a sore-tailed bear. How was I going to explain that?" But between the bear's intermittent cries, Bell reached a solution. The few Motorola Handy-Talky radios at the fire weren't working well and Dean Earl wanted new radios. So Bell decided he had an excuse: he was returning for radios; the little bear just happened to thumb a lift.

"Flying back to Santa Fe, the possibilities kept building up in my mind," Bell reflected. "When I got into that plane I kind of let my imagination run away. When you're flying by yourself, your mind gets on a subject; you listen to that old engine prop going; it's kind of like a dream so you just let your imagination go. I really got excited about it when I got into the air. All this stuff rolled around in my mind. I thought: How damn foolish can a person be to imagine all these possibilities? But the more I thought about it, the more I liked it, and when I got to Santa Fe I was more excited than when I left the fire camp. The basics were there; Smokey was what I had in mind—a living symbol of that bear. We would have taken care of any animal, but probably wouldn't have flown it to Santa Fe to see a vet. All I thought about was a living symbol. I knew there would have to be a lot of people sold on it. There would have to be people with a lot of pull to get behind it. I wanted to plant the seed to start it growing, and I figured I had the seed right there in the airplane."

And Bell was eager to get something started. "I knew I wasn't capable," Bell conceded, "but someone had to start it. The first thing I thought about was to see Mr. Barker. I figured if I could sell him, he was intelligent enough to know what could be done and then there would be people in the Forest Service that could pick it up. I didn't have enough experience and training to know how to do it. But I felt it was one of those situations that don't come up very often. One thing that *did* hit me was to get Harold [Walter] to take pictures. Law enforcement officers know that one picture is worth several thousand words of testimony."

Banking slightly into a landing pattern south of his city of 10,000 people, Bell brought his aircraft down into a west wind, landing smoothly on the dirt runway at Ragle Airfield. Bell had a long habit of refueling immediately after landings so, despite his urgency, he taxied to Paul Ragle's gas pumps and filled up with Mobil aviation gas. Then, as Bell rolled the plane into its corrugated-iron hangar, airport manager Lois Ettinger ambled over to chat.

Peering into the small box at the even smaller cub, Ettinger, heart-struck with the tiny bear, cooed and fussed over the fur ball. "By now, he was really whimpering and putting on a good act," Bell noted. "She felt sorry for the little fellow. She really had a fit over him." When Bell explained his plans to take the animal to Ed Smith's veterinarian clinic, Ettinger, an old friend, volunteered to call Smith and alert him about the burned bear. Bell agreed, but cautioned Ettinger that he didn't want publicity because the bear could die. He didn't want to build up too many expectations.

Carrying his box with its now restless bear, Bell walked to his two-year-old New Mexico state auto. The black 1948 Ford's back seat was loaded with shovels, an ax, blankets and a first aid kit. Patrol reports and diaries littered the front seat. A Browning .12-gauge automatic shotgun and a Marlin .30-.30 rifle peeked out from clipboards and purchase order books. Bell's white Stetson claimed its place of honor in the driver's seat. So Bell perched his companion on a paper throne on the front seat and turned the two-door sedan north for the ten-minute drive on dirt roads.

One of three veterinarians in Santa Fe, Doctor Edwin J. Smith already enjoyed a solid reputation at age thirty-five. Born in Mentorn, Colorado, and educated at Colorado State University and Adams State Teachers College, Smith migrated to New Mexico after leaving the U.S. Army at the end of World War II. Smith bought out a retiring vet and opened his own clinic on New Year's Day, 1946.

Serving family pets and farm animals, Smith quickly built a large practice. His days began at 6:00 a.m. with calls from farmers who uncovered problems while milking cows. With mornings devoted to large animals and afternoons to domestic pets, Smith scheduled surgeries at night when his wife Jean "gloved up" to help with instruments while assistant Emery Gerzanich supplied bandages and medicine. With surgery ending at 10 or 11 p.m., Smith recalled that he "worked seven days a week, forty-eight hours a day."

Smith traveled throughout Santa Fe and Taos counties to treat horses, sheep, cattle and pigs. Twice weekly, Smith visited Taos, where clients left messages for their peripatetic vet at the Walgreen Drug Store. In his spare time Smith treated dairy cows at the New Mexico penitentiary.

Smith's clinic on "Pen Road"—the street leading to the brick penitentiary two blocks away—was housed in a stuccoed single-story building erected in 1928. Smith divided the front of his spacious facility into a receiving room, two examination rooms, an operating room and a pharmacy, where he kept a large supply of medication. "A horse or cow could use a lot," Smith explained. In the rear, Smith could house fifty-six animals in two surgery kennels and his larger boarding kennels. Out back, he had twenty-six runs and corrals for larger animals.

Known and respected by New Mexico's game wardens, Smith had once been Bell's neighbor in Tesuque Canyon, just north of Santa Fe. An avid hunter and fisherman, Smith enjoyed the great outdoors as much as his game warden friends, who sometimes asked him to treat sick or wounded elk, geese, deer and other animals. Smith always helped out—always with enthusiasm and always without a fee. And Ray Bell believed Smith was the best vet in New Mexico; Bell just wouldn't fly a baby bear halfway across the state to be treated by someone he didn't trust.

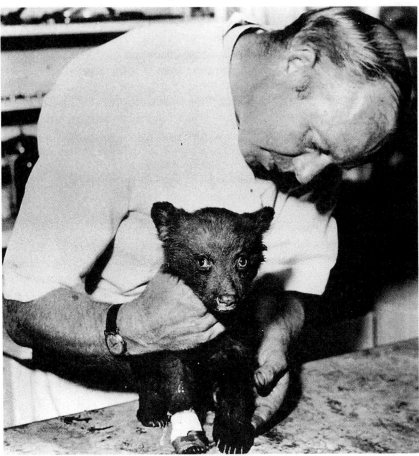

Santa Fe veterinarian Edwin Smith tends to the rescued bear cub. *(Courtesy USDA Forest Service. Photo by Patt Meara.)*

Luckily, Smith was in his clinic, so while Bell briefed his old friend about the Capitan Gap fire, Smith, wearing a white smock, began a routine "dog or cat" examination of Bell's wounded varmint.

He turned first to the obvious injuries. Both front paws had serious burns—the right, with the equivalent of second-degree burns, seemingly worse than the left. Although skin was peeling from the cub's right paw, Smith found no drainage and he decided the burns had not penetrated too deeply. Contrary to fire camp reports, Smith didn't remember burns on the bear's buttocks, although the hair between his legs and much of the hair inside the cub's arms was singed. But as he examined the bear, a spicy aroma from the singed hair began to waft through Smith's clinic.

Smith saw nothing unusual about the burns and didn't believe serious harm had been incurred. The injuries resembled those on dogs burned while biting extension cords, and the bacon grease and strawberry jam applied to the bear's paws at the fire camp had not aggravated the problems. Nevertheless, Smith cleaned the cub's paws, hindquarters and stomach with a liquid peroxide, a commonly used cleanser that helped prevent infection. As Smith carefully washed each tender paw, he talked soothingly to the bear, as if it were a child. "This might hurt a little. Okay, let's take a look at the other paw," Smith cooed softly.

Next, Smith smeared an antiseptic and then a healing salve on the burned areas, unrolled white gauze around the tiny paws and wrapped them with white adhesive tape. Throughout its treatment, the cub accepted Smith's attentions. If the bear felt pain, it didn't seem to mind. It didn't resist or show excitement as Smith continued his monologue: "There, there. Don't be afraid. You're a nice little bear."

Smith then felt under the animal's arms for swollen lymph glands, which, if enlarged, could have indicated an injury or infection to which the bear's system was reacting. As a precaution, Smith also searched for swollen glands in the bear's throat, although that exam would have been more revealing on an older animal. Smith used his stethoscope to check the bear's breathing, heart, and lungs, and made the bear take deep breaths simply by holding the cub's nose shut.

Next he looked at the bear's teeth, checking for sores, infection, malnutrition or injury. Smith rolled his patient over to look for ticks, lice and body sores. He examined the cub's eyes to see if they were refractory to light, but could find no signs of trauma. (If the bear had been in shock, his eyes would have been dilated like a human's.)

Finally, Smith checked for broken bones simply by feeling around to see if it hurt the bear. "You know in a minute if you hit a sore spot," Smith chuckled. Except for a minor torn tendon on the back of the right front paw, the bear appeared to have no skeletal or muscular damage. Although the bear would walk with a slight limp for the rest of his life, Smith found no injuries on that initial examination that would have caused that limp. Also, Smith found no burns or damage in the bear's genital area that would have rendered him sterile.

Despite reports the bear had been fed soft drinks and candy by the soldiers, Smith had his doubts. While an adult bear could have ingested just about anything, junk food would have been a poor diet for a baby bear. But the cub was not trying to vomit and it hadn't had diarrhea. "If he had anything, it was very little," Smith recalled. He believed the bear simply was hungry—a condition which, when combined with the anxious reaction to his burns—may have appeared to be a sick stomach.

Smith estimated the bear's age at two and a half months—too young for a rabies shot. And because the examination revealed no need for any other injections, the bear's forty-five-minute physical was complete.

Smith announced his diagnosis: the bear was sick, but except for his treatable burns, probable pain, hunger, anxiety and lack of rest, the cub wasn't badly injured. Ray Bell had a pretty healthy little animal on his hands. Despite reports that Smith saved the bear's life, Smith later said he believed the cub would have survived in the forest if no infection had set in and if it had been able to find food and water.

Smith put a soft pad in the cardboard box and locked it in a standard dog cage in his surgical ward. The waist-level cage measured only two feet square by two feet high—more than ample for the little cub who wasn't much more than a fist-size ball of fur when he lay down, curled up and promptly fell asleep.

12

A Bear Adjustment

*"Dad brought home wild animals all the time, so another one
was not something to get excited about."*
— Don Bell

Satisfied that his bear was in good hands, Bell drove a few blocks north to
join his family for lunch. "Home" for the Bell family, temporarily, was a
stucco, adobe-colored rental house at 129 West Coronado Avenue, on the
north side of the road, less than a block off Don Gaspar Avenue. The Bells
moved in after transferring from Capitan and planned to stay until they
could buy or build a home.

The modest five-room bungalow sported a covered, raised porch with
inset, dome-shaped mailbox. Rose bushes, a piñon tree and a small pine
adorned a grassy front yard opening into the back through an archway on
the home's east side. A five-foot wire fence hemmed in a backyard housing
a sandbox and one-car garage at the end of a shady driveway. Shedding
Chinese elms littered neighbor Juan Heurera's home on the east, but across
the dirt road, only wildflowers and prairie grass filled undeveloped fields.

Bell walked through the front door to a warm welcome from his wife,
Ruth, and five-year-old daughter, Judy. Although little Judy worshiped

Don, her fifteen-year-old brother, Bell considered Judy to be his closest pal. As "best buddies," Bell and Judy greeted each other with hugs, tickles and kisses. Judy had a new friend—Don's black cocker spaniel puppy named Jet, so after hugging Daddy, Judy resumed her romp with the little fellow while Ray and Ruth discussed the Capitan Gap fire.

When Ruth asked if the fire was out, Ray replied, "No, but I brought back a baby bear." Then Judy's ears perked up as she rushed to her father to hear about the critter. Over lunch, Bell filled in details, and the more he talked, the more excited Judy became. Listening intently and asking questions when Bell paused to take a bite, the little tyke begged her daddy to let her see the bear. Eager himself to see the cub again, Bell agreed, but because he had to go to work, they would wait until evening.

After lunch, Bell drove to town to file a report with his boss, Elliott Barker, New Mexico's legendary chief game warden. Barker ruled his small empire from an office in the east end of a converted barracks building brought in from Bruns Hospital. Because of a shortage of space, the nine Game and Fish headquarters employees had temporarily relocated from the State Capitol into their remodeled World War II structure. A storage room claimed the barracks' west end, and Bell's desk stood with six others in a large central bull pen. Sharing space only with his secretary May Walter, Barker had an office twenty-five feet long by fifteen feet wide that extended across the barracks' west end. Inside Barker's office, visitors' chairs ringed the desk where Barker, usually wearing coat and tie, held court.

Although born in Moran, Texas, on Christmas Day, 1886, Elliott Speer Barker arrived in New Mexico's mountains via covered wagon at age three. Raised on the family ranch, Barker fished for trout and hunted squirrels and rabbits with a Stephens single-shot .22-caliber rifle. Playing football and marching in his high school band, Barker learned Spanish so well from ranch hands that he often substituted for his Spanish teacher. As a farmhand, logger, cowboy and cook, Barker learned to trap and hunt bears, cougars, coyotes and bobcats, and he served as a back-country guide for hunters and fishermen.

In 1908 Barker passed a forest ranger examination with a grade of 86.4 and accepted an assistant ranger's post in the Jemez National Forest. Soon, the scrappy Barker was promoted to full ranger at a monthly salary of $92.66 plus quarters and horse feed—an income that allowed him to marry young Ethel Arnold, the daughter of a mountain rancher, in what would become a seventy-five-year union.

During World War I, Barker delivered patriotic speeches in Spanish and English and served as a first lieutenant in the National Guard, a deputy

U.S. Marshal and chairman of the Taos Red Cross. After the war, Barker farmed and ranched until he returned to the Forest Service in 1930.

New Mexico's Game and Fish Department was created in 1912, when the state was admitted to the Union. But only in 1930 did a comprehensive game code provide authority to manage wildlife resources on the state's vast public lands—10 million acres of national forests, 12 million acres of state lands and 14 million acres of public domain. Responding to a cry for aggressive management, the State Game Commission appointed Barker chief game warden and he took office on April 1, 1931.

Barker established himself as a zealous protector of game and fish laws by successfully prosecuting businessmen, a chairman of the Democratic party, two state troopers, a lieutenant governor, two legislators, a preacher, a nun and a member of the Game Commission. His tactics worked as the deer population tripled to 200,000 and antelope thrived enough to allow hunting. And by 1950, the fiery Barker was controversial, involved in legislative activities and frequently discussed by New Mexico media. Barker could be a formidable opponent or a powerful ally.

Although Bell usually wore his Game and Fish uniform under his white Stetson, he had left the Capitan Gap fire camp only that morning, so he wandered into Barker's office wearing jeans and a cotton work shirt. Bell explained the circumstances of the fire and briefed Barker about the Game and Fish people on the scene. As his report ran on, Bell realized he was stalling before telling Barker about flying in the bear with the burned butt.

But when Bell finally explained what he had done, Barker didn't voice an objection. So Bell continued, outlining the possibility of tying the rescued cub to the Smokey Bear posters used by the Forest Service. Bell emphasized that the idea could work only if the bear lived; although Doc Smith's prognosis was good, it was too soon to be sure.

"I didn't feel like I had to give Mr. Barker a sales pitch," Bell explained. "I just gave him the facts. I told him what Dean and Sam and I had talked about at the fire camp. I didn't exaggerate. You didn't bullshit Mr. Barker."

At first Barker just sat in his chair, then leaned back, stroking his chin, deep in thought. Then he began his irritating habit of rapidly tapping a pencil against his desktop. Finally, Barker leaned forward and delivered his decision: "You know, I think that may be a wonderful idea. Keep checking on it, and if the doctor charges us anything, just write a purchase order for the Game and Fish Department. We'll bear the expense."

In fact, Barker's cooperation was typical. He supported his people and he liked ideas, never shying from opportunities to try something different. "It all looked good," Bell recalled. "Mr. Barker was just as enthused as anyone. Several times he said to keep him posted." But Barker was careful with money and insisted that people consider the dollar cost of their actions. Perhaps it was dollars rumbling through the back of Bell's mind when, during his flight to Santa Fe, he grew concerned about Barker's possible reaction. Bell knew Barker wouldn't accept a flimsy excuse.

But as Bell drove home, he suddenly realized he had failed to mention the radio alibi to Barker. Bell assuaged his conscience anyway. "I did get them," Bell sheepishly confessed. "I took them to Capitan the next day and they were used on the fire line."

As darkness settled over Santa Fe, Bell found his daughter still agog with excitement about the baby bear. Judy couldn't stand it—she had to see the bear and she had to see it now! Grinning, Bell raced Judy to their car.

Judy's heart leaped when she first saw the live little "Teddy" bear. As far as Judy was concerned, it was love at first sight. But from the bear's perspective, Judy was just another intrusion. The tired cub wanted only to sleep; he had had a rough couple of days. For now, he had no interest in the little girl who soon would become his good friend. Nevertheless, Judy wanted to take the bear home. Ed Smith wasn't around, but Emery Gerzanich, Smith's assistant, had his instructions and, despite her fervent pleas, Gerzanich refused to let Judy handle the bear.

For thirty minutes, Judy cooed and giggled and jumped up and down while Bell and Gerzanich smiled at her enthusiasm. But when Gerzanich mentioned that the tiny bear wouldn't eat, Judy insisted they take the cub home to Mommy. Judy, who adored Ruth as much as she did Ray, believed Mommy could cure anything. But neither Bell nor Gerzanich agreed, so the excited five-year-old went home without her four-pound friend.

The next day, Bell opened his newspaper—the *Santa Fe New Mexican*—to find with dismay that the story of the bear's rescue had leaked to the press. With a photo of Dr. Smith and the little cub taken by staff photographer Patt Meara, the *New Mexican* introduced the tiny animal as the "Teddy With A Hotfoot," but didn't mention the possibility of tying the cub to the Smokey Bear posters. Bell was irate: "I was upset at the paper; I felt it would hurt things. But Mr. Barker said, 'No, that is not bad publicity. We can overcome that.' Mr. Barker was pretty well acquainted with publicity and he felt any publicity was good."

As with the actual rescue of Smokey from the Capitan Gap fire, there is some disagreement over the events of the next few days. Available evidence suggests the bear stayed at Ed Smith's clinic about one week. In a May 15 letter to Dorothy Guck, Bell indicated his intention to pick up the bear "in a day or two." Further, the famous photos of Smokey and Judy Bell, which were shot in the Bell home after Smokey left the clinic, appeared in the *Santa Fe New Mexican* on Sunday, May 21, and four people recalled that the pictures were taken in the middle of the week. It seems, then, that Smokey probably moved into the Bell residence on Tuesday, May 16, although the 15th and 17th are possibilities.

Smokey's week at Smith's clinic passed quietly. The bear slept most of the first three days, showing no interest in playing or walking—probably because it hurt him to do so. Both his age and the unsettling events no doubt contributed to his sleep patterns. At first, Smith kept the cub's paws well bandaged, but as they started healing and needed air, Smith took off the bandages from time to time to let the bear walk around his cage and strengthen its pads. Later, Smith put the cub in an outside run for a few minutes each day.

The bear apparently didn't spend all his time inside cages. Smith lived in Tesuque, a few miles north of Santa Fe, but his assistant Emery Gerzanich lived in a small white stucco house next door to the clinic. With only a living room, kitchen, bedroom and shower, the Gerzanichs shared the cramped space with their two young children. The thirty-one-year-old Gerzanich had been born in Madrid, New Mexico, and claimed a Yugoslavian ancestry. Although both Gerzanich and his slender wife, Libby, were raised in orphanages, Gerzanich learned seven languages and studied for the priesthood before he fought in Europe during World War II.

At least two reports indicate that Gerzanich kept the bear with him at night and, on the nights of the 12th and 13th, asked Juanita Fernandez (now Satches), his sixteen-year-old sister-in-law, to watch the little bear.

"I was a student at Loretto Academy," Satches explained. "The bear was scared of the dogs that were barking, so Emery made a bed in a box and took it to the house. Emery asked me to help him in shifts, so we took turns for about four hours each. Smokey slept at the foot of my cot, by a space heater in the living room. It can get cold in Santa Fe in May."

Later, Gerzanich's children remembered Libby sitting in a wooden straight-backed chair trying to give the bear something from a bottle. The little cub still was too sick to act up or bite, but the Gerzanichs kept a leash handy and wouldn't let their children play with the bear or get anywhere near him.

More than forty years later, Smith recalled diagnosing hunger as the bear's most threatening problem. Smith indicated that he might have fed the bear with a Pablum and milk formula or a mixture of egg yolk, milk and Karo syrup prepared by his wife. Smith thought he also might have sliced up bananas, blueberries and lettuce for the tiny cub.

Smith's ten-year-old son, Tom, enjoyed watching the little bear. "I gave him bread with a lot of honey on it," Tom Smith explained. "I'd push it into his cage under the door—there was about a two-inch opening there. He'd lick off the honey and push the bread back under the door. He wouldn't eat the bread, but he wanted that honey. I went in every day after I got home from school. He didn't have a name then; he was a novelty—just a bear."

Still, the cub was a wild animal and Smith wouldn't risk him around visitors. Kids who came to see the animal were turned away after brief visits; they were not allowed to hold the bear or put him on a leash.

But the story with by far the most corroboration, and the tale reported most frequently in newspapers, magazines and private writings, contends that the bear refused to eat for several days. Most reports stated that Bell returned every day, often with Judy in tow, to check on the tiny cub. When Smith told Bell the cub was healing fine but would die if it didn't eat, Judy insisted, "Let's take him home. Mommy will make him eat." At first, Bell refused to heed his daughter's counsel, but after Judy went to bed one night, Bell mentioned the matter to Ruth, who listened without responding.

When Bell and his small sidekick returned the next day, Judy renewed her lobby to take the bear home, and Bell finally agreed. So Smith gave Bell the bear, a supply of ointment and gauze, and explained how and when to change bandages.

After Bell put the bear on the rear seat of his Ford, he and Judy stopped briefly at the home of Harold and May Walter to let the bear walk around for a few minutes. But little Judy could hardly stand the excitement when they left for their own home. Giggling, talking, cooing and yelling, she bounced around, standing and looking over the seat back, never taking her eyes off the tiny cub.

Almost before the Ford stopped in their driveway, Judy flew through the back door, yelling to her mother that they had brought the bear home so Ruth could make it eat. Ruth wasn't surprised.

"Dad brought home wild animals all the time," Don Bell explained, "so another one was not something to get excited about. One time Dad had roared up, jumped out of his car and started hollering, 'Ruth, Ruth! Cold water! Fill the bathtub!' Then he ran into the house with a beaver in his arms, dumped it into the bathtub, took his billfold out of his pants, jumped into the tub, and gave artificial respiration to the beaver. Another time he pulled up with a bear in a trailer. Then one afternoon, when I was in my room, I heard a noise in the living room. I came out of the bedroom and I was face-to-face with a fawn; Dad had rescued it and shoved it in the front door."

Ruth Bell had lost count of the animals she nursed back to health, so she looked at the tiny bear, gave Bell a cold stare, rolled her eyes and started issuing instructions. Bell was sent to a grocery store for supplies, and upon his return, Ruth mixed milk, Pablum and honey into a thick paste, picked up the tiny bear and forced open his little mouth. With an index finger, she rubbed paste around the bear's teeth and the back of his mouth, and rubbed his throat until he began smacking his lips and swallowed. After the bear downed about a teaspoonful of the paste, Ruth stopped the feeding; she didn't want to force too much on the bear and make it sick. Finally, she put the cub back into its box to let it rest.

Then Ruth set her alarm clock to ring every two hours, and for two days and nights she fed the bear around the clock. After a few interruptions of his sleep, Ray Bell decided there had to be a better way to feed the bear, but Ruth was adamant. "I'll feed it my way or you can take the bear back to the vet," she insisted. If Bell didn't want to hear the alarm, he could find another bed.

Ruth lined the bear's box with a pair of white towels and assigned it to the floor on the home's rear service porch. The first day, the little bear quit crying soon after his arrival, opting instead for almost continual sleep. But when the cub screamed, even tolerant Juan Heurera next door could hear the fuss. "We were young and didn't care what the Bells were doing over there," Heurera explained with a shrug.

13

THE POWER OF A PHOTO

"He sure wasn't good looking, but he had a personality that wouldn't quit."

— May Walter

Before Ray Bell left Elliott Barker's office on the afternoon of May 10, Bell raised another matter with his boss. "If the bear lives, and just in case there's something there," Bell carefully explained, "it wouldn't hurt to document events—perhaps with a good photographer." Although Bell knew that Harold Walter, a close friend, was the best photographer available, he had two reasons to secure Barker's blessing.

First, Walter was an assistant state purchasing agent with no official affiliation with the Game and Fish Department or its activities, including bear rescues. Regardless of the individual freedom delegated to Bell, he was flying a Game and Fish plane and (except for bears) he wouldn't carry, without permission, anyone who wasn't connected with the department.

Second, for reasons known to no one, Barker and Walter didn't get along. Although Walter's wife, May, was Barker's secretary, a good chemistry never developed between the two men. So to avoid aggravating a sore spot, Bell thought it wise to see if Barker objected to Walter's involvement.

But Barker, who wouldn't let personal feelings interfere with his job, knew Walter was a good photographer, and he accepted Bell's suggestion. Barker also knew that Walter, an accomplished "amateur," wouldn't charge a fee. And if Barker knew Bell as well as he thought he did, Bell probably had already made arrangements with Walter.

Yes, Barker knew his man quite well. As Bell left Barker's office, he winked at May Walter, strolled to his desk, picked up a phone and called Harold Walter to tell him the trip was a "go"; they would leave for Capitan before dawn the next morning. "Harold latched on to that like a duck on a June bug," Bell grinned. "Walter had already turned his imagination to the possibilities and was eager to jump into the middle of the 'Smokey Bear' idea. He was concerned that I could have blown the whole arrangement, and he chided me for asking Mr. Barker's permission. But it was the proper way to get Harold involved."

Experience has taught many people that they have to rise mighty early in the morning to get up before Ray Bell. But when Bell arrived at Walter's house well before dawn, Walter was waiting outside with his gear.

At Ragle Airfield, the two men pushed the plane from its hangar, and a somewhat penitent Bell loaded six Handy-Talky radios into the rear baggage area and hopped into the pilot's seat. Walter placed his camera and gear in the left rear seat, jumped the prop for Bell and then scrambled into the right rear seat. With only his landing lights for guidance, Bell taxied down the dirt runway and lifted off into the gray sky for the 125-mile flight to the Capitan Gap fire camp.

Both men felt elation. Each was doing what he loved most. Neither realized they were flying into America's history books.

A June 1901 photograph of nine-month-old Harold Walter shows him grinning from ear to ear, and from the day of his birth in Aspen, Colorado, Walter loved life in all its wondrous forms. Mountains were for climbing; people were for loving; challenges were for learning. Smiling and laughing, Harold Walter had a hearty appetite for life and eventually began recording that life through photography.

May Augusta, Walter's bride in 1931, recalled that Walter first became interested in photography in the 1930s. "But he didn't do anything about it for two or three years," she recalled. "Then he bought a book and started reading up."

As a metallurgical accountant for the American Mill Company in Turrerro, Colorado, Walter talked to every chemical salesman that came through camp and ordered books and literature by mail. Soon, he accumulated a supply of developing chemicals from traveling salesmen and began developing film for everyone in town. Then, in the mid-1930s, Walter went west to the Art Center School of Photography in Los Angeles. "Harold found just what he needed there," May Walter explained. "The teachers were real photographers who taught practical, everyday stuff."

Harold Walter, the amateur photographer who captured the nation's imagination with his photos of the bear cub rescued from the Capitan Gap forest fire. *(Courtesy May Walter.)*

As Walter returned with newfound knowledge and formulas for developing, printing and enlarging photos, his collection of equipment grew, and soon he coupled his newer interest with his long-time favorite by hauling his box camera on every mountain-climbing weekend.

In 1939, Walter was appointed official photographer for New Mexico's celebration of the 400th anniversary of Coronado's 1540 arrival in the state. As part of his duties, Walter traveled the entire state—even tracing Coronado's route from old Mexico—and offered photos to newspapers and magazines across New Mexico. The hobbyist soon made a name for himself as a wildlife and mountainscape photographer.

With his growing reputation, Walter probably qualified as a professional photographer by 1950 except for one detail—he always had an excuse not to take money. Walter wasn't interested in money; he enjoyed photography for fun. If people liked his work, Walter gave them his photos. He never owned more than one camera at a time and swore by Goerzdagor lenses, but by chance Walter purchased a new camera only months before he met the bear he would make famous. Walter's new camera—a 4 by 5 Pacemaker Speed Graphic—was lighter than his old one and, as May Walter emphasized, "He was entitled to a new one."

The heavy fog helping Dean Earl tame the Capitan Gap fire also caused a navigation problem for Ray Bell, who struggled to see the ground. Familiar with Lincoln County's terrain, Bell took his plane down to within two hundred feet of the rolling plains before spotting a road he could follow to Capitan. Ten miles from camp Bell again lost visibility and missed the fire camp by half a mile before tracing an arc around the smoldering fire line and circling back for a second approach.

Sheriff Ortiz escorted Bell and Walter to camp, where Walter was greeted by several men he knew. Walter chatted and gulped down Ray Taylor's hot coffee while he waited for the sun to rise enough to light the camp. Meanwhile, Bell wandered over to Earl Moore's tent.

As supervisor of the Lincoln National Forest, Moore had arrived to view the damage, and if anyone was slacking off after several days of tough battle, he intended to boost morale. "Mr. Moore wanted his help to work around the clock," Sam Servis explained, "but he was one of the best supervisors I ever worked for."

"Mr. Moore had been a World War II captain and had no place for foolishness," Bell added. "He was, however, one of the fairest and most considerate persons I ever met." So Bell briefed Moore on the "little idea we had cooked up" of trying to tie the rescued bear cub to the Forest Service's poster bear. Moore reacted in much the same manner as Elliott Barker. "Mr. Moore sat on his cot a few minutes in silence and then said, 'Yes, I

152

think you may have something, and if I can help in any way, let me know. Right now I must be sure this fire is out and stays out.' But we would have talked it over if he had not agreed because we had already cooked it up—it was in the pot," Bell said.

Dean Earl (left) and Ray Bell in the ruins of the Capitan Gap forest fire in the Lincoln National Forest on May 11, 1950. *(Courtesy USDA Forest Service. Photo by Harold Walter.)*

As daylight came, Bell flew the fire lines and helped in camp as Walter shot photo after photo from an endless supply of film and an inexhaustible reservoir of patience. In midmorning, Dean Earl drove Walter and Bell up into the burned forest, where a hanging mist from the fog and smoke rising from smoldering embers bathed the charred forest in an eerie, diffused light, as Earl and Bell posed for Walter.

The three men did not hike to the area where the little cub had been picked up, so the actual rescue snag and rock slide area where Speed

Simmons and crew had survived was never photographed. The historic spot simply was too far up the steep mountainside to warrant a speculative trek. Smokey's fans, then, would never see the exact spot of Simmons's heroics and Smokey's rescue.

While returning to camp, Earl mentioned that not everyone was excited about their bear. Sam Servis and Earl Moore had sat in that morning when Dean Earl reported to Albuquerque. "Dean and Mr. Moore told Albuquerque they had a bear," Servis explained later. "Albuquerque said 'To hell with the bear. Put the damn fire out.'"

Walter didn't photograph the cub itself until the following week when, after taking the cub from Ed Smith's clinic, Bell knocked on Walter's door at 1410 Santa Rosa Drive with Judy and the bear in tow. Walter had his new Speed Graphic loaded and ready, so Bell turned the cub loose and watched Walter bird-dog the wandering animal as he followed his nose around the house.

From time to time the little explorer whined and fussed, but otherwise went about his business of trying to stop the flashbulb nonsense by finding his way out of Walter's home. "The little thing managed to run all over the house as well as he could run with the bandaged paws," May Walter recalled. "He was not very friendly, and he would not let me pick him up."

Just before the session ended with a tired and grumpy bear, Walter decided to get a shot of the bear with Judy. When the cub refused to cooperate, Walter grabbed a jar of honey and smeared a daub on the surprised Judy's boot. Did it work? "Sure it worked," May Walter laughed. "Bears like honey."

Most of Walter's photos that captured the imagination of America were taken the next night at the Bells' home. Kay Flock, supervisor of the Santa Fe National Forest, arrived first. A few minutes later, Walter popped in with his Speed Graphic, tripod, film and other photographic gear. He returned from a second trip to his car with an armload of paper.

Ruth Bell poured coffee for the three men, all anxious for fun after a day's work. Five-year-old Judy fluttered about; fifteen-year-old Don listened to his radio; four-month-old Jet barked himself silly; and the three-month-old bear slept, ignoring the boisterous intruders.

Walter outlined his plans and ordered Bell and Flock to rearrange Ruth's living room furniture while he checked lighting and camera angles. As Walter fussed over arrangements, Flock and Bell swapped fish stories, with Walter listening as he fiddled. Their embellished tales grew and grew, improving with age, but still the patient Walter took his time. Bell didn't mind, for this was what he enjoyed most—a "bunch of rascals" telling lies and having fun.

While Walter continued to set up, Bell noticed the sheaf of papers Walter had brought in, and as he unrolled them, Bell realized that every poster was Smokey Bear, courtesy of Flock and the Forest Service. Walter planned to tack the posters to Bell's living room wall and pose the injured bear cub under them! Bell was stunned. "It was all Harold's idea," Bell recalled. "Harold said, 'This is what's going to nail this thing to the bear—it's those posters over there.'"

Still, Walter took his time as the men tacked posters to the wall, only to remove or rearrange them under Walter's orders. They laughed, joked and moved posters and furniture again. But as Walter continued to prolong the evening's activities, Bell's thoughts turned to his family.

By any standard, the Bells may have been a model American family. The family thrived on closeness, enjoying picnics, hiking in New Mexico's mountains and taking short weekend automobile trips. Sometimes his family rode on patrol with Bell when he was on duty close to home.

Don helped his father stock fish and transplant beaver, and he flew on search missions, including a well-publicized rescue of a lost Boy Scout troop that Bell tracked from his plane. But Don found time for his kid sister, too. "Don and Judy were almost inseparable," Bell smiled. "Judy followed Don around like a puppy. Judy was quiet, but she was a monkey as far as physical activity was concerned, and she was an otter in the water."

Daddy and Daughter spent a good deal of time together too. "Judy flew with me a lot," Bell acknowledged. "I put her on a box—she was just a little wart—and let her 'fly' the plane."

Walter interrupted Bell's wandering mind by asking if Judy had any blue dungarees. She did, so Ruth helped her daughter change into dungarees and cowboy boots. "Judy wore boots and dungarees a lot, so that was pretty normal dress for her," Bell recalled. "Don and Jet sat in a chair watching while Harold prepped Judy. Don was pretty interested, but it all centered on Judy—a little girl with a baby bear. Harold didn't want to run in more people and complicate the thing. He was interested in sticking a little girl with a baby bear to make a connection with children."

Finally, everything suited Walter. Background was set; lighting was perfect; the angles ideal; the posters chosen. As everyone gathered to watch the action, Don turned down his radio, Judy huddled near Daddy, Bell and Flock turned sharp eyes to Walter, and Ruth brought the tiny cub into range of Walter's camera. Expectation hushed the gathering as Walter began to shoot. It's a shame the bear wouldn't cooperate.

The little fellow had not recovered from his ordeal and had no interest in serving as a focal point for the chuckling fellow with the flashing box. At best, the bear could muster only enough energy to nose around on the floor, from time to time angling his head toward a caricature likeness adorning the wall above him.

Walter snapped away, hoping for a lucky shot, but his five observers seemed disappointed, having expected more action after the extended warm-up. But the bear was too ill to be active, and when Bell tried to move the cub onto a green rug that Ruth thought might look like grass, the irritated little animal bit him.

So Ruth Bell wasn't pleased when Harold Walter suggested it was time to pose Judy with the bear. Ruth's eyes narrowed, glaring at Bell when Walter added, "Just like we did at my house." But Walter positioned Judy on the floor while Bell, scooting the bear toward his daughter, got two quick bites for his effort. Ruth hovered, ready to pounce, but the bear took no more interest in the little girl than he had in the posters. He just didn't understand.

In fact, there were a lot of things going on in the Bell home that evening that neither man nor beast seemed to understand.

Ray Bell couldn't understand the value of Walter's posters. Ruth Bell couldn't understand why her normally cautious husband didn't seem worried about the possible danger to their daughter. The bear didn't understand why he couldn't be left alone. As a self-respecting kid, Judy Bell understood her obligation to pose for photos, but she didn't understand the elaborate preparations or imagine that Harold Walter would make her so famous that she would be honored at the White House by President Eisenhower. And certainly Judy didn't understand the poetic beauty of the circumstances, for like her little bear friend, Judy, too, had been adopted into the Bell home when her natural mother—Ruth's niece—died in childbirth.

Perhaps only Don Bell understood the events as he watched his parents fuss over his kid sister. "It was really neat," Don Bell recalled. "My little sister looked pretty cute, but at the time Smokey was just a bear. Judy was *not* happy about the whole thing. She didn't know the bear well yet, and he was unpredictable."

"Honey," Walter ordered, breaking the stalemate. "Just like at my house. Get some honey, Ray." Without a glance at his wife, Bell grabbed the honey. He understood the need to lure the tiny bear to his daughter, so Bell stooped down, dipped his index finger into the golden honey jar and smeared a sticky glop on the bottom of Judy's boot.

Judy now understood the routine, and she stretched almost professionally into a casual pose. Clad in boots, dungarees, suspenders and open-neck short-sleeve print shirt, she watched Daddy spread the honey in front of the bear.

Five-year-old Judy Bell with the little cub that soon would be named the living symbol of Smokey Bear. *(Courtesy USDA Forest Service. Photo by Harold Walter.)*

Then the little bear twitched his nose toward Judy. Sniff. Sniff. They finally had his attention. Sniff. Sniff. Honey. At last, something a bear could understand.

Walter finally had what he wanted, and he snapped shot after shot while the bear ambled over to lick honey from the giggling little girl's black boot. After two more daubs of honey, a relieved Ruth Bell thought she could relax—until she realized that Walter's imagination never relaxed.

Ruth tensed again when Walter instructed Bell to smear the next finger of honey on Judy's knee.

As both Ruth and the bear came closer, Judy watched with curious interest. Slowly, slowly, the little bear followed his nose up Judy's leg, tiny claws digging into denim for support as he licked honey from the blue dungarees. Alternately giggling, watching her Daddy, then looking at the bear, Judy sat patiently while Walter clicked persistently toward his goal.

If Ruth had been concerned earlier, Walter's next command to Bell sent chills down Ruth's spine: "Okay, Ray, now put a little honey on Judy's chin."

"Judy wasn't too fond of that," Ray Bell conceded. "She was interested in the bear, but wasn't too well acquainted with it yet."

Judy's moment of truth. How brave was this little girl? Should she let these men have their way? Would the tiny bear hurt her? Skittish at first, Judy looked at Daddy for approval, leaned back on her hands, relaxed as best she could, then stuck out her chin like a trooper. Slowly, ever so slowly, the curious bear climbed into Judy's lap, sniffed at her jeans and shirt, ignored the little tress curling under her left eye, reared up on his tiny hind legs and began to lick Judy's chin.

Ruth took another step closer, but little Judy kept her chin up; Daddy was near. And as his friend's camera clicked away, Ray Bell finally understood the true genius of Harold Walter.

The evening's events left two casualties: Bell and his bear. Receiving only a chilly stare from his wife as she wiped Judy's face with a washcloth, Bell was in the doghouse and he knew it. "Ruth never said anything," Bell admitted. "But if something had happened, I'd have caught it."

The cub, ersatz star of the show, suffered a slight setback because Bell removed the bandages from the animal's paws just before the photo session. "That, too, was a mistake," Bell confessed, "because his wounds cracked open and bled a little."

Walter rushed home to develop his film and, slightly before midnight, called Bell with his announcement: "I think we've got something. These are really good." And by early morning, Walter produced an inch-thick stack of photographic negatives. America soon would have a new hero.

But Walter wasn't finished. The next afternoon found Bell and Walter on their way to Ragle Airfield with an angry bear cub. Bell rolled out his plane while Walter set up a tripod, but the bear still wasn't feeling well; he would have preferred to stay in bed.

When encouraged to stand or walk, or when lured with honey to a new spot, the bear moved grudgingly. Although he liked their honey, the cub wasn't interested in Bell or Walter except for an occasional bite. But the bear's attitude didn't stop Walter, who clicked shot after shot of the little bear and the clean-shaven, all-American Bell, resplendent in a freshly pressed green-and-tan New Mexico Game Warden uniform.

Ray Bell tries to make peace with his little friend. *(Courtesy USDA Forest Service. Photo by Harold Walter.)*

For almost an hour Bell, armed with his honey jar, and the bear, armed with its tiny razor-blade teeth, waged a battle as they posed in, on, under and beside the aircraft. Despite Bell's concern for the bear's safety, Walter shot the cub standing on top of the small plane, with Bell at attention by his side. When they took breaks, Walter snapped Bell feeding the bear a swig of Coca-Cola, which Bell later confessed he probably shouldn't have done. Again, Walter's photo session produced two wounded warriors: the cub's unwrapped paws began bleeding again, and the bear's bites were beginning to take their toll on Bell's hands and arms.

Back in Santa Fe, Bell and Walter stopped at Ed Smith's clinic to treat the cub's paws. Because Smith was out treating animals, Walter asked

Smith's assistant—Emery Gerzanich—to don a white smock and "play doctor" by wrapping bandages on the tiny bear's feet while Walter took several photos.

The "poster" Smokey Bear seems to be looking down at his new living symbol. *(Courtesy USDA Forest Service. Photo by Harold Walter.)*

Walter's final shooting session took place three weeks later, after Bell confronted the owner of a small store and Standard gasoline station in Cimarron, New Mexico. In an effort to attract attention and increase sales, the owner, claiming the mother had been poisoned, chained a bear cub to a gasoline pump. Bell didn't buy the story but couldn't find evidence of poaching, so he agreed to let the station owner keep the cub—but only in decent quarters.

But when he heard that the bear again was pumping gas, Bell and Edward M. "Mickey" Lang, a state biologist, flew to Eagles Nest. En route, they radioed Game and Fish patrolman A. C. Ledbetter, who met their plane and drove them over the pass to Cimarron.

"The station owner had been convicted on a felony for murder," Lang explained. "This really scuzzy bear was chained to a collar out in the hot sun. She was thirsty, so people were giving her soda pop and feeding her candy and bubble gum. The poor little thing was just skin and bones and had chewing gum stuck in her fur." Bell demanded custody of the bear.

Armed with a pair of brass knuckles, the owner decided he could handle the plucky Bell, and at first refused to surrender his furry station attendant. But Bell had handled loud-mouthed toughs before, and within an hour Bell was winging his way back to Santa Fe with another bear as navigator.

Unlike little Smokey, the new bear cub—officially named "Ruby" by the Bells—liked to play with humans. She enjoyed being petted and fussed over and quickly adapted to life in the growing Bell menagerie. Luckily, Ruby didn't share Smokey's disposition. "I saw Smokey two or three times at Ray's house," Lang recalled. "That bear was mean as hell, and Ray handled him with heavy fireplace gloves. After Smokey bit me I wouldn't fool with him any more; he made six holes in my arm and drew blood. But Ruby was gentle and sweet."

Unfortunately for the new guest, Smokey had staked out his territory and Ruby wasn't welcome. "It was really a shame," Bell sighed. "Ruby was a good bear, but Smokey fought her from the word go." Ruth kept Ruby in her kitchen, but after only three days the Bells had their fill of battling bears. They surrendered to Smokey and donated Ruby to the Albuquerque zoo.

Before Ruby was turned away, however, Harold Walter arrived with his hands full of photographic gear and his head full of ideas for posing the diminutive duo. So Bell, Walter and the two bears drove to Santa Fe's Hyde Park. There, Walter posed the cubs on signs—until Smokey took too many swipes at his beleaguered female companion. Then Walter posed them together on the ground—until Smokey drove off the mild-mannered Ruby.

Because the session was Smokey's first visit to a wooded area since his rescue, Bell carefully watched the scampering cub so he wouldn't disappear into the forest. But Smokey's paws still were tender, so he didn't wander too far, especially after they began bleeding again.

Harold Walter did his job well. Because of Walter's photographic skill, little Smokey was destined for a place of honor in the National Zoo in Washington, D.C.

But the Smokey photos added no meaning to Walter's life. In his eyes, things would come and things would go. Walter liked Smokey, but he wouldn't build his life around a bear. Walter had mountains to climb, and life would go on. And as the years passed, Walter passed out pictures of Smokey until he grew tired of reprinting photos and finally gave away the negatives.

14

FOUR BELLS AND A BEAR

"It was a little bitty fuzzy baby bear."
— Elida Ragle

*"I never understood what provoked the bear. He never did bite
Judy or Ruth. But I could be sitting in a chair—just like
this—and the little bastard would walk by and then suddenly
turn and latch on. He bit just as hard as he could."*
— Ray Bell

Most women who eagerly accept the challenge of raising children would
be unlikely to accept responsibility for rehabilitating a wild bear—even the
most famous bear in the world. But most women don't marry New Mexico
game wardens.

In early 1950 the Santa Fe household of Ruth and Ray Bell fit the
stereotypical definition of the American family: working father, homemaker
mother, teenage son, younger daughter and a dog. No bears. But in May
1950, life for the Bells changed dramatically when a tiny, orphaned bear

entered their home—neither confined to a cage nor parked in their garage nor exiled to the yard. The bear joined the Bells as a welcome addition to their family.

As the four Bells soon learned, a bear cub manifests its presence in a multitude of ways, and each requires a different response. Treat it as a baby: you can expect to lose sleep because it isn't guided by a clock. Treat it as a patient: it's injured and needs medical attention. Treat it as a dog: it eats and drinks on the floor and, well, doesn't wear diapers. Treat it as a normal house guest: extend basic courtesies.

Then study it to learn the ways of a bear. Feed it and watch it grow rapidly. Play with it and see it gain strength. Laugh at its curiosity. Marvel at its personality. Show it to friends. Get bitten when you change its bandages.

Then surrender the house to the bear and keep visitors at a distance. Fend off sightseers as the bear becomes famous. Rejoice when it finally receives a job offer from the Forest Service and a career opportunity in the National Zoo.

Ray Bell may have been a game warden and a man of vision, and he may have carried the cub home. But primary responsibility for the bear then fell onto the competent shoulders of his wife, Ruth. If Ruth Bell could handle a herd of cattle from horseback on the open range, she could handle a single bear on the floor of her own kitchen.

Intelligent, hardworking and blessed with a good sense of humor, Mary Ruth Bell, born in Shawnee, Oklahoma, in 1914, claimed a heritage of one-eighth Cherokee Indian and a seven-eighths blend of Irish and German stock. As a young woman, Ruth worked cattle and taught tap dancing. With her husband in the Pacific during World War II, she worked for a telephone company, later studied computers and then served twenty years as an accountant for the New Mexico Highway Department. Ruth enjoyed loud colors—especially red dresses to compliment her reddish-blond hair. But her bold sartorial tastes betrayed her basic personality—a tendency to keep her thoughts and opinions private.

Always supportive of her husband's career, Ruth Bell never objected to Ray Bell's job choices or his hobbies. "Ruth went to a lot of rodeos with me," Bell recalled. "She saw me almost get killed about five times, but she was supportive as a wife. She was level-headed and she didn't scare. It didn't bother her that I was flying, and she flew with me many times. Storms didn't bother her either, except that she smoked cigarettes and when the air got rough I wouldn't let her smoke, and that aggravated her."

Ruth Bell loved New Mexico. An avid camper, rider and hunter, Ruth took pride in her independence and felt comfortable on her own. "She drove by herself to Santa Fe a lot before we lived there," Ray Bell explained. "She always carried a bedroll, something to eat, a six-shooter and a bottle

Ruth Bell, nursemaid to little Smokey, with her daughter, Judy, and husband, Ray. *(Courtesy Ray Bell.)*

of Yellowstone bourbon. She didn't drink when she drove, but she always carried it—'ready for emergencies.'" Although usually polite, Ruth could be blunt and direct when necessary. "She didn't take any crap from anyone," Bell admitted.

Most important to Ray was Ruth's skill as a mother—a devotion to their two children that wove the family fabric. "She liked being a mommy," Bell emphasized, "and she was a good mother." Ruth liked to have fun with her family, and from their baby years through adulthood, both Don and Judy affectionately referred to Ruth as "Mu." But Ruth loved animals too, and from a bear's viewpoint, that may have been her most valued trait.

Once the decision was made to house the bear, Ruth took charge of the little tyke, treating it as another member of her family. But first, it had to regain its strength.

Throughout its first two days at the Bell home, Ruth confined the bear to its assigned quarters in a six-foot by eight-foot rear service porch. Beneath a large window, the cub's bed had to compete for space with a hot water heater, a washing machine, brooms, mops and a brown chest of drawers where Ray kept his tools and paint. Somehow the cramped porch still served as a hub of activity, generating traffic to the backyard, and serving as the family laundromat and home for Jet, the black cocker spaniel. Usually the puppy could be found sacked out on an old quilt to keep warm on the tan linoleum extending from the kitchen.

Ruth placed the newcomer's box, lined with two white towels, on the floor along the north wall next to her washing machine. Because the tiny bear was tired and sore and, except for an occasional bout of screaming, primarily interested in sleeping, Ruth just left it alone except for feeding time. Containing five-year-old Judy's enthusiasm was perhaps Ruth's most difficult task, but Ruth patiently explained that if the bear lived, there would be plenty of time to play; if it didn't live, there was no reason to hasten its fate.

Luckily for the Bells and their neighbors, the cub's earsplitting screaming lasted less than twenty-four hours, and tapered off as Ruth coaxed more and more food into its little belly. By the second day, the cub quieted down, and Ruth and son Don began its rehabilitation.

"I was a maintenance keeper," Don Bell explained. "Dad was gone most of the time, so Mom and I took care of it. Mom figured out what to feed it because she had done this before with other kinds of animals. One of us would hold it and one would feed it."

On the second day the baby bear crawled from his box for a brief look around. Slowly, carefully, he explored the exterior of his box, eventually wandering around the entire porch. He showed neither a sense of mission nor any particular interest. Exploring was just something to do while he stretched his little legs. Ruth simply watched, careful not to interrupt the cub's concentration. After a few minutes the cub retreated to his box and climbed back in to resume his sleep.

But late the next afternoon, Ruth watched her cub again crawl over the top of his box and roam the porch, and it began to show curiosity when it sat down at the edge of Ruth's kitchen. From time to time, the bear leaned forward sniffing, perhaps, the lingering aromas of bacon, eggs and coffee.

Ruth's domain spanned an area seven feet wide and fourteen feet long, including both kitchen and eating area. A new white electric stove, won by Ruth on a radio show, a white refrigerator, a square dining table and four chairs were all the cub could see as he looked across the expanse of linoleum extending from his porch. So Ruth casually chatted with her little friend, recognizing that the cub's comfort level would gradually increase if she let the bear dictate the terms of its emergence into everyday life.

On the third day, Ruth, although still concerned about the bear's wildness, nevertheless decided to try to cement Judy's relationship with the animal. "I need a little help," Ruth said to her daughter. "Would you like to hold the bear in your lap and feed him milk and honey from a baby bottle?"

Without hesitation, the happy little girl flew into a chair, smoothed her dress and waited. Grinning from ear to ear, little Judy fidgeted, hardly able to contain her glee when Mu carefully lifted the cub from its box and gently laid it in Judy's lap. "Now don't try to pet it—just let it lie there," Ruth admonished. "We'll just feed the bear and he can decide if he wants to be friends."

It's hard to say whose heart was beating fastest when Ruth handed the baby bottle to Judy. A delighted Judy stifled her squeals; a slightly concerned, but mostly beaming mother, stood back, thoroughly enjoying the scene. Judy pushed the nipple around the bear's nose, immediately capturing his interest. The cub only sniffed the honey twice before latching onto the latex. That bottle became the first of many that Judy fed the bear over the next three days, so the bear quickly developed affection for the creature feeding him milk and honey. Their sessions were short-lived, however, as Ruth soon weaned the bear from Judy's bottle by offering small pieces of puppy food pirated from Jet.

Jet didn't seem to mind sharing his food or sleeping area with the bear. Because he had been in the Bell home only one month, Jet was too new to have staked out a clearly defined territory. Besides, the bear was only slightly larger than Jet, had lots of fuzz and looked like it could be fun to play with when it stopped sleeping so much. During the bear's waking hours, in fact, the two animals became inseparable and Jet made his own contribution to the bear's education. By example, Jet trained the bear to heed his nature calls on newspapers surrounding his box. Imitating his canine friend, the cub quickly learned to use his papers for both urinating and depositing his scats.

As the bear gained strength, his periodic excursions finally led him into the Bells' comfortable living room. Measuring fourteen by eighteen feet, this playground featured a dark brown carpet and offered new opportunities for the little bear. Three brown easy chairs, a brown sofa under the window on the west wall and a wooden coffee table all had to be examined. A quarter-circle fireplace claimed the northwest corner while Don's radio occupied a small table in the southwest corner near the front door. A wall heater on the east side crowded a door opening into a hall leading to two bedrooms separated by a single bathroom.

The cub quickly took a liking to the living room. His fuzzy friend Jet liked to hang out there, and his new mentor Judy played there and could often be counted on to come up with a taste of honey.

Soon, the Bells were beaming with delight at the progress of the little bear's recovery, and because they knew of the effort to tie the bruin to the Forest Service's poster bear, they began calling their cub Smokey. But before Smokey could enlist in the Forest Service he had to get on a regular diet.

Ruth eventually began feeding Smokey three times each day when she fed Jet, and mealtimes proved exciting for both animals. At first Ruth fed them only dry puppy food in a ten-inch, cream-colored shallow porcelain bowl. Both animals ate together from the same dish on the floor next to their beds.

During their first meals, the two critters both ate quickly with little fooling around—just gobble, gobble, down the hatch. But despite their eagerness, neither animal tried to eat all the food. "They never fought over their food," Ray Bell explained. "They were pretty decent about it and meals were never a problem."

After three or four days, Jet continued to eat aggressively, but not competitively, because Ruth kept dry food in the bowl almost all the time. When Smokey realized he had an inexhaustible food supply he, too, slowed down and enjoyed his meals. "Smokey really began to take his time, as if he were savoring each mouthful," Ray Bell grinned. "Smokey liked to lift his head and look around while eating, and often interrupted his chewing to take a drink. Ruth kept a water bowl next to the food, and Smokey liked that because he drank a lot of water, although perhaps no more than the dog." Their drinking techniques differed, however. Whereas Jet lapped his water, Smokey sucked it in, as if drinking through a straw. After their meals, both animals liked to finish with a nice long drink.

Ruth never mixed table scraps into Smokey's meals because of her concern about upsetting the little bear's stomach. Ruth liked salads, however, and believing them to be a healthy addition to any meal, fed some lettuce to Smokey. Occasionally she added blueberries as a special treat.

With all those meals, Smokey found it necessary to deposit his scats far more often than Jet attended to nature's call. When he did his business, however, Smokey seldom strayed from the newspapers. Because Ruth immediately gathered up the papers and burned them in a backyard incinerator, virtually no odor permeated the house.

Before long, the bear had the run of the Bell home, and Smokey, Jet and Judy became eager playmates in Santa Fe's version of a three-ring circus. "Judy played with the bear every day," Bell recalled. "In Judy's mind,

Smokey was her 'little baby.' Judy, Jet and Smokey just ran and romped all over the house, and Smokey nosed around Judy's chin in hopes of finding more honey. Smokey didn't lick like a dog, but he nosed Judy enough to get her giggling and laughing."

Soon, the frolicking trio developed a game of chasing each other around chairs and tables. But just as quickly Smokey, stronger and far more agile

Ray Bell watches Smokey walk across the plane he flew in from Capitan to Santa Fe on May 10, 1950. *(Courtesy USDA Forest Service. Photo by Harold Walter.)*

than Jet, learned to take shortcuts by scampering over Ruth's coffee table, chairs and sofa. What a time they had running from one end of the house to the other! A little girl laughing and screaming with curls flying. A puppy barking. And a silent but hustling American black bear so fuzzy it was difficult to see his little legs. "Smokey ran with both front legs together flowing back between his rear legs," Bell explained. "From just a few feet away, Smokey looked less like a running bear than a rolling ball of chocolate-brown fur."

As the playful crew enjoyed their youth they grew increasingly aggressive, and leaping on furniture became de rigueur. So Ruth first cleared her living room of breakable possessions, then finally abandoned the room to Judy and her furry friends.

Because all four Bells occasionally needed an island of refuge, the small home's two bedrooms—Ruth, Ray and Judy occupied the front room, with the rear bedroom assigned to Don—were posted "Off Limits" to both Smokey and Jet. But despite her best efforts, it was difficult for Ruth to keep Smokey out of the family sleeping quarters. "If a door was ajar, Smokey would scoot in," Bell remembered. "He liked to go in the front bedroom where Judy slept. He was probably looking for honey."

As the bear began to wander freely, Ray Bell found more and more need to rub salve on the cub's rear end or on his arms or legs where earlier applications had come off. Bell also continued changing the bear's bandages twice each day, sometimes causing bleeding when scabs came off the paws. Despite Bell's caution, the bandaging sessions hurt the bear, and when it resisted, Don helped hold the cub. The cub never chewed off his bandages or licked off salve, but as the bear ran around more, Bell had trouble keeping on the bandages.

It wasn't any surprise, then, that the cub had a different view of Ray and Don than he did of Ruth and Judy. The women fed him, cleaned his box, fussed over him and let him do what he pleased. But the men were another matter, and while they didn't seem particularly mean, the bear knew it usually hurt to be handled by them.

Gradually, the Bells began to understand that many of Smokey's acts reflected more than just instinctive animal reactions to people. At times, the critter displayed a testy temperament, and both Ruth and Ray grew concerned as Smokey continued to gain weight. Some of the bear's habits reflected strong personality traits that would have to be respected if they were all to survive together.

Smokey's aversion to being petted became particularly frustrating to almost everyone. He had been accepted by humans, and people instinctively wanted to pet, cuddle or hold him as if he were a house pet. Although some bear cubs are known to enjoy physical attention, Smokey didn't fit into that category. Ray Bell explained with a shrug, "Smokey simply did not take to petting. He liked to cuddle up in Judy's or Ruth's lap, but would only tolerate a little rubbing before he would take off. It got to the point where they respected that and didn't try to pet him. We had hoped he'd be different, but basically, you don't pet bears."

Bell also recognized that Smokey had an attitude problem. From the time of his rescue the bear wasn't a friendly companion, and despite his later association with the smiling poster bear, the adult life of Smokey would demonstrate that he was a loner. Humans consistently treated Smokey with kindness and the consideration due a wild animal, but whatever his motivation, Smokey's temperament hovered like a black cloud.

It is characteristic of black bears to huff and blow as a warning signal to potential foes, but this bear either hadn't read the book or was too young for all his inherent traits to manifest themselves. This bear wouldn't be intimidated. This bear began to bite with all his fierce little might and without warning.

It became clear, too, that Smokey wasn't much of a showman. He didn't enjoy attention and was likely to walk away from anything in which he had no interest. Smokey had friends—Judy, Jet and Ruth—and couldn't see a need for anyone else in his little world.

Smokey's other basic traits were more "pet-like," however. If he wanted something, he might stand around expectantly for a while, then push Ruth or Judy with his nose and whine like a dog. Smokey's high-pitched whine got attention and sounded more human than canine. The bear had tiny eyes—typical of bears, which do not see well—and a noticeable, but neither strong nor offensive, odor. He never showed feelings by facial expression; usually, he maintained a blank, intent look on his face.

But Smokey always liked food handouts. Ruth and Judy often tossed him a few nuggets of puppy chow or forked over a dollop of honey—a treat Smokey truly enjoyed and never, ever ignored. "The little guy would follow you around for honey," Ray Bell grinned. "If he thought there was any chance for a snort of honey, he would bird-dog you until you gave up and let him have a taste. Ruth was always slipping him something sweet. When I tried that, Smokey would eat it and then bite me."

Smokey passed the biggest portion of each day asleep—usually curled into a ball in the center of his box. Ruth eventually weaned Smokey from his box, too, but the bear, who slept a lot more than Jet, never seemed to care where he was sleeping. If Smokey tired, he just went to sleep. That was that. Soon, the bear even began taking his frequent naps on the living room sofa.

After ten days, Ray Bell decided Smokey's paws had healed enough so that bandages were no longer required. By then, Smokey had staked out his territory. "Smokey had the run of the house—just like the dog," Bell conceded. And when he wasn't sleeping, Smokey preferred to hang out in the living room. Ruth, Judy and Jet were welcome. Ray, Don and anyone else would get what the bear thought they deserved. But if left alone, Smokey usually didn't object to the presence of people.

At times, Smokey certainly could turn on the charm. Whether playing or seeking a handout, the bear often pranced around on his hind legs. When

Judy gave him honey, Smokey made a "na na na na na" sound and licked her hands or played with her fingers. When the cub felt a call of nature, he bolted to the service porch to make his scats.

Smokey's relationship evolved to the point where he would approach Ruth or Judy—sometimes even jumping into Ruth's lap. If he wanted to play with Jet, Smokey simply darted over to goose his playmate and take off for a grand chase. "Jet and Smokey played and played and played," Bell grinned. "First it was dog on top, then bear on top. I honestly think Smokey thought he was a dog. He would go after the dog, then the dog would chase him. They rolled and tumbled over chairs, over the tables, over laps. They hauled it pell-mell through the house."

"We didn't have television," Don Bell added, "so we watched the bear play with Jet."

Increasingly, too, Smokey approached Ray Bell. "But only if he needed something to bite," Bell emphasized. "It got to be pretty regular. At first I handled the bear a little in addition to changing his bandages. But Smokey would go out of his way to bite me, so when he grew stronger and got to biting too hard, I didn't handle him much."

Don Bell got the same treatment. "Yeah," he confirmed, "and I wasn't too fond of getting bit. You had to handle him real carefully. It you aggravated him, he'd bite the hell out of you. His temperament wasn't exactly the best. He was just mean. He would walk around and grumble and gripe all the time. If you picked him up, you had to be careful or he would bite."

But Ruth Bell handled the bear's temper tantrums a little differently. "If he got nasty with Ruth," Bell laughed, "she just gave him a bath. His temper was like a fuse; he could get mad quick and then turn it off. But in all fairness, he usually got mean when he got tired and cranky."

With Smokey's recovering health, the outdoors opened as the Judy, Jet and Smokey free-for-all moved outside. With spontaneous glee, they chased each other up one side of the front yard, back down another, around the corner and into the back. "Sometimes they would collapse in a big pile, sliding through the grass," Bell smiled. "They spent a lot of time rolling around, with Judy giggling and laughing and Jet barking. Judy was pretty much a little tomboy, so it fit her well."

Surprisingly quick, Smokey liked to cut through bushes, dodge ahead of Jet, and then jump the cocker spaniel. Sometimes, especially after word of Smokey's destiny spread around Santa Fe, the three playmates drew small crowds to witness their antics.

As much as Smokey enjoyed his playing, however, he could tire suddenly. When he decided to quit, he quit, and no amount of coaxing could lure him back to the game. Then Smokey headed for the house—his place of refuge. If he found the screen door closed, the bear stood there whining until someone let him in so he could scoot straight to his quilt or climb onto the living room sofa to sleep.

Little Smokey gets a good view of Santa Fe from the top of the New Mexico Game and Fish Department airplane piloted by Ray Bell. *(Courtesy USDA Forest Service. Photo by Harold Walter.)*

Another personality quirk appeared on Smokey's first day outdoors. If Jet had to heed nature's call, he simply trotted into a corner of the yard. Smokey, however, had been trained to use the *Santa Fe New Mexican* and, ever loyal to that publication, refused to make his scats outdoors; instead, Smokey ran to the door. "If it was closed," Bell remembered, "the little wart would stand there and squawk until someone opened the door. Visitors thought he had been chewing on locoweed. Once inside, Smokey would made a run for his papers."

When Smokey's paws healed, the Bells sometimes took an after-dinner stroll around the block—a typical family out for a walk—Ruth, Ray, Judy, Don, a dog and a bear on a leash. But the promenades proved to be short-lived because Smokey exercised so much that he didn't need to walk.

Further, Ruth believed that the increasing traffic around their house was bad enough that there was no need to encourage visitors by advertising the bear's presence.

One Saturday afternoon, Ray Bell decided his running battle with Smokey had gone on long enough. So Bell grabbed the honey jar and wandered into his backyard to mend fences by offering the little bear a nice helping of honey. It didn't do any good. Smokey accepted the offering and then chomped down on Bell's arm. Bell kept trying, but with dismal results. "Sometimes he bit me if I didn't give him honey," Bell said. "Other times he took the honey and bit me anyway."

Bell's neighbor, Juan Heurera, puzzled at Smokey's attitude toward Bell. Heurera leaned on his fence to watch Bell trying to play with the cub, and it seemed clear to Heurera that Bell treated the cub well, only to receive bites in return. If Smokey cooperated, Bell chased the bear or allowed the bear to chase him. Sometimes Bell tugged gently on Smokey's ears just as Judy so often did, but with different results: the bear bit back.

So Bell tried another tactic. While playing their "honey game" in the grass, Smokey suddenly turned and bit Bell on his hand. Reasoning that Mama Bear must have cuffed her cub from time to time as a way of training or showing displeasure, and figuring the same tactic would work for him, Bell gently cuffed Smokey—a backhand on the side of his furry head. But Smokey's surprising reaction sent the neighbors running, while an astonished Bell stood with mouth agape: the startled little bear promptly threw a temper tantrum. "Smokey screamed, rolled over with paws plastered against his head and squalled just like a mean little kid," Bell related. "It was a real show. He must have carried on like that for two or three minutes."

At times, Smokey seemed to have dedicated himself to a life of terror against Bell. Like a professional hit man, the little cub developed three basic types of attack. When Bell's fingers, hands or arms were Smokey's targets, the bear relied on his "bite and scoot" technique. In a hit-and-run tactic, his idea was to bite unexpectedly from a seen position or sneak up undetected, perhaps by springing onto the sofa while the unsuspecting Bell was reading his newspaper. Either way, a rapid departure from the scene was paramount in Smokey's plan. If Bell's legs were his goal, Smokey preferred the "grab and hold" system in which he either crept up on Bell or took a sharp turn toward his quarry as he ostensibly chased Jet or Judy. Then he jumped onto Bell's leg, hung on with claws from all four paws and bit for all he was worth until Bell could shake him loose.

174

Apparently, the cub felt safe because he learned that Bell wouldn't hurt him in spite of anything he did. "I never understood what provoked the bear," Bell confessed. "He never did bite Judy or Ruth. But I could be sitting in a chair—just like this—and the little bastard would walk by and then suddenly turn and latch on. He bit just as hard as he could."

Bell's penchant for cowboy boots saved a good deal of wear and tear on his legs. Occasionally, however, Smokey jumped onto Bell's leg high above his boots. "That certainly got my attention," mused a chagrined Bell. "I didn't hurt him, but I usually pushed him off with my other foot. After a while it wasn't funny."

But Smokey's entrapment efforts were his most successful. With this technique, Smokey attacked only after luring Bell into a position where he could neither fight back nor repel his small antagonist. Trees and cars were primary crime scenes, as Smokey apparently thought it great sport to lure Bell into a tree. It usually started when Smokey climbed an elm tree in Bell's backyard, occasionally scaling so high that he either couldn't or wouldn't climb back down. Then a reluctant Bell grabbed his ladder, knowing full well what was about to happen. At first, Bell and the bear tried to outwait each other, with Bell ignoring his daughter's pleading to "save my poor little baby." Smokey, meanwhile, just sat there, looking down at Bell.

After a few minutes, Bell surrendered to Judy's request and started up his ladder, but as soon as Bell touched the bear, Smokey started biting. Then, when Bell actually lifted Smokey off a limb, the bear urinated on his rescuer. Finally, as Bell negotiated his way back down his ladder, Smokey put a few more bites into Bell's arms. "My fingers and hands were in pretty bad shape," Bell said. "Usually, I wore gloves, but I didn't always have a pair when I needed them."

Smokey also recognized the opportunities available in an automobile. But would Smokey really bite Bell in a moving car? "Darn right," Bell declared.

As word of the bear spread, Bell received many requests to appear with the soon-to-be-official "Smokey." Because of job demands and the volume of requests, Bell turned down many invitations; but with a soft spot for children, he tried to accommodate schoolteachers. When asked to visit a class, Bell grabbed Jet's harness and leash, put Smokey on the front seat of his car and drove to school.

Until Smokey recognized the situation in which Bell had inadvertently placed himself, this routine worked well. At school, Bell told the story of Smokey's rescue while he walked the bear around on his leash. Excited children loved the cub, although many were disappointed they couldn't pet the bear. Bell knew his rascal and wasn't anxious to take a chance on the bear biting any children. Each session ended after about an hour when Smokey, tired and bored, signaled his readiness to leave by screaming and squalling.

But one afternoon, Bell and his bear stayed longer than usual—too long, as it turned out. On that occasion, Bell and Smokey were accompanied by Leavon Lee, an unsuspecting Game and Fish biologist who rode along "just for fun." Later, Bell accepted responsibility for the subsequent incident: "It was my fault. We stayed there too long. That bear was just plumb worn out."

So as Bell drove home, Smokey suddenly lunged into Bell's right rib cage, slashing and scraping with his tiny claws. "Damn it," Bell roared and, in a reflexive action, pushed the cub away—directly into the lap of a surprised Leavon Lee.

Hardly pausing, Smokey took a quick series of bites on Lee's arm. Cursing in response, the startled Lee pushed the ruffian off his lap—and back into Bell's ribs, where he ripped Bell's shirt, only to be bounced back to Lee for his efforts. This time over, Smokey bit Lee on his belly.

"That bear really got Leavon's attention," Bell laughed. "He had been around Smokey but had never been bitten before. Later Leavon said, 'He's a mean little son-of-a-bitch. His teeth running down our ribs sounded like a screwdriver running down a washboard.' Smokey took some hide off both of us, and I got to laughing so hard I could hardly drive. Leavon wasn't taking it serious either—he got a big kick out of the bear. He was laughing as hard as me."

Then the tired bear began one of his temper tantrums, interspersed with biting teeth, tiny slashing claws and a storm of cuss words from Smokey's two victims. "That little bear really threw a fit," Bell recalled. "I suppose it seemed comical with two grown men driving down the street cursing and fighting a little fur ball. Leavon had the bear by the leash, trying to control him and keep him off me so I could drive. We wrestled all the way home." When they arrived, Judy ran out to see her fuzzy friend calmly chewing on Lee's hand.

After considerable reflection many years later, Marcelle Simmons agreed with Leavon Lee's disparaging assessment of Smokey. "That bear was a great psychological study," Simmons offered. "He lost his mother, he took a beating, he moved quickly into a different world and he was confused. Of *course* he was a mean son-of-a-bitch. What would you expect from the little guy?"

Regardless of the considerable doubt cast on his ancestry, Smokey's fame spread throughout Santa Fe. To accommodate crowds anxious to see the bear, Ruth let Smokey spend a day in the window of the Camera Shop in downtown Santa Fe, where he attracted hordes of bear-watchers.

Smokey also became a radio broadcaster when he accompanied Kay Flock and Elliott Barker to one of Santa Fe's local stations. After picking up Smokey at the Bell home, Flock and Barker drove to a broadcasting studio located in a small house on a hill nestled on the edge of town. "Elliott frequently was asked to talk on the radio about forest fires," Flock explained. "So Elliott talked first about forest fires. Then he smeared honey on the mike and let the bear start licking until, without warning, Elliott pulled the bear away from the microphone." With his snack unfinished, the bear squalled and screamed for his honey. "That was Smokey Bear talking on the air," Flock grinned.

Smokey once visited Game and Fish headquarters for a firsthand look at Bell's office. Jack Samson, in charge of public relations, recalled the event: "Smokey was not a very friendly bear. People from all the state offices came to see him, and he tried to bite anyone that came near. Smokey was meaner than hell. He tried to kill everybody."

But Smokey seemed to have a soft spot for five-year-old girls, especially girls who liked to run and chase and roll around on the ground. Barbara Ragle, Judy Bell's best friend, fit that bill perfectly. Barbara, the daughter of Paul and Elida Ragle, lived around the corner at 904 Don Gaspar. The Ragles knew of the bear's propensity to bite, so neither Elida nor Paul tried to pet him. But little Barbara was a different story.

Smokey took to Barbara as readily as he had Judy and accepted every ministration from the two young ladies. Together, the girls fed the bear—first from his bottle, then with bowls of milk. Later, when their parents weren't looking, Smokey knew he could count on his young friends for a steady supply of ice cream, candy or puppy chow. He never snapped at or bit Barbara or Judy, but Elida Ragle hovered close by during the girls' first few play sessions with the bear. "It was a little bitty fuzzy baby bear," smiled Elida Ragle, then age thirty-five. "He liked to run and he liked to lick. He was a real playmate, but he was rough. He never bit Barbara; if he had bitten her, I would have stopped it immediately."

Ragle's comfort stemmed from her close relationship with the Bells. "Ruth and Ray took wonderful care of that bear," Ragle insisted. "It was like a child. They were crazy about the bear. Ray Bell is a wonderful person. No other man would have let his kids have a bear in their house."

Ragle, too, enjoyed the little cub. "I thought it was wonderful to have the bear around," Ragle recalled. "The girls thought it was the most wonderful thing. Just Judy and Barbara would play here. Sometimes the girls wore little dresses—blue and red gingham checks. They would go running by with their little panties showing. Their hair was all over their heads—all rumpled up. But when the bear got tired, he would run and hide like a cat under a chair where they couldn't get him. It sure was a lot of excitement."

Ragle barred the bear from a downstairs bedroom and the entire upstairs. "We never would have been able to get him to come out from under a bed," Ragle smiled. "He romped and played with the kids. The girls giggled and laughed and yelled. The bear didn't make any noise. But he could jump into your lap and scare you half to death. He was cute as a bug. He had coal black eyes; he was always looking around. And he didn't get into any trouble or chew up anything because the girls kept him so busy. He was a good house bear—Ruth and Ray took real good care of him. Smokey ate honey like mad, and sometimes he would lie there just chewing on the girls' fingers. I never knew what the girls were feeding him. You know how it is with a bunch of kids; no matter how much you tell them not to do something, they will do exactly what they want to do.

"The Bells began to get possessive with the bear because of all the attention," Ragle explained. "They wanted to protect him." So visits to the Ragles ceased in favor of exclusive play periods at the Bell home.

Ray Bell's biggest disappointment occurred when he took home "Ruby," the female bear cub taken from the Cimarron gas station. As if one bear wasn't enough, Ruth Bell opened her door a second time to an orphan bear. But Smokey was not so welcoming.

"Smokey was a high-tempered little rascal," Bell explained. "He could get mad pretty quickly and his first reaction was to bite; other bear cubs that I had run into didn't do that. By comparison, Ruby was good-natured and liked to cuddle, but Smokey just fought her from the word go."

"When Dad brought Ruby home," Don Bell added, "she was a joy to have around compared to Smokey. Smokey was a pain in the ass, but Ruby would get in your arms and snuggle up. Ruby was like a pet—just as sweet as she could be. But Smokey wouldn't cuddle like a domestic animal."

Eventually, as Harold Walter's photographs of Judy and Smokey spread across the nation, the Bells realized that Smokey's days in their household were numbered.

"We opened the paper and there was Judy and the bear on the front page," Don Bell explained. "Smokey the Bear had been found! I didn't know there was any connection between that bear and Smokey until I saw the newspaper. I couldn't believe it was true. I couldn't believe it had happened to our family. We were simple people, but the phone started ringing and it was chaos. Mom and Dad said it had gone all over the United States."

As more and more people learned a Santa Fe resident was going to be the official living symbol of Smokey Bear, visitors increasingly infested the Bell home. "It was like Grand Central Station, especially after word got around that he was going to Washington," Ray Bell recalled. "People showed up with their kids, or just alone. We were new in town, so we didn't know that many people at first. But we sure got to be well known. It seemed like everyone wanted to play with Smokey, but we tried to keep the kids away because we were afraid the bear would bite. Most people weren't bad about it—they were just curious. Adults didn't try to pet him too much, but kids would, so we had to ask parents to keep their kids back. It got to be quite a chore to have dinner interrupted almost every night."

Traffic in front of the Bell house increased steadily as *Santa Fe New Mexican* photographer Patt Meara's photos of Smokey appeared repeatedly in the newspaper: Smokey eating from a saucer with Jet; balancing all four feet on Judy's doll cart; climbing up the back of a chair and tipping it over; playing in a bathtub; lugging (and biting) one of Judy's dolls; wrestling with Jet. "Traffic finally got so heavy," Bell explained, "that we had to be careful about playing in the yard. People driving past hoping for a look at Smokey would see the bear playing in the grass with Jet. Before you realized it, we'd have a regular traffic jam out there on that dirt road."

But family friends were welcome. Speed Simmons dropped by with Joyce, his ten-year-old daughter. Another evening, New Mexico's six-foot-eleven-and-one-half-inch-tall corporation commissioner arrived in a Volkswagen. "We called him 'seven-foot Pickett,'" Bell grinned. "Don had Smokey in the yard, and when Pickett got out of his car, Smokey ran right up Pickett's leg. I had to pry Smokey off that leg. Pickett got scratched a little, but he wasn't hurt. Pickett said, 'That leg may look like the limb of a tree, but it isn't.'"

When strangers were allowed to see Smokey, he continued to show that he preferred to be alone. He didn't seem curious about people and wouldn't put on a show. "He just didn't like to be bothered," Bell reflected. "Smokey just headed for the back porch. He never growled or snarled. He just left."

But time passed—perhaps too quickly—and a quiet, almost gloomy atmosphere began to settle on the Bell family. "Ruth thought quite a bit of that bear," Bell recalled. "She didn't say much about it, but I knew she was going to miss him. Judy was going to miss him too. She asked about his leaving all the time."

And finally, Ray Bell grudgingly admitted that he, too, was disappointed the bear had to leave. "I thought I would miss him in a way," Bell conceded, "but there usually were so many animals around that I didn't have to worry about Smokey." Already Bell had a replacement animal in his garage—an injured wild turkey gobbler. Because of an infection, Bell had amputated three of the turkey's toes, and was trying to nurse it back to health.

Then Bell realized that, except for a few newspaper clippings, the family had nothing to record their tenure with the little bear. So Bell borrowed a 16mm Bell & Howell movie camera from his friend Homer Pickens, and the two men filmed Smokey, Judy and Jet playing together. Both men noticed how much the animal had grown. "It was almost unbelievable," Bell recalled. "Smokey weighed more than eight pounds; he doubled his weight in just a few weeks."

And Smokey's disappearing stunt occurred the day before he was scheduled to leave the Bell household. "I came home," Bell explained, "and Ruth was upset and Judy was crying. The bear was gone." Fearing that Smokey had run away, Ruth and Judy had been searching the neighborhood. Bell joined in, looking in garages, backyards and under cars, and had begun to expect the worst when Judy rushed up with the good news: Smokey was safe. Ruth had found the bear in her washing machine. "Smokey had crawled up on top of the machine," Bell shrugged. "But the lid tipped over and he fell into a pile of dry clothes. So he just went to sleep where it was dark, cool and quiet."

15

THE GREAT SALES PITCH

"I was so sure it would be a good thing that I thought everyone was wrong but me."

— Kay Flock

Three days after he began eating, it became apparent the tiny cub was going to live. The Bells smiled. Harold Walter snapped photos. Traffic increased on West Coronado Drive. Honey suddenly seemed in short supply. And Elliott Barker had a problem: what to do with this bear? Barker found himself increasingly intrigued with the burned bear. Was it possible to tie the little animal to the national symbol of forest fire prevention as Dean Earl, Sam Servis and Ray Bell had planned at the Capitan Gap fire camp? How should it be done? Who would want it?

This was the type of puzzle Barker liked best—new ideas in uncharted territory—and Barker's staff knew the fallacy of underestimating the state's top game warden, who never recognized barriers that limited lesser men. Armed only with a high school diploma, the self-educated rancher eventually would author seven books, receive an honorary doctorate from New Mexico State University and be named a "hero of our time" by *Newsweek.* Outgoing, effervescent and an outstanding public speaker, Barker extended the ultimate compliment to almost everyone: he believed what people told him. "But he would not tolerate or forgive liars," Bell insisted. "Mr. Barker had a temper like a bobcat and would cross you off if you lied to him. But when people were honest, he stayed by his men till hell froze over. He was the best man I ever worked for."

A solid constitution blessed Barker with boundless energy, and he tried to use it all during his 101 years of life. While hunting or fishing, Barker focused not only on bagging his prey, but on learning terrain and the habits of game. He worked just as hard at his desk, but Bell believed that Barker's greatest skill may have been his ability to understand people: "You could tell him about a game violation and its characteristics, and he could just sit at his desk and figure out the probable reasons and whether a person was guilty."

Now Barker had an opportunity to apply his powerful reasoning skills to the little cub that Bell wanted to call Smokey. Barker liked the idea, and Bell's no-nonsense reputation didn't hurt his proposal. Barker agreed that the little critter had possibilities—a wounded "war hero" to dramatize the need to prevent forest fires. But how to make the tie-in? What was the best approach? How could the animal be used for the greatest impact?

As far as Barker knew, the poster Smokey was a federal bear, although he was used by some of the states. Certainly the Forest Service had been the bear's biggest promoter. So Barker grabbed his phone, called his good friend Kay Flock at the Federal Building in Santa Fe, and suggested the two meet for a chat.

Kester D. "Kay" Flock, supervisor of the Santa Fe National Forest, enjoyed Barker's company and ideas. Flock, too, enjoyed writing and penned a monthly magazine column for fourteen years. Intelligent, energetic and committed to top-level job performance, the slender Flock even shared Barker's penchant for longevity. "I guess we all got petrified out there," Flock later observed at age ninety-one.

But the two men earned their stripes through vastly different methods. Born in Greensville, Idaho, Flock won an undergraduate degree in forestry from the University of Montana before adding a master's degree in public administration from American University. As a rising star in the Forest Service, Flock was transferred to Washington in 1938, and served with the navy during World War II. Then Flock moved to Albuquerque for a series of assignments leading to his job as forest supervisor.

Besides their differences in formal education, Flock's personality was perceived differently as well. "People who didn't know him thought Kay was a little aloof," Bell recalled. "But everyone recognized Kay's honesty and fairness. When he believed in something and felt he was right, then he would go ahead. Kay just didn't smile a lot. He was serious-minded. Usually it was strictly business to deal with him."

Because of his strong personality, Flock sometimes intimidated lesser minds, and Bell often referred to Flock as "the smartest man in the Forest

Kester "Kay" Flock who had the idea to send the injured cub to the National Zoological Park in Washington, D.C. *(Courtesy Kester D. Flock.)*

Service." Maybe so; maybe not. But anyone sitting across a table from Kay Flock didn't take long to realize they were in the ring with an intellectual heavyweight. Honesty, integrity, attention to detail and careful review of facts permeated his manner. When asked questions, Flock leaned forward, sat on the edge of his chair, listened intently, thought deeply, and then, with formidable mental acuity, responded with succinct and thorough answers.

Kay Flock had been with the Forest Service for twenty-eight years when Elliott Barker ambled into his office that afternoon in May 1950. One represented the federal government and the other the state of New Mexico, but the two outdoorsmen were driven by a love for animals and motivated by a common desire to preserve their environment. Politics rarely emerged as a factor in their decision making; their only interests were to determine what was best for New Mexico's public lands and game animals.

But the issue now facing the two allies was unlike anything they had handled. New Mexico had a wounded bear cub. What role, if any, could that baby bear play in the federal government's forest fire prevention efforts?

Unfortunately, Flock had bad news for his friend. A few days earlier, Flock had learned about the rescued bear when Harold Walter asked for the posters of Smokey Bear, and Flock felt the burned bear was too good a chance to be ignored. During his 1938 assignment in Washington, D.C., Flock had visited the National Zoo more than a dozen times. "I did a lot of looking around, like all the dudes," Flock recalled. "I was impressed with the zoo because of what it was, and what it meant, and how the kids reacted. I don't think anyone else in Santa Fe involved with the bear had ever seen that zoo." So Flock had an instinctive reaction: why not send the bear to the Washington, D.C., zoo? There, it could serve as a "live" Smokey Bear— a living symbol to boost the Forest Service's fire prevention campaign.

In fact, Flock already had acted. Brimming with enthusiasm, he called his boss, C. Otto Lindh, southwestern regional forester in Albuquerque, told him about the rescue of the tiny cub and explained his idea to send the animal to Washington to be the living symbol of Smokey Bear. "That's a good idea, don't you think?" Flock asked.

Despite a reputation for affability, Otto Lindh didn't see eye to eye with his subordinate that day. Almost without hesitation Lindh fired back a negative reply: "That's a hell of a poor idea. Forget it."

Although surprised by the quick rebuke, Flock had no appeal. Lindh, a pleasant social friend but an authoritative boss, never invited dissent. "Otto was very sharp, very brief and very decisive," Flock explained. "But it was not easy to discuss matters with him. So when I proposed the idea of the zoo, and Otto cut me right off, there was no argument, no discussion and no follow-up. That's the way he was."

So Flock and Barker didn't accomplish much that day. Pausing from time to time to watch a squirrel or bluejay play in the city park outside Flock's first-floor window, the two thinkers discussed a number of alternatives. After an hour's discussion, Barker felt certain that Flock had a solid idea. Perhaps it could be sold in a different manner.

The two comrades regrouped the next morning in Barker's barracks office five blocks from the Federal Building. Because the men still couldn't develop a satisfactory solution, that session became only the second of many such meetings over the next two weeks as the men alternated between offices.

As days passed, Barker often discussed the matter with Ray Bell and, with Bell's daily reports of the bear's condition and Harold Walter's photographs on his desk, Barker couldn't get the bear off his mind. "We just talked it over a lot," Bell recalled. "But we were all pretty busy and, bear or no bear, Mr. Barker saw to it that our work didn't stop."

Barker apparently thought about the bear as he drove home each day for lunch with his wife, Ethel, at their home on East Palace Avenue that they had occupied since 1937. With a sunken office on the east side and a yard overflowing with flowers, Barker's home was a good place for reflective thinking, and there he discussed the bear with Ethel.

"Elliott was excited," Ethel Barker recalled at age ninety-nine, "but he didn't know what to do with the bear. The bear got so naughty and mischievous; he was a little devil. Elliott was influenced a lot by Ray Bell. Ray is a 'tops' man and Elliott thought the world of him."

Flock, however, kept his own counsel. The issue occupied much of his free time and repeatedly surfaced as a topic to mull over as he walked the two blocks home each day for lunch. In fact, Flock had a number of considerations to ponder.

First, Flock had to deal with the issue of ethics. Flock was loyal to his boss even when they disagreed. But Flock sensed he was getting caught up in something big. He didn't make a habit of jumping to conclusions, but Flock had seen a number of things to reinforce his growing feeling that he and Barker were on the right track.

Flock remembered the lump in his throat and the strong feelings he had the first time he saw the injured bear at Smith's clinic. Flock remembered his visits to the Bell home to watch the bear and dog play, and he remembered the Bells' devotion to the sick cub. And Flock had long respected Ray Bell's work and his judgment. Flock's wife, Flora, and Ruth knew each other well, and Flock viewed Ruth as "a joyous person—really a sweetie." Flock wasn't too concerned that the bear itself wasn't the world's friendliest animal. A bear that tolerated a little five-year-old girl fussing over him couldn't be all bad.

Flock also remembered the photo sessions with Harold Walter at the Bells' home. No one could fail to be moved by Walter's photos of little Judy Bell and the tiny cub. As circulation of the photos widened, increasing publicity would be inevitable.

Flock recalled, too, Barker's coaxing the bear to squall into the microphone at the radio station. After Barker pulled that stunt once, they could hardly get into the studio the next time because of mothers and excited kids swarming through the parking lot. "The first time, there were only a few people," Flock grinned. "The second time, we had to elbow our way through. That was when it really hit me."

Flock's mind began spinning. That bear had drawing power. What if it were in the National Zoo in Washington? Why did Otto Lindh not appreciate the potential? Had Flock failed to explain it properly?

Flock had a history of fighting for causes in which he believed, and he was rapidly becoming a strong believer in a living symbol of Smokey Bear. Could he follow his instincts and still be loyal to his boss?

Second, Elliott Barker, "an exceptionally positive person" in Flock's eyes, seemed determined to go forward. Barker believed that the poster bear was a solid fire prevention symbol, but he thought that its impact on forest fire prevention had been almost imperceptible. With his persuasive talents, Barker could argue effectively for a living symbol and he had a good chance of making something happen.

Third, Flock never doubted Barker's motivation. Over their many years together, Flock had repeatedly witnessed Barker's sentimental attitude toward animals and his devotion to conservation. The articulate Barker (who later testified six times before congressional committees in support of conservation) had established himself as a solid spokesman for conservation issues. Barker certainly wasn't seeking personal gain.

Flock represented the U.S. government, Barker represented New Mexico, and forest and game personnel in the two entities claimed a long history of cooperative effort. So Flock would treat this issue as any other in which New Mexico requested assistance. Flock would support Barker. "I was so sure it would be a good thing that I thought everyone was wrong but me," Flock admitted.

Reports later indicated that with this decision Flock "put his reputation and his career on the line," but Flock disagreed with that assessment. "In the Forest Service," he emphasized, "you were always able to [officially] disagree with your boss." Further, Flock felt comfortable with his decision because, like all field personnel, Flock kept a diary of his official activities. And Flock had his own ethical standard: if he didn't want to record an activity in his diary, he didn't do that activity. But Flock thought that he could support Barker, and he decided to detail that support in his diary. Then Flock took a further step. "If I worked on Smokey during the day, I signed out for vacation," he explained.

So as Flock and Barker met to plot strategy, Flock became the driver to plant the ideas; Barker became the man of action to implement them. They agreed that Barker would personally handle everything, while Flock would consult from a less visible position. In his writings, Barker acknowledged that it would have been unethical for Flock to go over the head of Otto Lindh and make the proposition directly to Chief Forester Lyle Watts in Washington, D.C. "However," Barker concluded, "there was nothing to keep me from doing it." So Barker placed the call to Washington, D.C. Although documents are inconsistent, Barker apparently made that call to Clint Davis, director of the Cooperative Forest Fire Prevention program in Forest Service headquarters.

By 1950, Clint Davis had proven himself to be extraordinarily gifted at public relations. "Clint was a great guy—just a natural PR man," J. Morgan Smith, Forest Service information director in Washington, D.C., confirmed. "Once, I went to Atlanta with Clint and it took two hours to walk a block. He knew everyone in town." Exceptionally talented at interpersonal relationships, Davis worked well with private enterprise and federal and state governments in promoting conservation of America's natural resources. From Barker's perspective, no better man than Davis could have been running the "Smokey Bear" program.

Davis was viewed by his enchanted associates as perhaps the most responsive person to new ideas they had ever known. Davis carried a well-earned reputation for creativity and innovation, and as a broad thinker, he developed his own ideas and sought ideas from others. With his fertile imagination and high energy level, Davis found ways to make ideas blossom.

Perhaps most important, Barker, who was careful not to let old friendships lapse, had established a personal relationship with Davis many years before. As luck would have it, Davis had once accompanied a party of Texans on an elk-hunting trip to the Santa Fe National Forest in New Mexico, and Elliott Barker was their guide.

As they roar through the state in comfortable automobiles, millions of travelers each year enjoy New Mexico's stunning beauty with no more effort than it takes to turn a head or raise an eyebrow. But the state's wonders can be felt, its smells appreciated and its spirit absorbed only on foot or horseback. And sometime—probably in the early 1930s when Davis was an outdoor sportswriter for the *Atlanta Constitution*, Davis rode with Barker on his visit to New Mexico. Davis certainly couldn't have forgotten the comradeship when the two men experienced nature together, creating a bond that neither would want to break.

On one of Barker's hunting trips, as many as three dozen riders saddled up and pointed their mounts into New Mexico's rugged mountains. Although camp life had a rustic flavor, two dozen pack horses and mules laden with food, bedding, cooking utensils and hunting and fishing gear attested to a slightly softer trip than memories later revealed. Passing through canyons, across ridges and below towering cliffs, riders couldn't help but be impressed with views so spectacular that long hours on horseback passed all too quickly.

Camping each evening in a meadow or forest glade near a chilly stream, animals grazed while hungry horsemen lined up for broiled steaks, fried chicken, baked ham, pork chops and platters of fruits and vegetables. But it was around the campfire that each trip took on its meaning, for the men truly valued their camaraderie. A demonstrative speaker and historian, Barker usually recapped the region's history or talked about its wildlife. And as the men sipped coffee, chatted about the day's ride, told stories and sang songs of the American West, spirits of brotherhood rose as deliberately as did the moon crawling into the New Mexico night. Slowly but certainly, friendships formed and then deepened each night.

Each morning at dawn a crackling fire and the aroma of hot coffee lured campers from warm sleeping bags into the cold morning air to feast on eggs, sausage, bacon, biscuits, pancakes, cooked cereal and plenty of coffee, tea and hot chocolate. Then the hunters saddled up, usually led by Barker, riding easily with his .32 Winchester Special in a saddle scabbard.

No other personal meetings between Barker and Davis were recorded prior to 1950. However, "they certainly were friends," Flock confirmed. "When you bunk, cook soup, swear, gut elk and drink with each other, you get pretty well acquainted. But it can be wet and miserable, too, so you become either friends or enemies. Anyway, Elliott told me, 'I may have some leverage with Clint Davis.'"

But Barker's call to Davis required tact, because Barker had to avoid placing Flock in a compromising position with Lindh; also, if Davis didn't like the idea, it was important that Barker at least keep the door open so he could appeal to Lyle Watts.

Memories of what became a lengthy dialogue between Santa Fe and Washington are hazy. Varied versions appeared in press reports, and participants sometimes contradicted themselves and each other, but reports tend to support the following course of events.

Fortified with the confidence that flows from an almost religious conviction, Barker called Davis to explain the story of the burned bear. With Ray Bell in his office, Barker suggested that the cub be adopted by the Forest

Service as a conservation symbol and explained that he would be pleased to offer the animal as a gift from the state of New Mexico. Only minutes into the conversation Barker, finding little need for his well-honed persuasive skills, smiled across the table at Bell. According to Barker's writings, Davis's response was immediate: "That is the greatest idea for beneficial publicity that I have ever heard of. Of course we will accept your offer." Davis was eager to shepherd the idea through Washington's bureaucracy.

Other versions indicate that Barker's first contact with Washington came on a call from Davis to Barker wherein Davis asked for the bear. Yet another version suggests that Barker first called Lyle Watts, who asked Davis to resolve the matter. In any event, there appear to have been several phone conversations between Santa Fe and Washington—all involving Barker and sometimes including either Flock or Bell. In addition, Dean Earl, although too far away to help, kept in touch with Santa Fe by radio and telephone.

Final authority to make the decision rested with Forest Service chief Lyle Watts, widely respected as an "old-style, do-it-all" forester. Born in Iowa in 1890, Watts received a B.S. in forestry from Iowa State College in 1913, began his Forest Service career in Wyoming, and returned to Iowa State College for his master of forestry degree in 1928. After serving in five additional states, several national forests and a variety of jobs ranging from district ranger to head of an experimental station to regional forester over two of the Forest Service's ten regions, Watts ended up in Washington in 1943 as the Forest Service's sixth chief forester. And Watts trusted the judgment of Clint Davis.

With the mind of a seasoned newshound, Davis recognized the value of a living symbol of Smokey Bear. Davis explained to Watts that although the poster image had been successful, a living Smokey to back up the image would be even more successful. "I don't know what went through Clint's mind," Flock said, "but he went right to work."

And finally the word came back. Watts had approved. Flock and Barker had succeeded. New Mexico's bear was going to Washington, D.C. The nation would have a living symbol of Smokey Bear. But as with other aspects of Smokey's saga, four versions of Watts's response drifted out of Washington and Santa Fe.

The first version claims that Watts immediately agreed with Davis that the little cub was a wonderful opportunity. "Go ahead and do it," Watts responded without deliberation.

Version two, which has authoritative corroboration, shows a more reluctant Watts responding to Davis: "Go ahead and do it, but it will be your ass if it fails."

The third version plays off Elliott Barker's efforts. As the media picked up the story with Walter's pictures, the incident attracted a nationwide following. "There's no question that Mr. Barker was really promoting the name of 'Smokey' and it was catching on," Bell admitted. "Mr. Barker was seeing to it that those photos of Harold's were well distributed to the Associated Press, the UPI and the *New Mexican*. Santa Fe was the state capital and Mr. Barker was pretty well known, so the Associated Press went to Mr. Barker regularly, and Will Harrison, a *Santa Fe New Mexican* reporter [Harrison actually was editor], came to the Game Department office every day to check with Mr. Barker for news."

Jack Samson, a 1949 graduate of the University of New Mexico and Barker's first public relations director, felt Barker played the issue well. "The timing was perfect," Samson recalled. "From a public relations standpoint, the Forest Service really needed a live bear to go with their national symbol." This version, then, insists that the Forest Service was backed into a corner, and Watts had no choice but to acquiesce to an expectant American public.

Version four credits the enthusiastic Davis for convincing Watts that bringing the little bear to Washington would be a master stroke for the forest fire prevention effort.

The actual truth probably lies in a combination of versions two and four. Virtually everyone in Forest Service headquarters recognized the imaginative and forceful Davis's instincts for public relations, and his Forest Service career developed because he so effectively imparted enthusiasm. "Clint Davis did things quickly, efficiently and with courage," an admiring Kay Flock emphasized. By sheer force of energy, Davis probably convinced Watts of the value of a living symbol.

"We got word about the rescue because the bear had gotten national recognition in the papers," J. Morgan Smith explained. "The pictures just got everyone. The AP picked up the photos of this poor little thing with his burned, wrapped-up paws. Then Elliott Barker said he would like to present the bear to Lyle Watts. Clint Davis and I both knew Elliott Barker, but we had a regional forester out there [Otto Lindh] who was against it, so that made it hard on Kay Flock. At first, Watts wasn't very happy about the bear coming to Washington, either, but Clint Davis was all for it." And Davis could be a persuasive man.

"Clint and I wanted to get this bear in," Smith explained. "We arranged the deal with [National Zoo director] Dr. [William] Mann—he was a good friend. We drove to the zoo to talk to Doc. His office had documents piled up in long lines—it was the damnedest filing system you ever saw. But

Doc could find anything; ask him a question and he would walk down the line and pull out the paper. Doc was a great man, and we loved him. Once, when he was sick in a hospital, old Doc was bleeding from one end to the other, and a circus delivered a baby elephant to his room to cheer him up. Doc was a good politician too. The chairman of the House Appropriations Committee would go down once a year and see what the Doc needed and then give Doc whatever he wanted. So when we told Doc about the bear, he loved the idea because he wanted publicity for the zoo."

But Mann didn't have the final vote. "Then when we went to tell [Lyle] Watts about the deal," Smith added, "he got irritated and said, 'You guys aren't going to make a fool out of me with a silly old bear.' But Watts was great after he got used to the idea."

In fact, the groundwork for Watts's decision may have been laid inadvertently by the Advertising Council. The possibility of a living symbol of Smokey reportedly was suggested in the late 1940s by Stuart Peabody, advertising manager of the borden milk company and a director of the Advertising Council. Peabody apparently believed that the poster Smokey's popularity could be increased if a "suitable" live bear could be adopted into the program. Although Peabody's critics accused him of trying to romance the fire prevention program, Peabody may have effectively planted the idea with Watts.

Washington Forest Service staffers Rudy Wendelin and Bill Bergoffen remembered excitement "spreading like wildfire" with word of the bear moving to Washington, and Wendelin credits the enthusiasm of Davis. "It was something no one ever thought to question," Wendelin said. "Clint had such a positive attitude that everyone just accepted it as a great opportunity."

Bergoffen agreed that "everyone was excited. The overall reaction was extremely favorable. Clint said, 'We've got a bull by the tail.' We all thought the idea of a live Smokey Bear was great. It was unexpected. Suddenly, it was in our laps. It stood by itself as a beautiful island."

Kay Flock, too, supports this thinking. "I don't agree that the Forest Service was backed into a corner," Flock insisted. "Clint Davis simply was very enthusiastic and very persuasive. Lyle Watts probably got caught up in that with everyone else."

After Smith ironed out details with the zoo, Davis wrote to Barker, formally requesting that the little cub be donated to the Cooperative Forest Fire Prevention program; the bear's permanent residence would be in Washington's National Zoo.

As state game warden, Elliott Barker had the final authority to donate the bear to the Forest Service. The cub was a New Mexico game animal and, technically, could not be transported outside the state without Barker's permission. But Barker, who had worked so hard to get the bear to Washington, suddenly developed reservations. As the national press

Elliott Barker, who convinced the Forest Service in Washington, D.C., to accept New Mexico's injured bear cub as the living symbol of Smokey Bear. *(Courtesy Kester D. Flock.)*

grabbed the story, it focused on the Forest Service and forest fire prevention, and stories began crediting the Forest Service—and not New Mexico's Game and Fish Department—with Smokey's salvation. So Barker leaned back in his chair, propped his feet on the writing board of his desk, adjusted his hearing aid, started tapping a pencil and began to rethink the matter.

Barker had no objection to the use of the bear for forest fire prevention, but he envisioned a wider use, including wildlife conservation. Barker wanted the nation's wildlife management efforts to get equal publicity, but he wasn't convinced that would happen. Ray Bell remembered Barker's objection. "If they get the bear," Barker opined, "it's going to be all Forest

192

Service, and there will be nothing to credit wildlife management as much as there is on forest fire prevention."

Barker apparently received several requests to sell or donate the bear to worthy causes. The first inquiry came from California in a 62-word telegram explaining that the state wanted the little bear as a living symbol for the bear on California's state flag. That interest caused Barker to have even deeper reservations. "If it's worth that to the State of California, maybe it's worth more to us," he reasoned.

Bell thought that Barker was about to renege on his pact with Davis. "I wanted to get the bear to Washington and the matter finished," Bell grimaced. "The thing had finally gelled, but gosh darn, I was sitting there about to have a fit. I thought Mr. Barker was going to change his mind." But with Bell and Flock campaigning in Santa Fe and Davis arguing from Washington, Barker finally agreed to the original plan. "Besides," Bell chuckled, "Mr. Barker couldn't figure out what New Mexico would do with the bear anyway."

Barker wrote that after Davis begged him to donate the bear, he agreed on condition that wildlife conservation be included in the long-range goal. Barker sent his official letter to Watts on June 9. "We are willing to release Smokey to you to be dedicated to publicity programs for fire prevention and wildlife conservation," he wrote.

Six months later, Kay Flock was transferred to Forest Service headquarters in Washington, D.C. Then word spread around Santa Fe that an apparently displeased Otto Lindh had told Flock, "If you like Washington that much, you can just go and live there."

But Flock refuted those reports. "My relationship with my boss was never bad," he explained. "We just disagreed on that one issue." Perhaps in testimony to that relationship, Flock and Lindh later traveled together with their wives on a vacation in Mexico.

However, Flock got a surprise two months after his transfer. "Chief Watts called me into his office," Flock recalled. "He was sitting behind his big mahogany desk and he threw two letters on the table in front of me; both had been signed. The first was a letter to me from the Chief commending me for doing a good job with the Smokey Bear project. The second letter was to the Chief from my old boss—Otto Lindh in Albuquerque—criticizing me for going over his head. Lindh was recommending that I be reprimanded for 'initiating action' with Elliott Barker. Lindh's letter had arrived the same morning the Chief had signed his own letter to me. The Chief asked me what he should do with the letters. Like a fool, I said, 'I don't know.' I wish now I had asked for the letters. After a few minutes, the Chief ended the matter by sweeping both letters into his wastebasket."

And Elliott Barker? He wrote at age ninety-six that he didn't believe the Forest Service had lived up to its end of the bargain to promote wildlife conservation equally with forest fire prevention. But Barker also wrote that donating the bear to the Forest Service had the most far-reaching conservation benefit of anything he had ever done.

Ethel Barker confirmed that Elliott Barker's private conversations tracked his public writings: "Elliott said that sending that bear to Washington made his life worthwhile. The kids were quite impressed, too, that Daddy knew someone in Washington that he could persuade to take the bear."

Although little Smokey now was assured of national prominence, Barker faced one more problem: Washington's zoo was 1,800 miles from Santa Fe. Lyle Watts and Clint Davis weren't going to come after Smokey, so Barker had to deliver New Mexico's gift. "It was left to us how to get the bear to Washington," Ray Bell confirmed.

Given his scrappy nature and penchant for quarreling, Smokey wasn't welcome in anyone's car for such a long drive, nor did a train trip seem feasible. A quick flight to Washington seemed the best solution.

"Our problem now was to find a plane to take Smokey to Washington," added Kay Flock, who signed out for a half-day's vacation and called United Parcel Service at his own expense. "I had this great idea to have UPS fly the bear to Washington in a plane with some acknowledgment about Smokey on the nose. I thought they could get a lot of free press about the flight, but UPS would only look at it from a commercial standpoint. If I wanted to ship an animal, it had to go as freight. I couldn't get through to anyone in management that might have had any imagination. I got a brush-off right away."

Then Bell tried a commercial airline. "We called Omaha from Mr. Barker's office and talked to a TWA manager and told him our story," Bell recalled. "Thirty minutes of conversation resulted in his saying Smokey could go alone on a freight plane as baggage, but he could not ride in a passenger cabin. Mr. Barker made a decision on the spot; he said, 'No. We are not going to do that.' Mr. Barker said it was beneath Smokey's dignity to travel as common baggage, and that when he went to Washington, someone would go with him. Then I thought of a good friend—Frank Hines—a Piper aircraft dealer in Hobbs."

Hines, owner of the B.F. Hines Flying Service of Hobbs, New Mexico, was known for his generosity and parties. A hard worker, Hines sold planes, ferried people and goods, sprayed crops and offered every aviation service his clients could demand.

"Frank never missed a party," Bell grinned. "Frank liked for everyone to have fun; he saw to it that they did too. One time he went to a food store and got a whole basket of groceries for each of his employees, and he put a quart of bourbon—Jim Beam, the cowboy's bourbon—in the middle of each bushel basket. Before I got the new plane, Frank rented planes to me for game surveys at $3 per hour, which was dirt cheap. Sometimes, when I landed in Hobbs on a weekend, I went with Frank to ferry planes back from Lock Haven, Pennsylvania, where they built Piper aircraft. Sometimes we flew all the way to the East Coast on weekends too. Ruth and Judy were at the Hines home a lot with Matty Hines [Frank's wife], and one Fourth of July, I took some leave and Frank and Matty picked up Ruth and me and we flew to Salinas, California. Frank taught me how to dust and spray cotton, too.

"When I called Frank and explained my problem," Bell continued, "Frank settled the matter real quick. He said, 'You bet your life I'll take the bear.' Frank said he would take Smokey to Washington with whoever wished to go along. Frank also volunteered to finance the trip and said he would contact Piper Aircraft because Bill Piper Sr. might want to take part in the program. Frank thought it was an ideal thing for Piper to get in on because the Piper Cub airplanes had the little bear cub symbols on them."

"When Hines called Bill Piper, president of Piper Aircraft," a delighted Flock recalled, "the word came back with great gusto. Piper said, 'Break out a new plane. But there is one stipulation. Paint a picture of the bear on the fuselage on both sides of the plane.'"

The matter of Smokey's chaperon also required some thought. Hines would pilot the aircraft, but four other men were candidates for the trip. As a pilot, Bell was a logical choice as a backup for Hines. Homer Pickens, assistant to Barker, was considered because his son was attending an FBI training school in Washington. Flock and Barker were other possible choices because of their role in convincing the Forest Service to accept Smokey. But Barker insisted that only one person should go. "We don't need a whole crew," he reasoned.

So Bell elected to pass in favor of Pickens and convinced Barker to let Flock go too. Flock wanted a new car, but the Korean War was starting and Flock remembered it had been difficult to buy cars during World War II. Because Flock had been planning to go to Indianapolis to buy a car, Bell argued that Flock could ride that far with Pickens and Hines.

"What about me?" Barker asked Bell. "Well, you're the boss," Bell responded. But after some thought, Barker offered seats to Pickens and Flock. The flight that would capture the nation's imagination was about to begin.

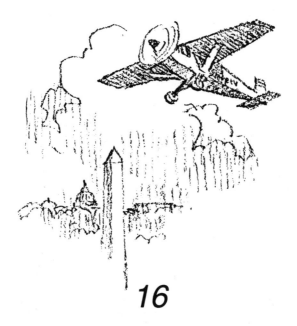

16

THREE MEN AND A BEAR — IN THE AIR

"Of all the darn fool things. They have enough bears here in Pennsylvania that we didn't have to go through all that rigamarole to get that New Mexico bear to Washington."
— Bill Piper Sr.

"Yeah, that's true. But the difference is that none of the bears in Pennsylvania had their butts burned in a forest fire."
— Ray Bell

Concerned that Smokey would hold a decisive edge in any battle of teeth and claws during his flight to Washington, Homer Pickens and Ray Bell agreed that Pickens should try to build a relationship with the little cub. Neither man had reason for optimism; despite his best efforts, Bell's own familiarity with Smokey had failed to endear Bell to the bear. "Smokey already had a pretty good taste of me," Bell laughed.

197

A long-time family friend, Pickens visited the Bells and knew Smokey's reputation and sharp teeth. After considering alternatives, the men agreed that Pickens should take the bear to his own home for two or three days before the flight.

But first, Pickens and Bell designed a small wire cage so the little bear wouldn't get hurt rolling around if his plane encountered air turbulence. Finas Beavers, a local artisan, volunteered to help. "Finas had a metal shop in Santa Fe," Pickens explained, "so Ray and I gave him the dimensions. Like most people in those days, Finas didn't charge us either." Then, for three days before he left Bell's home, Smokey spent time in his new cage to help acclimate him for his upcoming trip.

Nestled in a valley six miles north of Santa Fe, the village of Tesuque hosted the Homer and Edna Pickens family in a hundred-year-old pitched-roof adobe house amid four acres of irrigated apple orchards and one acre of lawn, livestock pens and outbuildings. Don Bell donated Jet's leash and red harness, and Ruth, Don and Judy took Smokey north.

Assigned to the Pickens's spacious yard, the cub eagerly made friends with Sarge, a black Labrador retriever. Much of the property was closed to Smokey, and he was allowed neither into the house nor free run of the farm. Smokey probably could smell their presence, but he wasn't allowed near the horses, chicken coops, cow, sheep, pigs or apple house. He did enjoy, however, an occasional romp with two mountain lion kittens Pickens had brought home for rehabilitation.

Smokey easily adapted to his new quarters—a part-adobe doghouse that he shared with Sarge. "We caged him in at night," Pickens recalled. "Smokey slept most of the time, anyway, but he liked to play with Sarge. They chased each other around and played pretty rough, but neither got hurt. We fed Smokey dry dog food pellets—Peerless dog food—and Pablum that I got from Ray. I thought it was best to keep him on the same food the Bells had used. Ruth Bell taught him to eat originally, so I figured she knew what she was doing."

Betty Pickens Cabber, then four years old, remembered the antics of the two animals: "Sometimes Sarge would just lie there, ignoring Smokey, but the bear would crawl all over Sarge. Smokey was a busy bear—a lot of fun to watch. He had a real curiosity about the farm, always sniffing and looking around and finding something to do. He usually played in the grass around the apple tree in our yard, but sometimes he ran up and down the steps on the front porch. Dad let him climb up and down the apple tree, too.

"Smokey acted like a puppy," Cabber continued, "except he wasn't sweet and lovable like a puppy. He was mean. He was so mean I couldn't play with him or get too close to him because Mom and Dad worried that he would hurt me. He bit Wilda Salveson, a neighbor, on her calf. He bit several other people too, but he never bit me because I wasn't allowed to handle him. I could hold the lions and play with them, but I couldn't get near Smokey. People could just stand there and he might go after them. They may have been playful bites, but it was scary."

Playful or not, Betty's blond cocker spaniel, the family's domestic cats and other animals kept their distance. "A lot of people showed up to see the little bear," Cabber remembered. "Dad cautioned people all the time to stay away from Smokey. Dad always kept the bear on a leash because he wasn't sure what he would do; Dad didn't trust him."

Edna Pickens had problems with the bear too. "As far as Mom was concerned," Cabber explained, "Smokey was a nuisance. It bothered her because he bit people. It was part of Dad's work and she put up with it, but she was glad when Smokey left."

The purpose of Smokey's stay in Tesuque was to acclimate the bear to Homer Pickens, but it didn't work. "Smokey never did take a liking to me," Pickens conceded. "He resisted from the first time I put him into that harness Don Bell gave us. Smokey didn't like that, so I had to be careful when I handled him. I *always* wore my buckskin gloves: yellow deerskin; size eight; made by Hodkins."

Final preparations began as Frank Hines developed a flight plan, and Kay Flock arranged to take a few days of annual leave. Withdrawing $2,300 from his bank, Flock carefully tucked two one-thousand-dollar bills and three one-hundred-dollar bills into a money belt. Flock had his eye on a new black V-8 Katerling Oldsmobile. Colored cars were just hitting the market, but Flora Flock issued her instructions: "Don't get anything except black. Colored cars are for 'jazzy' people."

Then an excited Santa Fe arranged a farewell party for the tiny rascal at Seth Hall, a community center in the city's north side. "It was a big place, like an opera house," Ray Bell explained. "They had the premiere of the *Santa Fe Trail* movie there, with stars like Erroll Flynn. Seth Hall could hold lots of people, so we had the big going-away party there the night before Smokey left for Washington. Needless to say, Smokey was the whole show."

An elaborate program honored New Mexico's famous little bear. Sponsored by the Boy Scouts and Girl Scouts, with assistance from the Safety Council of the Santa Fe schools, the party began promptly at 7:00 p.m. on

June 26, 1950. Jack Hester served as master of ceremonies, and Reverend M. E. Waldrum of the Church of Christ gave the invocation. Dignitaries included Frank Ortiz (mayor), Angus Evans (chairman, State Game Commission) and James W. Young (vice president, J. Walter Thompson advertising agency) representing the Advertising Council. Earl Moore, Speed Simmons, Major Bob Cooper, Ray Bell and Dr. Edwin Smith told of Smokey's rescue and his adventures in Santa Fe, and Homer Pickens and Frank Hines spoke about their flight plans for the trip.

"They invited a lot of people," Bell recalled. "We had quite a crowd— maybe 150 or 200 people. Ruth, Judy and Don were there. Dean Earl drove in from Capitan. We also had Kay Flock, Elliott Barker, Al Hathaway, Will Shuster and Harold and May Walter. Smokey sat up there on the head table, just watching and listening. They had a nice program arranged and decorations all over the room." And all of Santa Fe heard Smokey's famous farewell bite.

"The party was broadcast over a Santa Fe radio station," Bell winced. "I was answering questions from the audience at the same time I was trying to handle Smokey. But Smokey was beginning to get a little disgusted because I had put on a thicker pair of buckskin gloves. His chewing was not having the effect it had had in the past, so I guess I should have been on my guard. Finally, Smokey got tired, leaped at me, reached high up on my arm over the gloves and bit the hell out of me."

"Damn it, you little son-of-a-bitch," a startled Bell yelled as he pushed Smokey back. "That wasn't fit to go over the air," Bell laughed, "but that was Smokey's way of making a speech. He sure got everyone's attention. The crowd was quite pleased with this entertainment at my expense. They really roared with laughter. Smokey just sat there. I guess he figured he had evened things up."

Frank Hines still had to honor Bill Piper's request to decorate his plane with pictures of the little bear. So Kay Flock talked with his fellow Rotarian— fifty-year-old Will Shuster, a well-known Santa Fe artist, teacher and writer. "Will was the most prominent artist in Santa Fe," Flock explained. "He was an 'assignment' artist, much sought after, but he readily agreed to donate his services."

After the Seth Hall party, Flock, Shuster, Bell and Shuster's granddaughter drove to Ragle Airfield and found Hines's plane in a hangar next to a baseball field. "Frank had a new plane he was using," Bell recalled. "It was a short, heavy 125-horsepower 'tail dragger' [it had no nose wheel]." Shuster planned to paint replicas of the poster Smokey on the Piper Tripacer, but no one had remembered to bring the posters. Undaunted, Shuster used his imagination to paint caricatures of a small bear with his arm in a sling to emphasize Smokey's forest fire experience. As Flock and Shuster's granddaughter took turns holding a lantern, Shuster painted each side of

Homer Pickens and Smokey pose under Will Schuster's painting just before their June 27, 1950, departure from Santa Fe for Washington, D.C.
(Courtesy USDA Forest Service. Photo by Harold Walter.)

the canvas fuselage with regular artist's watercolors, then sealed his finished product with a protective coat of clear lacquer.

Before dawn on Tuesday, June 27, Smokey's friends assembled at Ragle Field to bid adios to their favorite terror. Despite the early hour, most attendees from the Seth Hall gala showed up with several children. Because everything had been said the night before, no speeches were delivered on the chilly grass airstrip, but Homer Pickens led the bear around on his leash and posed for photographs. Then, as daylight crept across the field, Shuster checked his artwork and Hines said to load up. Smokey's Santa Fe sojourn had ended.

At 6:30 a.m., Hines, Pickens, Flock and Bear taxied down the runway, easily lifted off and turned east toward Tucumcari, New Mexico. Ruth Bell wiped a tear from her usually stoic face, and Judy Bell just watched. Ray Bell had his own thoughts. "I remembered the trip from Capitan to Santa Fe when all the possibilities came into my mind. But it went further than I could ever have imagined. I guess it was a natural," he said.

Pickens felt elation at his great adventure. Hines searched for a smooth cruising altitude. Flock hitched his money belt. And little Smokey, oblivious to his new responsibilities as a public relations bear for the U. S. Department of Agriculture, slept flat on his back, all four tiny paws pointing toward the roof of his private plane.

Then the three men settled back for their 1,800-mile milk run to Washington, D.C. Five feet six inches tall and weighing "140 pounds with billfold, pocketknife and car keys," Pickens wore his tan Game and Fish Department uniform, complete with necktie, cowboy boots and a western-style, white felt "Sunday hat." Flock wore his green Forest Service uniform with tie. Not to be outdone, pilot Hines also had rustled up a tie.

Although Homer Pickens eventually earned a reputation as one of America's outstanding animal trackers, in 1927, at age twenty-three, he demonstrated no overt aptitude for his latent talent. With five dollars in his pocket, Pickens left Phillips Petroleum in Borger, Texas, to join his half brother Albert in Albuquerque. But as Pickens stepped from his train in the Indian village of Laguna, a conductor explained, jerking a thumb east, that Pickens had slept through Albuquerque, seventy-eight miles "back that-a-way."

Finally reaching Albuquerque—with its 27,000 residents nestled in the Rio Grande valley bottomlands—Pickens was enthralled from the moment he left the train. Thinking he was in a foreign country, Pickens stared in amazement at Spanish-style buildings, cowboys wearing blue Levi's jeans, Navajos sporting large black hats and other Indians wrapped in blankets. And when he first visited Santa Fe, Pickens marveled at the flat adobe buildings, spires of smoke, burros packing aromatic piñon wood, covered wagons and the blend of Spanish, Indians and Anglos.

Appointed as a game warden in Elliott Barker's new Game and Fish Department in 1931, Pickens was assigned to tackle the mountain lions that seemed bent on wiping out the state's deer population. Game and Fish wouldn't tolerate vigilante warfare by ranchers against mountain lions, and Pickens took on the job. But lion hunting isn't a sport for the timid, and on one occasion, during hand-to-hand combat with three dogs and a lion, Pickens found himself trapped. So he did the only thing a fellow could do—he walloped the lion over the head with the butt of his .32-.20 Bisley model Colt revolver. By 1936, Pickens had killed or captured 165 mountain lions—many of which stocked America's zoos.

In 1940, Pickens became assistant director of Game and Fish (and would become director upon Barker's retirement in 1953), where he supervised thirty-four trappers but focused on public relations and produced movies of department activities.

"I was Mr. Barker's assistant for twelve years," Pickens explained. "I didn't have anything to do with the phone calls to Washington, but it meant so much to me when Mr. Barker asked me to take the bear to Washington. My son had gone to Washington in 1949 to work for the FBI and attend George Washington University. Naturally I volunteered. But I sure never thought about Smokey Bear being a monument for the country until Ray flew that bear up here from Capitan and they began to discuss it with the Forest Service."

Pickens completely trusted his pilot. "Frank Hines was a nice, very principled person," Pickens smiled. "Sometimes, if we were out late, Frank would take us up to cruising altitude and then say, 'Here, take these controls. See this direction? See that highway? Well, just point it that way.' But the moment I varied from the route, Frank would jump at me. Frank was an outstanding pilot. He could do anything with an airplane."

But Smokey's flight to Washington was uneventful—at least in the air. "Smokey didn't seem to mind his little cage," Pickens reflected. "He usually got kind of excited when we took off from an airport, but he was always asleep by the time we leveled off."

Flock, too, was surprised at the tiny passenger: "We had figured Smokey would fight and raise hell on the trip," Flock grinned. "But he just laid on his back with all four feet in the air and slept. He turned out to be no trouble at all in flight."

So the three escorts swapped yarns, sipped coffee and enjoyed the passing countryside. "We ran into heavy clouds most of the way east," Pickens recalled, "so Frank flew above them when he could. I think we usually were around 3,500 to 4,000 feet high. The plane had four seats—two in front and two in back—and was pretty comfortable. Most of the time we kept the bear on one of the rear seats. When we dropped in for a landing, he would get restless and noisy and scratch his ears. He began scratching the moment we began to lose altitude."

A refueling stop had been scheduled for Tucumcari, but Hines bypassed that tiny town and flew straight to Amarillo, Texas, where, true to form, Smokey awoke and scratched his ears as soon as Hines began his descent.

"Game and Fish and the Forest Service coordinated the trip with the media," Pickens explained. "We agreed to fly a certain distance, then land and let Smokey exercise. So we had planned a brief stop in Amarillo to let the bear go to the bathroom. But I was surprised at the crowd—it may have amounted to two hundred people. The news media were making a real splash about the trip, so we stayed about an hour in Amarillo."

That afternoon, the foursome descended for another break in Tulsa, Oklahoma, and Pickens again was caught off guard. "Several hundred people greeted us at the terminal," Pickens recalled. "There were a lot of tourists and families. I was scared to death because I wasn't sure how to handle Smokey in crowds. Everyone wanted to see and touch the bear. The kids wanted to get their hands on Smokey. I kept them away and watched him very closely."

But it was a different story with Smokey's handlers. "That bear bit me every chance he got," Flock remembered. "My legs were all beat up by the time we got to St. Louis. Sometimes I got to be his chambermaid. We would walk toward a bush or something, and if I tugged on his leash Smokey would nail me. He had teeth like pins; one bite didn't hurt too bad, but they had a cumulative effect. Of course, Smokey never was very friendly. He didn't like to be petted, except he seemed to like little Judy Bell fussing over him."

But Smokey tried to bite each time he was hooked to his harness or whenever Pickens's attention wandered, so Pickens always wore his buckskin gloves. But his concern grew as crowds increased and kids clamored to pet the bear. The startled Pickens, who had assumed his role was to protect the bear, suddenly realized that his real responsibility was to protect Smokey's fans.

The day's final leg took them to Kratz Airport in St. Louis, Missouri, and several hundred new Smokey admirers. "By then I was beginning to get aggravated at the crowds," explained a frustrated Pickens. "They just didn't understand that this wasn't a friendly poster bear, that he was a wild animal that could hurt people, especially if he felt threatened. But the Chase Manhattan Bank people sent a large black limousine for us. Chase volunteered through the news media and they sure showed us a good time." Milo Perkins, an insurance company advertising man, apparently representing the Advertising Council, also helped host the trio of escorts in St. Louis. Smokey, meanwhile, enjoyed a teacup of Pablum mixed with honey and milk and spent the night in the basement of the reptile house at the Forest Park Zoo.

The next morning Flock said good-bye to his colleagues in Indianapolis. "As it turned out," Flock recalled, "a fellow named Roscoe Turner owned the airport where we landed. Turner was a famous barnstormer who had won national coast-to-coast contests three times. All barnstormers tried to do something different, so Turner traveled with a lion cub. Naturally, he liked the Smokey Bear idea. Roscoe drove me to an Olds dealer and introduced me. The dealer had only one Katerling left—a black one—and I got it."

Cincinnati was the next stop. "The crowds began to look pretty big to me by then," Pickens laughed. "A lot of business people were in the crowd. They sent a limousine out for Smokey but not for us. But we were treated to a grand reception in Cincinnati."

Later, Hines landed at Elkins, West Virginia, to buy fuel. "We even had a crowd waiting for us in Elkins," Pickens laughed. "Little Smokey had to go to the bathroom right there on the runway. It was kind of embarrassing because he had been living strictly on Pablum, so he sort of had the runs. It was a paved runway, but Smokey didn't care.

"It was really raining, but we had another big crowd in Baltimore," Pickens continued, "and they sent a car out to take Smokey to a veterinarian hospital for a routine check. Again, the media arranged hospitality; they took us to a nice restaurant and we stayed in another nice hotel. Frank was relaxed but I was nervous. I would have felt much more at home riding my saddle horse in the hills."

Because of pouring rain and strong winds the next morning, Hines delayed the final hop to nearby Washington, D.C. "It was raining and raining and raining, but Frank finally spotted a hole in the clouds, so we sent for Smokey," Pickens said. "Frank warmed up the plane a little, looked at the clouds, said, 'We can do it—we can make it now,' and took off. We were in D.C. in just a few minutes, and we landed at the correct time. Frank was a good pilot and took us in without difficulty." President Truman reportedly granted permission for the little aircraft to fly over the White House, and Washington newspapers reported that twenty-seven commercial planes were kept circling until Hines could land with his fuzzy cargo at National Airport. Then TWA moved a plane so Smokey's aircraft could pull up to its assigned gate.

At precisely 4:00 p.m., Frank Hines taxied his dripping wet Piper to a cheering crowd of two hundred admirers armed with umbrellas and ignoring the downpour. Their hero had arrived, and Will Shuster's paintings electrified the crowd. Leading the welcoming delegation were a beaming Lyle Watts, Clint Davis, Morgan Smith and Lloyd Swift, chief of wildlife resources for the Forest Service. Bill Piper Sr., his wife, Sue, and Homer Pickens Jr. couldn't suppress their grins. Boy Scouts and Girl Scouts elbowed aside the media to cheer the tiny bruin.

Alexandria, Virginia, Cub Scouts formed an honor guard and Homer Pickens Jr. held an umbrella as his father alit with the bear and hooked a

Arriving in Washington, D.C., Homer Pickens (right) held Smokey in a pouring rain for Stanlee Ann Miller (left) of Albuquerque, New Mexico, and Forest Service chief Lyle Watts. *(Courtesy USDA Forest Service.)*

silver-colored chain to Smokey's red harness. Then the ten pounds of mischievous cub immediately stole the show. To the delight of photographers, Smokey reared up on his hind legs and began strutting through water puddles along the tarmac, holding forepaws aloft, sniffing the air and catching raindrops on his stubby snout.

The Secretary of Agriculture had arranged for Smokey to use the terminal's Presidential Suite, and there, where visiting dignitaries usually met reporters, fanfare continued unabated. Under a large "Welcome Smokey" banner surrounded by Smokey posters, his fans finally got a good look at the heralded animal as they watched the tiny critter nibble on the suite's green carpet and bite a Venetian blind before being lured to a table by a milk bottle.

TWA Hostesses Donna Christ (left) and Catherine Wright give Smokey a drink while Homer Pickens restrains the little fellow at Washington's National Airport on June 29, 1950. *(Courtesy USDA Forest Service.)*

Photographers snapped Bill Piper Sr. and Lyle Watts watching as TWA hostesses Donna Christ, of Chicago, Illinois, and Catherine Wright, of Rome, Georgia, fed the little bear while Pickens held the leash with both gloved hands. As Christ fed warm milk to the round-eyed bear, who happily sucked away, one paw steadied the bottle while Wright looked on approvingly. "First Washington Lunch," newspaper captions concluded the next day.

Then, his meal finished, his belly full and a ring of white foam around his mouth, Smokey simply lay down and dozed off until the screams of delighted children and the popping of flashbulbs woke him.

Climbing from the table, the cub chewed on an ashtray—the nearest thing, one newspaper reported, to an after-dinner smoke. "Smokey got the same treatment as the President of France," Morgan Smith explained. "In fact, he even got more because he had a couple of pretty girls to feed him." But after almost two months of celebrity status, the little cub handled his fame rather modestly—usually by ignoring surrounding activity. Smokey didn't care about the rain, photographers, posters, dignitaries or the attendant excitement. He seemed interested only in the milk bottle.

As the fascinated crowd pressed in for a closer look at the surprisingly healthy critter, they noticed that, despite his traumatic ordeal, the bear sported no singed hair, bandaged paws or casts. Then reporters besieged Pickens and Hines for flight details. Pickens confirmed that the bear had been a pretty good flier and didn't get airsick, perhaps because he had been rescued from a height of 8,000 feet on Capitan Mountain.

But as reporters fired questions, the tiny animal managed to hold attention. Whimpering occasionally, the bear took a swing at Pickens's arm just as the game warden, trying to put Smokey's best paw forward, explained how gentle the little bear could be. On the other hand, Pickens pointed out, dodging another swipe, the cub's teeth and claws certainly had to be respected. The crowd roared each time Smokey tried to take a bite out of his handler. Although Pickens continued to insist that the cub was friendly, he repeatedly ducked to evade the lunging bear.

The flashbulb blitz indicated that, just as he had captivated Santa Fe, Smokey was now the darling of the nation's capital. And eager Washington newspapers outbid each other with superlatives: "It took Smokey exactly one second to become another Washington institution"; "All but took over National Airport"; "Walking Teddy bear captivated a Presidential Room reception"; and "Brown, fuzzy and the incarnation of a Teddy bear."

An hour later, a motorcade took Smokey to the National Zoo for an introduction to his new cage mate Gene, a well-known seven-month-old hybrid bear. As the offspring of a cross-breeding experiment between a brown bear and a Kodiak bear, Gene (a nickname for "Genetics") surprised animal experts first by being born and then by surviving. Dr. William Mann, zoo director, and Clarence Arata, manager of the Greater National Capital Committee, who would preside at the next day's ceremonies, had planned a testing period to ensure that the two animals wouldn't upset the proceedings with a battle.

But because of Smokey's reputation, Mann changed his mind and ordered that Smokey be kept in a separate cage. On the theory that Smokey was an "uppity rascal," Mann decided that Smokey and Gene should be allowed time to accustom themselves to each other; the animals would first be kept in separate quarters, then placed in a shared cage separated by a wire fence until they could acclimate themselves to company.

But notwithstanding his celebrity status, like a guest at a posh resort, Smokey first was required to register with his new hosts, and the heralded bruin was entered into the zoo's official animal acquisition records. "General classification: Carnivora—Ursidae. Specific name: Euarctos americanus. Common name: Black Bear—'Smokey.' Sex: Male. Catalog number: 21,463. Received from: Forest Service and State of New Mexico. How acquired: Gift. Remarks: Weighed 11 pounds upon arrival."

With enrollment formalities complete, Smokey was turned loose into his new quarters. Of course, the little cub didn't realize that it had not always been so easy to secure quarters at the Smithsonian Institution's National Zoological Park.

When the first live animals were donated to the Smithsonian in 1855, the unfortunate beasts were promptly turned over to the supervisor of the U.S. Insane Asylum. Although the idea of a national zoo was broached in 1870, it wasn't until 1887 that Dr. G. Brown Goode organized the Department of Living Animals as part of the U.S. National Museum. With 58 animals living in the Washington Mall by 1888, President Grover Cleveland signed an 1889 District of Columbia appropriations bill that provided funds to acquire land (once owned in part by President John Quincy Adams) for the National Zoological Park.

Several animals officially were turned over to the zoo in June 1890, but they stayed on the Mall until June 27, 1891, when three elk and six prairie dogs led the exodus to their new home in a wagon drawn by four horses borrowed from the Humane Society. Upon arrival, however, the new denizens were greeted by an American black bear that had already taken up residence. But by the time of Smokey's appearance in 1950, the National Zoological Park had developed into one of the nation's finest and best-known zoos.

Although no problems developed during his first night in Washington, Smokey staked out his territory early the next morning. "I had unsnapped his harness when we turned him loose in his cage at the zoo," Pickens grinned. "He didn't like the harness and I was trying not to aggravate him because that was when he got nasty. So I carefully went into his cage to catch him and gently put on the harness. I didn't have much luck, so an attendant said, 'You can't catch that bear. Let me handle it.' Well, he didn't know Smokey like I did. The attendant grabbed Smokey and Smokey grabbed back. Smokey got him on the leg and tore his pants. The blood just streamed down and the attendant said a few cuss words."

At 11:00 a.m. on Friday, June 30, 1950, in a well-planned welcoming ceremony, the state of New Mexico and the Forest Service officially presented Smokey to the National Zoo. In contrast to the previous day, Washington enjoyed a beautiful morning for Smokey's dedication. It was a meaningful event and people dressed appropriately—men in suits and ties, and women in dresses.

"We got the head of the Chamber of Commerce to be emcee," Morgan Smith explained, "and we notified all the stations and newspapers. A lot of people that had worked on the program were there, and we had gotten in touch with Senator [Dennis] Chavez's office and asked the Senator to go. They were all for it; they were tickled to death. Chavez [a Democratic fixture in the Senate since 1935] was involved because his granddaughter was there, and Chavez was a good friend of the Forest Service. Several hundred people—maybe up to five hundred—attended. There were lots of kids, but that was the purpose—kids."

With the event heavily attended by Washington and national media, Smokey walked into another salvo of flashbulbs. On a grassy area outside his cage, a dozen Smokey Bear posters were displayed on wire racks flanking a green-covered table. With a background of spreading trees, a speaking area equipped with microphones hosted Pickens, Mann, Chavez, Bill Piper Sr. and Lyle Watts.

But no speaker could compete with Smokey. "Pickens put Smokey on the table and he just went to sleep," Morgan Smith recalled. "But the TV people and photographers wanted to see what Smokey would do; they didn't care about speeches. The photographers said to make him do something, so I put my Forest Service ranger's hat on the little bear. Then he just rose up on his hind feet and put his front paws on the hat as if he were trying it on for size. We couldn't have arranged that—he just reared up and it was one of those lucky shots." (Typically, reports disagreed on the hat. Smith said it was his ranger hat; one paper said it belonged to Watts; another said it was Mann's gray fedora.)

Regardless, Smokey kept his fans happy. Whether rolling in the grass to the screams of tickled children, or playing with a ribbon, the bear ignored the palaver. Even when Pickens paraded the cub around on his leash to the

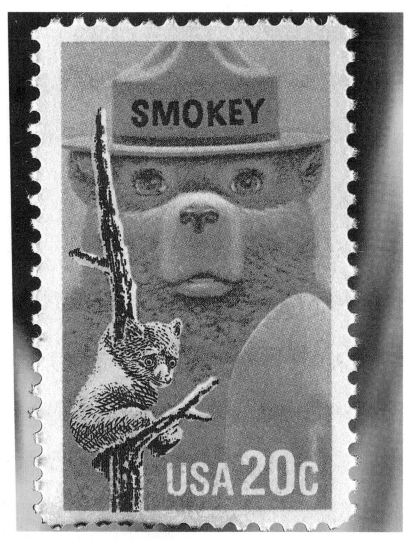

The Smokey Bear Stamp, issued on August 13, 1984. *(Courtesy USDA Forest Service.)*

delight of a roaring crowd, the cub seemed oblivious to his admirers. He focused only on his search for something to chew—his chain, a pencil dangled near his snout or Morgan Smith's hat.

Because of the cub's reputation and Pickens's careful attention, people kept their distance. "Smokey didn't bite anyone, but I didn't see anybody trying to pet him either," Smith explained. Even Dr. Mann had noticed Pickens's heavy gloves and elected not to shake paws with his new star.

As Joseph Kaylor, president of the Association of State Foresters, and Frank Hines, resplendent in a new double-breasted suit, stood by, Stanlee Ann Miller, twelve-year-old granddaughter of Senator Chavez made the presentation for the Forest Service. And after eight-year-old Spicer Conant accepted the ten-pound cub on behalf of the children of Washington, Smokey was ushered into his official cage adorned with a Smokey poster with the caption "Thanks for helping prevent forest fires."

Smokey's first photo inside his cage showed a curious little cub acting as if he were trying to bite the head off the poster bear. Then Smokey ambled into a corner of his den, ignored an exercise tree with sawed-off stumps, curled up out of sight and settled down for a late-morning snooze. Smokey had done his job by giving, as one Washington paper reported, "300 squealing children a fairy-book day at the Zoo." But hybrid Gene was unimpressed; in his nearby cage, Gene slept peacefully through the entire event.

Little Smokey became an instant hit. Just as he had beguiled the folks in Santa Fe, the little cub with the forlorn look captured the hearts of Washingtonians. "Thousands lined up to see Smokey," reported the *Times-Herald* on July 3. "Lines stood four and five deep to see Smokey," claimed the July 3 *Washington Post*. "Zoo police were kept busy directing visitors to his cage above the Reptile House. 'If one person has asked me where Smokey is, a thousand have,' said one policeman."

Smokey, in fact, gained top billing in a star-studded zoo, outdrawing Gene, Ham the space monkey and another bear—a hundred-pound grizzly cub that arrived from Yellowstone National Park the day before Smokey. And the Forest Service seemed pleased with its publicity coup. Washington papers reported that Forest Service officials felt their live Smokey was "worth more than 10 tons of pamphlets" when it came to preaching a forest fire message.

With the official ceremonies completed, Pickens stayed with Lloyd Swift in Arlington, Virginia. After dinner, Pickens gave Smokey's harness to Swift's young daughter, Clara. Later, Clara Swift Aiks donated the harness to the Smokey Bear Historical State Park in Capitan, New Mexico, where it hangs today on permanent display.

A year later, Hines's plane crashed in an alfalfa field when a pilot on a search-and-rescue mission lost power after failing to switch gas tanks. When word of the crash reached Santa Fe, Ray Bell called Frank Hines. "I knew that was the plane with the pictures on its side," Bell explained. "I asked Frank if I could get the pictures. He said okay, so I flew down and landed on a gravel road between Capitan and Roswell." With his pocketknife, Bell ripped through the thin canvas sides and removed the painted panels of Smokey. "Matty Hines said to have Ruth frame them," Bell added. "She kept one and gave the other to me. I gave mine to the Forest Service in Washington, and Frank gave the other one to the Smokey Bear Museum in Capitan after Matty died."

Later, Bill Piper Sr. couldn't resist teasing Bell about Smokey's flight. "Of all the darn things," Piper chuckled. "They have enough bears here in Pennsylvania that we didn't have to go through all that rigamarole to get that New Mexico bear to Washington."

"Yeah," Bell replied, stifling his own grin. "That's true. But the difference is that none of the bears in Pennsylvania had their butts burned in a forest fire."

17

ADVERTISING'S BEAR NECESSITIES

*"We busted our butts on that account. We had a lot of fun
and I think it showed."*

— Jack Foster

*"Around the evening campfire we passed a bottle of bourbon
from one mouth to another, and the next day we flew with
throbbing hangovers in a plane held together by Scotch tape.
That was camaraderie."*

— Jim Felton

As Foote, Cone & Belding's Los Angeles office developed the campaigns
promoting forest fire prevention, hundreds of the firm's employees worked
with Southern California producers, actors, singers, technicians and artists.
Creative talents such as Don Belding, Ervin Grant, Charley Coleman, Lou
Scott, John O'Toole and Dick Stow led FCB's dedication to Smokey. But
FCB's Los Angeles office varied in size from perhaps fifty to three hundred
people, and procedures sometimes changed over Smokey's first half-century.
By allowing a few FCB staffers to represent their colleagues, however, a

composite overview of typical campaigns can illustrate the marketing of Smokey Bear to the American public.

Each year in late summer, a Forest Service delegation representing the Cooperative Forest Fire Prevention program flew from Washington, D.C., to visit FCB in downtown Los Angeles. Around a long table in a windowless conference room, the foresters met with creative director Jack Foster and several FCB staffers to plan the next fire prevention campaign. Previous years' materials were pinned on fabric walls or propped on ledges; movie and slide projectors and a video screen stood nearby.

Over glazed doughnuts washed down with hot coffee, the foresters reviewed statistics from past years and pointed out special concerns for the coming year. Although fundamental issues never changed, the CFFP's concern with specific problems requiring special attention almost always changed. One year's campaign might have to remind communities encroaching on forests about trash burning. Another might focus on hikers and campers.

Sandwiches were brought in at lunch as spirited discussions continued with both sides freely questioning. FCB probed deeply to identify problems faced by the foresters and to understand what advertising had been successful, what had been ignored and what the foresters thought should be changed.

Those sessions usually included Smokey's "national coordinator"—a post ably held from 1965 to 1977 by Jim Felton—an FCB alumnus. Virtually everyone associated with forest fire prevention respected the contributions of other parties, and it was Felton's responsibility to see that it stayed that way.

Born in Mt. Vernon, Washington, in 1914, James P. Felton became a statistic of the Depression, dropping out of the University of Washington after only two semesters to work as a copyboy for the *Seattle Times*. Felton's first reporting job—with the *San Diego Sun* for $17.50 a week—started his career as a writer and newspaper man in a variety of assignments. Felton edited the *Oxnard Press-Courier*, wrote for the *Los Angeles Daily News*, served *Time* magazine as a Los Angeles correspondent and as a New York editor, and then edited *Script* magazine in Beverly Hills. As a reporter, Felton looked askance at the advertising business—until FCB hired him in 1949 to work on its Lockheed, Sunkist and Thomas electronic organ accounts. "Right away I asked if I could work on the Smokey Bear account," Felton remembered. "I didn't get to work on it until 1952, but I eventually stayed with it for twenty-one years."

Felton served on FCB's "new business" committee. "FCB was the largest and most successful advertising agency in Los Angeles," Felton explained. "If you had a good product you automatically went to FCB. So when I heard that Seaboard Finance Company [now AVCO Financial Services] was looking for an agency, we put a presentation together and won the account." Then, when offered a job by Seaboard's president, Felton moved to Seaboard in 1961 as vice president for advertising and public relations. Four years later Russell Eller, who since 1942 had served as the only national coordinator for the forest fire prevention campaign, retired and recommended that Felton succeed him. Felton, already enamored with the program, readily agreed.

"As national coordinator, I devoted five or six weeks a year to the campaign," Felton estimated. "I traveled to New York, Washington and several state capitals to meet with state foresters every year. Russ and I had long discussions on just what a coordinator does. Mostly it was a case of being sure that the Ad Council was doing its job and the Forest Service was getting its kits out and that FCB was delivering on time. But if there was conflict between any parts, they would call me in to act as arbitrator. I could be more objective because I wasn't personally involved in any of it. If there was any disagreement of, say, the controversy over controlled burns, I would be the spokesman on behalf of the Smokey campaign to help educate the public. Sometimes a few Forest Service people wanted to use the campaign to help solve their political problems. But that was the role the national coordinator had to play—keep the campaign directed toward the group we were trying to influence. Forget the politics; the objective was still the children."

An FCB account executive also participated to ensure smooth relations with FCB's forestry client. From West Hartford, Connecticut, Nancy Budd saw advertising as an opportunity to combine her interests in communications, psychology and business. After graduating from Boston University's school of communications, Budd declared her disdain for cold weather and wound her way west to Los Angeles. Working first for an advertising agency and then as advertising manager for a small bank, Budd signed on with FCB as account executive for United California Bank. Her work with Smokey Bear began in 1977.

"Account people handle clients' needs to coordinate activities within the agency," Budd explained. "Account executives make sure everything happens when it is supposed to—that deadlines and budgets are met. It's fundamental housekeeping work. They listen to clients' needs and interpret them for the creative department. Once the campaign is developed, the account executive goes back to convince the client how the work will accomplish the client's objective. But with Smokey Bear, the creative people are very much involved in the account. There is a lot of direct communication between the client and the creative people. It's a more modern way of working with clients."

With business between the advertisers and foresters concluded by early afternoon, evenings were reserved for socializing. Sometimes they gathered at a popular Los Angeles restaurant; sometimes they congregated for beer, barbecue and Smokey business at Jim Felton's home in Altadena—the CFFP's "western headquarters." Solid friendships developed as the foresters, often on a tough per diem travel allowance that didn't go far in pricey Los Angeles, were welcomed as house guests by FCB staffers. As a natural interdependence developed, business was discussed openly and directly and neither side felt it necessary to worry about tact. Clearly, a special relationship existed.

"I cannot overstate the fond memories I have of those people," Jim Felton emphasized. "The foresters I have met and lived with are the finest bunch of people I have ever known. You get to understand them while huddled around a campfire on a snowy mountain peak in Montana or fighting chiggers in the South or inspecting a beaver dam or studying erosion control in North Carolina. Once we flew into the Bitterroot Forest in Montana on a Ford Trimotor. Around the evening campfire we passed a bottle of bourbon from one mouth to another, and the next day we flew with throbbing hangovers in a plane held together by Scotch tape. That was camaraderie."

FCB executive Lou Scott claimed that knowing the foresters was the best client relationship of his career: "I remember most the absolute dedication and commitment of the Forest Service to the Smokey program. I remember their sincerity and the love and deep affection they had for anybody contributing to the program. In my judgment, a good part of our success was the dedication of the forestry people."

"It was inspiring to talk to the people who protect our natural resources," Nancy Budd added. "They gave us a feeling that what we were doing was very worthwhile. We felt we were contributing to the country."

After the Forest Service delegation returned to Washington, it was left to FCB's creative director to bring Smokey to life, and Jack Foster filled that role from 1967 through 1988. Born in Chicago in 1930, Foster studied statistics en route to a degree in business administration from Northwestern University before serving with the U.S. Army as a prison camp guard in

218

Korea. Foster began his professional career by selling advertising for the *San Francisco Examiner* and working in sales for Mobil Oil. "Then I discovered that advertising agencies paid you to write," Foster explained. "All my life I had been writing plays, novels, poems and short stories. So I got a job in the mail room of a Los Angeles ad agency. Then I spent a year in their research department before I finally started writing advertising."

Bring out the bear in your dad.

Jack Foster, creative director for
Smokey Bear posters and
commercials at Foote, Cone &
Belding in Los Angeles, California.
(Courtesy Jack Foster.)

In 1964, FCB lured Foster to its agency, immediately lost him when his first employer doubled his salary, and then enticed him back to FCB. "I first saw Smokey Bear in the early sixties when a lot of us were developing social consciousness," Foster recalled. "We were using our talents to sell soap, but here was something we could be proud of—do our absolute best work with no limitations. But I was not the lead figure on Smokey; I just kept the flame alive. Twenty-five years of hard work had gone into Smokey Bear before I came along."

As creative director, Foster oversaw development of ideas and led the creation of polished advertising for FCB clients. "Ad agencies have a number of departments, including research, merchandising, TV production, copy, art and account departments," Foster explained. "At FCB, art, copy and TV are combined into a single 'creative department' populated by artists and writers. Art directors think of visual ideas and do layouts or storyboards. Then, if they require photos, they hire a photographer; if they require illustrations, they hire an illustrator; if they need music, they hire musicians. Some art directors could not even draw very well, but with this freelance system, agencies can pick out the right person for each project. Some agencies had illustrators on staff, but we didn't."

Among the people creating Smokey's advertising were Peter Angelos, Ann King, Judy Johnson and Len Levy.

Born and raised in New York City, Peter Angelos began writing journals at age ten. He won a journalism degree in 1975 from the University of Oregon, then worked in an ad agency mail room before becoming a copywriter. In 1977, Jack Foster hired Angelos, who became creative director after Foster retired.

Ann King, from Battle Creek, Michigan, studied art at DePauw University in Indiana before moving to New York City and graduating from Parsons School of Design in 1955. After stints at Bonwitt Teller and an advertising agency, King was hired by Foster in 1970 for what became a seventeen-year hitch. "I felt lucky to get a job there," King admitted. "I came in as an art director—the lowest of the low."

A native of Idaho Falls, Idaho, Judy Johnson was interested in art as a small child. Following her instincts, she graduated in 1971 with a B.A. degree from the Art Center College of Design in Los Angeles, and Jack Foster hired her to work for FCB. "I was very young and very cheap help," Johnson laughed. "I started as an art director and worked on Smokey Bear and some other accounts. Then a writer got fired and I had all these ads that needed to be written, so I went to Jack and he said, 'Well, you write them.' Within six months I was writing more than art directing, so I switched."

Len Levy, born in Chicago in 1926, graduated with a marketing degree from the University of Illinois in 1954 after a tour of duty in the U.S. Air Force. Working first in Chicago for a film production company and several ad agencies, Levy moved to Los Angeles to be closer to the major production centers. Jack Foster hired him in 1973.

To kick off a forest fire prevention campaign, Foster assembled his entire staff of two dozen writers and art directors. "Jack would say, 'All right. Smokey time. Let's do it,'" Angelos recalled. "Jack mobilized the whole agency, but we needed the whole agency. There were a lot of assignments."

"Smokey was an 'everybody's account,'" Foster emphasized. "Normally, artists and writers are assigned to a specific account—Mazda, Sunkist, a bank—but Smokey was a public service account and I felt everyone should have the opportunity to work on it."

On each of the dozen creative teams, an art director structured ads by focusing on layout, color, illustrations, photos and general themes. "An art director is not an artist per se," King stressed. "We are creative people. We have an art background, and we can draw. But it's more the conceptual ability that counts."

"You may have a picture of a smiling bear," Johnson added. "But how big is the bear? What will the bear look like? What kind of typeface? Those questions are the responsibility of an art director. But writers are responsible for the words. A writer would write a headline about why the bear is smiling." Always, the two professionals worked on concepts as a team, feeding off each other's creativity.

As they assembled, each staffer knew that he or she would commit the equivalent of ten full working days to Smokey. Although pleased to provide public service time, FCB received no money for its efforts and couldn't stay in business if it didn't meet its contractual obligations to paying clients. So while Foster's staff theoretically could work on forest fire prevention at the office, little time actually was available for Smokey because of the firm's frenetic work pace. Smokey simply had to be squeezed in between jobs or at night and on weekends. So what did FCB's creative people think of that arrangement?

"Smokey Bear was the most fun we had at the agency," Angelos contended. "It was a great cause and everyone believed in it."

"It was a relief to work on [Smokey]," King agreed, "because you could get ideas through. You could have a wonderful idea for a bank, but you wouldn't be allowed to do it. You got beat up a lot on the regular stuff, so it was great to work on Smokey."

"Smokey Bear was a great opportunity," Levy concurred. "I consider it one of the most heart-felt things I have ever done. I felt it had a deeper meaning, and records showed the campaign was working; at least someone was listening. Both the nature of the program and the freedom were important—we had no creative supervision by the client."

"We always stipulated that it was volunteer work that must not interfere with regular work," Foster explained. "But we never found anyone that did *not* want to work on the Smokey account. It was hands-down, no contest, the best account I ever worked on. The account gave everyone in the creative department a chance to shine. All those people loved that account; they had the feeling that it was their account, and it was unbelievable how it worked."

"There was a magic about the account," Jim Felton acknowledged. "There's no question that the up-and-coming people in the agency wanted to be involved with that campaign. There was a lot of competition to work on the account."

"The budget was determined by the Forest Service," Nancy Budd explained. "We ran on a two-year budgeting process. We might do poster and TV ads one year and reissue old printed materials. Then, the next year, we'd use old TV and new print materials. The budget allocation started with television because that was the most expensive. Whatever was left over would determine how much original print or radio material could be produced for that year."

Planning strategy for a national campaign quickly becomes a juggling act. Multiple objectives, audiences and regional needs conflict with budgets and time limitations, and the persuasiveness of different media is evaluated. But strategy development helps an agency focus on the people they want to reach, what they want to say and how to position their client against competition. Only after strategy was planned could FCB create Smokey's advertising.

"Sometimes a creative strategy takes on its own personality," Jack Foster explained, "but this was not true in Smokey's case because Smokey had so many different audiences. We had the same basic creative strategy each year because the basic message—'prevent forest fires'—never changed. The competition—carelessness—was always the same too. Smokey wasn't like packaged goods or an automobile."

Although basics never changed, FCB still crafted new ideas each year as Foster assigned individual teams to particular areas—radio, TV, magazines, billboards, newspapers and, of course, the poster—the very personification of Smokey Bear.

Smokey's campaigns began with, and often revolved around, a basic poster. Those colorful posters adorned hardware stores, decorated post offices, signaled park entrances and plugged Smokey wherever automobile passengers could see him. Although multiple posters might be used, each year's primary poster reflected a special emphasis identified by the foresters. "Sometimes the Forest Service liked to have a 'green' year and then a 'red' year," Jack Foster revealed. "In a green year, the message would be positive, and posters would show beautiful green forests, with messages to the effect of 'Let's keep them that way.' In a red year, posters would show destruction, with messages about the dangers of carelessness. It was a nice idea that continually varied the message."

A green, upbeat poster might show a smiling Smokey in a lush forest with birds and deer adding color to imagined music wafting on a gentle

One of many Smokey Bear posters created
by Foote, Cone & Belding in Los Angeles,
California. *(Courtesy USDA Forest Service.)*

breeze. But a red poster would illustrate a burned, ruined forest with starving, homeless animals and a grim Smokey sternly chastising careless humans for their assault on his forest home. "The strategy," Len Levy explained, "was to tell people that all of the destruction—not only the raw destruction of timber, but also what it does to the environment—can be no more than a carelessly tossed cigarette or an unattended campfire. Some was educational; some was hitting with dramatic impact. We were scaring them, essentially, into being careful."

"The poster was very important from a Forest Service standpoint," Foster added. "They posted it everywhere and gave it out at schools. TV dominated after a while, but we always started with the basic poster and sometimes a range poster—not necessarily about forest fires—for states like the Dakotas and Montana. The kids' posters that went to schoolrooms for kindergarten, first and second grades almost always were built around the theme that Smokey's friends don't play with matches, and they almost always had Smokey in them. Then we would do an education poster—about trees or how to be careful in the woods with fire—to help teachers teach kids about safety. Then Ann King developed a whole series of nature posters that were a huge success. Ann is a magnificent designer and she thought them up all by herself. Ann's enthusiasm for Smokey ignited the whole agency."

But regardless of their charm, Smokey's posters weren't the vehicle to reach most Americans. Limited poster distribution simply couldn't influence human activities in thousands of wooded areas on private land or on the fringe of state and national forests. In a sense, the posters provided collateral support for a larger campaign.

Television is viewed by the advertising industry as the single most powerful medium. TV assaults senses with both sight and sound, adds a dimension of motion, offers high-quality color and graphics and allows for the element of surprise. Through its networks, TV functions as a mass medium reaching tens of millions of people, but it also permits geographic selectivity through regional broadcasting.

TV has drawbacks too. Viewers swamped with commercials cannot absorb every message, and their minds may be in a low inquisitive state as they channel surf or dash to the refrigerator. So effective TV ads must be unique, recognizable and personal.

"The whole strategy was to know the consumer," King explained. "We were trying to be respectful. No one asked us into their homes. We had to be considerate; we had to entertain or enlighten; we didn't want to talk down to people. Smokey Bear made our point because he was recognizable and friendly, but we still tried to get a mental pledge—what we talk about as the 'call to action.' That's why we used the phrase 'Repeat after me' so often."

Many Americans assume that Smokey's TV commercials must be aimed at kids. They also assume that TV would have capitalized on the enormous popularity of the live Smokey in the National Zoo. But neither assumption is correct.

"Smokey's TV spots are not designed for kids," Len Levy, producer of thirty Smokey commercials, insisted. "They are designed for a broad spectrum because we have no control over when the commercials run. TV stations run them when they can't sell ads or have some spare time. They can be run at two o'clock in the morning, so ads *have* to be designed for the general population."

Although many FCB staffers liked the living Smokey Bear, most thought that a living symbol had no value from an advertising standpoint. Smokey was, after all, a purely fictional advertising creation that had done his job well. Rarely, in fact, did the caricature Smokey appear on television. "We didn't use the Smokey figure a lot in TV," Ann King explained. "We signed off with his head, but generally didn't use the whole bear."

"The Smokey campaign was much more than a live bear," Peter Angelos agreed. "We never used the live bear in our advertising. With an ad, you have one chance; Smokey's face is as recognizable as Santa Claus; you gotta go with it."

So FCB created forest fire prevention TV commercials with adults in mind. "We initially developed perhaps twenty ideas," Levy recalled. "Through internal reviews with the creative director, those ideas were distilled to perhaps six or seven for presentation to the Forest Service."

As with commercial clients, FCB did not incur the expense of actually producing TV spots at that preliminary stage. "We developed storyboards," Judy Johnson explained. "Storyboards are simply a series of pictures drawn on paper that show what a commercial would look like."

Although FCB sometimes tried to develop commercials reflecting the annual poster theme, a tie-in often became irrelevant despite the best efforts of FCB and the Ad Council. "One of the problems," Levy added, "was that we advised stations to run the ads within one year because that was the time for which the talent had been cleared. But they ran what they liked. Some ads struck a responsive chord or station directors just had a personal preference for an ad. Sometimes we saw a spot prepared two years earlier, so we had to paint with a very broad brush."

But the ultimate viewers—the American public—were not FCB's primary consideration. The issue was simple: would anyone ever see Smokey's ads?

"All the Ad Council could do was send out materials," Foster shrugged. "Then the media had to ask themselves two questions: Do I run anything? And if so, what do I run? The media are not required to run public service ads. So Smokey materials had to be good enough to attract attention and then beat out other public service issues. We interviewed TV station managers to get a feel for what kind of people they were and what they wanted."

"The name of the game is to get the stuff run," Johnson concurred. "That's the whole secret. TV stations will run public service ads, but it doesn't have to be your stuff. It could be something for the American Cancer Society or drugs. The subject is up to them, so we tried to do ads they would like."

In contrast to television, radio offers only one dimension—sound—but can aim it at both the masses and selected geographic areas. As with TV, listeners expect intrusion, time limitations restrict an ad to a single point and the element of surprise can be used to an advertiser's benefit. Because people listen to radio while showering, driving or cleaning house, however, an advertiser can't count on intense interest.

Radio's greatest advantage from Smokey's viewpoint is the access it offers to attitude groups. "On radio, we did a lot of 'narrow casting,' as opposed to true TV-type 'broadcasting,'" Foster stressed. "Radio stations have target audiences—everything from top forty to classical to rock to sports. We tried to have a radio commercial for whatever narrow band some radio station was using. In a given year, we may have created twenty different styles of radio commercials for different audiences. It was really successful; we got more public service time and space than anyone else did for a long time."

"TV and newspapers have to be able to run 'horizontal' over a wide spectrum," Johnson added. "But on radio, the idea was to make it vertical rather than horizontal so that we were formatting for individual radio stations. We would do news spots, and then a country and western spot, and then rock and roll so they fit the format of stations. Then we would prepare a write-up so the stations could see that the ads were formatted. With vertical marketing, you focus on very narrow targets like you do with magazines. But the idea wasn't aimed at the audiences, it was aimed at getting the station managers to run our ads."

Foster insisted that everyone generate ideas for radio ads. "Developing radio spots is best with a team," Johnson added. "Radio isn't just writing. With a team, you're using another ear. Art directors have a great sense of nuance and have a feel for sound effects." And when preliminary radio ads were selected, FCB recorded sixty-second demonstration spots with attendant sound effects—an inexpensive but effective way for the Forest Service to review proposed ads.

Magazines—which allow extensive use of photos, illustrations and the best color—offered friendly territory for FCB because reader interest could be more intense than in other media. Readers can ignore ads or quickly turn pages, but readers also may flip through a magazine several times. Advertisers typically view magazines as a selective medium because most magazines focus on narrow interests. Running, fashion, food, soccer, environment, travel and literature magazines offer splendid opportunities for narrow casting.

"We segmented audiences with magazine ads because we could focus on special interests," Foster explained. "An ad for *Field & Stream* might address campers and hunters; a teen magazine would address youngsters; and a motorcycle magazine would address bikers. We liked to focus messages so they were specifically talking a reader's language."

"An ad in a woman's magazine," King added, "may include a needlepoint pattern that readers could make themselves. The headline would say, 'Stitch yourself a lesson. Teach your children to be careful.' But we tried to do general things—more serious and newsworthy—for *Time* magazine. We did different things for sports magazines too—ads with old wooden golf clubs, baseball bats—sports equipment made from wood."

Foster's group also developed newspaper and billboard ads. Newspapers offer geographical selectivity and, in multi-paper areas such as New York, attitude selectivity as well. And because they allow uninterrupted concentration, newspapers provide ideal conditions for advertisers. A morning cup of hot coffee and a newspaper can put a reader in a receptive frame of mind. A railway commuter may linger over each page; another reader may be trapped in a bathroom. And surveys reveal that ads can be a primary reason for buying newspapers.

"Everyone in the creative department contributed ideas," Foster explained. "We would get together on Saturdays and review progress, and if we found holes I made additional assignments. If no one did, say, motorcycle magazine ads or the school posters, then I would assign those."

But Foster kept his staff focused. "Whenever someone tried to be avant-garde or smart ass or wisecracky, it never seemed right," Foster asserted. "Smokey was a serious bear delivering a serious message. We always thought of Smokey as a person; I never consciously thought about him as a bear. Of course, we would argue, as ad people are wont to do, about minutia. I remember the time [account executive] Ed Wilson and I spent an hour arguing over the underline in 'Only *you* can prevent forest fires.' I wanted it out; he wanted it to stay in. I won and he didn't speak to me for a month. Yes—a month. It just shows, I guess, the strong feelings Smokey Bear generated."

In late fall, three FCB staffers visited Forest Service headquarters at 14th and Independence in Washington, D.C. For a day and a half, FCB showed proposals for the next campaign, explaining plans for posters, radio, TV, newspapers, magazines and billboards.

"If the Forest Service wanted one basic poster," Foster explained, "we presented ten or twenty or even thirty sketch ideas in color and correct size, but not finished. We had storyboards for TV. Radio ideas were recorded, or someone read them. Sometimes we brought in a piano or guitar player to sing the lyrics to a ditty. We didn't spend a lot of money on these presentations; our client didn't have the money and, given the relationship, it wasn't necessary. We made recommendations, and the Forest Service usually followed them."

"Some ads would strike a responsive chord more than others," Len Levy added, "but we would eventually end up with two to four thirty-second TV spots and at least four to eight radio spots. The budget ran from maybe twenty thousand to fifty thousand dollars for the entire package."

"We always got a lot of help from the Forest Service too—especially in the artistic areas," Foster confirmed. "Rudy Wendelin was keeper of the flame. Rudy was the person who kept everyone honest. Sometimes creative people wanted to take off on a tangent, or artists would go a little too far, but Rudy kept them with the image. As styles changed, we sometimes tried to keep Smokey up to date; once we tried to do Smokey in airbrush to keep him modern, but the Forest Service thought it was too bold a step forward. Over and over, if I weakened, someone in the Forest Service would not weaken."

But sometimes the tempering faction was on the other side. "Grass and range fires sometimes may be the most devastating," Peter Angelos explained, "so in 1986 there was a proposal to change the slogan to 'Only you can prevent wildfires.' We said we would do specific ads for wildfires, but asked them to please not change the line. We understood that a state such as South Dakota may not have as many forests, but we believed that people could get the message generically."

"If they [the foresters] had an objection, it was usually valid," Foster emphasized. "If they said it would not work, we would not even argue. It was a rare relationship. In advertising, you're almost always dealing with buttoned-up, sophisticated MBAs; you're up against city folk. But the Forest Service people are down-to-earth country folk; it was a joy and a breath of fresh air to deal with them."

Then FCB refined the chosen items and presented them to the Advertising Council in New York. "The Ad Council scheduled a whole day for public service presentations," Angelos offered. "Our presentation lasted about two hours, and we showed TV storyboards, radio spots, the poster and print ads in different size configurations. We usually had about twenty ads for newspapers, ten for magazines and two or three for outdoor boards."

"The Ad Council is supposed to approve campaign materials before they go to the client," Nancy Budd stressed. "The Ad Council is supposed to be sure it is the best it can be, because a client usually doesn't know enough to judge. But the Forest Service and FCB worked together so much that the Ad Council didn't approve much. Later, the Ad Council reproduced the material, which is the largest part of the cost of items such as billboards, and handled all national distribution, although the Forest Service distributed within the Forest Service and maybe the state forestry associations. The Ad Council billed back 'hard costs,' as did FCB. They both donate man-hours only."

"After approval," Foster continued, "we returned to Los Angeles and hired artists, recording stars, cameramen and producers. Nearly all the art was cheaper than it would have been for a regular client. Selecting artists was not contingent on their doing it for free, but we did not want to pay full costs. When art directors hired outside artists, almost always they said, 'We are doing this for free; we don't expect you to take a bath, but it should be much, much less than you would normally charge.'"

Shooting a thirty-second Smokey Bear TV commercial could consume a full day after location, cast and backdrops were selected. FCB sent a writer, an art director and a producer on location to review lighting, filming techniques, dress, color and other details with the director. An FCB internal producer such as Len Levy hired a director and a production company, shot the commercial, hired and recorded a "voice," added sound effects and edited the finished product.

"We used a lot of different studios," Levy explained. "It depended on current relationships. If we had a crew shooting for three days for another client, we could buy the rest of the week for very little extra. Sometimes we asked studios if they could shoot on downtime or when their crews were there with nothing to do; then they usually did it for their direct out-of-

Hundreds of Hollywood's brightest stars flocked to Smokey's cause.
(Courtesy W. W. Bergoffen and USDA Forest Service. Drawing by Rudy Wendelin.)

pocket costs. We had an advantage because we had a fairly long period of time to prepare the work."

Over time, FCB incorporated contributions from hundreds of celebrities into fire prevention ads. Louis Armstrong, John Wayne, James Mason, Ella Fitzgerald and Leonard Nemoy were just a few who willingly cooperated. "I was never turned down by a celebrity," Levy acknowledged. "Fire is part of the culture in California, so an offer to help Smokey Bear was always accepted. The biggest problem was scheduling. We would want to film during a certain week, and the star would be on a shoot, but we could get them if we were flexible. We got celebrities to do the voice work for radio, but TV usually took too much time to expect them to act in the commercials."

"We used people you would never think of for Smokey Bear," Peter Angelos added. "Once we used Mickey Hart of the Grateful Dead, and all he wanted was a Smokey poster. We used Aretha Franklin, Kareem Abdul Jabbar and dozens of singers."

"Lordy, what a kick," Jack Foster exclaimed as he looked back at the many recording sessions. "Joanne Collins arrived without a guitar because she wanted to sing 'America the Beautiful' a cappella. Rudy Vallee sang through a megaphone. After singing a song we had written in English, Vicki Carr wanted to sing it in Spanish, so she sat down and translated it right there while the orchestra waited. When I complained to Bob Hite, the wild-haired leader of Canned Heat, that I couldn't understand the lyrics to his Smokey Bear song, he said, 'The kids'll dig it, skinhead.'"

"Because Smokey Bear is public service," Judy Johnson added, "you can get famous people to do commercials and they charge one dollar and, under union rules, can waive residuals. We paid Jonathan Winters one dollar and he invited us to his house afterward. But a commercial Johnson did with Ray Charles perhaps best illustrates FCB's creativity.

"I originally designed a Ray Charles commercial for radio," Johnson beamed. "I called him, and he said he'd do it, but that 'We'll call you.' A year later, they called and said, 'Tomorrow, but bring a braille script.' So I scrambled around and got the script in braille and then went to Tangerine Studios in Los Angeles and taped the script. It went real quick and took only a few minutes. Then, on impulse, I asked Mr. Charles if I could use it for TV as well. He said, 'Yes, as long as you use it—that's all I care about.'"

But Johnson needed help polishing her idea. "I asked Jack Foster what picture to use," she continued, "and after a lot of talking we finally decided to use no picture at all. But the networks went crazy. They said we couldn't do it—that people would think their TVs were broken. But I wanted just a black screen with Ray Charles's voice. Then [account executive] Charley

Coleman came up with the idea to put a title that said, 'A personal viewpoint' in white type on a black screen. I had to go to New York and meet with the Ad Council for a whole day to talk them into it, but it was a classic. I am proudest of that of anything I have ever done. What a beautiful man Ray Charles was to work with! What an experience! I was twenty-three years old."

"Then we took the materials to Washington early in the spring," Foster explained. "It was a perk for the people who worked on the account. Usually the chief of the Forest Service would attend with a hundred or so participants. We presented the materials and got their comments." With all the trappings of a mere formality, the three-hour morning meeting nevertheless generated intense interest.

"The Forest Service always had an open presentation," Levy added. "Information would be published in advance. Lots of organizations would be there representing private interests such as the timber companies and environmental groups."

So what did FCB produce? How can its posters, ads and commercials be characterized? In one phrase: a continuing triumph.

Although the great Smokey Bear posters tended to follow common themes—instructional, a word of thanks, shameful waste, religious—they became instant collector's items each year. Colorful, attention-getting and forceful, FCB's posters repeatedly hammered home the fundamental themes of forest fire prevention. But it was in the national media where FCB did its best and most memorable work.

Television demanded the very best work from FCB, and the agency delivered year after year after year as it attacked the issue of carelessness in the nation's forests through widely varying approaches. In the process, FCB produced some of the most imaginative, powerful and persuasive messages ever seen on American TV. FCB aimed thought-provoking ads directly at the hearts of the nation's citizens with visuals and text that often kept people thinking long after Smokey's signature logo had faded from the screen. Perhaps each commercial earned its own descriptive characterization.

Instructional. The earliest commercials in 1950 and 1951 featured a caricature of Smokey lecturing and emphasizing principles of proper fire behavior in forests.

Patriotic. Over the sound of a drumroll and visual renderings of famous American paintings, "Liberty Tree" appealed to the viewers' sense of history. "The first stirrings of America's freedom began under the Liberty Tree. The

232

pine tree schilling was our first coin, and George Washington's cherry tree our first tall tale. Names like 'Old Hickory' and 'Abe the rail splitter' just naturally seemed to fit our country's giants. Our legends—Johnny Appleseed, Paul Bunyan, Davy Crockett—come from the forest. We built our churches, our homes, our tools, our rifles, our toys, our books—all from trees. We traveled West on wooden wagons and canoes, and blazed a path to the ocean on wooden ties. America and America's forest have grown up together. So please be careful with fire, because a country without its forests is a country without its future."

Accusative. As giant dominoes toppled with thundering echoes, "Dominoes" explained the facts of life. "A fish died because it couldn't breath. Because its gills got clogged with silt. Because mud ran into the river. Because there was nothing to trap the rain. Because all the trees were gone. Because someone got careless with fire."

Shuddering. In "Slow Burn," a single match ignites, and a fire spreads wider and wider while the attendant sound of burning grows into a spine-tingling roar. "Matches don't start forest fires; people do. Next time, think before you strike."

Threatening. In a tranquil forest of owls, squirrels, deer and ponds, a crunching footstep echoes in "Deadliest Animal" before a lighted match drops into a bed of pine needles. "The deadliest animal in the forest isn't the biggest, or even the strongest. The deadliest animal rarely travels alone. It fears the darkness, but it's cunning and it strikes without a moment's notice. Each year, nine out of every ten forest fires are started by these animals. The deadly ones. The ones with the brains."

Tearjerker. As "America the Beautiful" plays in the background, a lighted match drops onto a red, white and blue flag map of America, and the entire map burns: "One careless second with a match and America the Beautiful becomes America the Ugly."

Lump in the throat. A camera pans a giant fir tree in "Vanishing American" while music and voices recreate America's history. "In the time it takes to grow a tree, you can grow a country. It only takes a minute to wipe out a century. A flash, and then nothing. Then even the birds won't come any more."

Gut-wrenching. Feet of a small girl and older man plod across a desert in the opening of "Oxygen Mask." "When I was your age, pumpkin, there were trees everywhere. But people got careless, and every year they started forest fires. All the trees burned down and all the birds died. 'Cause without trees, there's no air, so everything dies." The camera then pulls back to show both figures wearing gas masks in a barren countryside: "Grandpa, I wish I could bring back the trees for you."

Beautiful. Ray Charles plays his piano, with "A Personal Viewpoint" displayed in white across the bottom of an otherwise blank screen. "I like the way the forest sounds. The way the leaves rustle in the wind and fall to the ground and crunch under your feet. The way the birds sing and the chipmunks chatter. The way a squirrel scrambles up a tree. That's why I'm asking you to please be careful with fire, because when we lose a forest, we lose a lot more than meets the eye. I ought to know. I'm Ray Charles."

Comical. In "Jonathan Winters," the comic stands decorated with evergreen limbs and recites a litany of problems he faces as a tree—wind, cold, and pesky insects. "The worst danger I face is fire. Everybody wants to live a long time. Even a tree."

Admonishing. In "Campfire," two men hover near a fire in a wooded glade. "Over two million years ago, prehistoric man discovered fire. He learned how to cook with it, stay warm with it, even light up the darkest night with it. But he never learned how to be careful with fire in the forest. After two million years in the forest, isn't it time we acted our age?"

Grim. In "Rock Hudson," the actor holds the reins of his horse in the smoking, charred remains of a burned forest. "Hello. I'm filming in Sequoia National Forest here in California. This area was once green and alive. Have you ever seen a forest destroyed by fire? Do you know what it takes to restore the beauty and productivity of the land? Take a good look at the destruction here. Fire safety is so easy."

Without visual impact, radio commercials couldn't hit as hard as their TV counterparts, but they usually featured Hollywood celebrities and were no less effective.

Gregory Peck offered his distinctive voice: "For everything there is a season. A time to live, and a time to die. A bird's time in the forest may only be four years—a squirrel's perhaps five. A deer may only see eleven summers—a rabbit just four. Life is short enough in the forest. Please, don't make it shorter."

Rodney Dangerfield chimed in: "Hey, did you ever think what it's like to be a tree in a forest? Well, let me tell you: as a tree, I don't get no respect."

"Hi. This is Glenn Campbell and I'm here to do a little down home talking for old Smokey the Bear."

"Okay, Chipmunks. Let's all sing Smokey Bear's ABC rules song."

"Homer? Yes, Jethro? You know matches don't cause forest fires—people do. Any dang fool knows that. Homer, let's give old Smokey a break."

"This is Jack Webb." "I'm Barbara Mandrell." "I'm Mickey Hart." "This is Lorne Greene." "This is James Mason." "This is Lee J. Cobb." "This is Andy Griffith."

The Ad Council typically mailed TV kits in early April. The 1968 kits, for example, cost the CFFP $20.02 each for four-color spots featuring "Smokejumper" a 60-second dramatization with action footage from a Walt Disney film. Other spots included 60-, 30-, 20- and 10-second versions of a cartoon message from "Bullwinkle" and reprints of Rod Sterling in "Careless Killer." Kits included a cover letter from national coordinator Jim Felton, forest fire fact sheets, "live" scripts and a color slide for on-camera use.

Through 1965, most stations were sent black-and-white ads, with colored spots mailed on request. But in 1966 the Ad Council sent color materials to 179 stations that broadcast in color, and in 1967 distributed color materials to all TV stations—even those broadcasting only in black-and-white. Mal Hardy, CFFP program director, reasoned in his 1966 annual report, "We consider it good business to be a little ahead of demand. Most of the stations that don't get color equipment in 1966 will convert in 1967."

In March, the Ad Council distributed radio packages to 4,800 radio stations and to state and federal foresters. In 1965, for example, a seven-inch, 33 1/3 rpm pressing in a two-color jacket featured the New Christy Minstrels singing their famous "Green, Green" with special Smokey lyrics, in 60- and 30-second versions. In addition, a range fire prevention kit and live scripts were mailed to 1,006 stations in western states.

The 1968 kit featured ten recordings of popular messages from prior years, a sales pitch from Felton, a forest fire fact sheet and six scripts for live readings. In April, the CPPF mailed kits and platters to field offices at an average cost for pressings, materials and postage of 73 cents per kit. Surveys indicated that the money was well spent: radio stations in forest areas broadcast an average 138 forest fire prevention messages per station.

In a typical year Smokey's print ads were mailed to 3,900 "house" magazines, 350 consumer magazines, and such popular periodicals as *Time, Fortune, Field & Stream, Good Housekeeping, Farm Journal, Reader's Digest, Ladies Home Journal* and even *Penthouse* ("Remember, there are babes in the woods"). Highly focused supplemental ads sometimes were distributed; in one year a special "Tough Guy" ad was sent to 175 men's magazines.

No matter how solid the response, the Ad Council kept trying to do better. In 1966 the council issued magazine ad proof books in lieu of color separates used in earlier years. First sent to 400 selected publishers, the proof books were credited with almost tripling the contribution of Smokey advertising pages in 1966.

On the newspaper side, more than 8,000 editors typically received fire prevention ads. Most were offered a choice of mats or reproducible proofs, with the sheets printed on a coated paper of sufficient quality to allow ads to be directly reproduced. Again, special materials often were produced, for example, in 1967 when FCB created thirteen ads for an Ad Council newspaper promotion; those ads combined splashy art with provocative messages, resulting in 538 newspapers donating space for more than 5,000 Smokey ads. In appreciation, cooperating editors received prompt thank-you letters from Smokey.

Finally, "outdoor" materials for as many as 3,500 Smokey Bear billboards typically were distributed annually.

When each year's results were tallied, it was clear that FCB and the Ad Council continued to be phenomenally successful. Ad Council surveys for 1971, for example, showed that network TV recorded more than 3 billion viewer "impressions" for Smokey, network radio impressions approached 10 billion and newspapers ran more than 2 million lines of copy. Consumer magazines ran hundreds of ads, and almost 100,000 car cards were posted.

Impressive as they are, these numbers do not reflect the public's entire exposure to Smokey. Not included were fire prevention messages shown on the syndicated series of Smokey Bear animated shows, gratuitous TV plugs, exposure on cable TV systems or thousands of locally promoted community newspaper ads. Also uncounted were supplemental materials produced by state and federal agencies.

"We had no control over Rudy Wendelin and the Washington office," Nancy Budd explained. "They had their own group of things, such as school kits, that the Forest Service distributed. We looked at them and gave comments on direction, but usually they were items that did not require the level of creative talent that was available from FCB. It was a matter of using resources where they were best suited. But it worked out well; different talents were used in different areas for different products."

Many radio commercials were produced outside FCB. In addition to the radio ads prepared in Washington, D.C., state fire prevention authorities frequently developed their own commercials. "States tend to do their own radio," Ann King acknowledged. "Everyone has different fire seasons, but we tried to overlap the nation as much as we could."

"The Forest Service continued to produce radio commercials with Jackson Weaver too," Jack Foster added. "But we didn't view that as a challenge. With Smokey, if anyone wanted to do anything, I was thrilled.

Just get the message across that we were burning up our forests. We had no proprietary interests."

Anyone questioning FCB's dedication to forest fire prevention only had to measure FCB's work against that of its peers, where FCB regularly won award after award. Smokey Bear radio and TV commercials and print ads repeatedly reaped honors from such diverse groups as the Art Directors Club of Los Angeles, the Western Region of the American Advertising Federation competition in San Francisco, the Don Belding contest, the North American Forestry Commission's International Festival, the Hollywood Advertising Club, the Exhibition of Advertising and Editorial Art in the West, the National Safety Congress, the American Association of Agricultural College Editors and the Cannes International Film Festival.

Awarded under different names and for different reasons, top honors went repeatedly to FCB: "One of the 100 Best Television Commercials"; "Award of Distinctive Merit"; "Certificate of Merit"; "Best in the West"; "Sweepstakes Award"; "Supreme Award"; "Bronze Lion"; "Silver Lion"; "Top Ten"; "Best Individual Public Service Ad"; and "Excellent." It didn't seem to matter—FCB won them all. One year, of all the TV spots submitted for the Cannes Film Festival competition by all FCB offices, only three won awards—and two of those were for forest fire prevention. (CFFP headquarters reacted by sending telegrams to 459 TV stations asking for continued use of the ads.)

"Public service accounts cost the agency money," Len Levy admitted. "But it is good public relations—great prestige. FCB won *many* awards [for Smokey Bear work] for print, writing, radio and TV. They won Clio awards, ANDY awards, Communicating Arts awards, New York Radio awards, Advertising Foundation awards and awards from the United States Television Commercials Festival. There was a period of time when FCB stepped out of the awards applications because they took so many that it became meaningless."

So what accounted for FCB's continuing success with forest fire prevention? "For one thing," Jack Foster admitted, "people loved Smokey. For another thing, we busted our butts on that account. We had a lot of fun and I think it showed. With Smokey Bear, we knew we could do the best work in the world because there were no restrictions on creativity. We were motivated because it was a meaningful account—it was helping make the world a better place. Not all accounts are like that."

Although they never charged the Forest Service for their time or that sparkling creativity, FCB harvested a landslide of awards and reaped other

237

benefits—a sense of contribution to the nation, a chance to spread their organizational wings, a window for people development and an opportunity to open doors to new accounts.

Jack Foster believed forest fire prevention helped his agency more than any other account. "FCB on the West Coast was sort of autonomous," Foster explained, "so we could practically do what we wanted. A creative department is not a profit center, so I didn't have to worry about making a profit. Although Lou Scott, John O'Toole and our management were trying to make a profit, they still supported us; I really admired them for that. Management was as much if not more committed to the program."

"Public service advertising illustrates what your people can do," Lou Scott, former chairman of FCB's executive committee, acknowledged. "We took it very seriously and put our best people on the account. It was a creative challenge; they loved it and some great work came out as a result. It was a valuable thing for FCB too, and it opened a lot of doors. We never regretted a dime of the money we invested in talent for the forest fire prevention program."

"The fact that the Smokey campaign was born on their back porch was a major factor too," Jim Felton added. "If you open the door some morning and there's an orphan there, you take care of that orphan the rest of your life and don't let anyone else in on it. The Smokey campaign was praised so highly and became so popular that FCB used it in every new business pitch they ever made. If FCB went to Ford Motor Company, Ford didn't know beans about FCB, but they sure knew Smokey. Because it was so highly successful, FCB wouldn't dare let anyone else try to get a piece of it."

Former FCB chairman John O'Toole agreed: "We used the Smokey advertising on our demonstration reels because it was the highest quality. We regarded forest fire prevention as one of our most important accounts regardless of the fact that it did not bring in any income. It was really prestigious because when you are a Los Angeles agency, most of the work is regional. But Smokey Bear was national, and business prospects would say, 'Wow, I didn't know you people did that.'"

18

THE GREAT SMOKEY BEAR ARTISTS

"Smokey is very personal to me. I always felt like he was somewhere down the hall directing the operation."
— Rudy Wendelin

Communication is the cornerstone of America's forest fire prevention effort, and despite his humble birth as a mere poster bear, Smokey demonstrated his communication skills through television, radio, magazines, newspapers and billboards. By 1955, Smokey's familiar face reached almost every American family, and it all began on artists' drawing boards.

Because of the tidal wave of mail swamping Washington, D.C., the Forest Service recognized the impact of Smokey Bear as an effective communicator. When those perceptions were relayed to Foote, Cone & Belding in Los Angeles, that agency, too, understood the power of its crusading bruin. And because they realized that Smokey influenced children to a far greater extent than expected, FCB copywriters took special care to carefully craft the bear's personality.

But consistent representation of Smokey's appealing figure weighed heavily in determining public acceptance, so the nuturing of Smokey's character and the preservation of his public image depended upon the great Smokey Bear artists.

Although the Smokey Bear Americans see today sports the same determined, dedicated attitude about fighting fires as he did in 1945, his physical characteristics have changed significantly since that first public appearance.

Albert Staehle's 1945 and 1946 bears looked like, well, bears. Staehle drew Smokey with a pointed snout, limpid eyes surrounded by fur, cylindrical ears crawling over his hat, long hair, protruding claws and a massive, grizzly-style humped back. Smokey's head looked a little small on his powerful torso, and a chin strap held his hat in place. But the Smokey that became famous was a much different character from Staehle's, and most of the evolution to today's familiar face occurred over a short period of time.

Smokey's development lay primarily in the very capable hands of Dick Stow and Rudy Wendelin. Working behind the scenes in Los Angeles, Stow carefully directed the early interpretations and graphic conceptions of Smokey that were portrayed by the artists he hired. In Washington, D.C., Wendelin became the most productive and, eventually, the best known of the great Smokey Bear artists. In Atlanta, Georgia, Harry Rossoll became perhaps the most visible Smokey artist. But dozens of others—including Russ Wetzel, James Hansen, Chuck Kuderna, Craig Pineo, Merv Corning, T. Wright, Richard Foes, Ken Smith, Elmo White, Joshua Meador, Robert Poole and Ren Wicks—were involved.

To a certain extent, Smokey Bear developed simultaneously in both Los Angeles and Washington, D.C., and admirers of Stow and Wendelin happily point to each man as the person most responsible for the evolution of Smokey. It can be argued, however, that no single person is "most responsible" for Smokey's image. The great Smokey Bear artists were quick to accept suggestions from colleagues and may not have even realized that they were influencing, or being influenced by, other artists. Regardless of who created the ideas or who applied the brush strokes, the Smokey Bear we know and love is the product of the collective talents and creative minds of several artists.

Pleased with the public acceptance of Staehle's early bears, FCB hired Russ Wetzel, a Chicago cartoonist and illustrator, to finalize the 1947 Smokey poster. Wetzel's interpretation featured a cartoon-type caricature with a rotund stomach and a shiny bulb nose topping a short, deep snout that claimed the lower two-thirds of Smokey's face. Arched eyes with tiny pupils, a full lower lip, smaller and lower ears, a shorter neck and a comical expression completed the transformation on Wetzel's larger head topped with a more pointed hat sans chin strap. "Possibilities seemed endless for this type of characterization," Rudy Wendelin explained. "Animation would be easily effected, incorporating a wide variety of situations suitable for communicating ideas appealing to children." But Wetzel was not destined to continue with Smokey. "The national committee rejected the Wetzel interpretation the next year," Wendelin added. "It thought the character was too cartoonish and could not communicate a serious message."

James Hansen's 1948 "praying bear" may have been the most popular early rendition of Smokey. Originally drawn with sharp, protruding claws and no hat, Hansen's version was a direct ancestor of today's bear and completed the preliminary transition to a human-looking bear. Hansen placed small ears high on the rear of Smokey's head, shortened the depth of his snout, pulled fur back from his eyes, shortened his lower lip and removed his bulb nose and most of the expression from his face. "Hansen was a well-known animal illustrator and sculptor from San Francisco," Wendelin recalled. "He could render fur and expressions very well. Hansen did beautiful work and drew a number of the early posters, including the praying bear—a mature, bareheaded bear in a kneeling position with folded paws surrounded by small woodland animals on the edge of a forest. The caption ["And please make people more careful"] communicated an appealing message, which hit the public fancy. The pattern was set by Hansen more than anyone."

In 1949, Hansen added back Wetzel's high-pointed hat, increased the size of Smokey's paws, and in his original drawings, included sharp fangs and claws. Hansen drew Smokey again in 1950 and created a close cousin of today's bear with fur surrounding slightly larger eyes and a smaller, shorter snout. On this imposing bear adorned with tiny ears, powerful arms and thick neck, fingers replaced claws and Smokey's name appeared on his hat and belt buckle. Because of the success of his praying bear, Hansen later drew additional posters, sometimes with religious themes.

But after Chuck Kuderna created several Smokey illustrations for the 1962 campaign, he was credited with producing in 1965 the final version of the "classic" Smokey head. Kuderna's work—viewed by Wendelin as "a beautifully rendered head that became a classic model for the logo that incorporates every loved characteristic of the imagined Smokey face"— still is used on posters. With a slightly larger snout, smaller nose, medium-length hair, large eyes, ears under a shortened hat and just a hint of a smile on a friendly but business-like face, Kuderna's Smokey is the version today's kids recognize.

"I met Chuck while I was in the navy," Wendelin recalled. "Chuck drew several Smokey posters. He was a wonderful commercial illustrator from Chicago who had been hired by the agency [FCB] and he hit on a face that clicked with everybody. It was a face that I approved completely without change. That was one of the most famous heads and they still use it. It was a major influence in my rendering of the head for the commemorative stamp I designed in 1984 on Smokey's fortieth birthday. The Kuderna head withstood the test of time and continues to serve as the official logo as well as a guide for construction and visualization of the entire figure. Chuck never did a full-length painting of the bear, but he was the best at drawing Smokey."

And so Smokey evolved from a husky, young Teddy-type bear to a working bear with serious job responsibilities, to a middle-aged bear with a middle-aged bulge and then back to a fit, hard-working protector of the nation's forests.

Richard Woods Stow certainly claims a spot on the roll of great Smokey Bear artists. Perhaps he was head of the class, but too many years, too many artists and too many memories have passed to be certain. Stow apparently didn't do final art for any Smokey campaign posters, didn't draw Smokey's image on book covers and ashtrays and didn't create Smokey figurines or draw Smokey cartoons. Stow never was known to the American public as a Smokey Bear artist. Yet, as a behind-the-scenes force, Stow may have been the most influential of that exceptionally talented group of Smokey artists. Dick Stow apparently was the artist who quietly guided the creation of the bear familiar to generations of Americans.

Stow was born in Colorado in 1910 and studied engineering at Colorado A&M University before completing his education in journalism at the University of Arizona. Then, with an interest in art, Stow studied at the Chicago Art Institute, but it was a tough go for a Depression-era student. Struggling financially, Stow worked as a doorman at McVicker's Theatre and shared an apartment with Joshua Meador, a colleague from Mississippi, until Meador moved to sunny California to work for Walt Disney. But Stow stayed in Chicago, found work, and married his landlady's daughter. "Dick did a lot of freelance art work," wife Betty Stow explained. "He drew ads for newspapers, produced art for private companies and drew an oil company cartoon strip." Most important, Stow's 1940-43 stint as art director at National Transitads laid the groundwork for his future association with Smokey Bear.

Stow followed Meador to Southern California in 1943, where he plied his trade as a story gag man producing storyboard art at Walt Disney's Burbank studios. "Joshua Meador got Dick to move to California and got him into Disney," Betty Stow recalled. "Joshua worked for Disney, and Dick started there in 1943. Dick worked mostly on Donald Duck."

Dick Stow (left) accepts the presidency of the Los Angeles Art Directors Club in 1951. *(Courtesy Betty Stow. Photo by John Meredith.)*

But the anonymity of Disney's artists took its toll on Stow. "All Disney cartoons were Disney cartoons," a sympathetic Jim Felton explained. "Disney's cartoons were created and drawn by as many as forty different artists." So Stow sent out resumes and began work with FCB in 1944. Assigned first to the RKO lot in Hollywood, Stow created lobby posters and newspaper advertising layouts before transferring to FCB's Los Angeles office where, in February 1944, he accepted a job as an art director. In that position, which he held until November 1957, Stow assumed responsibility for the artistic development of Smokey Bear.

Likable and outgoing, Stow established a reputation as a good-tempered and hardworking contributor and easily recruited talent for the nascent program. "Dick had a whole world of friends," Jim Felton recalled. "They knocked themselves out for him. Dick was one of the most popular figures in the Smokey campaign. We called him our seven-foot elf." Not quite, but at six-foot-six, Stow picked up the usual sobriquets: "a long drink of water" and "Los Angeles's longest art representative." A solid admirer of Stow, Rudy Wendelin, too, looked up to his colleague: "He was such a tall guy that I could almost walk under his legs."

Although not fond of office gatherings, Stow could be the life of any function. "Dick lived a robust and full life," Felton explained, "and he was extremely humorous. Around a campfire, Dick told shaggy-dog stories." Shaggy-dog stories?

"Shaggy-dog stories were quite the vogue back then," Betty Stow confirmed. "They weren't particularly about dogs, but they ended with tag lines about dogs. Dick picked up original stories and added his own ideas. He elaborated on the stories and they kept getting longer and longer."

But at work, Stow drew bears, and so successful were his efforts that, along with account executive Ervin Grant, Stow sometimes was lauded as the "creator of Smokey Bear." Of course, this acclamation must be kept in perspective. Albert Staehle drew the first Smokey character, and although the concept was embraced, Staehle's bear wasn't particularly admired. Thus, Smokey faced the danger of becoming a political orphan if artists such as Stow had not intervened.

Jim Felton probably best summarized the matter: "Many people claim to be the originator of Smokey Bear. The delineation of this majestic figure over many years was a natural evolution that fell into the hands of FCB through Dick Stow and the Forest Service through Rudy Wendelin. Dick cleaned the bear up and made him a majestic figure. Rudy did Dick's bear some good, but Dick actually created the image as we know it. Others may have doctored the impressive head somewhat, shortened the hair or narrowed the chin, but the basic image is like Michelangelo's David, which may have been polished or refined or adjusted some by subordinate sculptors, but it was still Michelangelo's David. And Smokey is Dick Stow's creation."

Dick Stow's colleagues agreed that with the exception of the Smokey head drawn by Chuck Kuderna in 1964 (seven years after Stow left FCB), the bears attributable to James Hansen, Russ Wetzel and other early artists in fact reflected the interpretation and guiding hand of Dick Stow. Although skilled at producing finished art, Stow, like most art directors, rarely did so. He simply preferred to draw Smokey in his mind and let other artists produce finished art. Perhaps Stow picked up ideas from the artists that tried their hands at painting Smokey, and perhaps that's why Stow liked to use a variety of artists. In any event, a look at two of those artists shows how Dick Stow influenced their work.

At Stow's request, artist Bob Poole developed two Smokey posters—a "matchbook cover" and a frontal view portrait. A native of Tacoma, Washington, where he was born in 1913, Poole took his early art training at the Cornish Art School in nearby Seattle before moving to Southern California in 1939 to study at the Art Center of Los Angeles. "The Art Center specialized in advertising art," Poole explained. "They were very thorough about teaching figure drawing, fashion, illustrations for stories and things like automobile designs."

Leaving the Art Center at age thirty-two, Poole moved into his studio near Wilshire and LaBrea. "We got together—seven of us—and organized a corporation called Group West," Poole recalled. "Ren Wicks was the hub and instigator." And as Group West developed into a top-notch art and design group of thirty people, Poole's work became known around the city.

"I worked with the agency that had the Carnation account," Poole recalled. "They cooked up recipes in the Carnation kitchens and I did ice cream still lifes for that account. Lyman Powers, an art director at FCB, saw some of my sample work in a show and I started working with him. Then I worked with Dick Stow on a bacon product account. They liked my baked ham illustration, but they asked me to draw Smokey Bear. They had some Smokey illustrations already there and they said to give it a try. The art had to follow a pretty good bear design, but sometimes they made minor changes from one year to another. They liked a poster that Merv Corning had done—a stylized portrait of the bear. Merv did a very nice job, so it was customary to copy his bear or come close to it. As art director, he [Stow] outlined the plan or theme for the year. He already had the idea, so the first meeting was only an hour or so. It took a couple of days to get the 'comprehensive'—a replica of the finished job—together because comprehensives are not carefully done like finished work."

After Poole produced a rough draft of his Smokey poster, it had to pass Stow's critical eye and fit his mental image of the bear.

"I took the 'comp' back to Dick, who indicated on a tissue sheet what should be changed—maybe the size of the hat to the head, for example," Poole explained. "It only took another hour at Dick's office to change or list the changes. Color was all worked out in the comp too. Stow might say 'do a warmer black' or 'use a little light for the side.' There were no restrictions on my work, but if something stood out that Dick didn't want, he would have said something like, 'That's not Smokey's nose' or `Change the bear's expression.' The comp is the whole picture in a nutshell without being down to the gnat's eye with perfect swatches of color; that comes later with the finished art. Of course, there would be a lettering man involved. If there was any change on the illustration, it might affect his lettering too, so we all worked with Dick."

Then Poole finalized his art. "The finished product took at least another two or three days," Poole explained. "I painted in tempera color—a gouache mixed with water. The poster size was drawn up for about a one-third reduction—up enough so that the rough edges come out on reproduction. By reducing the original, it takes on a more finished shape and the colors blend a little more. Then I figured on at least a day for the lettering. I left the pay up to Dick; he knew what the job would stand—probably around five hundred dollars. Sometimes I paid the letterer; sometimes FCB paid."

Born in Syracuse, New York, in 1911, Ren Wicks moved to Seattle when his father, in the automobile business, transferred. "I knew I wanted to be an artist when I was eight years old," Wicks recalled. Like Poole, Wicks attended the Cornish School in Seattle and the Art Center in Los Angeles for a simple reason: "The Art Center was the premiere art school in the United States." As he developed a reputation for helping young artists, Wicks designed postage stamps, drew aerial art illustrations, handled a heavy load of government work and was the driving force behind Group West.

"Those were indeed the golden years for advertising—and for artists and illustrators too," Wicks remembered. "That was before television took all the money that was formerly spent on publications and the camera took over for the illustrators. We worked with FCB for many years. We did work for Hughes Tool, RKO, TWA, Lone Star Beer and Sunkist. FCB was a magnificent agency—they had top art directors and professional, knowledgeable people. In my book, it was the greatest agency ever around. They had the biggest and best accounts in the area for twenty-five years. They were the top agency in western America. I was an outside contractor— one of their regulars. I worked for Dick [Stow] a lot, so he called me in on the Smokey Bear account. I drew a forest with a fawn and a deer in a clearing, with a cabin in the background. Then I did the same scene with everything burned down. Another poster was a big head of Smokey with his hat on. Dick was involved in everything. Agency art directors were instrumental in designing all graphic material; they set the direction and details and made decisions about what the message and general design would be. Dick did the creative thinking and I developed the comprehensives from that," Wicks added.

"Comprehensives took only a day to complete; finished art on the burned-down forest took three or four days; the head only took two days. I used a mixed media—mostly gouache—and painted on Whatman one hundred percent rag paper mounted on poster boards. Most artist's illustration boards have rag and wood pulp in the paper, but Whatman was the very finest available. You couldn't hurt it with masking paper, and it had an absolutely impervious surface. It cost three and a half dollars for a twenty-seven by forty piece of heavyweight board; I used the entire board because we had to draw large figures to get at the detail. I was paid about seven hundred dollars for a final product."

But FCB didn't monopolize Smokey Bear art, and across the continent, the Forest Service produced its own Smokey artists.

Harry Ludwig Rossoll's first memories after his birth in Norwich, Connecticut, in 1909, were of his desire to draw. "I was drawing by the time I was eight years old," Rossoll recalled. "Mom encouraged me; she let me paint landscapes and seascapes on the walls at home. I painted on the walls in the bathroom, kitchen and on some of the doors."

After attending the Norwich Art School and the Meyer Both College of Commercial Art in Chicago, Rossoll enrolled in the Grand Central School of Art in New York City in 1929. "That was the age of the great illustrators," Rossoll remembered, "and I wanted to be an illustrator. Grand Central had the top illustrators. Our instructors were practicing, professional artists working for a living." So Rossoll financed his education by playing trumpet in New York City dance bands, then married in 1932 and moved to Mississippi—his wife's home. In his own studio in Jackson, Rossoll painted billboards, polka dots on ladies dresses and polka dots on ladies shoes. "It was a fad at the time," he shrugged.

But forests had long been a true love, and Rossoll joined the Forest Service in Atlanta, where, except for the war years, he stayed until his retirement in 1971. "When I first joined the Forest Service," Rossoll recalled, "they didn't have any appreciation for what an artist could do. Then I got a boss—Clint Davis—who was not a forester. Clint had a background in newspapers and advertising and he understood the value of an illustrator."

Discharged from the navy in 1945, Rossoll turned to a fellow artist for guidance. "Ed Dodd, who drew the comic strip 'Mark Trail,' and I were good friends," Rossoll recalled. "I sent Ed material on forestry to help him look for ideas for his strip. Ed told me to get out in the field more and learn the business instead of waiting for it to come to me. So I did. Pretty soon, I knew almost everyone and I was on TV, radio and giving 'chalk talks' throughout the thirteen states in the region."

But before Rossoll returned from the navy, a freelance artist began producing "Smokey Says" cartoons for the Forest Service. Unfortunately, the early history of the series has not been documented. "Folks in the regional office in Atlanta say that a Forest Service man named H. F. Sears had the idea for the first 'Smokey Says' cartoons," Rudy Wendelin explained.

Forest Service artist Harry Rossoll created Smokey Bear's Story of the Forest, which was distributed to more than 24 million schoolchildren across the South. *(Courtesy Harry Rossoll.)*

"The idea called for a series of one-column cartoons to be distributed to newspapers in the South. The first fourteen cartoons were rendered by an artist named Plummer [his first name seems to have been lost for posterity], on the staff of the *Atlanta Journal*."

"I don't know who originated 'Smokey Says,'" Rossoll admitted. "It may have been an adaptation of my earlier 'Ranger Jim Says' idea. Plummer had been crafting the cartoons for a few months, but they assigned it to me because I was on salary and they could save money. I had to draw 'Smokey Says' plus do my regular job—folders, booklet illustrations and layouts, recreation maps, annual reports, conservation pamphlets and exhibits." With a schedule calling for four cartoons each month, Rossoll's challenge was to generate new ideas to stimulate readers to follow the advice of a cartoon character.

"I read newspapers to see what was current and tried to adapt issues to see how Smokey could convince people to be careful," Rossoll recalled. "There was quite a lead time and I traveled a lot, so sometimes it was tough to make deadlines." Initially, Smokey Says appeared as space fillers in regional newspapers, but the cartoon's popularity increased as Rossoll drew more than a thousand Smokey Says panels.

"The first bears I drew were horrible-looking," Rossoll admitted, "but Clint Davis allowed me to use the one I created before I went into the navy. So at first I used my 1943 bear with the bulb nose. Later, Rudy Wendelin came along and made the bear look much better, so then I used the standard bear that Rudy created. Rudy took off the bulb nose, which was lousy anyway. He took off the hat strap too. He probably added the shovel. Rudy Wendelin deserves the credit for what Smokey Bear is today."

But the evolution of Rossoll's bear took a few years, and Rossoll's Smokey carried a bulb nose off and on until 1953. Rossoll's Smokey carried a middle-age spread, featured big round eyes and offered a wealth of wit, wisdom and admonishments against carelessness in the forest.

Over time Rossoll developed an aggressive, practical and versatile animal. A determined Smokey nailed up warning signs, a tender Smokey protected tree seedlings and a political Smokey campaigned in an election year against woods burning. Rossoll portrayed a teaching bear warning an opossum about fire dangers, a farmer bear square dancing in coveralls and an aggressive bear walloping a careless smoker's rear end with a smack of his shovel. Rossoll pictured Smokey in a desert, on skis and on the face of an alarm clock. But whatever the situation depicted, Smokey had a one-track mind that focused on nothing but human carelessness with fires. By transposing Smokey's "thoughts" into that array of settings, Rossoll reminded Americans that they had to assume responsibility for their actions.

"It was quite a task," Rossoll conceded. "The hard part was trying to simplify what I had to say. I made eight-inch by ten-inch line drawings with pen and ink. We sent them to the Forest Service in Washington, where they reduced them to two inches by three inches and had mats made for direct printing by newspapers. Later, when offset printing came into common use, the Washington office mailed out proofs of four cartoons on one sheet of paper. Originally we started with about sixty sets in Atlanta, but newspapers started to pass them around and interest spread."

"We don't know just how many cartoons were distributed in the early days of Smokey Says," Rudy Wendelin added. "The big increase came in late 1951, when we arranged with the Government Printing Office to extend this feature to weekly newspapers across the nation. In 1967, we adopted a suggestion from Walt Ahearn of South Carolina and replaced the newsprint proofs with glossy reproducible proofs. This permitted the many weeklies who print by the offset method to use Smokey Says." By 1972, 3,000 copies of Smokey Says were distributed each month at a cost of $500—an inexpensive way to reach millions of readers.

"I worked on it for about twenty-five years," Rossoll explained. "Rudy filled in when I was sick or doing other things. When I retired in 1971, Rudy took over for a while [four years], but Rudy was busy and thinking about retiring too, so it just melted away."

Another Rossoll contribution developed through two small booklets. In the late 1940s, Rossoll produced a pamphlet called "Forest Friends" for distribution in southern schools. Because of its success, Rossoll expanded "Forest Friends" into a 16-page coloring book entitled "Smokey Bear's Story of the Forest." Determined to provide a useful educational tool, Rossoll consulted with education specialists at the University of Georgia. "They told me that most coloring books don't teach kids anything," Rossoll explained. "They said, 'Harry, make it so the kids can learn something from it.'"

With simple writing and engaging illustrations of deer, quail, rodents and trees, Rossoll developed his booklet with Smokey teaching from a slate blackboard. Rossoll drew leaves, asked the names of birds, explained forest and lumber uses and emphasized that trees cannot run from forest fires. In 1950, with endorsements from state foresters and educators, more than 8 million copies of "Smokey Bear's Story of the Forest" were distributed to schools across the nation. Tennessee's Department of Conservation offered the booklet free to third-graders in all 150 public school systems and all parochial schools in the state. One 1953 Tennessee educator's newsletter reported: "Nothing tried so far in the field of conservation education materials has made a greater hit with both teachers and pupils at this important grade level." The newsletter claimed that 70,000 Tennessee children each year were learning Smokey's lessons: "Its 16 pages are packed full with appealing illustrations. It is dedicated to the understanding of the great damage done by forest fires." And at last count, more than 24 million copies of the book had been distributed to schoolchildren.

Certainly the most prolific of the great Smokey Bear artists was Rudy Wendelin, a Kansas artist not involved in Smokey's creation. But over almost fifty years Wendelin guided the CFFP's visual thinking through graphic studies, suggestions and his own alterations of the Smokey concept. Assigned in 1946 to work with the CFFP, Wendelin became Smokey's official caretaker—the man directly responsible for maintaining the cartoon bear's image as America's champion of forest fire prevention. While Smokey labored to guard America's forests, Rudy Wendelin worked just as diligently to guard Smokey, ensuring that Smokey illustrations reflected the personality and message the bear was created to convey.

As Wendelin produced more than 4,000 Smokey works of art, his Forest Service associates viewed him as the man who trained Smokey to be graceful and charming. Quiet and sometimes painfully modest, Wendelin had difficulty accepting the tag line "great Smokey Bear artist." For many Americans, however, Rudy Wendelin is forever entwined with Smokey Bear, and over the past half-century Wendelin became so closely associated with Smokey that many people are reluctant to accept the fact that Wendelin didn't create Smokey. So former CFFP program director Mal Hardy offered a palatable substitute: "If Rudy isn't the natural father of Smokey Bear, it would be okay to call him his stepfather. God bless a great guy!"

But Bill Bergoffen best articulated his colleagues' feelings: "Rudy Wendelin is the most selfless individual I have ever met. He just oozes devotion and dedication."

Rudolph Andrew Wendelin, the grandson of Austrian immigrants, grew up in northwest Kansas hunting jackrabbits in the snow with a .410 shotgun. Born in Herndon, Kansas, in 1910, as the oldest of four children, Wendelin learned violin, baritone and trumpet and started his own town band—a popular pastime in rural Kansas. But at an early age Wendelin found another hobby: drawing.

"I was always drawing," he recalled. "My mother did embroidery work and she had put one little design—a couple of rabbits on a seesaw—on a school book sack. I copied her design and that's the first thing I remember drawing." Soon, Wendelin created cartoon characters and a comic strip featuring a sailor boy. When his cartoons won prizes at county fairs, Wendelin began drawing political cartoons and took the Landon correspondence course in cartooning from a Chicago school.

Wendelin's first exposure to disciplined drawing (mechanical drawing with instruments) came in high school. "My uncle, a building contractor, always had plans and blueprints around our home and the idea of building things was in my mind," Wendelin recalled. "I didn't think I wanted to be an artist because it wasn't a masculine thing to do, but I still continued drawing. I just couldn't keep away from it." So by the light of a coal-oil lamp in a small home cellar, the determined Wendelin sketched cartoons on the back of his dad's accounting papers. He also whittled figures from Ivory soap bars and, on a trip to nearby Denver, Colorado, combined carving skills with a solid imagination when a Denver movie house sponsored a soap sculpture contest to promote the star of a new film; Wendelin carved a nude model of Marlene Dietrich to take top honors.

After high school he attended the University of Kansas, living modestly in Lawrence for $7 a month for room and $5.50 each week for meal tickets. Enrolled in the school of architecture, Wendelin won prizes in sketching and design and became known for his art supporting the Jayhawks' basketball and football teams as he painted rival Missouri Tigers and Nebraska Cornhuskers on store-front windows. He drew covers for alumni newsletters and university magazines and designed posters and flyers to support his Lutheran church.

In 1932, in the midst of the Great Depression, Wendelin ran out of money and dropped out of KU. But while mapping the KU campus in an ROTC course, Wendelin had learned the principles of surveying and, upon returning to Herndon, he drew a map of a proposed lake at a Civilian Conservation Corps camp. "I drew this map for the county and I got a little money," Wendelin explained, "but I had a nice blueprint sample of my engineering work." So Wendelin sent his sample to the Forest Service regional office in Milwaukee, Wisconsin, and was hired as a draftsman for $90 a month.

In Milwaukee, Wendelin drew CCC manuals and wildlife identification guides and designed engineering guides. As teachers demanded conservation information, Wendelin built exhibits of CCC camps and conservation projects and sent them to teachers' and sportsmen's conventions in Chicago, Madison and other Midwest cities. When his work drew national attention, Wendelin was transferred to Washington, D.C., in 1936, arriving with everything he owned in a 1932 Ford.

Although few of his new assignments were on national campaigns, Wendelin quickly got involved in forest fire prevention. "Mostly, they expected rangers to handle fire prevention in the forests," Wendelin recalled. "Typical posters in those days were printed on yellow cardboard without illustrations. There wasn't too much fire prevention except about pipes and tobacco and smoke, and the printed messages were simple admonitions to be careful with them and put them out."

At first, Wendelin didn't have much time to help change those posters. As a Yeoman First Class, he spent the war years drawing training manuals and intelligence books depicting enemy equipment. But the war also brought Wendelin his bride—young Carrol Bergman, an Indiana native who grew up in California, attended UCLA, and signed on with the U.S. government in San Francisco to draw maps. She transferred to Washington in 1943, met Wendelin, married him in 1945, and settled down in their Virginia home.

Wendelin returned to his Forest Service job in January 1946, to be greeted by Staehle's posters of Smokey Bear. "That was the first time I saw the new symbol of Smokey," Wendelin remembered. "I never knew anything about the symbol or the development of Smokey while I was in the navy. But these old friends of mine were on the [CFFP] committee. Fred Schoder, who helped me tremendously in Milwaukee, pushed this bear work on me because he knew I could come across with something." So as he produced mechanical drawings, charts and maps, Wendelin also began to work for Smokey Bear.

"I spent about seventy-five percent of my time on forest fire prevention and Smokey Bear in the early years because there was no one else to do it," Wendelin explained. "Over my career, I probably spent sixty percent of my time with Smokey and the rest with other Forest Service work. In 1946, I made line drawings of Staehle's material for my first drawings of Smokey. It was a packet that would contain reproductions of news ads that the advertising agency had prepared. Posters and other materials would be distributed in it. Using one of Staehle's posters as reference, I made a line drawing for the cover using brush with ink. That period was the beginning of the use of color in government campaigns. The forest fire prevention program was one of the early programs where color was beginning to be used. This material had to go through the Government Printing Office, and it took some real persuasion to convince the GPO it was necessary to print in color. The navy and some of the defense agencies had already printed some things in color, but no private agency in the government had done color work until the forest fire prevention program came in. I didn't try to persuade the program to use color—it was the advertising agency and the demands of the national media that promoted the use of color."

Throughout his career, Wendelin loved working with "the agency" [Foote, Cone & Belding]: "I felt a great respect for the organization because they were professional people who were contributing their time and energy and talent to this program. They hired nationally known freelance artists to portray Smokey. When they did the news ads, we issued a proof sheet of line drawings for reproduction in local newspapers. Most of them were just black-and-white drawings. The agency prepared large ones and I did many of the small ones. When it came to Washington, I got it ready for printing. As a general rule, the artwork was almost finished upon arrival, and I tried to accept the art unless it was just way out of line. Then I had to check on printing. Much of Smokey's color material was contracted out by the GPO, but it still had to be approved by our office. Because of tight schedules, I frequently visited printing plants—Chicago, St. Louis, New York, Erie—to approve final proofs. The printers worked on it at night and I saw proofs the following night or two days later, and then I approved them."

Wendelin's artistic eye was uncomfortable with the first Smokey Bear posters because they portrayed a wild bear with a hunch back, long snout, claws and fangs in the mouth. "During those early years Smokey wasn't an extremely friendly looking bear," Wendelin recalled. "I finally got the courage to begin to dig into other people's artwork. With Hansen's praying bear poster for the 1948 campaign, I put Smokey's hat on the ground because Hansen drew him bare-headed. That was my first manipulation of another artist's work. Inspired by the concern of Clint Davis for tactfully respecting everything the agency produced, I was very reluctant to suggest changes in artwork produced by its creative people. Faced with periodic printing deadlines, however, and when some changes were deemed necessary, I offered to do them. Because some of these posters were created in Southern California, for example, the background might have mountains or the Pasadena hills and be too high and, therefore, not acceptable nationwide. Clint Davis might say, 'See if you can lower those hills, Rudy.' So I retouched the art and lowered the hills or removed fang-like teeth from Smokey's mouth. That was delving into someone else's artwork, but usually there wasn't time to go back to the original artist for those corrections.

"Over the years," Wendelin continued, "the part I had was the humanizing conversion. I started putting a friendly face on Smokey. Over time we replaced Smokey's claws and paws with more human-type hands; the paws became rough fingers—not delicate fingers, but fingers that could point, and that was used by some of the other early artists too. We softened his sharp pointed teeth, shortened his long bear snout and trimmed his long hair. We also broadened his shoulders, took the hump out of his neck and changed his sloping head to a rounder head to fit better on his new shoulders. Then we widened his leather belt and put the name Smokey on his hat and brass belt buckle for better identification if his hat was off his head. By then, Smokey didn't look so much like a wild animal. We had created a more human, friendly and acceptable appearance. My contribution was in the development of these changes and establishing licensing guidelines for creating visual interpretations of Smokey."

Wendelin couldn't always identify exactly which of his alterations were adopted by other artists. "Sometimes changes I put on the bear seemed to influence their art the following year," Wendelin explained. "Sometimes we discussed changes on the spot in Los Angeles. It may be that what little I did influenced some of the artists that worked on Smokey. That I don't know. I didn't necessarily try to influence the work of other artists so much, but concentrated on my own drawings of Smokey for the schools and other special drawings. However, in special instances—the Golden Books, for example—I was sent to New York to advise the artist on what Smokey should look like. That was not an easy job, because artists have their own conceptions."

Wendelin certainly admired the work of artists selected by Foote, Cone & Belding. "Generally, I never had contact with artists hired by the agency to do annual campaign posters," Wendelin added. "I would alter just a little bit, not too much, if I felt it was necessary. After a while, they began to understand what I was looking for. It was kind of a mutual thing; it just grew out of the efforts of all of us. We all contributed to this rendering of Smokey, and we all had some little part in it. But since I was in the Forest Service office here in Washington that managed the program, it became my responsibility to check all the art and visuals and put everything out for printing, which put me in a position where I had the final say. In the early years of Smokey's portrayal I wasn't sure what he should look like myself. I don't like to look at my early drawings of Smokey because Smokey looked so different. He was evolving."

Still, Wendelin didn't like to alter the work of other Smokey artists. "It bothered me," he admitted. "Since it was an agency-created campaign, I was just an intermediary to put it into production. I did specifications and prepared it for printing and made models in the poster margins. I don't know if my alterations bothered the artists or not. Most of the artists were hired by the agency in Los Angeles. With increasing awareness of the great popularity of the program and realizing we had a lion by the tail, everyone became overly cautious about not rocking the boat."

Gradually, almost imperceptibly, the Smokey Americans know and love evolved. "There was no driving force, no motive, for Smokey Bear changes," Wendelin explained. "The more I drew Smokey, the more little things became important. For example, at first the ears were outside the hat. Later, the ears were under the hat. Later I developed different brush strokes. Sometimes things just didn't seem right. I spent a lot of time just thinking about Smokey and what he should look like. It was the little things that added up to the final picture over a number of years."

As Wendelin labored diligently to make Smokey Bear real in the minds of the American public, the bear became real in Wendelin's own mind. "Smokey is very personal to me," Wendelin explained. "I always felt like he was somewhere down the hall directing the operation, and I was responsible to him. I was his principal caretaker. As the years passed, I continued to feel a *real* responsibility for carrying on the image. Over time, a lot of the bear development was shaped in my own mind and was being accepted by the public. When you draw a character, you create characteristics that need to be used and exploited to show his personality. The real test of how well Smokey's visual image has been projected is in areas where we have no control—such as cartoons in publications."

So while other artists portrayed Smokey only occasionally, the bear became a way of life for Rudy Wendelin and his work with Smokey developed into a routine part of his job—neither dramatic nor visible to the American public. "The state foresters, for example, were interested in something to attract schoolchildren to fire prevention, so the schools demanded a lot of work," Wendelin remembered. "The teachers wanted kits, so we started putting together a lot of kits every year and I drew many coloring sheets. I created some on my own and adapted others from materials for the national campaign. Then, when the [CFFP] committee decided to try Smokey in range and grass fire protection, we changed locale and scenery just a little on some of the posters. I drew burnt fence posts and grasslands, and we broadened Smokey's message to 'Prevent forest and range fires.'"

Wendelin's Smokey work included developing award materials, working with commercial licensees, creating a Smokey costume and working on supplemental materials for each year's campaign. He created posters to recognize the contributions of the Boy Scouts, Girl Scouts and Campfire Girls. Using Jackson Weaver voice tapes to shape lip movements, Wendelin also created the first animated Smokey Bear black-and-white television spot with Smokey's one-line message. "This was an important step in the progress toward the humanization of Smokey," Wendelin emphasized. "To shape an animal's lips framing words to communicate a message was a critical link in the metamorphic process."

"At one time, Clint Davis asked me to come up with some criteria for Smokey," Wendelin laughed. "We had a package from Borden in which their artists had outlined the criteria for Elsie the Cow. They were very careful to see that Elsie the Cow would look like Elsie at any kind of a position or any kind of a movement of the head. But I never did get to that, largely because, at the time, I never was exactly sure myself what Smokey should look like."

Thus, some observers felt that Wendelin had a tendency to romance Smokey outside of his role as a "business" bear, but Wendelin remained confident of his art. "I take liberties with Smokey," he conceded. "I put him in different positions or I put a knapsack on his back. I'm not a wildlife artist; my drawings of animals are just on the edge of realism. They show character and personality. They're not cartoons; they're personal."

Although Wendelin enjoyed the live bear at the National Zoo, he didn't change either his art or his perception of Smokey. "I didn't make any changes when the live bear came along," Wendelin said. "He was not an inspiration or a model. Smokey had already evolved into this humanized version and we didn't need a live bear. To me, they were two separate programs and they remained that way. The Smokey Bear program was a popular program and it carried on a high level of interest without dropping. This other was a supplementary program; he had his own kind of image. It was a *cub* bear that was the main interest. As he grew up he became an adult bear and he lost a little bit of that appeal.

"He wasn't real friendly, either," Wendelin continued. "When the first bear was still in a caged area I designed a glass door and we silk-screened a fire prevention message on it so you could take a picture of Smokey with the words on the glass door. There was a little closet to hang his clothes— his coat and his pants and a little hat. Once they built a concrete tree with limbs to simulate a gnarled tree, and the bear would climb around on that. Then they put honey in it, but the honey attracted bees. You couldn't go near the place because of the bees. They had to take that tree down."

Because he drew Smokey for so many years, Wendelin enjoyed the confidence of CFFP program administrators and was given almost a free hand to do what he wanted, and what he wanted to do was serve the cause of forest fire prevention. Even in his free time, Wendelin's art focused on children's and conservation issues as he illustrated magazine covers and children's books. He designed a towering Smokey statue for International Falls, Minnesota, illustrated a series of newspaper articles on trees, adapted campaign posters for *Reader's Digest* and other magazines, illustrated "Smokey Says" and gave dozens of chalk talks to schoolchildren. At times Wendelin garnered so much publicity for Smokey that the mild-mannered

Forest Service artist Rudy Wendelin in his Washington, D.C., office. *(Courtesy USDA Forest Service.)*

artist seemed to be on a crusade. He received awards from the Department of Agriculture, both the Golden and Silver Smokey Bear Awards, the Horace Hart National Award for Graphic Arts and dozens of prizes for art and graphics in exhibits as his paintings found their way into government and private collections.

"I produced a heck of a lot of Smokey art," Wendelin explained. "But something like that is hard to save. I don't know where the original art went. We never had an organized effort to record and tabulate that stuff." (In 1993, however, the Forest Service, through former Forest Service historian

Jean Pablo, finally developed an inventory of Wendelin's memorabilia, posters, reproductions, photos and correspondence.)

Over time Wendelin's unceasing efforts on behalf of his bear generated unplanned—but certainly welcome—favorable press for the Smokey Bear program. Each time Wendelin's art was displayed, a magazine article written about him or one of his six U.S. postage stamps (including the 1984 Smokey Bear stamp) was issued, attendant news reports focused on Wendelin's activities with Smokey.

As Wendelin became a celebrity at Forest Service headquarters, he coupled intensity with a high energy level, often working late into the night on his creative interpretations, or perhaps just thinking about his work instead of sleeping. "I loved the Forest Service," Wendelin confessed. "I never had any desire to get out of it. I wanted to be there for my entire career. I was so connected with this character that I was often overwhelmed with the responsibility. I was compelled to do what I could for the bear."

And because he recognized his responsibility to promote Smokey, Wendelin was careful to take time for people. Often, when plagued by visitors looking at Smokey art, Wendelin graciously accommodated his guests, but worked until after the Arlington buses quit running. Then his wife drove into town—sometimes as late as 10:00 p.m.—to take her husband home.

Officially, Wendelin retired from the Forest Service in 1973. Realistically, he never quit—perhaps because he couldn't walk away from the character he had portrayed for a good portion of his adult life. Because he was never replaced, Wendelin began serving as a consultant to the Smokey program and accepted repeated requests for commissioned art from commercial licensees and the Forest Service. Wendelin's post-retirement credits include illustrations for forestry journals and magazines, historical societies, environmental groups, posters for the State of California and a series of calendars for the Vernon Company in Newton, Iowa.

Although Wendelin's retirement slowed down his official Smokey Bear work, that event passed unnoticed by Wendelin's fans across the United States. Even as his age crept into the eighties, Wendelin still labored away in his home studio many nights answering requests from children for drawings of his favorite bear. Was he tempted to ignore those requests? Did he ever turn down people who asked for drawings? "Not very much," Wendelin confessed in his studio. "It's always an open door for Smokey."

19

A Business Bear

"Somkey [sic], Goddam you why don't you sent kit? All the Goddam other kids got one."

— *"James"*

After Foote, Cone & Belding and the Advertising Council completed their annual placement of forest fire prevention campaign materials with media across the nation, it was left to the Forest Service and the National Association of State Foresters to capitalize on that groundwork. For more than half a century, the lead force behind that effort has been the Cooperative Forest Fire Prevention (CFFP) program's executive committee operating from Forest Service headquarters in Washington, D.C.

From the time of its creation as an advisory panel in 1942, the CFFP's executive committee has been composed of federal and state foresters—usually three of each. Duties varied, but since its inception that committee has developed the basic policy for American forest fire prevention, approved commercial licenses, reviewed advertising programs and coordinated special projects under the umbrella of the "Smokey Bear" program.

Typically, the committee meets twice annually, first for a planning session held at locations throughout the country, then for a subsequent program review meeting in Washington. All meetings are designed to cement working relationships between the CFFP, FCB, the Ad Council and fire prevention field staffs. With the director of Information & Education generally chairing the committee, and the CFFP program manager serving as secretary, the executive committee has a role far greater than that of a rubber stamp organization.

"The Forest Service set the direction, but it never was an adversary situation," explained Mal Hardy, who worked with the CFFP for fourteen years. "Mostly, we didn't vote; we acted on consensus and usually had someone from the Ad Council and someone from FCB sit in. Open meetings helped build consensus, so state foresters had plenty of opportunities to be heard."

A look at the evolution of the CFFP must begin with Mal Hardy. Of hundreds of foresters associated with Smokey over fifty years, only a few acted to preserve the program's history. Mal Hardy recognized that need and documented Smokey's behind-the-scenes support.

Born in Newton, Massachusetts, in 1919, Hardy nurtured an interest in forestry even as a young boy, and determined to devote a career to the profession, he studied forestry at the University of Maine. Graduating in 1942 with a B.S. in forestry, Hardy was called for a tour with the U.S. Navy. After training on Stearman biplanes and SNJ and SNV monoplanes, Hardy served as a navy flight instructor in Florida and Texas before flying passengers and bananas across the Pacific Ocean.

After the war, Hardy completed his forestry education at the University of Washington, graduated with a master's degree in 1946, and partly because of his thesis, "Use of Aircraft in Forest Fire Control," was hired by the Forest Service. First detailed to two of Oregon's national forests, Hardy eventually earned an appointment as supervisor of the Chugach National Forest near Anchorage, where he combined his twin loves of forests and water to become one of Alaska's "saltwater rangers."

In 1960, Hardy transferred to Washington, D.C., where he found a life different from that of a dirt forester. Assigned to the CFFP program as assistant director, Hardy was promoted to director three years later. In most respects, the CFFP had evolved into a mature, smooth-running program by the time of Hardy's arrival. The campaign's fundamental concepts, direction and thrust had been well established for almost twenty years, and programs such as licensing and the Junior Forest Rangers had been in place for a decade. It was Hardy's responsibility, then, to continue administration of a highly successful campaign. But Hardy added a new dimension: a sense of history.

First, Hardy authored detailed annual reports summarizing CFFP activities during each year of his leadership. He highlighted individual achievements, discussed problems and liberally sprinkled in editorial observations to create one of the program's few sources of contemporaneous documentation. "I did it to give credit to state foresters and others who were cooperating," Hardy explained. "I found that giving every bit of credit to the state foresters paid off because they implemented the program."

Hardy led production in 1969 of a historical record of the campaign, when color negatives and transparencies were made from fifty forest fire prevention posters created from 1942 through 1969 and reproduced in a brochure.

Then Hardy initiated the first two (of three) "National Smokey Bear Workshops" attended by dozens of federal and state foresters in 1970 and 1973. Those workshops left a 150-page paper trail of speeches and panel discussions that carefully detail the CFFP program's history and operations. As part of his own preparation for each workshop, Hardy researched Forest Service and CFFP files to develop the most comprehensive history of the Smokey Bear program extant as of those dates.

Although commercial support of Smokey Bear never has been viewed as particularly important, Smokey's official licensing program often accounted for a large share of CFFP time. But because of the widespread exposure of Smokey's message, licensing has required careful handling, and another New Englander led the way.

While growing up in Holyoke, Massachusetts, where he was born in 1909, John Morgan Smith learned gardening and yard maintenance by working for "people a little richer than we were." Jettisoning both his first name and his hometown, Smith studied landscape gardening at Syracuse University and won his degree in 1930, before undertaking additional studies at Oregon State University. After learning forestry basics for five years in New York, Smith joined the Forest Service in 1935, first for a stint with the CCC, and later as a ranger in national forests in Wyoming and Colorado.

"Then I was called to Washington for a one-year detail by Clint Davis," Smith recalled, "but I stayed for nine years working on all phases of the Smokey Bear program: radio, television, posters—the complete program that was just starting."

"Smokey Bear was important," Smith asserted. "Letters came in from all over the world. Some mail came in with no address—just 'Smokey Bear.' Then we started getting requests from companies to produce belts, shirts and things like that, and the CFFP got worried that some people were using Smokey Bear commercially and improperly. So one of my jobs was to get the 'Smokey Bear bill' through Congress."

Smokey Bear may have reigned supreme in America's forests, but an unprotected poster caricature cannot hold his own in the business world, and marketers had recognized Smokey's popularity with children. Although welcoming commercial interest, the CFFP grew concerned about possible abuse of their bruin and a distortion of his message. Certainly, some marketers understood that the Smokey character was part of the public domain; no cooperation with the CFFP was required to use the bear's image. Afraid of potential damage to Smokey's message, Department of Agriculture attorneys investigated the matter but determined that copyright or design patents probably wouldn't shelter their bear. Protective legislation was needed.

"The bill was put on the consent calendar—that's where there is no money involved," Smith explained. "The Democrats had three people that handled that calendar and the Republicans had three. Congressman [Byron G.] Rogers from Denver took me to meet the Democrats and then the Republicans—one of whom was Gerald Ford. Then we got Senator Pat McCarran from Nevada to sponsor the bill. A congressman from New York introduced the bill in the House and we also got a Pennsylvania senator to help." (Representatives Harold Ostertag (R-N.Y.) and James Lind (D-Pa.) introduced the House bill; Senators Edward Martin (R-Pa.) and Richard Russell (D-Ga.) introduced the Senate version.)

"I was told to help write up the law," Smith added. "Department of Agriculture lawyers took a shot at the first draft, then they asked me what I thought. I said, 'Just say that any money that comes from Smokey Bear commercial ventures must be used for forest fire prevention.' It took a little more than a year to get through Congress, but eventually it worked out very well. Afterward, as part of the deal, the Forest Service sent a lot of press releases to Nevada newspapers and TV and radio stations praising McCarran." McCarran even earned a bonus from Forest Service chief Lyle Watts: a Smokey Bear doll.

Passing both houses by unanimous votes, the "Smokey Bear Act" (Public Law 359 of the 82nd Congress), which outlined the mechanics for commercial support and established Smokey's legal name as "Smokey Bear" (*not* Smokey *the* Bear), was signed by President Truman in May 1952. Quickly, the CFFP drafted a licensing policy requiring that Smokey products (1) educate the public about forest fire prevention, (2) be consistent with the bear's image and message and (3) generate a reasonable royalty (originally set at five percent of wholesale revenues) to help fund forest fire prevention.

The actual licensing process has varied. Sometimes the CFFP directly analyzed proposals; sometimes it recruited assistance from, say, Weston Merchandising Company in Los Angeles (retained in 1968) or Harold Bell Associates (1970), also of Los Angeles, or Joseph Pellegrino of Cambridge Consulting Company (1993) of Reston, Virginia. After a product and its distribution and promotion plans were reviewed, sometimes with approval from the Ad Council or the national coordinator, the CFFP typically issued a license for a limited period so that close control could be exercised. License terms generally required that all artwork, price schedules, fire prevention messages and promotional materials associated with the product be approved in advance.

Because of cyclical public interest in Smokey, competition from movie products and their own experience, the CFFP revised its regulations a number of times over the years, seemingly adding restrictions on top of restrictions. There could be no direct or implied endorsement by Smokey of any commercial product or service; Smokey could not be used as a brand name; unauthorized Smokey products could not be imported, and customs officials were instructed to confiscate all such items. Some observers believed the CFFP was draping its brown-colored black bear in too much red tape, but CFFP insiders held a different view.

CFFP administrators faced the same issues as their counterparts in the executive suites of Walt Disney, Ideal Toy, Kenner and hundreds of other manufacturers. What was best for the program in the long run? How could they prevent the bear from soaring to a high level of popularity, then quickly fading from public interest? Would Smokey benefit from maximum exposure, or would he wear out his welcome? How closely could a product be associated with Smokey without diminishing his pristine image?

Those difficult questions often had uncertain answers. But the CFFP appears to have been consistent in its attitude about licensing revenues: more is not necessarily better. The fact that a license may generate substantial funds from royalty payments has never been accepted as a valid reason to waive regulations. The licensing campaign isn't motivated by cold cash; applications have been considered only on the basis of their potential contribution to public education about forest fire prevention.

"Of course the dollar amount wasn't what we were most interested in," Jim Sorenson, Mal Hardy's assistant, emphasized. "What *did* mean quite a bit to us was the amount of exposure Smokey and his wild fire prevention message were getting through sales of the licensed items. By watching the increase in royalty payments, we had some way of estimating that exposure."

Smokey Bear's official song took the nation by storm even before the Smokey Bear Act was passed. Because of success by the songwriting team of Steve

Eddy Arnold (with guitar) sings about Smokey Bear as artist Harry Rossoll (with chef's hat) watches on April 1, 1954. *(Courtesy Harry Rossoll.)*

Nelson and Jack Rollins with their hits "Frosty the Snowman" and "Peter Cottontail," their publisher, Hill & Range Songs, was looking for new material. When Jean Aberbach, president of Hill & Range, vacationed in Yosemite National Park with his brother-in-law, he happened to spot a Smokey Bear poster on a bulletin board. Back at their lodge, the men roughed out song ideas, then gave them to Nelson and Rollins, who crafted words and music.

Responding to pressure from singers and disc jockeys, Aberbach agreed to pay the CFFP 50 percent of the songwriters' royalties, so the CFFP approved the idea to test Smokey's marketing potential. Nelson and Rollins's four-verse "Smokey the Bear" was released nationwide in April 1952 by the Junior Red Cross, and the words and music were reproduced and distributed to 450,000 classrooms throughout America. After Victor, Columbia, Golden and Decca Records recorded the song, it claimed fifth place in record sales during the 1952 Christmas season.

By the end of 1952, dozens of license applications began appearing in CFFP headquarters. After licenses were issued, Rudy Wendelin was assigned responsibility to review Smokey artwork—including the products, packaging and advertising. But considering the marginal artwork submitted, Wendelin often found it easier to actually create the art himself. Thus, the Kansas artist generated a stream of designs for dolls, clothing, belts, cookies, ceramics and statuettes. Sometimes he drew Smokey, sometimes he created clay or plaster models, sometimes he altered submitted samples, but Wendelin checked each piece of artwork and all materials to ensure safety and high quality.

Eddy Arnold sings the Smokey Bear song as Bill Bergoffen (first row, left) and Clint Davis (second row, left) listen in. *(Courtesy W. W. Bergoffen.)*

"The commercial support program is especially indebted to Rudy," Mal Hardy explained. "Some of the material received was mediocre, especially from those licensees without an art staff. Thanks to Rudy's patient manipulation of their ideas, some very handsome silk purses have been made out of some low-grade sows' ears."

"That [the early 1950s] was a wild time," Wendelin remembered, "because we had a parade of people applying for licenses to do various things. A large part of my job was to help those licensees in designing what they wanted to produce and sell. Games, Golden Books, stationery, birthday party materials, toys, inkstands, plastic banks, ceramics, ashtrays, mugs—

just a variety of things. All of them either used drawings that I already had made, or I made special drawings for them. Not only that, they needed containers or advertising material to promote their products."

The first official product was a Smokey Bear doll. "Late in 1952," Hardy explained, "Ben Michtom, chairman of the board of Ideal Toy Corporation, came to Clint with a proposal to market Smokey Bear stuffed dolls. Ben's parents, fifty years before, had gotten President Teddy Roosevelt's approval to market the first stuffed Teddy Bear."

So Wendelin focused on a stuffed animal. "I was sent to New York to work with the professional artists of Ideal Toy to design their Smokey doll," Wendelin recalled. "One fellow was a German sculptor that made delicate doll's heads, so I went to his studio. The sculptor's first head of Smokey was a clay model which was to be formed into a whole plastic head with a soft furry body; the two didn't go together very well, but that was his way of creating a doll—by separating the head from the body. It was a cute look of a bear, but not quite like the bear we have today, either. He had his own conception of what Smokey should look like, so it was kind of a delicate job to tell someone else what Smokey should look like."

To encourage support for the Smokey Bear program, a large replica of the first doll was given to President Eisenhower at the White House in 1953. The president presented the bear to his five-year-old grandson David, who later donated the well-worn doll to the Smokey Bear Museum in Capitan, New Mexico.

By 1971, 46 commercial Smokey licensees were producing 160 different Smokey items appealing to virtually every American pocketbook. Toy stores offered a Smokey Bear plastic jeep, wooden toys, play furniture, a ceramic bank, a board game, a Viewmaster reel, mosaic kits, plastic hats, stuffed and inflatable dolls and a plastic toy play set. Kids wore Smokey's image on shoes, pajamas, T-shirts, sweatshirts, wristwatches, slippers, head scarves, jackets, cloth and leather belts, felt hats, neckerchiefs, bolo ties and backpacks.

Admirers decorated rooms with Smokey Bear electric clocks, drapes, bedspreads, pennants, balloons, calendars, book covers, banners, cloth patches, decals, a wall plaque, bulletin boards, posters and signs. Children ate a Smokey Bear breakfast cereal with Smokey Bear spoons and forks or snacked on Smokey Bear cookies served on Smokey Bear dinnerware while their dads grilled steaks with Smokey Bear charcoal briquettes and Smokey Bear barbecue accessories. Their parents cluttered homes with Smokey Bear jewelry, rulers, warning lights, cigarette lighters, towels, sheets, ashtrays, silver souvenirs, pillowcases, figurines, lunch boxes, patio buckets, pens and pencils, and then cleaned it all up with a Smokey Bear litter bag. Kids bathed in Smokey Bear bubble bath and washed their hair with Smokey Bear shampoo while singing from Smokey Bear sheet music or listening to a Smokey Bear record album. And they could write this entire list on Smokey Bear stationery, stay at the Smokey Bear Motel in Capitan, New Mexico, and tell their friends about it on Smokey Bear postcards.

Over time, American companies such as General Electric, Milton Bradley, MGM Records, Standard Knitting Mills, Mobil Chemical, Owens-Illinois, Fieldcrest Mills, Kinney, General Foods and Tonka Corporation joined the parade of Smokey Bear licensees. Even the state of West Virginia was licensed to produce a Smokey Bear trading post.

Application flows varied, but a typical year found the CFFP processing perhaps a dozen applications, with about half being accepted. Over time, licensees added and deleted products or dropped out of the program. Some products didn't sell well, and one year, nine of the fifteen licenses dropped had generated royalties of only $140; in other instances, the CFFP wanted to raise the quality of Smokey's products. While a typical year found four dozen active licenses, almost 150 licenses were issued in the program's first twenty years. But even Smokey had his deadbeats: by 1967, efforts were underway to collect almost $5,000 in delinquent royalties.

Authority to produce and sell Smokey products in Canada also was extended to the Canadian Forestry Association, with all royalties to be used in the Canadian forest fire prevention effort.

Although tough with commercial applicants, the CFFP could be a soft touch for organizations asking to use Smokey for noncommercial, educational purposes. In a typical year, perhaps twenty-nine of thirty such proposals were accepted, so Smokey's picture and message appeared on telephone directories, maps, milk cartons, grocery bags, scouting patches, educational publications, calendars, filmstrips, floats and even hand puppets distributed in potato chip packages.

But some folks didn't know or care about image protection, so violations of the Smokey Bear Act sometimes occurred. Illegal Smokey stationery appeared in Cincinnati, unauthorized Smokey art popped up on T-shirts in Rochester, Smokey helped sell products in a Tacoma newspaper and bogus dolls found their way into Tennessee stores.

Most violators simply were ignorant of the law and, when advised of their improprieties, usually stopped their activities, withdrew offending products and destroyed remaining inventory. If a large number of illegal items had been sold, a payment often was charged as a condition of settlement. But the Smokey Bear Act has teeth, and recalcitrants faced investigation by the FBI and criminal prosecution by the Justice Department, and were subject to both a $250 fine and a six-month jail sentence. Further, it wasn't easy to escape notice when selling illegal Smokey products. Because of the sheer size of the network of federal, state and local participants in the forest fire prevention effort, few violations remained undetected.

A Columbus, Ohio, firm selling Smokey T-shirts with the words "Help preserve wildlife—throw a party" paid $75 as a royalty. The "Smokey Bear Beef Jerky" company, the "Smokey Bar and Grill" and a stripper ("Smokey the Bare") were forced to change their names. A Denver candy store stopped selling a tasty (but unauthorized) chocolate Smokey. In California, a poster with a moonlighting Smokey attired in a gas mask, with the inscription "Smoggy the Bear Says—Only You Can Prevent Pollution," also was withdrawn. And when the FBI arrested a Buffalo, New York, poet for publishing obscene poetry using Smokey's name, the case took an unexpected turn: "Defendant died, case closed," Mal Hardy reported.

Perhaps the most entertaining "violation" occurred in the late 1960s. In an article, "Will the real Smokey Bear please stand up," Mal Hardy related the entire episode in his 1969 Annual Report.

> What we have come to call the Folsom Fracas started with a photograph printed in the *Sacramento Bee* on January 28, in which a bear was shown with a tiny cub in her mouth. The caption read, "Smokey the bear is a father again." When I called this to the attention of the folks at the National Zoo, they sent off a letter telling the Zookeeper in Folsom that "the 'Smokey Bear' name is designated, by an Act of Congress, for use only for the 'Smokey Bear' we have here, and Federal law states that no other bear is to be known by the same name." Of course, the Smokey Bear Act does not prohibit all other bears from being named Smokey (as the Acting Zoo Director's letter indicated), but it does take Smokey out of the public domain and puts the supervision of his name and character under the wing of the Secretary of Agriculture, who passed the authority along to the Chief of the Forest Service, who generally agrees with what the CFFP Committee recommends. Without any further checking, the Zookeeper went to the Mayor, who went to the press and to his Congressman. The way the National Zoo's letter was phrased, it almost

invited the press to go to town. It had three winning elements—big government picking on a little town; a second bear that had been burned in a fire, cared for, and named Smokey; and the family aspects of Momma Bear, Poppa Bear, and Baby Bear. The press loved it, and many newspapers carried the story, especially in California. We had about 50 letters to answer, most of them addressed to the Zoo or the Department of Interior, and almost all of them insulting. Highlights of the coverage were a foot-long story in the March 9 *Sports Illustrated* and a three-page photo story in *Life* magazine for April 3. The *Life* article suggested that readers demand patience of Washington and that their letters go to the Chairman of the Smokey Bear Executive Committee, Henry W. DeBruin (no relation). So far we have heard from 40 people who read *Life*. The only word from Folsom so far is a telegram from the Mayor offering his latest cub to carry on the Smokey name when the original Smokey goes to Bear Heaven. The Chief agreed to give the offer serious consideration.

Generally, Hardy displayed no sense of humor when his favorite bear came under attack. In that same 1969 Annual Report, Hardy challenged the continuing libeling of Smokey's good name. "Derogatory or obscene Smokey Bear cartoons have appeared in more periodicals this past year than in any other year I know of," Hardy wrote. "We have ignored these in the past, but I now believe that at least some of these could detract from Smokey's status and endanger the public service support that is so vital to the program's success. I recommend, therefore, that we adopt as our policy that the Director shall in each such case advise the Editor of the provisions of the Smokey Bear Act and Regulations and shall ask his cooperation in limiting future editorial use of Smokey to material that is not offensive to good taste."

Licensed Smokey products often were used as gifts on Capitol Hill, throughout the United States and around the world. White House, Agriculture and other government officials presented Smokey dolls, books, patches and snuffer-lighters to their counterparts in Denmark, South Korea, England, Laos, Italy, Australia, New Zealand, Japan, China, Mexico, India, Turkey, Honduras, Brazil, Argentina and dozens of other countries. And never forgetting their funding source, the CFFP sometimes passed out Smokey dolls to supporting politicians, and once distributed 3,000 Smokey pocket planners to members of Congress and committee staffs. Additional materials were sent to the Ad Council for industry and advertising leaders.

Although Smokey's royalty income began with a meager $30,848.85 in 1953, his annual income reached $100,000 by 1969, and cumulative royalties topped the $1 million mark by 1972. By 1975, Smokey licenses were generating more than $200,000 each year—more than one-half the budget for the entire Smokey Bear program. Smokey's financial success inspired favorable editorial comment in such publications as *Life*, the *New York Post*, the *Christian Science Monitor*, the *Wall Street Journal* and the *Chicago Daily News*.

Jack Anderson of the *Washington Post* reported that although Smokey began his career in dungarees and a weather-beaten hat, the bear now could afford Brooks Brothers suits: "To its credit, the government has taken pains not to allow Smokey's puritanical image to be abused." *Playboy* summarized the liberal view: "The moral is obvious: We need more cartoon characters in Government—and fewer real ones." *Time* trumpeted the bear as "Smokey the Capitalist." An admiring *Forbes* noted that Smokey "pulls in $100,000 a year just for talking gruffly about saving trees," and across the Atlantic, a British magazine touted Smokey as "the billion-dollar bear," a label repeated stateside in *Family Weekly* and *Reader's Digest*.

But *Sports Illustrated* put the entire matter into perspective: "Let's hear it for Smokey the Bear. On page 213 of the 1972 federal budget we learn that Smokey is expected to earn $172,000 for the U.S. Treasury next year in fees from private users of his name and image for things like Smokey dolls. Wonderful. That means the rest of us are going to have to cough up only $229,100,828,000."

Certainly, increased exposure of Smokey's message occurred. Western Publishing Company, for example, reported selling more than 3 million Smokey Bear books, puzzles, magic slates, comics and other materials during 1970 alone.

Licenses could be issued for limited promotions too, but a few "one-time" promotions far exceeded expectations, as when the CFFP found itself in the balloon business, courtesy of a General Electric TV special.

For several years the CFFP had considered flying a Smokey balloon in the Macy's Thanksgiving Day parade in New York City, but didn't feel it could justify the investment. In 1966, however, the "Ballad of Smokey the Bear" was proposed as the third in a series of GE Fantasy Hour specials that included "Return to Oz" and "Rudolph the Red-nosed Reindeer." The Ad Council and FCB reviewed story ideas, and *Scholastic* magazine and *My Weekly Reader* helped generate national interest. To further promote the animated musical fantasy that was scheduled for airing on Thanksgiving night, GE contributed $26,000 for construction of a 59-foot Smokey balloon and half the first year's cost of flying it. Then the CFFP agreed to fund costs of flying the balloon in subsequent Macy's parades when GE was not promoting the "Ballad." So, weighing in at 320 pounds, the monster Smokey, with its design approved by Rudy Wendelin, required 8,000 cubic feet of helium to inflate and a team of three dozen volunteer firemen to control his march through New York's streets.

The triumph of the "Ballad of Smokey the Bear"—narrated by James Cagney, with lyrics and melodies by Johnny Marks—exceeded all expectations. The Ballad's first showing reached 15 million homes—a 40 percent viewer share, despite competition from a major football game. It ran again in 1968 to an audience of 35 million people, and again in 1969 to another 10 million viewers. And for several years, Smokey continued to

SMOKEY THE BEAR   **by WES WOOD**

Smokey the Bear comic strips were distributed to about 80 newspapers.
This strip was written by Paul S. Newman and illustrated by Morris Gollub.
(Courtesy Columbia Features, Inc. and USDA Forest Service.)

float through New York on Thanksgiving Day at a cost to the CFFP of $5,000 for each appearance.

Inspired by the Ballad's 1966 success, Secretary of Agriculture Orville Freeman and ABC-TV president Elton Rule announced at a 1968 Washington, D.C., press conference that ABC had signed a two-year contract for a series of animated Smokey Bear comedy-adventure shows. The weekly show premiered on Saturday, September 6, 1969, and each installment included a pair of conservation messages and a single hard-sell fire prevention message directly from Smokey. In 1970, the Smokey show was switched to 8:00 on Sunday mornings and then discontinued as planned in 1971. More than two dozen Smokey Bear comic books were published from

1955 to 1973, and a daily comic strip was distributed nationwide from 1957 through 1960. Again, Smokey attracted the country's top talent.

Born in New York City in 1924, Paul S. Newman graduated from Dartmouth in 1947 and, over the years, accepted hundreds of freelance writing assignments. "I wrote marketing proposals for Seagrams, TWA, and Lever Brothers, and designed films, videos and audiovisuals for Lord Calvert, ABC, Nabisco and the American Petroleum Institute," Newman recalled. Then he began writing comic books in his spare time. "I'm a writer—not an artist," Newman insisted. "I cannot draw, but I wrote comic books for more than forty-five years."

Newman eventually became America's most prolific author of comic books. In 1993, he was crowned "king" of comic book writers by Robin Snyder, editor of *Robin Snyder's History of the Comics*, published in Bellingham, Washington. "Newman is the King of the Comics," Snyder determined after a three-year survey. "Though research will continue for some time, here are the preliminary figures upon which I base my claim. Paul wrote 4,016+ scripts which amounts to 35,000 pages of comics."

Randall Scott, comic art bibliographer at Michigan State University (America's national repository and archive for comic books), agreed in a confirmation letter to Snyder: "I've reviewed your 150 page printout of Newman's 4,000 plus story titles, and I can confirm that all is in order. Michigan State University's Comic Art Collection is filled with his work (over 38,000 pages) for such titles as *Superman, Doctor Solar, Mighty Mouse, Prince Valiant, Jungle Jim, Fat Albert, Tweety and Sylvester*, and in every genre of comics. The sheer extent and variety of his work amazes me, as it must have amazed you as you were working through it."

Newman's list of comics exceeds three hundred titles, including *Turok, Son of Stone* (for twenty-eight years), *The Lone Ranger* (for twenty-four years), *I Love Lucy, Gunsmoke, Sherlock Holmes, Ghost Stories, Archie, Bonanza, Daffy Duck, Flash Gordon, Little Lulu, Zorro, Tom & Jerry* and dozens of others. Newman also penned a variety of syndicated comic strips such as *The Lone Ranger, Laugh-In* and *Smokey the Bear*, and wrote more than half a dozen books, screenplays, plays, TV sketches and articles for newspapers and periodicals.

When creating Smokey Bear stories, Newman relied on the Forest Service for his raw material. William W. Huber, CFFP program director after Clint Davis, provided Newman with information on spruce bark beetles, woodpeckers, timber management and other topics from which Newman formulated stories for comic books and comic strips. "I would create a plot," Newman explained, "but it would go to Huber at the Forest

This Bambi poster was the most memorable of the eight created for the 1944 campaign. Forest fire prevention took a major step forward when enthusiastic kids wanted to take the poster home from school. *(Courtesy USDA Forest Service.)*

Albert Staehle, one of the best-known animal artists of his time, was selected to draw the first forest fire prevention symbol. After submitting several animals for consideration, including an owl, chipmunk and squirrel, a bear was chosen. This 1944 drawing of Smokey Bear first appeared in the 1945 campaign. *(Courtesy USDA Forest Service.)*

Some people thought Albert Staehle's squirrel (shown in this 1945 poster) would be the best symbol for forest fire prevention. *(Courtesy USDA Forest Service.)*

Because the forest fire prevention campaign came alive when Staehle's Smokey Bear was released, he was commissioned to draw another Smokey poster. This poster appeared in the 1946 campaign. *(Courtesy USDA Forest Service.)*

The Cooperative Forest Fire Prevention Campaign (CFFP) and the advertising people tried different approaches for the yearly campaigns including this 1948 "praying bear" by James Hansen. *(Courtesy USDA Forest Service.)*

The forest service occasionally alternated between a "red" and a green" theme. In this 1952 "red" poster—designed to show destruction and present messages about the dangers of carelessness—Smokey points out the terror of forest fires. *(Courtesy USDA Forest Service.)*

In a 1954 "red" poster, Smokey shows his disgust with careless humans. *(Courtesy USDA Forest Service.)*

"Green" posters contained positive messages and portrayed beautiful, green forests to encourage people to "keep them that way." In this 1957 "green" poster Smokey offers his thanks. *(Courtesy USDA Forest Service.)*

In an effort to attract school children to fire prevention, the state foresters and the CFFP developed posters portraying smokey as a teacher as in this 1955 poster. *(Courtesy USDA Forest Service.)*

In 1960, Smokey recognized the commitment of America's Boy Scouts and Girl Scouts to help prevent forest fires. *(Courtesy USDA Forest Service.)*

Smokey reminded us in 1963 that it is easy to prevent accidental forest fires. *(Courtesy USDA Forest Service.)*

Smokey welcomed forest visitors in 1967, but politely asked Americans to be careful. *(Courtesy USDA Forest Service.)*

Rudolph Wendelin honored Smokey's "living symbol" upon the Bear's retirement in 1975. *(Courtesy USDA Forest Service.)*

With 30 years of good work under his belt by 1975, Smokey thanked Amercians for their help in preserving the nation's forests. *(Courtesy USDA Forest Service.)*

Smokey is so will known that in 1985 and 1989 he only had two words for forest visitors. *(Courtesy USDA Forest Service.)*

Rudolph Wendelin's 1991 painting emphasized Smokey's special relationship with children. *(Courtesy USDA Forest Service.)*

Service for approval and any suggested changes. Then I would write the script, detailing in each panel what the artist should draw. Then Matthew H. Murphy [Western Publishing Company editor] would review the finished artwork."

Morris Gollub, a nationally known cartoonist, drew most of the supporting art for Newman's Smokey stories. Early in his career, Gollub worked for Walt Disney as an animator on such classic films as *Pinocchio*, *Fantasia* and *Bambi*, and later served as president of the Motion Pictures Screen Cartoonist Guild from 1978 to 1982. No stranger to comics, Gollub illustrated such comic books as *Lassie*, *Trigger* and *Prince Valiant*. As an admirer of Gollub's work, Newman is confident that Gollub helped influence the development of Smokey's character: "I believe that Gollub helped humanize Smokey's ad logo. I think that some of Smokey's personality is based on Gollub's drawings."

Newman wrote more than half of the Smokey Bear comics, created secondary characters such as "Specs" the raccoon and helped characterize Smokey. But he remained unknown to the American public. "There was no problem with bylines in the comic books, because Western [Publishing Co.] did not print any bylines at that time," Newman laughed. But he didn't receive credit for his comic strips either.

"Originally, Matthew Murphy decided to use the first names of the writer—Paul S. Newman—and the artist—Morris Gollub—for the byline 'Paul Morris,'" Newman recalled. "But the Forest Service didn't want anyone else identified as Smokey's creators, so Matthew came up with Wes (for the 'West') and Woods (for the Forest Service), which was used on the newspaper strips."

Smokey Bear comics were published by Gold Key and through the March of Comics, while Dell published its companion *Smokey the Bear* comics. *Smokey the Bear* comic strips featuring a scrappy "Little Smokey" and his comical raccoon friend Specs were printed and distributed by Columbia Features in New York and Adcox-Lenahan in San Francisco to about eighty newspapers. And CFFP director Bill Newman thanked Huber on behalf of the Forest Service: "We very much appreciate the fine job you are doing in combining education and humor in these very attractive comic books."

To capitalize on the strong appeal of stuffed Smokey Bear dolls, Ben Michtom of the Ideal Toy Company proposed in 1953 to include with his dolls an application card for youngsters to become "Junior Forest Rangers." Clint Davis eagerly accepted the idea, so each child writing to Smokey received in return an official kit of fire prevention materials. Although items varied over the years, kids typically received a treasure trove of Rudy Wendelin-designed articles—a Junior Forest Ranger membership card, a pledge card

Smokey received so much mail—sometimes 1,000 letters per day—that he was awarded his own ZIP code, 20252. *(Courtesy USDA Forest Service.)*

and badge, a Smokey song sheet, a bookmark, stamps and a Smokey photograph.

Administration varied, but kids' requests generally were serviced principally from CFFP headquarters in Washington, D.C. If CFFP staffers had foreseen the response to Michtom's idea, however, they might have made other arrangements. With surprising speed, the new program exploded into a major fire prevention tool. "Aside from personal visits to schools," Mal Hardy explained, "probably the most effective way to reach the grade school population was through the Junior Forest Ranger program. Children who wrote to Smokey felt a special sense of belonging when they got their kits in the mail. As the years go by, they are more apt to retain the principles of forest fire prevention than is a person seeing a Smokey poster once or twice."

Letters to Smokey arrived from the West, the South, the Northeast, from urban high-rises and rural farms, printed, typed and scrawled. From big kids and little kids, from girls and boys, a flood of letters swelled to a torrent until a tidal wave of paper washed into CFFP headquarters. By 1964, Smokey was receiving so much mail—reportedly more than anyone else in Washington, including the President of the United States—that the Post Office decided that special action was required. So on April 29, 1964, deputy postmaster William M. McMillan presented a card to Forest Service chief Ed Cliff that assigned a personal ZIP code—20252—to Smokey Bear.

In a typical year, more than 200,000 individual cards and letters arrived in Washington, D.C., and another 30,000 applications were processed by more than a dozen cooperating states. By 1970, 260,000 Junior Forest Ranger applications—a rate of more than 1,000 each business day—arrived. By 1972, more than 6 million children had enrolled in Smokey's posse as his national advertising kept up the pressure. Smokey's ABC-TV show alone prompted requests for kits from schoolteachers in New Hampshire to nearly double to 29,000 in a single year. As the program spread into Canada, CFFP staffers struggled to cope with the onslaught.

"The Junior Forest Ranger Program," Mal Hardy wrote in 1971, "continues to demand nearly half of our 7 to 7 1/2 man-years of personal services." But despite the resources required, the CFFP felt compelled to accommodate requests.

"The Junior Forest Ranger program is one of the important foundations upon which rests the entire Smokey Bear campaign," added Jim Sorenson, Hardy's assistant. "Through it children are not just exposed to the wildfire prevention message, but rather become committed to the entire concept because it is now their project. They are now the ones in the family who make sure that Mom doesn't burn the trash on a windy day; or that Dad pours water on the campfire before they leave an area. The young member of a camping family is often much more likely to be able to get a fire prevention message across to that family than some stranger riding around in a government truck. If he or she happens to be a Junior Forest Ranger, the chances are good that such a fire prevention message *will* be delivered."

Children growing into adults fit CFFP strategy. "These Junior Forest Rangers won't be little for long," Sorenson elaborated. "In a few years they will be starting families of their own, and the fire safety principles implanted through the Junior Forest Ranger program will still be available, at least subliminally."

If there was any doubt about the impact of the Junior Forest Ranger program on the minds of children, consider the 1960 case of nine-year-old Eric Riggenbach of Williamsburg, Iowa. After starting a fire that almost got out of control, Riggenbach, believing himself to be unworthy of membership, mailed his coveted Junior Forest Ranger badge back to Smokey. In a reply, "Smokey" told Eric he would return his badge in three months if the youngster didn't play with matches and was careful with fire. In a story distributed nationwide by UPI, Gaylord P. Godwin reported that Riggenbach accepted both the letter and the spirit of Smokey's warning, made a fire prevention speech at his school, appeared on a local radio station and then watched his story spread through newspapers across the nation.

Cleansed, Riggenbach petitioned Smokey for reinstatement. "I haven't played with matches or fire," Eric promised. "I want the badge back. I will carry it everywhere." After reviewing accompanying certification from the lad's mother, Smokey mailed Riggenbach a shiny new Junior Forest Ranger badge—and a special Rudy Wendelin drawing of Smokey with the caption "Welcome back, Eric."

All kids weren't like Eric, though. "James" wrote twice, first from Leaksville, North Carolina: "Somky [sic], Goddam you why don't you sent kit? All the Goddam other kids got one." The second letter came from Hendersonville, North Carolina: "Smokey Bear. I moved now. Sent that kit or else." But because James didn't provide his address, he never got a kit.

In almost every business, successful operations eventually generate progeny, and the Junior Forest Ranger program was no exception. Itself a spin-off of the licensing program, the Junior Forest Ranger program sired another concept to help educate children about forest fire prevention.

"An activity related to the Junior Forest Ranger program is the Smokey Bear Reading Club," Mal Hardy explained. "Several states set up these programs to reach children during the summer months, in addition to the normal exposure Smokey receives in schools." These clubs typically ask children to read ten books on conservation and the environment. Upon joining a club, members receive a Smokey Bear bookmark, button, and a Smokey comic book, along with a reading record book. Upon meeting the requirements, members receive a Smokey reading certificate.

Millions of delighted Americans who have seen Smokey at rodeos, county fairs and parades eagerly accept the furry creature as the ursinification of his poster counterpart. Like every aspect of his program, the walking Smokey is the product of an artist's fertile imagination, and it's no surprise that the talent behind the creation of the official Smokey costume lay with Rudy Wendelin.

It's also no surprise that some folks may challenge that statement. Wisconsin claims that the first Smokey Bear costume was created by Frank Brunner Jr. in Mercer, Wisconsin. But Virginia State Forester Jim Garner believes that the costume was created by Ed Rodger of Virginia. According to Garner, Rodger apparently found a Philadelphia company to make the first costume sometime around 1950. When Rodger showed it to the Forest Service a year or two later, mass production soon started.

But the official version holds that Wendelin created the Smokey costume with assistance from his wife, Carrol, in the kitchen of his Virginia home in 1952.

"Clint Davis apparently had a request from the Macy's people in New York for Smokey to be in the parade," Wendelin recalled. "Clint was always ready to do anything to promote Smokey; if there was a demand, Clint was ready to do it, so he asked me if we could make a costume of some kind. I said sure, and I got a roll of fur fabric from the Ideal Toy Company that made the Smokey Bear dolls. I worked on the costume at home in the evenings because I needed my shop downstairs; we didn't have proper facilities at the office for me to do the necessary woodwork. I shaped the head first. I carved a mouth out of wood, molded chicken wire into the proper shape, soldered it and then shaped the nose. Carrol and I soaked old newspapers in water and covered the chicken wire with papier-mâché. Then I used plaster of paris to smooth out the nose and cut up a plastic egg crate and used two of those plastic eggs for the eyes, with holes cut in the eyeballs."

For a week, Wendelin tinkered with his creation each evening. "I was always putting it on my head to see how it worked," Wendelin acknowledged. "I decided to make the mouth work, so I hinged the inside of the mouth and ran a cord down inside so it could be pulled by hand. I wish I could have made the eyes blink to give it a lifelike look, but I didn't, so Smokey looked glassy-eyed. I got the hat from a licensee in Philadelphia that made Forest Service hats. Then Carrol took the fur fabric, shaped it around the chicken wire and papier-mâché head and sewed it to the framework. She made the ears, filled them with cotton and sewed them onto the head. Then we made sleeves, arms and mitten fingers. We bought oversize dungarees at a department store; the belt was a licensed product. Carrol sewed during the day, then I came home and worked on it and we checked it over together at night."

Wendelin took his creation to the office, but insisted that he was not tempted to wear it on his commuter bus. "No one at the office had seen it," Wendelin acknowledged. "They left it up to me to come up with something. But when I took the final product to the office, someone tried it on right away. They were all excited because that was a new development in the appearance of Smokey. That outfit was first used in the Macy's parade in New York in 1952. Ben Sanders [of the Forest Service] wore it; he sat in the back of an open-air limousine, waved to the crowd and moved the mouth up and down like he was saying something. From a distance, he looked real—just like the image of Smokey. It was the first three-dimensional appearance of Smokey!"

Because of its instant success, demand for the costume grew rapidly. "They needed more costumes," Wendelin confirmed, "so the exhibit shop of the Department of Agriculture was assigned to reproduce the original. They made twelve or fifteen copies and I went down and checked on them. The head was the important part—creating the head and shaping the mouth and getting the lettering on the hat. Then, we had to stuff pillows in some of them to increase the bulk. Some people would wear a down vest to give more bulk around the shoulders too. A costume can be hot and uncomfortable, so someone put a little battery-operated fan in there to cool the head. Today they are pretty common and readily available."

Partly because his speech on the topic was recorded at the First National Smokey Bear Workshop, James Ricard, a training officer with New Hampshire's Division of Resources Development, is recognized as a tutor for effective use of Smokey costumes. As an authority on Smokey's personal appearances, Ricard combined official guidelines with common sense to instruct others on how to use the Smokey costume.

For openers, Ricard urged Smokeys never to appear in public alone. A bear can roam free in the woods, but not in civilization, where he should appear with a uniformed assistant connected with fire prevention. The best Smokey is an active Smokey, so Ricard expected each Smokey to move his paws, nod his massive head and adjust his hat. "Don't stand with arms hanging limply at your sides—be alive," Ricard preached.

But a maze of guidelines can choke a putative actor as quick as a four-hour summer stint inside the suit. Only state and federal agencies can own Smokey costumes, and anyone other than state and federal employees are discouraged from wearing the costume, although firemen, scout leaders and industrial foresters can act as Smokey if they follow the guidelines. Costumes can be used only in programs involving wildfire prevention, and although Smokey's "sponsor" may be identified, the volunteer inside the suit must remain anonymous. Perhaps most important, Smokey's costume must be kept under wraps before and after use. "Smokey should never appear in less than full costume," Ricard warned.

And why not, pray tell? "Smokey's head tucked under a forest officer's arm is shocking to a child, and is not to be tolerated," Ricard explained.

It wouldn't do, either, for a grungy bear to harm Smokey's image. Costumes must be kept clean and in good repair, Ricard emphasized, pointing out that Smokey's blouse should be dry-cleaned but his pants could be laundered. Smokey isn't a city slicker, either, so Ricard insisted that shiny shoes be left at home (until the furry feet were added) and that Smokey carry a shovel at outdoor appearances.

And Ricard warned against foolishness; the bear must be treated seriously. "Clowning, horseplay, insinuations and wisecracks have no place in a costumed Smokey presentation," he remonstrated. "Smokey should be dignified, friendly, but firm in presenting his fire prevention message. The use of alcoholic beverages by Smokey is out just before or during a Smokey appearance. It is well to remember that you can't make a joke out of Smokey without making a fool of yourself."

Perhaps Smokey's most difficult challenge is to not scare children— sometimes a tough assignment for the friendly but imposing bear towering over small fry. "Never force yourself as 'Smokey' on children or other timid people," Ricard cautioned. "If children or others appear frightened, turn away and talk or shake hands with someone else. Move slowly, try to discourage parents who attempt to force a child to meet or shake hands against the child's will. Never walk rapidly toward small children."

Smokey's assistant was charged with watching for wires, potholes, cars, motor scooters, toddlers, drunks and practical jokers. It wouldn't do to have Smokey dancing with a hotfoot. So Ricard's final plea is as basic as apple pie: "Never take the job of appearing as Smokey lightly. Be alive, vigorous, alert and remember that you are representing one of the greatest of national symbols."

Many volunteer "Smokeys" beefed about their costumes. Most wearers claimed the zipper was too small and jammed in the costume's hair. But the primary complaints were that the head was too small and the outfit was poorly ventilated. "The fabric and the headgear can be hot," confirmed

Ken Bowman of the Forest Service's southwestern region. "Get inside that thing in July and you lose ten pounds."

One of the hundreds of volunteers who suffered in that hot Smokey costume is Robert Conrad. A Pennsylvania native and graduate of the University of Upper Iowa, Conrad ran a gauntlet of media jobs, first as a disc jockey in Pennsylvania, then through radio and TV news in Texas, Colorado, Nebraska and the armed forces network in Spain and North Africa. Along the way Conrad edited a Texas newspaper and authored numerous magazine articles before joining the Forest Service in 1976.

"They wanted someone with a media background to run their national media office," Conrad explained. "The Forest Service had a 'Media West' office in California to deal with the *Lassie* series, but I was supposed to handle the media on a national scale. The Forest Service had a big appetite for news coverage, but I only had one secretary to help. Undaunted, Conrad rolled up his sleeves . . . and met Smokey Bear.

"One of my fun jobs was to develop the Smokey Bear and Woodsy Owl programs and increase their visibility," Conrad added. *Howdy Doody* was coming back to life, so I contacted the producers and suggested they could have Smokey and Woodsy appear on their show. They were enthused about it, and we scheduled a date in Miami for an appearance. The Forest Service had never had anyone on national TV in the bear costume. I could imitate Jackson Weaver, so because of my radio voice I was chosen to be in the costume." And Conrad's Smokey was an instant success, leading to twice-yearly showings on *Romper Room* and so many other shows that Conrad eventually appeared more than a hundred times in the bear costume on national television.

"Usually I got on any kind of kids program," Conrad explained. "It wasn't difficult back then [1976-1987]; it was fairly easy because there wasn't as much competition with other public service announcements. But it's been a little tougher since 1987."

Conrad certainly enjoyed prowling around as Smokey Bear. "Some of the old plastic costumes are horrendous-looking," he admitted, "but my costume was state of the art—fur, feet, jeans and shovel." Even then, the best-laid plans of bears and men sometimes don't work out as planned. April 5, 1978 was the big day.

"Don Hansen [CFFP program manager] said we were going to the White House to meet the president," Conrad recalled. "Smokey Bear always has to appear in complete costume, so you can imagine the looks on the guards' faces when I went walking through the White House gate. We were supposed to meet the president and Mrs. Carter and Amy, but unfortunately there was some kind of crisis. While we were waiting, all the staffers came down to get their pictures taken with Smokey. I never got to meet the president, but they gave us the VIP treatment and took us on a tour. I was really getting hot in that costume—it's like wearing a fur coat, plus it has furry feet and furry paws and a hat. When we got outside the White House, tourists wanted to get photos with Smokey. After four and a half hours, I was basically dying. Sometimes when I wear the costume I put a cooling band—a jogger's band—in a freezer and then wrap it around my head; it's good for six or seven hours, but I didn't have it that day."

Conrad loved his role. "I was always amazed at how kids reacted," he emphasized. "Smokey is six-foot-two and has a sixty-four-inch waist. He's a big bear. But even preschoolers were not afraid; they came up and hugged me. They knew it was a costume. I don't think even preschoolers would associate Smokey with a bear in the woods."

Conrad's primary problem was his inability to see the little tykes. "Visibility is terribly limited," he confirmed. "You can look out through the eyes or nose, but you have to be careful if you move a lot. Once, on the *Howdy Doody Show*, I walked to the peanut gallery and trampled on a kid's foot. You wouldn't do a fifty-yard dash in that costume. But you can feel kids if they grab you from behind, and you can hold a pen or hand out autographed posters. It's fun—a labor of love."

20

A GRASS-ROOTS BEAR

"If you go meet a program director, take a Smokey Bear patch
and tell how important the message is, there's a good chance
your material will get played."

— Jim Sorenson

Smokey Bear patrols America's woodlands with far more support than that of the Forest Service. The nation's fifty state foresters, the largest leg of the Cooperative Forest Fire Prevention program, take Smokey to America's grass roots—the local contributors who represent Smokey's lifeblood.

Because individual communities face unique problems, states use Smokey in different ways and often develop their own creative methods to promote forest fire prevention. And Smokey's legions of state allies include foresters who become directly involved at CFFP headquarters in Washington, D.C.

Born in 1940 in Kansas City, Missouri, James C. Sorenson developed an interest in forestry when he began asking why eastern Kansas farmers didn't use woodland resources to make their land more productive. After a stint with the army's 101st Airborne Division, Sorenson studied forestry at the

University of Montana, graduated in 1965, and was hired as an assistant district forester by Missouri's state forester—another former paratrooper.

Sorenson first worked with farmers to develop Missouri's forests, then began speaking to interested groups about fire prevention, started a new fire protection district and worked with fire departments on training and procuring firefighting equipment. Soon, Sorenson found himself far more involved with fire prevention than forestry, and after completing a special assignment for the Forest Service, Sorenson caught the eye of CFFP personnel in Washington.

"They were looking for someone under the Intergovernment Personnel Act [IPA], which helped government and universities share people back and forth," Sorenson explained. "They had a problem with Smokey Bear in the early 1970s because people throughout the profession were using Smokey to do things besides prevent forest fires. They wanted him to pick up litter, protect animals and be available for other uses for conservation. The Forest Service thought this was diluting Smokey's message, so Woodsy Owl was developed as an answer for an anti-litter campaign."

Mal Hardy, asked to run a Woodsy Owl campaign similar to the Smokey Bear program, had no budget or manpower to handle the workload. "So Mal stumbled onto the IPA to help him," Sorenson continued, "and I was offered the chance to become his assistant from June 1972 through June 1974."

"The Smokey Bear program has three partners," Sorenson emphasized. "The Ad Council makes it workable and spreads the word, but they don't have the technical fire expertise. So we have to involve the Forest Service and state foresters. Those people have the on-the-ground responsibility to implement the program. The states make the CFFP program work; they carry the biggest share of the responsibility. In Missouri, for example, the central office in Jefferson City orders materials in large quantities, and divides it up by fourteen or fifteen fire districts with up to ten or twelve counties per district. I had a district office at Lebanon with four and a half counties." And Sorenson started with fire prevention basics.

"I picked up my share of the supplies and then made up packets," he recalled. "Kids like kits—they go crazy over them. So I took a litter bag and put in a comic book, a ruler, some stickers and a couple of coloring sheets. Over time, I got letters and calls from teachers in the district asking me to come by and talk about forest fire prevention. We concentrated on kindergarten through fourth grade so we could get them early. We went to schools on the appointed days, making sure we had a kit for each kid and a special kit for each teacher with bigger posters and more adult items. We introduced ourselves, talked a little, showed a movie and then answered questions. The kids invariably talked about their dads starting fires in the woods, so we got them thinking about fire prevention and they took that message home. That night, the kids talked with Mom and Dad about what they had seen. The kids weren't involved with fire, of course, but Mom and Dad were, and as the kids got older they would remember."

Sorenson insists that local efforts can make Smokey's national advertising effective: "Let the Ad Council send the videos and audios because they have the recognition. But you need personal contact because local [radio and TV] program directors have their desks covered with public message stuff. If you go meet a program director, take a Smokey Bear patch and tell how important the message is, there's a good chance your material will get played. Otherwise, it may be just another tape gathering dust."

Sorenson's experience illustrates the value of the private/federal/state approach—a true cooperative effort despite its tongue-stumbling, bureaucratic name. The Smokey Bear program works because states support it and cooperate closely up the line with federal agencies and down the line with subdivisions of state government. In typical years, the states have distributed as many as 30 million items specifically designed and produced for the Smokey program. "Clearly, the program is geared toward personal contact," Sorenson confirmed, "but each state is different," as a review of states across the nation reveals.

Robert Burns, of the California Division of Forestry, proffered a snapshot of California's situation in 1970. With almost 100,000 square miles of land requiring wildfire protection, several entities share its administration. The state assumed responsibility for 34 million acres, the Forest Service protected 25 million acres, counties and contractors covered 7 million acres, the National Park Service oversaw 4 million acres, the Bureau of Land Management 1 million acres and the U.S. military another 4 million acres. Cities, towns and Indian services protected additional acreage.

Although fire authorities faced about 8,000 wildfires each year, California's forest fire problem was certain to grow. "Population is increasing by a half million people per year," Burns explained, "and people are moving into the wild lands by the thousands." Even by 1970, wildfires on state lands alone were increasing by three hundred per year. Alarming data revealed that children were causing 25 percent of fires on state lands and 12 percent of the fires in California's national forests, and that both figures were increasing.

"Obviously, we need to do a great deal more work with children," Burns observed, "and Smokey Bear and forest fire prevention materials are part of this answer." But Burns acknowledged that Smokey wasn't always the solution: "Smokey Bear is not too much value when it comes to incendiary [fires] and a good part of the machine use problem."

So California attacked its wildfire problem through engineering, research, law enforcement and education. The state's educational, or Smokey Bear, program worked by ensuring effective distribution of fire prevention materials. "The Information and Education office purchases CFFP materials," Burns explained. "This represents about two million pieces. Another two to three million pieces are printed in the state printing plant. All told, about ten million pieces are distributed annually by all agencies in California. Children-oriented materials and programs are our main thrust."

California Division of Forestry (CDF) printed materials came from a variety of sources. "We print former CFFP materials that were discontinued or those we can print cheaper, such as song sheets and reflectorized bumper strips," Burns offered. "We also print items originated by our own employees, such as wallet calendars, absorbent coasters, coloring books, posters, etc. Sometimes we borrow the artwork for materials . . . and print an additional supply of needed items."

CDF personnel distributed most of that mountain of material through the California Fire Prevention Committee. "The committee consists of over four hundred volunteer member organizations representing industry, civic groups, clubs, associations, and agencies," Burns explained. And what a roll call! That roster included representatives of railroads, oil companies, power companies, telephone companies, manufacturing firms, radio and TV stations, newspapers, magazines, Boy Scout and Girl Scout councils, automobile associations, women's clubs, chambers of commerce, banks and public libraries.

The state's library program—replicated throughout the nation—enjoyed a high visibility because of the California Library Association. "Because this organization and all its members are a part of the California Fire Prevention Committee, they are a strong segment of the fire prevention program," Burns explained. "A librarian organizes the clubs annually with children from eight to twelve years of age. Several thousand children go through the course each year."

Then a pair of nonprofit organizations chipped in. "Keep California Green and the Redwood Region Conservation Council cover the state with a fire prevention poster contest," Burns said. "Winners are printed by the

CDF. The Division of Forestry furnishes fire prevention materials as a contribution. They supply the artwork, and we print the material. Volunteer county committees handle much of the actual work—sometimes hand in hand with CDF and U.S. Forest Service field people."

With Smokey's fire prevention message spreading like, uh, wildfire, an army of supporters marched across the state each year. As clubs, schoolchildren, scouts and businesses enlisted in the cause, they, too, distributed Smokey materials. Posters appeared statewide, and stuffers and pamphlets were used by companies as inserts with bills and ads.

Sometimes Smokey joined in the fun. A baseball fan, Smokey appeared at all five of California's major league ballparks, thanks to the California Division of Forestry and Joe DeLucchi of Los Angeles, a member of the California Fire Prevention Committee. Smokey usually enjoyed a pre-game ride around the field on a fire truck, and because of his special fondness for people skilled at putting out any kind of fire, Smokey presented "Fireman of the Year" awards to the top relief pitchers of the various teams.

Public contributions were uncountable. *Sunset Magazine*, Pacific Gas and Electric, Bell Telephone, Bechtel Corporation and McCulloch chain saws featured fire prevention articles in their newsletters. Pacific Telephone included Smokey's picture in a mailing insert and followed up with 5 million stuffers in monthly billings. "The Bank of America distributes wallet calendars in all their branch banks," Burns added. "The automobile associations distribute material. Border stations give out-of-state cars a litter bag, and their inspection tag for out-of-state vehicles has a fire prevention message from Smokey. Bell Telephone Company not only hosts the annual California Fire Prevention Committee meetings but also put a fire prevention poster on each company vehicle and a window display in each office during June. The Junior Women's Clubs purchase Smokey Bear costumes for the CDF and the U.S. Forest Service. We have two animated fiberglass Smokeys that are used at fairs and conferences."

Even California's politicians supported the effort. "In 1968, the state legislature passed a law requiring that conservation education and fire prevention education be taught at all primary and secondary grade levels," Burns explained. And in his 1970 State of the State address, Governor Ronald Reagan asked for a formal fire prevention program in the California public school system.

At least one idea garnered publicity for Smokey across the entire nation. Sponsored by the Native Sons and Daughters of the Golden West, a Smokey Bear float first appeared in Pasadena's Tournament of Roses Parade in 1959. Gaining support from the CFFP, the NSD furnished manpower and funds, with the CFFP sharing costs and Rudy Wendelin's artistic talent. If 1964 is a valid measurement, the CFFP reaped good value from its $4,000 contribution: an estimated 100 million Americans watched that year's parade on television. In 1966 the NSD float won the Grand Marshal's trophy for exceptional merit. By 1971 the two groups had cooperated on eight floats, with that year's $12,000 entry featuring Smokey overlooking a floral forest from a fire lookout tower; two cubs helped rotate five poster frames displaying floral renditions of ten Smokey Bear posters. And numbers-oriented Smokey fans appreciate knowing that Smokey's hat in the 1973 parade was covered with more than 10,000 oat seeds.

California also developed a traveling Smokey Bear museum, thanks to a Utah immigrant and a vacuum-cleaner salesman. Richard C. Just, deputy chief of fire prevention for California's Department of Forestry and Fire Protection, was born in Brigham City, Utah in 1947, but moved to California when he was three days old. And Just learned about Smokey Bear before he understood forest fires.

"Back in the fifties," Just explained, "Hoover salesmen in California would give Smokey Bear dolls to anyone who would agree to watch a demonstration of a Hoover vacuum. Mom liked to have salesmen show her new products, so she listened to a Hoover sales pitch. She didn't buy a vacuum, but we got a Smokey Bear doll and I grew up treasuring that thing."

After graduating with a degree in biology from Chico State University in Chico, California, Just later won his teaching credentials. Then when Just began working for California's Department of Forestry and Fire Protection, he developed an appreciation for fire prevention. "With my background in education," Just explained, "I naturally had more of an interest in teaching fire prevention rather than focusing on fire suppression. And Smokey Bear is a good teacher."

So Just began collecting Smokey Bear items. "I started with posters, because my initial focus was on CFFP items that were free," Just recalled. But Just soon branched out into dolls, patches and anything else with the bear's image and message. His collection grew and grew until he spent more than $15,000 and, among other items, eventually accumulated more than 150 Smokey dolls. "About sixty different ones have been produced," Just explained. "I'm only missing a couple."

Just soon was swamped with Smokey paraphernalia. "I had most of it in my office, but it finally overran my office and my house," Just confessed. "The display cases in my office were so full that you couldn't distinguish one item from another. People were coming by my office to look, and peering in through the window if I wasn't there. It was easy to see that people were really interested in Smokey, so I started looking for a way to share the collection with the public."

Then Just hatched an idea for a traveling Smokey Bear display. The state first acquired an old twenty-eight-foot trailer that had been used in remote locations by the Forest Service. Then, with Dave Doughty doing most of the volunteer labor for two years, California spent more than $7,000 to refurbish the trailer, line it with redwood for a rustic flavor, build in several display cases, add carpeting and install a stereo system to play Smokey radio commercials. In late 1988, the Mobile Smokey Bear Museum began traveling around California.

Enormously popular, the museum's five dozen Smokey posters and hundreds of Smokey bookmarks, dishes, dolls, handkerchiefs and other items began appearing at state fairs, schools and public events. Kids and adults alike lined up to see Smokey's memorabilia. Even Disneyland, Knotts Berry Farm and Pasadena's Tournament of Roses parade were worked into the itinerary.

"The two original Smokey costumes may be the biggest attractions," Just offered. "They're about six-feet-six, so kids are pretty impressed. Also, we have a two-hour loop of Smokey's radio commercials that plays continuously, and visitors listen to them as they look at the exhibits. And the California Federated Women's Club donates money for the handouts that promote the museum."

In addition to Just's original collection, licensees and others have begun contributing items that are used to rotate out Just's personal items. "We go to vendors each year and ask for donations, but we offer to hand out their brochures in return," Just explained.

Because of the museum's success, management of the California Department of Forestry and Fire Protection allocated funds to purchase and staff a new thirty-two-foot trailer with about thirty percent more display room that will allow showings of videotaped Smokey TV commercials. More than 1 million people are expected to visit the museum each year.

"The image of Smokey brings something with it—all those fire prevention messages that we have seen through the years," Just emphasized. "It only takes a glance at his face, because Smokey Bear personalizes forest fire prevention. When you see Smokey, you are seeing Rudy Wendelin, the Ad Council and everyone else that works on forest fire prevention.

"Because of the catastrophic events here in California," Just added, "we have to have something to hang our hats on, and Smokey Bear works well for us. California's renewed emphasis on educating the public will put Smokey out there more than ever. Smokey helps everyone band together."

But what about the original Smokey Bear doll from Hoover? "Yes," Just laughed. "It's still a focal point of the collection."

Three thousand miles east, the nation's older states were just as dedicated to forest fire prevention. Eugene F. McNamara, chief of Pennsylvania's Division of Forest Protection, proudly spoke in 1970 of his state's commitment: "The Keystone State still has seventeen million acres or roughly sixty percent of its total land area in forest. This large forest acreage, combined with the fact that the state has a population of twelve million people gives the Keystone State the second largest combination of people and forest in the nation."

With an estimated 99 percent of its forest fires caused by people, Pennsylvania annually battled 1,300 fires burning 12,000 forest acres. Aware of the value of prevention, the state welcomed the nation's spokesbear for forests. "I am very proud that we can honestly say that we strongly support the Smokey Program," McNamara emphasized. "Each year we purchase and use the second largest amount of Smokey Prevention material of any state in the nation." But Pennsylvania didn't stop there.

"In an effort to take a new look at our overall prevention program," McNamara explained, "we have developed our intensive Metropolitan School Program. This had two objectives: one, reach a large number of children with the importance of and need for fire prevention; two, impress upon them that our department has the responsibility for forest fire prevention. We started this intensive prevention program in 1967 in the Harrisburg Metropolitan area. During one week in March, with four teams of Smokeys we visited sixty-seven schools, with sixteen thousand children in grades one, two, three and four."

Arthur Creelman, another Pennsylvania forester, believed their program was highly effective: "Smokey and the forester spend five minutes in each room, give a short presentation, answer questions and leave handout materials with teachers. During this program, we try to involve any local fire companies in the area. We have received excellent media coverage from newspaper, radio and TV."

But Smokey didn't limit his Pennsylvania efforts to that single week in March. "Smokey visits other schools, visits county fairs, rides in firemen's parades, sells his message from store windows, participates in Halloween parades, opens shopping centers, participates many times in sportsmen's shows, and is present at the annual Pennsylvania Farm Show, which is the largest of its kind in the nation," McNamara added. "Smokey is a welcome guest at any public affair in the Keystone State. We give Smokey a great amount of credit for the progress that we have made in the fire prevention program."

Like California, Pennsylvania supplemented CFFP products by printing its own materials, sometimes incorporating literature from the California program. Pennsylvania also adopted California's use of Smokey at major league baseball games and extended that idea when the state and the Philadelphia Fire Department sponsored a fire prevention show at half-time of a Monday night football game between the Philadelphia Eagles and the New York Giants. Smokey, naturally, received more attention than the fire prevention queen.

Creelman also arranged for Smokey to visit *Romper Room* TV shows broadcast during Fire Prevention Week, but Pennsylvania's state government took even a bigger step. "During 1970, instead of having just a Fire Prevention Week, we had a Fire Prevention Year," Creelman boasted. "This not only kicked off our program but opened up all the doors of state government. We tried to involve as many people as possible, which is really the name of the game in prevention."

Certainly, many people did become involved, and Pennsylvania's efforts even generated Smokey's own postage stamp in 1984, thanks largely to the efforts of Mike Marchese. A life-long resident of Williamsport, Pennsylvania, Marchese became a fireman in 1970 at age thirty-six, and developed an interest in fire prevention. Soon, Marchese was taking Smokey Bear coloring pages to schools, asking kids to color them, and encouraging firemen to judge the art and award Smokey stuffed dolls to the winners.

With his wife's help, Marchese broadened his fire prevention effort. He made speeches using borrowed films (until Burger King paid for new ones) as visual aids, worked with thirty-six area volunteer programs and continued recruiting kids into the cause of fire prevention.

But Marchese had become irritated that a stingy Congress wouldn't pay to move the living Smokey back to New Mexico before his death in 1976. So one day in 1977, Marchese was sitting at the firehouse weighing ideas on how to honor Smokey. When a U.S. Postal Service truck pulled into the Post Office next door and Marchese saw the eagle stamp displayed on the truck's side, he had his answer: a Smokey Bear stamp.

Certainly, the idea wasn't new; a Smokey stamp had been proposed by the Capitan, New Mexico, Women's Club as far back as 1960, and others had raised the idea, but nothing had materialized. Undaunted, Marchese started his campaign.

"I wrote letters to the Postal Service, President Carter, all the senators," Marchese explained. "I got the *World Almanac* and wrote to everyone I could think of—movie stars, the Boy Scouts, *Good Morning America, Reader's Digest.* I sent sixteen letters to President Reagan. Then I went to the schools and asked kids to write letters that I could send to Congress. I wrote to Governor Thornburgh of Pennsylvania and Governor King of New Mexico. I wrote to Elliott Barker and the New Mexico congressional delegation. I typed all the letters on a manual typewriter—several thousand, if not more. I was mailing fifty to sixty letters a week. My gosh, between gas, writing, duplication and stamps, I bet I spent five to six thousand dollars."

It took Marchese six years and more than a dozen appeals to the Citizens Stamp Advisory Committee, but his bandwagon finally rolled to victory. The Postal Service announced in the summer of 1983 that Smokey Bear would be feted with a fortieth anniversary stamp designed by Rudy Wendelin.

Proud of Marchese's efforts, the people of Williamsport collected donations to send Marchese and his wife to Capitan for the first-day-of-issue festivities. At the event, the Postal Service failed to mention Marchese's name or give him any recognition, but the CFFP didn't forget; Marchese later was awarded the Silver Smokey.

And why did Marchese push so hard for a Smokey stamp? "I'm a fireman," he affirmed, "so fire prevention has to be part of everyday life. If you see the stamp, you will think of fire prevention."

Many states directly supplemented the Ad Council's national media effort. Walter Gooley Jr., of Maine's Forestry Department, explained that his department sent its own radio spot announcements to Maine's thirty-seven AM radio stations in 1972. Each tape addressed topics such as fisherman-caused fires, debris burning, camper fires, hunter fires and eight other sixty-second reminders. "The spots carried a lively tune using a guitar and other instruments and a bridge message of approximately twenty-four seconds," Gooley recalled. "The cost of the spots was $822, which included an attractive box for the reel and postage. This figures out to $22 per station and $1.83 per spot. Many stations used the spots more than a hundred times and one was used over five hundred." Of course, what else could be expected of a state where, because of state forester Austin Wilkins, Smokey Bear had been appointed an honorary life member of the Civil Air Patrol?

They loved Smokey in Florida, too—especially in the General Federation of Women's Clubs, which passed its first resolution on conservation in 1896. "Not many people are as well known as Smokey Bear," explained Mrs. J. C.

Pratt of Florida's Department of Agriculture and Consumer Services. "Any schoolchild could tell you all about Smokey." Florida's women's clubs began distributing Smokey materials in the early 1950s and continued to support the program through the following decades.

"During the administration of 1970-72, environmental education was a prime concern," Pratt explained. "In the Junior Division alone there were over 388 projects or programs. Over a hundred Smokey Bear programs were given, ranging from library reading groups . . . to original productions reaching over 5,000 children. One club has a Smokey suit on permanent loan from the Forest Service. More than 84,700 pieces of literature were distributed during 1968-70. More than 500 books during this period have been donated to libraries for the Smokey the Bear Reading Clubs."

But in Florida, as in much of the United States, Smokey symbolizes more than the forest fire prevention effort, regardless of whether the bear intended to moonlight. "Through the years Smokey has become to the members of the Florida Federation of Women's Clubs the symbol not only of fire prevention but of conservation," Pratt added. "We have used Smokey as a symbol in programs dealing with all phases of conservation: Arbor Day programs, anytime trees are planted, nature tours, puppet shows demonstrating other areas of conservation and fire prevention. At the end of these presentations, Smokey will make an appearance and distribute coloring books. The children listen and we feel that they learn. Smokey is used in our safety campaigns, paint-up and clean-up programs, skits, convocation programs in the schools, ranger tours, fire tower tours, for every conceivable teaching method. About 2,000 conservation programs were held during a two-year period. Most of these included Smokey in some way. This, I think, indicates how FFWC feels about the Smokey Bear program."

Back in the West, Idaho's basic problems of coordinating efforts paralleled those of many other states, but the cooperative spirit of the Smokey Bear program helped resolve the issues. Barney Wozniak, of Idaho's Department of Public Lands, outlined his state's approach.

"In Idaho," Wozniak explained, "there are a number of state and federal agencies interested in forest and range fire prevention. The federal agencies include the Forest Service, the Bureau of Land Management, the Indian Service and . . . the National Park Service. The principal state agency involved, of course, is the Forestry Division of the State Land Department. There are also three associations of landowners concerned with forest and range fire prevention. All these agencies involved in fire prevention constitute a problem of correlation and coordination. This is done, to a large extent, through the governor's Keep Idaho Green program. With all these agencies involved in fire prevention, there was a need for some effort to prevent confusion, repetition and unnecessary work by the various agencies."

A typical problem involved coordinating the posted fire-danger rating among various agencies for the news media. Because of Idaho's array of elevation and topography, apparently inconsistent reports were issued to a baffled media and public.

"For example," Wozniak added, "the Bureau of Land Management is concerned to a large extent with the desert areas, which become dry and a critical fire hazard very early to late in the season, while the upper elevation lands on the National Forests are often still covered with snow. It was not uncommon for the Bureau of Land Management to report to a TV station that fire-danger was high and then the Forest Ranger to report to the same station that the fire danger was low. Usually, the state-protected lands would fall somewhere in between these two extremes and result in reporting fire-danger rating of moderate. The public, looking at one article out of context with the others and not understanding the elevational differences, would often conclude that the agency people were not accurately reporting or else they did not know what they were doing."

But Idaho helped develop a solution. "Within the viewing and listening areas of the various TV and radio stations in southwestern Idaho," Wozniak explained, "all the fire danger reports and ratings are funneled in to the Division of Forestry Office, which correlates and coordinates them and prepares one overall fire hazard situation for the news media. This has eliminated the confusion that once appeared and has also served to make radio and TV stations pay more attention to the fire-danger ratings they receive. We used to literally beg them to publish these notices, and now they frequently call the Division of Forestry to see what the situation is."

One of Idaho's many blessings is the dedication of so many of its citizens to preserving the state's forest and wilderness areas. As in California, many organizations pitched in to help. Concurrent with the beginning of Keep Idaho Green in the late 1940s, Idaho Jaycees identified forest and range fire prevention as their primary statewide project. Campfire Girls and dozens of other volunteer associations soon blanketed the state, with the strong support of fire prevention officials.

"One of the principal values of involving agencies," Wozniak emphasized, "has been the personal involvement of children and their parents in the prevention effort, not only making them more effective in getting other people to prevent fires, but they themselves more fully recognize their own personal role and responsibility in forest and range fire prevention."

Even within Forest Service regions, the Smokey campaign encouraged local initiative and creative solutions to forest fire prevention. Forester Franklin Carroll spoke of the southwestern region's problems with faulty spark arresters. (Every internal-combustion engine produces exhaust that contains extremely hot, tiny solid particles that, if not trapped by a spark arrester, can start a fire in brush. Faulty or missing spark arresters in chain saws, motorcycles, locomotives, construction equipment, cross-country vehicles and agricultural equipment have all ignited fires.)

"The new program was designed to expand on the Smokey Bear theme of *why* fires must be prevented," Carroll commented in 1973. "The new theme explains *how* to prevent wildfires in the area of public education, risk engineering and fire precautionary measures. The most successful has been the spark arrester exhaust system inspection and approval program. This has reduced fires from an average of twenty-eight annually to nine per year."

But the region's personnel found that a simple warning system could be as effective. "Another part of the program," Carroll continued, "was the establishment of fire prevention information check stations at all high hazard and risk area entrances within National Forests. The stations, manned during critical fire danger periods, have been effective in reducing man-caused fires by seventy-five percent."

The southwestern region also adopted special posters with word-symbol combinations, and its printed brochures illustrating how to safely build and extinguish fires proved so popular that more than 500,000 copies were used by other Forest Service regions.

But Forest Service fire prevention efforts ranged far beyond the boundaries of the nation's forests, as the search for support reached into America's cities.

Born in Santa Barbara, California, in 1940, Harry R. "Punky" McClellan began seasonal fire fighting after high school and moved up to Forest Service fire crew foreman in 1961. Over time, McClellan was recognized for his forest fire prevention efforts and won both the Silver and Bronze Smokeys. Then, in 1987, he became the only person to win all three statuettes when he was awarded the Golden Smokey for his leadership in developing "Smokey and the Pros."

In 1983, McClellan fashioned the idea of getting Smokey into major league ballparks, and with assistance from Rod Kindlund implemented the program in California in 1984. "In our first contacts," McClellan explained, "we mailed letters to all five California baseball teams on Monday and got the first response on Thursday. All were positive. This door-opening capability of Smokey is awesome." Then McClellan realized his idea wasn't new.

"Some people with the Dodgers remembered Joe DeLucchi having Smokey come into Dodger Stadium in a fire truck [in the 1960s]," McClellan confirmed. "I didn't know that had occurred, and we couldn't find much about it, so we didn't advertise our program as new. But we did try to capitalize on the fact that they had a total promotion effort for baseball.

"We had scorebook, scoreboard and public address messages, promotional materials for kids, TV public service announcements and an appearance by Smokey Bear," McClellan added. "It was a total media blitz. We think that if we had stood outside a stadium and asked questions, eighty-five percent of the people would have realized they had just experienced a fire prevention program.

"The baseball teams themselves—particularly the California Angels—made a big push to take it nationally," McClellan continued. "John Hays, vice president of the Angels, made presentations at baseball meetings to set the stage. Then Al West and I went to New York to make a presentation to the commissioner's office.

"The first national involvement with Smokey Bear in baseball occurred in New York on July 3, 1986," McClellan recalled. "The commissioner's office was so excited that they asked if we wanted to participate in the old-timers' series. Smokey appeared in eighteen stadiums that year—sort of as an ambassador for the commissioner—and presented trees to the cities. We didn't get much press attention because of the short notice.

"But the deal was set up with Peter Uberroth, the commissioner, to support a national Smokey Bear Day for Major League Baseball in 1987," McClellan continued. "Uberroth gave us the key contact names, so we just called the teams to set up appointments. In most cases, a phone call to a team's public relations director was enough, because Uberroth's letters paved the way. About ninety percent of the teams were extremely cooperative; for a couple, we had to get the commissioner's office to put a little arm on—but nothing too heavy."

Soon dubbed "Smokey Sports," the effort to garner partners in forest fire prevention eventually found Smokey throwing opening pitches, tossing coins at mid-field for football and throwing jump balls at basketball games. "We expanded into the West Coast teams—the NBA, the NFL, soccer, the NHL and the Oakland Invaders of the USFL," McClellan explained. "We produced just printed materials—posters and trading cards—in the early stages and later went to Smokey baseballs and batting helmets. With a baseball cap, kids walk around with Smokey Bear billboards on their heads.

"The costs were picked up by Forest Service, the Bureau of Land Management and the states, and sometimes the Park Service was involved," McClellan added. "But the Philadelphia Phillies handed out a Smokey Bear baseball glove; they paid $30,000 and we only paid $10,000. There was a pretty good budget, but we got player endorsements, the use of stadium facilities and everything else."

At last count, McClellan estimated that Smokey Sports had generated ninety-four different sets of trading cards, thirty-five posters and about five dozen baseball gloves, caps and other items.

Then a colleague crafted a similar concept. "Gene Dowdy came to me in the late 1980s with an idea about the cowboys," McClellan recalled. "I thought it was a good idea, so we sat in the training center in Clovis [California] and brain-stormed for a day and a half. Gene moved forward with it and tried to develop his own materials. Gene was an ex-rodeo guy. He had a lot of influence and he got it done."

With assistance from Jerry Barney, Dowdy, a former rancher, moved quickly to establish another partner in forest fire prevention: American cowboys. And in 1988, Dowdy's program—Smokey and the American Cowboy—emerged when the National Professional Rodeo Cowboy Association threw its support behind Smokey's effort. Because rodeo participants and rodeo fans tend to be heavy forest users, the new relationship seemed to be a natural. In any event, McClellan explained, "The cowboys feel pretty good about it."

Another creative group brought Smokey's image and message to the American public in a big, big way. Up in the sky—it's a bird, it's a plane, it's Smokey Bear?

Born in Globe, Arizona, in 1935, William L. Chapel III majored in forestry at Oklahoma State University in Stillwater, graduated in 1958, and followed his father's footsteps into the Forest Service. While serving his thirty-five-year Forest Service career at more than twenty locations in Arizona and New Mexico, Chapel began ballooning in 1975. Then, in 1977, he hatched an idea: why not create a giant Smokey Bear hot-air balloon?

"Coincidentally," Chapel confirmed, "I learned that Betty Carroll [Franklin's Carroll's wife] was interested in ballooning and also fancied a Smokey Bear balloon." Twice, in 1977 and again in the early 1980s, Chapel unsuccessfully broached the idea in Washington, D.C. But as Chapel kept ballooning, he couldn't dismiss the idea from his mind.

In 1987, Chapel was appointed New Mexico State Forester, and for several months commuted between Santa Fe and Albuquerque with assistant regional forester Dave Jolly. "I had a pretty good captive audience with Dave. We talked about the balloon quite a bit, and he agreed to help. When the Forest Service chartered the Friends of Smokey Bear Balloon in early 1991, we gathered six or so of Dave's staff and other folks that supported the idea. Larry Henson [southwestern regional forester] kept the spirit going, and we all started working in our own ways to make this come together." The idea, at least, had finally floated off the ground.

Then, Michael Rains led the effort in Washington, D.C., to put together a matching grant, and the FOSBB oversubscribed with contributions from almost five hundred people and organizations. When the manufacturer—Aerostar, Inc., of Sioux Falls, South Dakota—contributed $23,000 to the project, the balloon finally became a reality.

Chapel, Aerostar president Mark West and Aerostar engineer Rich Andrew designed the balloon on April 15, 1993, in room 226 of the Hampton Inn in Mesa, Arizona. "We sat down with a software package that is unique for ballooning and provides a three-dimensional picture," Chapel recalled. "We worked six hours that evening and till way early into the next morning, by looking at Smokey Bear posters and artwork."

Test-flown in August and delivered in September, the balloon is valued at $78,500. Its 120,000-cubic-foot envelope (with a lifting capacity of 90,000 cubic feet—typical for a special-shaped balloon) rises 87 feet high (97 feet with the basket) and measures 72 feet across the hat brim. The system weighs in at 1,100 pounds.

"It's the biggest bear you're ever going to see," Chapel grinned. "The balloon will create excitement for forest fire prevention and natural resources conservation. Our [FOSBB] mission is to create a medium that will interest kids and adults alike, that will bring them forward to listen to fire prevention messages. The balloon represents Smokey's message—it's a medium for communication; it will be a magnet to attract people to that message." And it seems to be working.

The Smokey Bear balloon made its debut before one million visitors at the 1993 Albuquerque balloon festival. "It was an absolute, roaring success," boasted Chapel, the pilot. "We got terrific TV coverage and the balloon was heavily photographed." Immediately, FOSBB phones lit up with callers pleading to schedule the balloon for events as far as three years in advance. "I could go on and on crediting the hundreds of volunteers that worked

The Friends of Smokey Bear Balloon--the biggest bear you'll ever see in the air—measures almost a hundred feet high. *(Courtesy Friends of Smokey Bear Balloon.)*

their hearts out for the balloon," Chapel emphasized. "A lot of people made this thing possible."

This activity around the states and Forest Service regions didn't occur without assistance, encouragement and coordination from CFFP headquarters. The campaign director and staff, representatives of Foote, Cone & Belding, state officials and other Forest Service people visited all fifty states for conservation meetings, inspection trips, Ad Council functions, TV shows and foresters meetings.

The CFFP also sponsored the First National Smokey Bear Workshop in Atlantic City, New Jersey, in 1970. Sixty forestry and forest fire professionals and advertising experts from the United States and Canada participated in the program. Mal Hardy designed the meeting to stimulate coordination between state and federal fire prevention agencies and to establish direction for the CFFP in the 1970s. Second and Third National Smokey Bear Workshops were held a few years later.

The CFFP supported special local needs as well. In one such effort, 10,000 copies of a school poster were given to the American Red Cross Youth. When Alaska suffered a disastrous fire season, the CFFP shipped a dozen TV kits, ten radio kits, ten extra radio platters, a hundred newspaper ad proof sheets and an assortment of 16mm and 35mm filmed prevention spots to saturate Alaska's media. When several northeastern states experienced a bad year, the Ad Council packaged a special emergency TV kit for stations in the affected areas. When thousands of surplus posters weren't needed by federal agencies, they were distributed by states. This massive effort wove Smokey into the fabric of America's everyday life, and citizens began supporting Smokey on their own initiative.

Prodded by Lou Graf, a producer of fire prevention commercials for Foote, Cone & Belding, Smokey posters appeared on film sets throughout Hollywood, and Smokey plugs began appearing on TV. *The Carol Burnett Show*, *Captain Kangaroo*, the *Wizard of Odds*, *Laugh In*, *The Danny Thomas Show*, *Mr. Rogers*, *Hollywood Squares*, and *Pete & Tillie* all talked about Smokey or used Smokey props. Dean Martin, Johnny Carson and Red Skelton plugged Smokey. Jackson Weaver appeared in a Smokey costume on *What's My Line*.

Smokey statues appeared in Texas and Minnesota forests and in the rotunda of the Utah State Capitol building. Smokey popped up at Arbor Day celebrations, centennial galas, and fishermen's breakfasts, and pinned badges on small fry at logging shows. Department stores included Smokey in environmental displays, and the National Council of State Garden Clubs sponsored Smokey coloring contests that typically generated half a million entries.

The AFL/CIO distributed forest fire prevention ads to 350 labor press editors, and local #758, United Brotherhood of Carpenters and Joiners in Indianapolis, made Smokey an honorary life member. Tulsa, Oklahoma's KVOO-TV advertised that "TV gets results in Tulsa! For 12 years we've been running spots for Smokey the Bear. Results? Tulsa has not had one single forest fire!!!"

And in a ceremony at his cage, the living Smokey was presented with Lassie's 10th Anniversary Gold Award in 1965. "That was just an occasional thing," Dr. Ted Reed, zoo director, emphasized. "People wanted Smokey to endorse and advertise everything, but the Forest Service didn't want him to get too far from forest fires. Nevertheless, Lassie came and made Smokey an honorary dog." Lassie also planted a slobbery smooch on Dr. Reed. "Of all the people that go through the zoo," Reed confessed, "I had to get kissed by a dog."

21

Bear Hugs

"With half the exposure Smokey gets, any politician could have any office in the land."

— Mal Hardy

Life at the CFFP's Washington, D.C., headquarters wasn't all routine licensing, mailing Junior Forest Ranger kits and designing costumes. The CFFP issued awards to hardworking Smokey supporters, handled Smokey's midlife crisis and let staffers freelance their own ideas.

One of Hollywood's biggest names was recruited into the effort by J. Morgan Smith in Washington. "The cub had not been at the zoo very long when Morgan had an idea," Bill Bergoffen explained. "Morgan heard that the Cole Brothers circus was coming to town with William Boyd starring as Hopalong Cassidy. The bear was new in the zoo, and Morgan wanted to tie the two together."

"I suggested to Clint Davis that we ask Hoppy to do a radio commercial for Smokey," Smith confirmed. "Clint liked the idea and told me to get over there and see what I could do. So I met Hoppy and talked with him for a while, but then he had to perform with the circus, so I was left with his public relations man—a slick Hollywood type, if you know what I mean. I told the PR guy what I wanted, and he said, 'Hell, I ain't got time for that.' Well, I got angry and showed him photos of President Truman talking about the bear and explained that the President of the United States had time for the bear. So the PR guy snapped back, 'Give me your phone number.'"

Harry Collins, Smith's Forest Service colleague, offered an observation of Smith's personality. "Morgan is an absolutely fearless guy," Collins conceded. "If Clint Davis said, 'Morgan, you go over to the White House and get the president to sign this,' Morgan would go—and get the president to sign it, too." So Collins reported a different version of Smith's challenge to Cassidy's agent: "Morgan said, 'Okay. Suppose I tell all the children in America that Hopalong Cassidy doesn't care for Smokey Bear?'"

Smith's tenacity worked. "Clint Davis got a call on Saturday morning," Smith laughed, "and was told to be at the Mayflower Hotel at two that afternoon. But Bill Bergoffen and I went with a recording technician instead. Hoppy was there with his sixth wife—she called him 'Daddy' and he called her `Mother.'" But the story that became legend wasn't made at the Mayflower Hotel.

"Morgan wasn't through," Bergoffen grinned. "He wanted to stage a publicity shot with the live bear, and Hoppy went along with it. I think it was the only time the little bear was permitted out of the zoo. A handler brought Smokey to the circus in a cage in the back of a pickup truck [on July 15, 1950] and carried Smokey over to us in a small blanket. Two beautiful bareback riders in scanty outfits were standing there beside Dr. Mann."

"We had to wait until Hoppy finished with the kids," Smith chuckled, "but then the fun started."

"So out comes Hopalong Cassidy, resplendent on a white horse, wearing a white hat and white cowboy costume," Bergoffen continued. "Rather impatiently, Hoppy said, 'Okay, let's get this over with. Let me have that bear. Hand him up.'"

But Smith balked. "I said 'Watch out, Hoppy. He's a mean son-of-a-gun.' Then Smokey's zoo handler took off his gloves and offered them to Hoppy and said, 'You may want to use these gloves, Mr. Cassidy.'" But like so many before him, the unsuspecting showman had to learn the hard way.

"Hoppy threw the gloves away," Bergoffen explained. "He said, 'If I can't handle a little critter like this with my bare hands, then I'm not worth my salt. Bring that bear up here. Let me have him.' So Hoppy reached

down and grabbed the feisty little character by the scruff of the neck and
plopped him down on his saddle pommel. Then three things happened:
Smokey urinated down the front of Hoppy's beautiful costume; Smokey
reached around and bit Hoppy on a wrist; and Hoppy flung Smokey down
to the ground. Then one of the bareback riders turned to Dr. Mann and

Hopalong Cassidy (William Boyd) laughs about his rough treatment at the
paws of Smokey while Bill Bergoffen (left, rear), Clint Davis (right, rear), J.
Morgan Smith (left, front) and Boyd's agent (right, front) chime in. *(Courtesy
W. W. Bergoffen and USDA Forest Service.)*

said, 'Did you see what that son-of-a-bitch did to that cute little bear?' That
just shows you what strong feelings people had for that bear. Later, Hoppy
laughed along with everyone else."

"Hoppy got over that incident in a hurry," Smith agreed. "He was a
hell of a good sport about it. The next year, Hoppy came back to Washington
to lead a big parade, so we met him at the zoo. The assistant chief made
Hoppy an honorary forest ranger in front of Smokey's cage, and we asked
Hoppy about the pants that Smokey had urinated on. Hoppy told us he

was wearing them that day for old times' sake. We really thought the world of Hoppy. Later, he even narrated a film about Smokey."

As foresters such as Bergoffen retired and Smith transferred to Albuquerque, the Forest Service continued to identify people within its ranks to support the Smokey Bear program. Among the best known was Chuck Williams, summoned from Hollywood, California.

Born and raised in tiny Delta, Colorado, Williams graduated from Colorado State University in 1957 with a degree in forestry and spent thirty years with the Forest Service. Serving first in Colorado, Williams transferred to South Dakota as a ranger in the Black Hills National Forest. Smokey became part of Williams's life in both states, as he wore a Smokey costume while his six-year-old daughter led him around for an admiring crowd.

In 1968, Williams moved to the glitz of Hollywood to work for the *Lassie* TV show. "The show's working agreement with the Forest Service required a real-life ranger to serve as technical adviser," Williams explained. "They wanted story lines, terms, uniforms and everything else to be as accurate as possible. I worked with producers, writers and television people developing scripts, but we filmed many of the shows on location in national forests in Washington, Oregon, California, Colorado, Arizona and New Mexico."

As Williams learned TV broadcasting, he often met Foote, Cone & Belding staffers who taught him the process of producing Smokey commercials. "So in 1971," Williams added, "I was assigned to the Forest Service public affairs office in Washington and placed in charge of radio and TV. In the eyes of the Forest Service, I was an expert."

When working with forest fire prevention, Williams's assignment was to assist CFFP director Mal Hardy. "Smokey Bear was such a powerful program that it pretty much handled itself," Williams continued. "However, I went to New York and worked with the Ad Council. The Ad Council distributed material nationally and the Forest Service distributed within their network. Then the Washington office would do follow-up work to make sure that the mailings were in the ranger districts and the field offices. If a local ranger showed up in a small town, they nearly always would have him say something or interview him."

Then, because Smokey's living symbol at the National Zoo continued to draw more than 4 million visitors each year, the CFFP worked to enhance the grumpy critter's appeal. To assist photographers posing children with the famous bear, a plate-glass panel designed by Rudy Wendelin was installed across the front of Smokey's cage in 1968. Three years later, at a cost of $3,000, "Smokey's True Story"—the text and pictorial display outside his cage—was overhauled. In 1974, $3,500 was spent to add Smokey's gear locker, with a burned snag contributed by Virginia and, at Jim Sorenson's initiative, a honey pot donated by Missouri.

CFFP staffers gobbled up ideas to focus attention on forest fire prevention. They updated Smokey films, changed billing procedures to expedite orders to states and held special meetings to develop long-term policy. One year they released 275 slide-script featurettes to selected TV stations. Another year they used the Department of Agriculture's newspaper service to distribute a 1,100-word, three-picture story updating the activities of Judy Bell. The staff arranged for Senator Lee Metcalf, Jackson Weaver, "Ranger Hal" Shaw and District of Columbia fire chief Henry Galotta to join Smokey at the National Zoo during Fire Prevention Week. On another occasion they scheduled a Smokey visit by Lady Bird Johnson.

In other years, the CFFP contracted for an animated talking Smokey figure, ordered new Smokey costumes (only $197 each, FOB Chicago), ordered "forest fire preventer" exhibits (at $1,945 a pop), developed reproductions of annual posters, and printed 50,000 copies of Smokey's song for the Boy Scouts (with a design on the back for whittling a Smokey neckerchief slide). Smokey's song was even translated into French for use in Quebec.

CFFP officials appeared countless times on Washington radio and TV and recorded fire prevention messages for the Department of Agriculture consumer report show released to more than 300 radio stations. And, guided by a 1970 report by Foote, Cone & Belding that summarized comments from 281 television stations, 328 newspapers and 1,485 radio stations, the CFFP changed the format of campaign materials to meet the needs of media supporters.

"We developed our budgets—usually around $300,000, not including Forest Service salaries—largely on costs of previous years and estimates of which way they were going," Mal Hardy explained. "Of course, the commercial income reduced our budget from Congress." Nevertheless, Smokey plaques were displayed in Capitol Hill offices and pocket planners and wall calendars were distributed to members of Congress.

To acknowledge appreciation for supporting forest fire prevention, a series of Smokey Bear awards were created to recognize achievements and encourge others to keep trying. The most prestigious of the many awards are Smokey's "Oscars"—Golden, Silver and Bronze Smokey statuettes. Originally, Golden Smokeys were to be awarded to organizations whose primary function is not necessarily forest fire prevention; Silver Smokeys would be presented to wildfire management professionals; Bronze Smokeys would recognize individual achievements outside the professional ranks.

Forest Service artist Rudy Wendelin designed--and later was awarded--both the Golden and Silver Smokey awards. *(Courtesy William Clifford Lawter Jr.)*

Naturally, the job of creating the statuettes fell to Rudy Wendelin, who had been active in developing three-dimensional figures of Smokey since the beginning of the licensing program in 1952. "I think the initiative for the Golden Smokey came from Clint Davis, but I'm not sure," Wendelin recalled. "I had been making a scroll parchment award every year that went to organizations such as the Boy Scouts and Girl Scouts, but Clint wanted something special, and it was natural to think of a three-dimensional thing." So Wendelin rolled up his sleeves.

"First I did pencil doodling sketches," Wendelin explained, "then I grabbed a glob of clay, wrapped it around an armature of aluminum wire with a central support and just built the clay around it. Smokey is not just something on a piece of paper, so this was kind of exciting to add the third dimension to the character to get an all-around view of his rear and side. That helped shape in my own mind the image of the figure too. Sculpture is a real aid to graphic work because it helps give a third dimension to drawings."

The first Golden Smokeys were awarded to Capitan, New Mexico (on behalf of the children of America), the Advertising Council, the American Forest Products Industries and the American Forestry Association. When twelve-year-old Judy Bell agreed to represent America's children, President Dwight Eisenhower agreed to bestow the foot-high statuettes.

At 2:30 p.m. on Thursday, May 8, 1958, presidential aide Sherman Adams, Forest Service Chief Richard McArdle, Secretary of Agriculture Ezra Benson, Secretary of the Interior Fred Seaton, and a crowd of dignitaries gathered under sunny skies on the White House lawn for Eisenhower's presentation. Young Judy Bell, her trip to Washington financed by the Ad Council (although a Washington newspaper reported that the Tuesday Musical club of aviation writers paid expenses), accepted the award and a hug from her president. Although protocol apparently dictated that young female White House honorees wear white dresses, no one bothered to tell the Bell family, so the pre-teen New Mexican smiled resplendently in moccasins and a red "squaw" dress.

After leaving the White House, Judy's Forest Service hosts escorted her to the National Zoo, to pose with her old friend Smokey, and then to Forest Service headquarters, where she penned replies to children who had written to Smokey. As had occurred eight years earlier, Judy captured attention from the press and her pictures with Smokey—both the 1950, five-pound edition and the 1958, 300-pound version—appeared in newspapers across the country. But back in Santa Fe, her family and friends had difficulty learning about Judy's activities.

"Judy was a quiet, shy person," explained Don Bell, Judy's older brother. "Mom and Dad had to work like hell to get her to go. Then we heard about it on the radio and saw her pictures in the newspaper, but it was hard to get information out of Judy. She didn't talk much." One newspaper reported that Judy kept a respectful distance from Smokey's zoo cage and even stepped back when the bruin reared up on its hind legs. Other newspapers, however, indicated that Judy walked dangerously close to her former pet. Judy's chilling handwritten letter of May 9, 1958, supports the latter version.

Judy Bell receives the first Golden Smokey award from President Dwight Eisenhower on the White House lawn on May 8, 1958. The award is now on display in the Smokey Bear Museum in Capitan, New Mexico. *(Courtesy Rudy Wendelin and USDA Forest Service.)*

"Dear Mu & Dad," Judy wrote on paper from a stenographer's notebook. "Well yesterday I met the President and everything came out just fine. He even put his arm around me. Then after I got the award and everything, we went to see Smokey and I tell you if he isn't the cutest thing you've ever seen. They let me go inside the fence. I had this poster and Smokey reached out for it, and I've got his claw marks on it."

Back in New Mexico, Judy presented the Golden Smokey to the city of Capitan. Today, it is displayed in Capitan's Smokey Bear Museum.

Over time, the CFFP gratefully presented Golden Smokeys to a roll call of key national contributors: Foote, Cone & Belding; Walt Disney Productions; Rudy Wendelin; Liller, Neal, Battle & Lindsey; the National Council of State Garden Clubs; the radio and television broadcasters of America; and national coordinator Jim Felton. Other recipients included

Russell Eller; the American Forest Products Institute; the U.S. Post Office; the newspapers of America; the General Federation of Women's Clubs; the Native Sons and Daughters of the Golden West; Ideal Toy Corporation; the National Zoo; Macy's Department Stores; Art Creelman; Nancy Budd; Punky McClellan; and two dozen others.

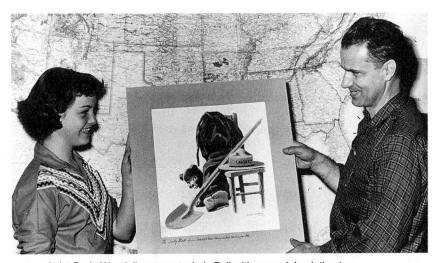

Artist Rudy Wendelin presents Judy Bell with a special painting to commemorate her 1958 visit to Washington, D.C. The painting is now on display in the Smokey Bear Museum in Capitan, New Mexico. *(Courtesy Rudy Wendelin and USDA Forest Service.)*

On April 18, 1968, the first Silver Smokeys were awarded to Clint Davis, Albert Wiesendanger (of Keep Oregon Green) and Raymond Conarro (Mississippi Forestry Commission). The next year, Rudy Wendelin, James Ricard and Barney Wozniak received Silver Smokeys. Later awards went to such notables as Mal Hardy, Eugene McNamara, Richard Thomas, Harry Rossoll, Bill Bergoffen, Jackson Weaver, Michael Marchese and many other dedicated professionals.

The Smokey Bear Plaque (replaced by the Bronze Smokey statuette in 1980) featured an original Rudy Wendelin drawing of Smokey standing with his shovel. "It had nice hand-lettered calligraphy printed in gold, and names were inscribed in Chinese Red lettering," Wendelin remembered. Vellum certificates mounted under plexiglass on a walnut or mahogany base, the plaques and statuettes were awarded to James Sorenson, Nelson Peach and virtually every element of the fire prevention effort—state forestry commissions, counties, individuals, forestry associations, private companies, Forest Service employees and the media.

CFFP director Mal Hardy didn't shy from recommending aggressive efforts to court the media—the backbone of the entire Smokey Bear effort. "Consider such people as newspaper editors, outdoor writers, radio and television weathermen, sports reporters and stars of children's TV programs," he urged. "By our recognition of good service, recipients will make further efforts—not only in publicizing the award, but in continuing the fire prevention effort."

So media support for Smokey was justifiably recognized as dozens of TV and radio stations, newspapers and individual reporters were awarded Smokey Bear Plaques. But if the media is the backbone of the program, the nation's fifty states are the protective ribs, so deserving state and local agencies, private businesses, community associations and conservation groups across the nation became frequent recipients of the treasured plaques. Individual achievement, too, was recognized as plaques were awarded to Forest Service personnel, schoolteachers, artists, prosecuting attorneys, machine inspectors and volunteer firemen.

Other awards for toiling on Smokey's behalf include a Smokey Bear Certificate, a Smokey Appreciation Award and any of the officially licensed Smokey desk sets, tie tacks, pen and pencil sets and dolls. Organizations were also free to design their own awards as long as the program's basic objectives were honored.

Bear season. No one pinpointed how it began or when Smokey's critics first voiced objections to his innocent work. Like any public figure, a bear can't expect to cavort too long in the public eye without losing some of his luster, and Smokey sometimes found his smiling face maligned and ridiculed in the media.

Smokey had first appeared as a cute cartoon bear peering out from posters. But Smokey grew into a formidable force in America's forests and emerged as big business, hauling in surprising amounts of cash and reinvesting every cent in his continuing awareness campaign. And year after year, Smokey's impact grew as supporters responded to his call.

Perhaps it was inevitable, then, that Smokey began to stand for more than his creators had intended. By the early 1950s, certainly, Smokey was doing more than helping prevent forest fires. A hero in the eyes of children, the friendly bear appeared everywhere—in cities as well as forests—and, except for the American flag, his exposure may have exceeded that of any other nationally used symbol. However, some people didn't understand

Smokey's narrow message, and he began popping up in situations or advertising not associated with his real intent.

Some extension of Smokey's role perhaps helped his image. Smokey's only job was forest fire prevention, but Americans began to view their bear as a leader in all conservation matters—a bear with influence far beyond forest fire prevention. Smokey was a friend of wildlife, water supplies, grasslands, recreation areas and rangelands, and some people expected Smokey to protect those areas too. Even within the Forest Service, thoughtful people disagreed on Smokey's role: some argued in favor of expanding Smokey's responsibilities; others insisted on a narrow job description.

The extension of Smokey's job was not illogical. No other nationally known person or character had emerged to lead America's conservation effort. Conservation values are reinforced through forest fire prevention, so the association is natural and corresponding responsibilities easily intermingle. And for children, the concept of Smokey Bear is easily understood and thus helps young minds understand conservation issues.

Simultaneous with Smokey's growth, moreover, such wilderness associations as the Sierra Club and the Audubon Society built more proactive memberships with greater influence in environmental affairs. Often that power challenged Forest Service management and, by extension, Smokey Bear. As Smokey became well known, many foresters realized that he was becoming a symbol of their profession, making it easier for the public to use Smokey as a scapegoat and the press to use him to get attention. Sadly, these challenges degenerated into personal attacks on the nation's favorite bear.

Although the Forest Service enjoyed respect among many conservation agencies, some groups opposed the service's multiple-use policy—and blamed Smokey Bear. Some environmentalists objected to roads in wilderness areas and timber overcutting—and blamed Smokey Bear. Preservationists yearning to set aside more forest acreage ran into barriers—and blamed Smokey Bear.

Then forest professionals who relied on natural and man-ignited fires for control found their ability to manage forestlands under attack—and blamed Smokey Bear. Smokey preached that all forest fires were bad, claimed this group, and the public wouldn't allow controlled burns. Smokey's popularity, they alleged, badly damaged this land management practice and contradicted ecologists who pointed to the beneficial effects of forest fires. Smokey, some thought, was overprotecting America's forests and condemning burning of any type. "The Smokey the Bear program is riddled with exaggeration," Mal Hardy reported that one observer had claimed. "It appeals to emotion. The forest isn't really a fairyland or Disneyland where all the wildlife babies live happily ever after."

One magazine ad featured a sinister Smokey partially concealing a chain saw behind his massive shoulders with an attacking text alleging that Smokey was destroying the nation's heritage. An article was illustrated by a fearful Smokey Bear shaking in a courtroom witness stand while an attendant caption directly challenged the Forest Service to sue the magazine.

These claims reflected an obvious gap between professional foresters and their public. Reg Ivory, public relations director for the Florida Forestry Association of 90,000 forest landowners, emphasized in a 1973 speech that it wasn't fair to landowners, the forest industry or even the public for Smokey Bear to be educating children to oppose every kind of fire in the woods.

"During a station break in a recent Saturday cartoon festival," Ivory explained, "a station in Atlanta ran a Smokey public service announcement, the gist of which was that Smokey's little friends don't play with matches because matches start forest fires and fires are bad for forests. My son, who is nine, watched the spot with interest, then turned to me and asked why Smokey had said fires were bad for forests when, just the week before, I had gone to his class—a local fourth grade—and explained to the children how fire could be a great help in managing forestland. I explained to him carefully that Smokey was talking about destructive wildfires, not prescribed burning, but I'm sure you all realize what effect that had on a child. I lost him completely. It was 'grown-ups talk'—contradictions. Smokey had said one thing, and I had said another, and there was no way my son would believe that we weren't calling each other liars."

Smokey not only had to absorb challenges to Forest Service land management practices, but he had to account for his focus on children. Some critics felt that the CFFP campaign was too juvenile—and blamed Smokey Bear. Smokey was, some charged, a simple figure with an oversimplified message who couldn't reach adults.

Other critics reacted to human injuries from wildlife—and blamed Smokey Bear. These attackers alleged that imparting human characteristics to Smokey misled the public into believing that bears and other wild animals were not to be feared and caused tragedies in national and state parks. Smokey's passive image was dangerously misleading, they claimed. "See motorists feeding those nice bears, and even trying to lift them into station wagons," argued a critic in a letter to the editor of *Advertising Age*. "I expect nine out of ten persons mauled by bears are those who think Smokey the

Bear is a nice, gentle and kindly animal, instead of the fact he is a fierce one."

Headlines appeared across the country. "Smokey the Bear Under Fire," insisted the *Los Angeles Times*. "Has Smokey Bear stomped out too many fires in the forest?" asked the *National Observer*. "Smokey Bear's Bosses Now Say Natural Fires Help the Forests," claimed the *New York Times*, explaining the Forest Service's new concept: "As an updated Smokey the Bear might say, Burn, baby, Burn." "Does America Still Believe in Smokey Bear?" headlined a thoughtful article in *Virginia Forests*.

Was Smokey really behind the times, as some claimed, or incorrect in preaching that forest fires are bad? "It would have been easy for Smokey to have felt like he was in a hostile camp this past year," Mal Hardy wrote in 1973. "Almost any given month the newsstands across the country displayed magazines and newspapers containing articles proclaiming Smokey as a liar. *Sports Illustrated, The Smithsonian*, and other magazines joined in to encircle Smokey with fingers pointing at his newly discovered hypocrisy."

Many foresters believed those attacks were unfair. "The Forest Service was the leader of the conservation effort in the United States for wise use of resources," Rudy Wendelin contended. "When I worked in Milwaukee in the 1930s, conservation was the theme. 'Save the land and plant trees.' The Forest Service was the leader in it and the rest of the country is catching up now. A paper company claims to be the tree-growing company; the Forest Service is really the tree-growing company, but they can't publicize their work."

Nevertheless, attacks continued—sometimes even from "friendly fire." The *Salt Lake City Tribune* noted, for instance, that the Forest Service had no one to blame but itself when a Utah fire was not battled aggressively enough. "It [the Forest Service] has convinced the average American that when fire erupts in the woods, every penny, every tool or device, and every person available is used to put it out," explained the *Tribune*. "This is the result of the Forest Service's all-too-effective fire prevention campaign."

Mal Hardy could only shrug. "With half the exposure Smokey gets, any politician could have any office in the land," Hardy speculated.

Was Smokey worn out, tired and old-fashioned? Should he be fired? Was Smokey really making it too difficult to use controlled burning? Did he make the public believe bears are not dangerous? Did we need Smokey? Was he relevant? Did Smokey fit the nation's interest in conservation? Were the character assaults fair?

First, Smokey certainly shared common values with his Forest Service handlers. "The Forest Service is an agency of the government that is related to the natural resources—woods, grass, soil, water, wildlife and recreation," Wendelin explained. "It's a conservation movement that has a real moral basis to it beyond just doing something for a job. Most of the people get involved deeply in that. They're not there just for their salary. It's a chance to carry on part of the movement that was started so many years ago by other leaders."

But although Mal Hardy loved both his bear and the Forest Service, he didn't feel comfortable with any type of adoption. "Smokey, that formidable, furry, foe of forest fires, has really been in the eyes of the news media," Hardy wrote. "His head doesn't swell at the praise he receives; and his shoulders are broad enough to bear the burden of attacks on his anti-wildfire pronouncements. Where he feels a little frustrated, however, is in the fact that the press tends to identify him as the general representative of all Forest Service activities."

But Hardy was willing to concede the obvious: "There is a surprisingly strong movement to use Smokey as a spokesman for the timber industry, the advocates of clearcutting, the opponents of clearcutting, and a dozen other causes. It's nice to know that Smokey is so respected that so many people want him to speak for them. However, that's not an ambassador's hat Smokey wears; it's a campaign hat—a *Cooperative Forest Fire Prevention Campaign* hat. He is the world-famous symbol of forest fire prevention, nothing more."

Second, a review of the Forest Service position suggests that the service consistently supported the concept that controlled burning could have a positive effect on range and forest lands and should be part of land management efforts. It is clear that the Smokey Bear campaign never aimed at preventing this type of management. From his birth in 1944, Smokey focused his entire career on a single target: unnecessary, accidental fires caused by human carelessness.

William Towell of the American Forestry Association persuasively argued Smokey's defense in a 1973 speech, rejecting claims that forest fire protection had been oversold.

"Let's not undermine the tremendous good that has been done by Smokey Bear and the fire prevention program," Towell insisted. "Protection of our forests from wildfires has probably been one of conservation's greatest achievements. Controlled fire as a management tool is one thing, but uncontrolled burning is something entirely different. Let's not confuse the two. Let's use fire where and when we need it. Let's exclude fire where and when we don't want it. But, most important of all, let's learn to know the difference. We can't afford to tear down a whole century of progress for a half truth. Perhaps fire was a natural part of the environment before the white man came to this country, but we have so altered land patterns and land use that adequate control of wildfires is an ecological necessity."

Mal Hardy agreed: "The public isn't stupid and, if it is given good information, it is going to make the right decision nine times out of ten. Smokey does not say all fire is bad. He even says, 'Use fire with caution,' and 'When you burn, follow my rules.' There is nothing incompatible about the educational thrusts of the woods burners and of the wildfire prevention crowd."

Third, the issue of whether Smokey was responsible for wild animal attacks on people seems senseless to many observers. Ascribing human characteristics to animals has occurred for many years, but as Robert Compeau, a Michigan forest fire supervisor, noted: "In most cases where incidents have occurred between man and animal, it is usually the case of down-right foolishness on the part of the human being."

It may also be a case of the American penchant for failing to accept responsibility for personal actions; many people will not admit to poor judgment; they must point a finger of blame at someone else. It seems inappropriate, therefore, to hold Smokey Bear accountable for personal foolishness, and Compeau seemed to agree. "I'm not sure that the problem lies in the human characteristics that have been given to animals," Compeau opined. "Possibly it is in the animal characteristics that are still in man."

Fourth, the CFFP filed a nolo contendere plea on the juvenile issue. "Smokey's message is not limited to children," Hardy wrote, "but it is fairly well accepted that children are more easily persuaded than are adults. It should also be pointed out that kids who started school the year the Smokey program began are now raising families of their own."

"All prevention efforts are a matter of education," Compeau concurred, "and Smokey Bear's campaign is one of the most outstanding public education enterprises that have ever been devised. It gives us complete coverage of all age groups [and] leads Smokey's campaign toward a never-ending job. As each new generation goes through our school systems, it will be our job to bring Smokey's message to them."

And fifth, the Forest Service knew that most of Smokey's friends stood behind him as staunch allies. Kids, forest professionals and much of the press continued to support their furry friend at every turn. "Aw, Come On!" headlined the *Atlanta Journal-Constitution*, "Why Pick on A Good Guy Like Smokey?" *Newsday* pointed to Smokey Bear as the "kind of guy you like to see kids look up to because he has scruples." Acknowledging to Smokey's success, the *Wall Street Journal* suggested other government agencies create animal characters to sell messages; perhaps the Department of Transportation could create a horse suggesting that riders "Don't Say Nay to the Amtrak Way"; an IRS thrifty squirrel could ask taxpayers to "build a cache for our April snatch."

Recognizing that Smokey had just reached maturity, Nelson Peach, of South Carolina's Commission of Forestry, summarized the situation: "Smokey has evolved from a beast of the forest to an intelligent being. He walks and talks and wears pants, a hat and carries a shovel. He can help us build the 'reverence for life.' In Smokey Bear, we have a winner. I'm for staying with him."

Despite Smokey's success across much of the United States, his message missed arsonists and landowners clearing underbrush by irresponsible burning. A special effort was needed to reduce these fires in the South, where, in 1956, 85 percent of the nation's incendiary forest fires occurred. Bill Huber, of the Forest Service, and Hux Coulter are credited with the solution. "Ideas for the southern program began to formulate after a special forest fire prevention conference in New Orleans in 1956," Huber explained. "But it wasn't until two years later, May 1958, at a meeting of the Southern State Foresters that Florida's State Forester, C. H. Coulter, brought the matter before the group."

Hoping to emulate the national CFFP program, the chairman of the Southern State Foresters appointed three colleagues to a new Southern Cooperative Forest Fire Prevention program (SCFFP) that included Forest Service representatives—one from Washington and one from the southern region—and two representatives of the Ad Council. The Ad Council had not previously sponsored regional programs, but it selected Liller, Neal, Battle & Lindsey, an Atlanta advertising agency, to develop the SCFFP's advertising. Richard Hodges Jr., named as the LNBL account executive for the SCFFP, expressed his firm's delight: "It's a high honor in our business to be associated with the Advertising Council."

"The Southern CFFP Committee held its first meeting September 12, 1958, in Atlanta, Georgia," Huber added. "The committee's first decision was that the southern program would not . . . compete with the efforts of the National CFFP Program. To ensure coordination between the two CFFP programs, the committee agreed that the Southern State Forester on the National Committee should also serve on the Southern Committee."

320

"Mr. Burnit" was created to supplement the Smokey Bear campaign in the Southern states. *(Courtesy USDA Forest Service.)*

"Smokey Bear materials still went to the southern states," Mal Hardy explained. "The Atlanta effort was purely supplemental; it did not supplant the Smokey Bear program." But while the SCFFP acknowledged that Smokey had successfully preached to youngsters against carelessness, they knew the South's forest fires were largely caused by adults, so the SCFFP aimed its program at adults.

"We also agreed that economic factors would have to be a part of our message—another important departure from the national Smokey Bear program at the time," Hodges added. "We agreed that the major problem involved persons who intentionally set fires to the woods and, when occasionally caught, were not being dealt with by the justice system. Too many people in law enforcement, the judiciary or in the jury boxes didn't see woods burning as a problem. Our objective, then, was to reach the people who create public opinion, who elect officials and who sit in jury boxes rather than the perpetrators themselves."

Although the SCFFP intended to tie in with other Ad Council campaigns stressing law enforcement and good citizenship, Bill Huber explained the committee's caution: "We have been careful in the use of Smokey in these ads. We don't want Smokey to portray a cop!"

"Until the southern program was launched, Smokey had never been in a position of being more than a kindly dispenser of advice about carelessness with fire in the woods," Hodges reasoned. "He certainly didn't have a policeman's role, which seemed to be called for in the South. Over time, it became acceptable for Smokey to be connected with some of the hard-nosed messages called for if we were to ease the problem. That first year we introduced a little character called Mr. Burnit, the Malicious Woods Burner. Mr. Burnit was much talked about, not always understood, somewhat controversial and eventually dropped from the program. We have always felt, however, that he served a valuable role in the early days of the SCFFP in helping to identify something that was basically not understood by far too many southerners—and perhaps some foresters who seemed unwilling to admit that there could be such mean, irresponsible citizens."

Bill Huber remembered Mr. Burnit as a tough character: "He was a little man with two eyes on one side of his face. Crouched secretively in darkened woodlands, holding a match with a large orange flame, the odd little man on the poster popped out in public places all over the South in the early sixties. He was used on newspaper ads, an envelope stuffer, and a 'burning dollar.' He was an animated cartoon character for two television spots." Though Mr. Burnit had been planned as a continuing campaign theme, he was dismissed after only two years. "Southern audiences were repelled by the sneaky little man," Huber explained.

"Our early programs, then, had two parts," Hodges added. "One aimed at influencing the public to be aware of the devastation and destructiveness of malicious burners, the other to remind persons who felt they must burn debris or underbrush just what the rules of burning were. It was a pretty difficult assignment." LNBL did well with its early ads with such themes as "Every time a Forest Fire Strikes, You Get Burned," "Help Stamp Out Malicious Burning" and "The Malicious Woods Burner Robs the South."

But states and some federal offices were not comfortable using the term "malicious burner," so the SCFFP substituted the word "arson" in its advertising—a term more acceptable to media. Thus arose the economic themes that proved to be highly effective: "Accident or Arson . . . the Results are the Same" and "Whoever You Are, Whatever You Do, the Forests of the South are Important to You."

To fund its annual budget, the SCFFP's original financing formula was allocated five-eighths to the southern states and three-eighths to the federal government, but the states agreed in 1969 to alter the formula so they would pay more. In a typical year those contributions financed a poster, two television spots (one each for fall and spring), one radio platter, a few newspaper ads and perhaps a wallet card.

SCFFP materials generally were distributed to 2,000 newspapers, 2,175 radio stations, 278 TV stations and 75 magazines. And in the end, two campaigns proved to be better than one, as southern forest fires were reduced by 20 percent within the program's first fifteen years.

22

BEAR CONTROVERSIES

*"Though Smokey belongs to everyone in the United States, the
people of Capitan love him just a little more."*

— unidentified New Mexico spokesperson

An instant hit from the day of his 1950 arrival in Washington, D.C., the
living Smokey quickly developed into a star attraction at the National Zoo.
By September, Smokey claimed celebrity status as tourists flocked around
his cage, letters arrived from people claiming to have discovered him and
the Forest Service denied repeated requests for personal appearances. Just
as Harold Walter's photos allowed the burned cub to capture the heart of
the nation's children, so did little Smokey's actual presence generate
adulation from an enchanted Washington.

Reporters outbid each other with praise for the little hero, public
speakers held him up as a symbol of the true American spirit of
perseverance, photographers clicked away and kids stood gawking in
adoration. But Smokey cared nothing about basking in the spotlight. He
did not appreciate the all-star treatment, did not read the millions of comic
books printed about him, could not chat with his millions of visitors and

could not reply to his thousands of letters. Certainly he couldn't understand his place of honor high on a pedestal erected by a doting public.

Just as certainly, the unfortunate animal never understood his fall from grace, the sneers of contempt and the disparaging jokes. America's living symbol of Smokey Bear seemed to have a knack for generating controversy without even rolling over in his cage. In fact, it all started innocently enough—with another bear.

For twelve years, Smokey ignored detractors who felt it inappropriate to have a living symbol of the poster bear. But the bruin's image slipped in 1962 when the CFFP elected to perpetuate its living symbol and ordered Smokey a mate from his native New Mexico.

"Goldie Bear," an American black bear with gold-colored fur, hailed from Magdalena, New Mexico. After her adoption as a tiny cub by a group of saw millers, game warden L. A. "Bear" Turner confiscated Goldie and drove her to the Little Beaver Forest Service museum on the Ghost Ranch near Chama, New Mexico.

"Then one day the CFFP director in Washington called and asked for a mate for Smokey," remembered Ray Bell, by then the New Mexico state forester. "I got Goldie and took her to Santa Fe in a cage in the back of a pickup. I took her to Dr. Smith's veterinary clinic, but we had to put a harness on her before we left. Goldie was a good bear, but putting a harness on a bear is a little something else. Norma Kellog [Moore] was working for Dr. Smith, and she just grabbed that bear and threw Goldie on her back and held her while I put the collar on."

"Tranquilizers were fairly new," Norma Moore added, "but they gave Goldie a whole bottle and it barely fazed her. Goldie was a very nice, practical bear; she wasn't mean or nasty, and people fed her by hand. But you don't want to rile a bear, so I suggested a muzzle. I got on top of the cage and put a noose over her head to pull her into the traveling cage, but no one told the bear to cooperate. She was a hundred and fifty pounds and she could have done some damage."

Then, with a leash strung through a four-foot section of PVC pipe, Bell and pilot Clyde Hoyt flew Goldie Bear to Washington, D.C., for her betrothal to Smokey Bear (no relation, despite the same last name). The New Mexico state land office furnished a Cessna 210 twin-engine plane, and Bell rode in the back with his caged bear. "We stopped several places on the way to Washington," Bell recalled. "But when we stayed overnight in Des Moines, Iowa, we left Goldie in the hangar and the damn fellows there fed her apples all night long. That bear was the dirtiest thing you ever saw the next morning—those apples had gone right through her. Goldie was a mess but, on the other hand, she was cleaned out too. She smelled terrible, so I had to give her a bath. She didn't particularly like that."

When the flying trio arrived at Washington's National Airport to a warm September reception, Bell walked Goldie around the tarmac to oblige photographers but insisted that the crowd keep a respectful distance. "Goldie didn't hurt anyone," Bell explained, "but she didn't like wearing a collar." But apparently game for new experiences, Goldie seemed to enjoy her motorcycle escort to the National Zoo. There, in an attempt to legitimize Goldie's anticipated union with Smokey, zoo officials presented Goldie a "wedding ring" and escorted her into Smokey's cage.

Bell enjoyed seeing his old nemesis. "I'd just sit there and watch him," Bell smiled. "But they wanted me to go into Smokey's cage and pose with him; some people from Pennsylvania had sent him some honey and they wanted me to give it to him. But I stayed out of his reach. I didn't know if he remembered me, but I remembered him, and there is a big difference between eight pounds and five hundred pounds. I figured I had to give him credit for all that extra bear."

But events didn't occur as planned. Nature didn't take its course. Nothing happened. Smokey hardly gave Goldie a glance—except when she took more than her share of the food shoveled into their cage. Year after year, officials waited with eager anticipation. But year after year, with Smokey and Goldie's ursine union apparently never consummated, no one heard the pitter-patter of little paws, and no royal heir appeared. The jokes began.

Apologists blamed Smokey's lingering injuries from the 1950 fire or claimed that the poor animal was too old. But critics alleged he simply couldn't perform his marital duty, or argued that Smokey was too stupid to understand the basic laws of nature. Others concluded that Smokey believed he and Goldie were of the same sex. And critics could always point their righteous fingers at Smokey's sour disposition: perhaps his personality—plain, pure cussedness—served as a prophylactic. Witnesses noted that Goldie acted friendly and, each June (when black bears go into season), even accommodating. So right or wrong, the blame for lack of issue fell on Smokey's broad shoulders, and the Washington press handed down its verdict: Smokey was a failure.

Perhaps only Dr. Theodore H. Reed, zoo director, spoke up on behalf of Smokey. Thoughtful and witty, Reed was born in Washington, D.C., in 1922. He won his degree in veterinary medicine from Kansas State University in Manhattan, Kansas, and later taught in the pathology department there.

After serving as Oregon State Veterinarian, Reed decided that zoo work was the "Cadillac of veterinary medicine," was hired by the National Zoo and replaced Dr. William Mann upon the latter's retirement. As director of the zoo's 130 employees and 3,000 animals, Reed attended numerous meetings with government "cookie cutters"—men in white shirts and blue suits—so as an oddity, Reed sported a beard modeled after General U.S. Grant. Why? "Because General Grant was the most uptight institutional man there ever was," Reed confessed. When beards later became fashionable, Reed, of course, began shaving again.

"Smokey just didn't breed Goldie," Reed shrugged. "I'm not sure she even came into heat. And remember, Smokey was raised by human beings from a very small cub, and certain behaviors probably had been imprinted by humans. We find that occurs in a number of animals that are raised by humans—they do not want to have anything to do with other animals. Leopards and other cats are like that. Maybe Smokey didn't know what bears were; he certainly wasn't interested or he just didn't know about sex. Besides, Smokey was so busy trying to stop forest fires that he didn't have time for sex."

It didn't help Smokey's image, either, when he lost status by living on the wrong side of the tracks. Although probably adequate for bears, Smokey's 1914 stone grotto at the zoo increasingly was perceived as dingy and unattractive, and many Americans have difficulty respecting anyone living in what could have been called "substandard" housing. But Smokey's home wasn't substandard, some insisted; it was a slum.

Consideration of upgraded housing had begun in 1957, when Rudy Wendelin designed a concrete cage with a background to be painted to resemble a log ranger station. But with zoo officials continually pleading financial embarrassment, Smokey's new quarters never materialized, and by 1961 he had become the center of a controversy that reached Capitol Hill. Senator Lee Metcalf of Montana asked the Housing and Home Finance Agency to consider a single-dwelling home loan for Smokey, and the Forest Service affirmed its intent to file Smokey's application. But the HFA threw cold water on the idea as quickly as Smokey drowns forest fires: no loans to bears—even one with an income of several hundred thousand dollars. With Metcalf's failure, the nation's schoolchildren rushed to Smokey's aid and mailed in more than $4,000 in pennies—a nice gesture, but inadequate to finance a new cage or persuade Dr. Reed to revise his budget.

Bearing down on the issue, New Mexico Governor Edwin Mechem reasoned that if Washington, D.C., didn't want to properly care for Smokey, New Mexico certainly did. "Bring the bear back to Capitan" became the rallying cry, with attendant proposals to turn Smokey loose in the Lincoln National Forest, house him in Capitan or find suitable quarters elsewhere in Lincoln County. Believing Smokey would gladly swap his run-down facility in Washington for a new home in the cool Lincoln National Forest, Mechem issued his orders to Merle Tucker, director of New Mexico's Department of Development: "Get Smokey back to New Mexico."

Jumping on the band, er, bear wagon, Alamogordo's city council entered its bid to assist with Smokey's relocation. Bypassing the bearocrats, Alamogordo Mayor Richard Stanley sent a telegram directly to Smokey (in care of Forest Service Chief Richard McArdle) asking the New Mexico native to "come home."

Caught up in the flap, zoo director Reed tried to keep the matter in perspective. The National Zoo ranked as one of the top zoos in the United States, and while admitting that Smokey's quarters were "old-fashioned," Reed refused to concede that Smokey's den was a slum. Smokey had a simple, but entirely adequate cage, Reed explained, arguing that Smokey's ego could be harmed if he surrendered his superstar status and moved to the remote Lincoln Forest.

"As a zoo director," Reed elaborated, "you sit around and worry about your star attractions because they have such high public visibility. But a zoo only has so much space. It only has so many bear cages. You can't have excessively large groups because it is expensive and the public wants to see variety. But personality is a big deal. 'Named' animals add to the involvement of the public, and those animals become public figures.

"We didn't have the best bear dens in the country," Reed admitted, "but you get into what is called the 'exhibit.' An exhibit has to meet the psychological and physiological needs of the animal. Basically, be safe. Zoo animals are well taken care of; their needs are met. They have freedom from being preyed upon by man or other animals; lions do not kill zebras in zoos. Zoo animals have social protection from their own species. Zoo animals have freedom from starvation; most animals scrape all their lives for food. Zoo animals have freedom from disease; no wild animal has a vet taking care of him. Zoos are enormously protective of animals.

"Smokey's den was old, with nice stonework and cement floors," Reed continued. "Now, some zoos have bears on grass, but much of that aesthetically pleasing stuff is for the benefit of the public—not the animals. What do animals need? What satisfies them? If a living area meets the animal needs for privacy, a pool and sleeping quarters, then they have what they need. Public perception is not necessarily accurate. You cannot prove

Despite his advancing age, Smokey could be an imposing bear. *(Courtesy USDA Forest Service and National Zoological Park.)*

that animals enjoy life more if their quarters meet the public perception of a jungle or forest."

So Alamogordo officials weren't surprised by a two-sentence telegram from Smokey: "Deeply touched by your offer of a new home. Preventing forest fires is still a national problem and calls for my attention here in the nation's capital."

Confronted with Washington's recalcitrance, Merle Tucker summarily dismissed reporters, admitting that he had rejected the only conceivable solution—sending a two-hundred-man posse to Washington to forcibly return Smokey to the Land of Enchantment.

America's penchant for new heroes also took its toll on Smokey's popularity. Although once the capital's fair-haired bear, the public always clamored for new stars, and the National Zoo claimed its share with such attractions as Ham, the first chimpanzee in space. Ironically, the poster Smokey had been created to help fight an Asian imperialist government, but an Asian communist government helped undermine the living Smokey. In fact, it was Smokey's own kind—the new bears on the block—that usurped him.

Responding to President Richard Nixon's diplomatic overtures, the People's Republic of China donated two giant panda bears—Hsing-Hsing and Ling-Ling—to the United States in 1972. Despite pleas from zoos across the country, Nixon ruled that the two bears should reside in Washington, D.C., so, as the president reasoned, *"all* Americans can see them." And see them they did. The new media darlings quickly claimed top billing, with panda signs placed throughout the zoo, panda souvenirs selling like honey cakes and—adding insult to Smokey's status—residing in a $425,000 cage of air-conditioned splendor.

Meanwhile poor Smokey, wallowing in his slum, didn't even own exclusive rights to his lair and sometimes was moved to even smaller quarters to allow colleagues room to give birth.

Next, Smokey was criticized for his indifferent attitude when, as in Santa Fe, Smokey refused to sport about for the pleasure of his fans. He wouldn't play, clown or beg, although he enjoyed peanuts and donuts and never, ever, passed up one of the honey sandwiches he so dearly loved. Again, Dr. Reed stood up for Smokey.

"Some bears are playful—they're clowns and beggars and they work the public," Reed explained. "But Smokey was an executive bear. He didn't play like a clown. He was a great personality in the papers, but he was just a straight bear behind the scenes."

But soon the world seemed to deny Smokey's importance. The large red sign depicting Smokey's life story was not updated or maintained and fell with peeling paint into shabbiness. Smokey's putative defender, the CFFP, seemed to change its public attitude, insisting that the living symbol was perhaps a welcome auxiliary to—but certainly not an integral part of—the campaign against forest carelessness. The living Smokey had fallen into ignominy.

Although the CFFP had harbored high hopes for a fruitful union between Smokey and Goldie, the passage of time told the painful truth—Smokey was not going to produce an heir. After examining Smokey, a Washington veterinarian opined that Smokey could have been sterilized when his hindquarters were so badly burned in the 1950 Capitan Gap fire. So if a living symbol added value to the CFFP program, a different tactic was required.

Electing to capitalize on the one-time enormous popularity of the living symbol, the CFFP began a search for a replacement bear. As luck and tradition would have it, in June 1971, New Mexico game rangers located another black bear cub in New Mexico's Lincoln National Forest—the same forest that produced Smokey in 1950. But this bear didn't have Smokey's impeccable pedigree and heroic firefighting credentials. This bear was a bum. Found wandering around a housing area near Cloudcroft, sixty-five miles southwest of Smokey's Capitan, the one-year-old cub was emaciated from hunger and eagerly welcomed his human rescuers.

"He was an orphan," Ray Bell explained. "Some people were putting out feed for coons, and the bear was fighting for their food. Roy Owen, the local game warden, got the bear and put it in the zoo at Alamogordo. About that time Mal Hardy called and wanted a replacement bear for Smokey. I told Mal about this little bear that was brown-colored like Smokey and weighed thirty-five or forty pounds, and Mal was interested." In a poetic overture, Bell again was asked to take the cub to Washington.

"Fred Fox flew me down to Alamogordo to get the bear in his Cessna 180," Bell continued. "But when I went into the cage, that damn bear liked to eat me up. I had on gloves, so I got hold of him and held him down while we taped his mouth so it could open an inch or so and he wouldn't smother, and then we taped his claws so he couldn't scratch. Then we wrapped the bear up in an old mattress cover and I got in the front seat and held him on my lap while Fred flew us back to Santa Fe."

By now, the novelty of New Mexico bears flying to Washington, D.C., had worn off, so "Little Smokey" (or, sometimes, "Smokey Junior") was forced to fly as cargo on a commercial airliner. What had been beneath the dignity of the first living symbol was now okay. So in November 1971, Bell left New Mexico with Smokey's replacement. "When they unloaded him in Washington," Bell recalled, "they wanted me to parade him around with that leash like I did Goldie, but I didn't do it; I was afraid he would tear me apart. He wasn't a good little bear like Goldie; he was kinda like old Smokey." So with far less fanfare than that bestowed on his predecessor, Little Smokey was quietly ushered into his own cage at the National Zoo to understudy the famous Smokey.

Although the ravages of time eventually shoved Smokey out of the national limelight, he never wore out his welcome in Capitan, New Mexico. There, Smokey's hometown folks used every resource within their limited means to show their love for their heroic friend. The Capitan Women's Club (an affiliate of the Federation of Women's Clubs) and Capitan's Smokey Bear Club often led the efforts to memoralize Smokey.

Under the leadership of Angelina Provine, Geraldine Randle, Frances Shaw and others the CWC won awards for spearheading the erection of portals on Highway 20 at both the east and west entrances to Capitan. Erected in 1954 and 1955, the portals depicted a large Smokey pointing to a sign urging motorists to prevent forest fires and identifying Capitan as his "birthplace." Clint Davis flew in from Washington, D.C., for the dedication. The Ad Council was represented by president Allen Wilson and executive secretary Henry Wehde Jr., and Homer Pickens, new director of New Mexico's Game and Fish Department, drove down from Santa Fe.

Soon thereafter, Bill Huber, new CFFP director in Washington, D.C., and Everett Doman, Lincoln National Forest supervisor in Alamogordo, visited Capitan. During a meeting with civic leaders, Huber and Doman apparently planted the idea to erect a Smokey museum, and the little community quickly sprang into action. Using her husband's Forest Service manuals, Dorothy Guck, chairman of many Capitan Smokey Bear activities, drew construction plans for an 18-by-32-foot log cabin. Patricia Flatley, who had hosted Smokey's first night in captivity, handled the shovel at ground-breaking ceremonies, and the entire village offered assistance.

Pearl Soderback and Margaret Rench led fund raising. Trankie Silva, J. G. Otero and H. C. Otero hauled and cut logs, and Charlie Pepper, a Forest Service retiree, took charge of construction and the dozens of volunteers who donated their labor. Men and women from the CWC, Smokey Bear Club, Lincoln National Forest, Game and Fish Department, Chamber of Commerce, Ruidoso Rotary Club, Lincoln County Fair and others lined up to help. But seventy-eight-year-old Abel Pino perhaps best demonstrated the local attitude as he peeled twenty-five logs a day, attracting both tourists and locals to watch his work. Pino took a simple view of Smokey Bear: trees were Pino's livelihood, and Smokey was their protector.

Although heavy rains delayed the museum's completion, its 1958 dedication occurred as scheduled, and the CWC hosted state and federal

Dorothy Gray Guck used her husband's Forest Service manuals to design the Smokey Bear Museum in Capitan, New Mexico. *(Courtesy William Clifford Lawter Jr.)*

representatives with Ray Bell, Judy Bell, J. Morgan Smith and Charlie Sutton. "Smokey" (Ed Guck in costume) made an appearance, but Rudy Wendelin's chalk talk highlighted the ceremonies while Albuquerque newspapers and a TV station documented events.

About the time Capitan began its annual Smokey Bear Stampede and rodeo, Smokey's log cabin museum actually opened its doors in 1961. With no federal or state financial aid, Capitan's 1,100 people honored their most famous citizen through private donations and volunteer efforts and carefully reconstructed Smokey's life. There, in the heart of "Smokey Bear country," visitors born long after Smokey began his tenure as America's fire-preventin' bear, learn how the living Smokey's luck and impeccable timing fueled his remarkable career, which was actually launched before his birth. Depicting

Smokey's story from birth to burial, virtually every aspect of his twenty-six-year reign has been reconstructed.

The rustic one-room building almost bursts with Smokey memorabilia, photos and posters chronicling his life history. Engaging drawings by Rudy Wendelin and Harold Walter's enlarged photos catch visitors' eyes first. In

Rudy Wendelin painted special art for the Smokey Bear Museum in Capitan, New Mexico. *(Courtesy William Clifford Lawter Jr.)*

one of Walter's photos, the cub Smokey looks up at the first poster of Smokey Bear. In another, the tiny Smokey crawls over Judy Bell's knee. Smokey's personal effects include his baby bottle with faint tooth marks.

Throughout the cabin, reminders of Smokey's extraordinarily powerful marketing impact offer a nice touch of nostalgia. Milton Bradley's Smokey Bear game, Smokey canteens, books, hats, dolls, watches, pens, scarves, rulers, and Viewmaster reels are piled beside Smokey mugs, patches, ranger station banks, shovels, Junior Forest Ranger badges, magic slates, ashtrays, coins, stamps, comics and sweatshirts. Four thick scrapbooks trumpet Smokey's achievements as if he were a high school athlete. Newspaper clippings, magazine articles and fan letters bring Smokey's fairytale story to life.

Outside, in a small front yard, a fiberglass young Smokey clings desperately to the stump of a fiberglass tree. Kevin Wolff, a Capitan woodworker, built the replica of the young Smokey in 1980 to replace a wooden one destroyed in a windstorm.

For most of its early years, responsibility for the Smokey Bear Museum fell to caretaker Willie Hobbs. "For seventeen years, she gave her heart to that museum," Dorothy Guck emphasized. "Willie was wonderful at publicizing and bringing that museum to the attention of the public. She kept visitor records, oiled the logs, kept up the building—just everything imaginable. She worked for expenses only, and never has been given as much credit as she deserves."

As Capitan developed its portals, Smokey's museum and many other projects, the city often received strong support from Ruth Bush Jones of the Forest Service offices in Albuquerque. "She was just wonderful to help us as much as she did," Guck stressed. "Ruth Bush Jones deserves an awful lot of recognition."

Through a congressional resolution, Capitan's Mountain Gap, Forest Lookout, and Ranger District were renamed after Smokey, and the CFFP granted permission to name a local inn the Smokey Bear Motel and Cafe. And at least one newspaper paid tribute to Capitan as the first community to dedicate itself to forest conservation.

Every bear—even a multimillionaire with his own ZIP code and 5 million annual visitors—eventually goes to the great honeycomb in the sky. So, aware of Smokey's creeping age, representatives of the CFFP, the Forest Service, the National Zoo, the state of New Mexico and the village of Capitan met to plan funeral and burial arrangements for their beloved bear. There may have been as many ideas as participants.

The CFFP's original plan—for Smokey and Goldie to return to New Mexico and sleep away their days at the Ghost Ranch Museum in the Carson National Forest—fell apart in the early 1970s. William Hurst, Forest Service southwestern regional forester in Albuquerque, reported that plans to build Smokey's grotto at the Ghost Ranch had been dropped because contractor bids exceeded the Forest Service's budget. Six bids ranged from $64,218 to $93,602, and despite Smokey's contributions to the nation's forests, Congress refused to allocate the funds. Smokey would have to stay at the National Zoo.

"There was a lot of interest in what should happen to Smokey," Chuck Williams acknowledged. "There was some talk of cremation and scattering his ashes over the forest. Elliott Barker wanted him stuffed. We found that offensive, but Elliott wanted him on display in a high-visibility place—perhaps the State Capitol in Santa Fe. We were uneasy about Elliott; he was eighty-nine years old, but even at that age he was a powerful individual. He had the ear of the governor—Bruce King. Elliott showed up at one meeting with a letter signed by the governor that said Elliott was representing the governor and the state of New Mexico and that whatever Elliott said was the state's position." But, nudged by the Forest Service, Ray Bell visited with Barker about the pros and cons of stuffing Smokey; soon thereafter, Barker dropped his support for the idea.

With that controversial proposal defused, CFFP headquarters breathed easier. "There were all kinds of news articles about what would happen," James Sorenson added, "and most of it was speculation. But Roy Rogers had stuffed Trigger, so kids wrote in with comments like 'If you stuff Smokey, I'll stuff you.' We got some really hostile letters. Even a radio station in Florida called us. The public was not interested in Smokey being a stuffed creature with glass eyeballs, but from adults to kids they were extremely interested in what we were going to do with the bear. That reinforces the idea that the live bear was important to the program."

Nonplussed by the press, radio and TV coverage on Smokey's health, Mal Hardy expressed some support for cremating Smokey's body and scattering the ashes over the Lincoln National Forest: "This . . . alternative . . . may be the best we've looked at so far. It does away with the morbid publicity inherent in preparing the body for shipment and the actual handling of the 'coffin' all along the line."

Smokey, of course, never voiced an opinion. "As for the bear himself," Hardy reported, "he is going along his creaky routine, eating well, and in apparently satisfactory condition."

From the outset of the debates, Capitan's citizens pushed for a simple burial in Smokey's hometown. City clerk Doris Jo Engleking, Mayor J. T. Johnston, and his wife, Dorothy Johnston, spearheaded the efforts. "After we heard that Smokey was in bad health, the crew here at City Hall wondered if we could get that [burial in Capitan] done," Mayor Johnston recalled. "Doris and Dorothy had the idea."

J. T. Johnston, who hailed from Portalis, New Mexico, was in the midst of a six-year stint as mayor. Johnston served as greens superintendent at the Alto Lakes golf course and operated a rock quarry northwest of Capitan. Dorothy, J. T.'s wife of 25 years, had been born in Telephone, Texas. Long-time residents of Lincoln County, the Johnstons first tried their hands running the Parsons Hotel near Bonita Lake and then bought the Top Hat bar in Ruidoso, which they remodeled and renamed the Wild Snail.

Working closely with Doris Engleking, the determined Johnstons elected to take on the CFFP. "We wrote letters to state representatives and everyone in Washington that we could," Dorothy Johnston recalled. "Anyone we thought could help—we went after them. We wrote maybe a couple of dozen letters, but most of them were ignored; no one even replied."

J. T. Johnston outlined Capitan's proposal in a March 26, 1974, letter to Mal Hardy, director of the CFFP program in Washington: "I am sure that you are aware that the Village of Capitan in New Mexico is the birthplace of Smokey the Bear. We are very proud of that fact. We have heard that Old Smokey probably does not have much time left to live. It is the wish of the residents of Capitan and the surrounding areas that Smokey be returned to his birthplace for burial when he does pass on."

Unfortunately for Capitan, the bear's final fate had been planned during a 1971 policy meeting in Penn's Woods, Pennsylvania. There, Smokey's national coordinator and representatives of the Forest Service, Foote, Cone & Belding, the Ad Council and New Mexico decided to bury Smokey high on Capitan Mountain. To minimize adverse impact on the forest fire campaign, the committee agreed not to publicize its plans until death actually occurred.

Hardy's reply to Johnston stood by that decision: "As the committee sees it, the best interest of the Cooperative Forest Fire Prevention campaign will be served if Smokey's passing and replacement by his adopted son are handled quietly and with dignity. We have provided for the succession of 'live Smokeys' but want it to be accomplished without creating the impression that the Smokey Bear campaign will be less important or less effective because of the change. The plan is to return Smokey's remains to the Lincoln National Forest, where he was born. There he will be buried with only a modest marker at the spot where he was rescued from the fire."

But New Mexico Congressman Harold Runnels introduced legislation to allow Capitan to make the final decision for its hero. And after seeing Hardy's response to Johnston, Runnels offered his own views in a May 3 letter: "This letter [Hardy's] is a perfect example of why I felt it was necessary to introduce legislation. I am of the opinion that if we are successful in getting this bill passed, it will carry more weight than Mr. Hardy's opinion."

Debate widened as the Ruidoso Valley Chamber of Congress jumped into the fray. In a June 18 letter to the New Mexico congressional delegation, the chamber argued simple logic: "To return Smokey's remains to the location he was found in, the Capitan Gap area, would benefit no one. We feel vandals would in no time take their toll and the area would be too remote for fans and admirers of Smokey to visit."

Although this reasoning eventually proved persuasive, several considerations may have been ignored, conveniently overlooked or passed unrecognized by the folks in New Mexico and those in Washington, D.C.

First, New Mexicans may not have understood that CFFP officials reflected a widespread belief by knowledgeable people in the Forest Service, the advertising industry and some state forestry offices—the very people charged with promulgating the message of Smokey Bear—that the CFFP program had evolved to the point where the living symbol detracted more from the message than he contributed. Some critics argued that Hardy's associates were isolated from the real world. Others wrote them off as single-minded advocates of a narrow school of thought. Still others dismissed Smokey's guardians as simple bureaucrats. But Hardy had valid concerns about the future of America's forest fire prevention spokesbear.

The problem was that many Americans had begun to identify the living representative of Smokey as the true Smokey—an improper association capable of chipping away at the amazing effectiveness of the Smokey Bear program. Kay Flock, for one, remembered sitting on a bench in front of Smokey's cage watching children tell their parents that the scrungy animal purporting to be Smokey must be a sham. Why wasn't his fur glossy and groomed? Why wasn't he wearing dungarees and a hat? Why didn't he carry a shovel?

And what would happen when the live Smokey died? Would the program die with it? That answer was yes in the eyes of many Americans, and Hardy's concerns eventually were proven to be justified. Hardy and his colleagues simply weren't interested in their highly successful caricature being lost on a tidal wave of emotion over a deceased animal that some felt hadn't really done much except (a) get his butt burned and (b) bite Ray Bell.

Second, the Washington crew may not have appreciated that the people of New Mexico—and Capitan in particular—had such strong, sincere feelings about their famous colleague. Many New Mexicans speak with reverence about their fellow citizen, and many of those people apparently never wanted to—or perhaps never could—disassociate New Mexico's living symbol contribution from the poster personification of Smokey Bear.

Third, one can argue that there is little difference between burying Smokey's remains on a remote mountainside or in downtown Capitan. Although filled with friendly folks, the fact remains that Capitan is very much off the beaten tourist path; in a good year, perhaps 50,000 tourists may wander through town, but many are hustling to Ruidoso's ski slopes or nearby Lincoln with its Billy the Kid history. A far cry from the 5 million annual visitors Smokey enjoyed at the National Zoo, Capitan simply is not a primary competitor for the public eye.

Fourth, concern over vandals damaging a grave on Capitan Mountain seems to have been misplaced. The site believed to be the location of Smokey's 1950 rescue is virtually inaccessible, and as late as 1993, local Forest Service rangers had never attempted the climb. To reach the site high on the north slope of east Capitan Mountain, a hiker must walk along steep slopes, traverse treacherous rock slides and hack through dense oak brush reaching as high as twelve feet.

Clearly, the CFFP knew exactly what it wanted—an invisible succession of living symbols that wouldn't damage their business of preventing forest fires. But on May 2, 1974, Congressman Manuel Lujan Jr. wrote to Forest Service chief John McGuire: "Smokey the Bear does not 'belong' to the Forest Service or to any one individual—he 'belongs' to the entire population of the Country and he deserves the honor the people wish to bestow on him for years and years to come. The Government has no more right to dictate his burial spot than they would a deceased elected official."

Although Mayor Johnston refused to concede defeat, he developed a greater appreciation for the seriousness of Washington's approach. "I went to Washington with Chuck Williams," Johnston explained. "He was going to a meeting of the Smokey Bear committee, so I went with him. It had never soaked in on me that Smokey was quite as important as he was until I attended that meeting. It was all business with those people, and the committee was very careful. I was impressed. But we didn't get any satisfaction at all. They just ran backwards on this."

Finally, the Ford administration agreed to support New Mexico when the House report accompanying Congressman Runnels's resolution estimated the cost to federal government to be zero: "The Department of Agriculture estimated that expenses for transportation and burial would be $2,500, all to be provided by donations or royalties from the Smokey Bear Fund."

In July hearings before the House Agriculture Subcommittee on Forests, care was taken to stipulate neither a burial nor an exact location; "proper disposition" would be left to the people of Capitan. Speaking in support of his resolution, Runnels explained that it was appropriate for Congress to recognize the inevitability of Smokey's demise and plan for the "time of his call to that great honey tree in the sky." Apparently only one representative objected to the resolution, expressing concern that constituents would look askance on Congress for worrying about a bear when problems of more significance were being ignored. But an unidentified New Mexico spokesman opined on behalf of the city of Capitan: "Though Smokey belongs to everyone in the United States, the people of Capitan love him just a little more."

James Felton, second national Smokey Bear campaign coordinator (left), Dr. Theodore Reed, director, National Zoological Park (center) and Mal Hardy, fifth director of the Cooperative Forest Fire Prevention campaign, in 1974. *(Courtesy Mal Hardy and USDA Forest Service.)*

Runnels's resolution passed the House on August 5, and the Senate concurred one month later. For the second time, Smokey Bear had become the subject of congressional action, as the bipartisan House Concurrent Resolution 564 resolved: "That it is the sense of the Congress that upon his death the body of Smokey Bear may be returned to Capitan, New Mexico, for proper disposition and a permanent memorial in or near Capitan."

With the burial issues settled, it was left to the CFFP and the Forest Service to make the final arrangements. One of those involved—James Abbott—was unaware of the role he would play in Smokey's burial.

Born in Spokane, Washington, Abbott became interested in forestry during high school. Hired by the Forest Service after graduating from

341

Washington State University in 1959, Abbott had served in the Washington office since 1972 and, as a member of the fire management staff, was active in developing Smokey's burial plans.

"We discussed the dying bear in staff meetings," Abbott recalled, "and it was an active debate. Meanwhile, the bear was getting older and scrungier—pretty decrepit, in fact. So we developed a 'morgue kit' with an outline of what to do. The zoo would call the 'State and Private' group in the Forest Service; the Forest Service would call the airline; the zoo would box up the bear and get it to the airport. Flights had been selected ahead of time and matters had been arranged with TWA. The people knew what to do."

"Press releases were drafted and airline routings picked," Chuck Williams confirmed. "It was decided to keep funeral arrangements simple, with only a basic service involving local people." Mal Hardy even wrote Smokey's obituary.

Although Forest Service policies have no mandatory retirement for bears, time marched on in Smokey's cage. Smokey's life span in captivity extended beyond that of a normal black bear because his regular food supply obviated the feast and famine cycles attendant to ursine pseudo-hibernation. But as aging continued, Smokey began suffering from arthritis and increasingly elected to hide in his den. While Smokey's fans probably expected to see an old bear sacked out, they frequently never saw him at all, unless he could be lured from his den by honey sandwiches.

So as old age and arthritis claimed Smokey's body, it became obvious that he was on his last legs. He rose later and later each morning and became increasingly reluctant to leave his den. A bear that won't sit up, climb trees, catch peanuts or act as if he gives a beehive about his surroundings certainly can't inspire putative young forest conservationists. Moreover, it became clear that the listless bear could even detract from the nation's fire prevention program.

Again, the press called more attention to the matter than the CFFP would have preferred. In a thoughtful, heart-grabbing 1974 *Washington Post/Potomac* article, "The Last Sad Days of Smokey the Bear," Kenneth Turrin explained that not only was Smokey's message under attack, but that the old, sick fellow had been upstaged by pandas and downgraded by the zoo. Distributed nationwide through the *Los Angeles Times–Washington Post* syndicate, the story appeared across the country under headlines such as "Problems, Pain Fill Smokey's Last Days," "Smokey the Bear Sulks As Fans

Prove Fickle Friends," "Smokey: Symbol in Decline" and "Smokey Bear Lolls in Cage at Twilight of his Career."

That publicity spawned more activity as WMAL-TV interviewed Jackson Weaver at Smokey's cage, and Mal Hardy appeared on several TV and radio shows—which in turn generated even more attention. "Dozens of concerned Smokey Bear fans wrote and phoned, expressing concern and affection," Hardy explained. "Many sent money, or remedies for arthritis. One offered undertaking services and a plot in their pet cemetery."

So on May 2, 1975, a clear spring day in Washington, the living symbol of Smokey Bear officially retired from the Forest Service after almost twenty-five years of dedicated labor. The National Zoo hosted the retirement ceremonies as Department of Agriculture officials, Forest Service colleagues, tourists and several hundred schoolchildren witnessed the passing of the torch to the younger and livelier Little Smokey.

Jackson Weaver presided as Smokey's title, ranger hat, blue dungarees and firefighter's shovel were ritually passed to the frisky youngster. Showing his appreciation, Little Smokey stood on hind legs and snapped proffered peanuts as children jockeyed for position to lob their offerings.

And when it all ended, Smokey and Goldie were quietly moved to a simple grotto on the zoo's Bear Row. As a final indignity, Smokey's new identification was a simple "American Black Bear." As Little Smokey pranced for the cheering crowd, Smokey seemed to sulk, and from Smokey's viewpoint, he should have stayed in bed. Not only did Smokey lose his job, but United Press International reported that his day began poorly too, when Goldie slapped Smokey on his snout just before he fell into a pool of water. "He's not in pain, but he isn't very happy," a zoo spokesman reportedly stated.

But had anyone asked his opinion, Smokey might have confessed to not being too aggravated. He had been, after all, a reluctant celebrity almost from the beginning—his national role had been forced on him. Smokey never cared to be the center of attention, but he won adoration primarily because he was small and injured at first, and as famous as the president later.

In any event, Smokey wasn't quite through; he gained another distinction that day. Because twenty-five bear years roughly equal seventy human years—then the mandatory retirement age for federal employees—Smokey was honored as the first bear to become a full-fledged member of the National Association of Retired Federal Employees. Rudy Wendelin commemorated the occasion with a touching painting: on the left stood a quizzical Little Smokey looking wide-eyed at the ranger hat in his paws;

on the right, a sheepish, ragged, bandaged and mottled Smokey hands his shovel and dungarees over to Little Smokey and speaks the words "Carry on, Little Smokey"; at Smokey's feet lies a well-used suitcase with travel stickers of "New Mexico," the dates "1950" and "1975," and autographs by Rudy Wendelin, Jackson Weaver, Mal Hardy, Clint Davis, Hopalong Cassidy and other colleagues.

Perhaps not by coincidence, the 1975 CFFP campaign poster featured an aged Smokey tipping his ranger hat under the heading "Thanks for Listening." At Smokey's retirement, however, an admirer had altered the caption to read "Thanks for a great job!"

While debating Smokey's possible replacement with Little Smokey, many Forest Service officials had questioned whether the popularity of the original living Smokey could successfully be transferred to a new bear. Certainly, not everyone agreed with the idea of a replacement, nor did everyone believe that a living symbol was needed. CFFP worries were soon dispelled, however, as Little Smokey inherited the many years of goodwill generated by Smokey. An adoring public accepted their new living symbol, gawked at his cage and read displays relating the dramatic rescue of the first Smokey. In contrast to the first Smokey, who never seemed interested in showmanship, Little Smokey perhaps became even more popular than his predecessor as children jammed against a glass partition to watch the rambunctious bear run and climb to their delighted squeals.

With Smokey destined to return to Capitan, an idea for the Smokey Bear Historical State Park apparently originated with the Capitan Women's Club. Working with state officials, the CWC and City Hall developed plans to acquire more than an acre of land from the Smokey Bear Museum and part of the "Branding Iron" property for a walled park on Capitan's Main Street. With costs projected at $331,000, $100,000 for Phase I was financed by the New Mexico Legislature and matching funds from the U.S. Bureau of Recreation. New Mexico's Forestry Department also contributed $30,000 in federal CM-2 funds for design and interpretive work.

Within New Mexico, however, controversy developed. After the state legislature appropriated $165,000 for the park in early 1975, an Albuquerque TV commentator challenged the propriety of spending so much money to "bury a bear." But the announcer failed to reckon with Elliott Barker.

Eric McCrossen, in a story in the *Albuquerque Journal*, reported that in a spirited defense of the park, Barker offered his view of the station's comments: "Uncalled for, deceitful and disrespectful. To refer to Smokey Bear of national and international fame as just a bear is an insult to the millions of young folks who idolize him." Instead, Barker insisted, the funds would "honor and perpetuate the image of the most celebrated animal that ever lived and the one that has done the most good to a worthy cause than any other animal in history."

Emphasizing that he had Congress as an ally, Barker argued his cause: "New Mexico would be inexcusably remiss in its duty if it did not provide a suitable memorial state park to perpetuate his memory and image. It

The Smokey Bear Historical State Park in Capitan, New Mexico, opened its doors in 1979. *(Courtesy William Clifford Lawter Jr.)*

must be comparable to Smokey's stature and the appropriation is by all standards fully justified." But if the TV station missed his point, Barker launched a final salvo to characterize the station's position: "Deprecatory, disrespectful, deceitful and utterly inappropriate editorial broadcast on the subject."

"It took legislation to create the State Park, and the effort was intensive," Chuck Williams recalled. "We worked with the mayor of Capitan, who worked with state legislators, who sometimes called the Forest Service for information. Eventually the bill passed unanimously and was signed by Governor Jerry Apodaca."

At the time of its dedication, Smokey's park didn't impress too many people—probably because it didn't look much like a park on that Saturday morning, May 15, 1976. But the three hundred spectators were not dedicating the dirt lot, unfinished stone wall and the lone sign. They were rededicating themselves to the spirit of their favorite bear and his role in forest fire prevention.

Two hours of ceremonies included music by the Capitan High School band and a presentation by New Mexico's Department of Forestry of a sycamore seedling taken to the moon in 1971 on Apollo 14. Plaudits from fifteen speakers extolled Smokey's virtues and the efforts of the people of Capitan, and Mayor Johnston spoke his feelings: "This park is proof that people in high places in this country can listen to people in small places and work together to fulfill a project like this."

The park's spacious visitors' center finally opened in 1979. Only fifty yards from Capitan's log cabin, New Mexico's modernistic center focuses on forest fires as a national problem and tells the story of Smokey's conservation efforts.

Visitors stroll through a simulated burning forest with black silhouette foreground and red blaze backlighting. Audio and graphic presentations emphasize the intensity of a wild forest fire, and well-crafted educational displays explain the three parts of forest fires. Exhibits on arcing walls explain how the forest fire prevention effort began during World War II. Early forest fire prevention posters include the grinning Japanese fanatic and leering German and Japanese military figures near Smokey's harness worn on his flight to Washington, D.C.

In a circular theater, visitors watch a special film about forest fire prevention, and outside the east door a winding boardwalk leads to Smokey's grave. Marked by a simple boulder sporting a bronze plaque, Smokey rests peacefully. When the U.S. Postal Service announced in 1983 that Washington, D.C., had been designated for the coveted "first day of issue" ceremonies for the 20-cent Smokey Bear stamp, no one anticipated the reaction from Capitan. When Smokey Bear Museum curator Willie Hobbs learned in October of the Postal Service's plans, Hobbs, Martha Thiedt, and her daughter, Rose Garner, immediately caused an uproar.

Thiedt and Garner formed a committee within the Lincoln County Republican Women's Club and circulated a petition to ask the Postal Service to change its mind. Hobbs enlisted Congressman Joe Skeen into the crusade and asked him to coordinate efforts with the rest of New Mexico's congressional delegation. Then Hobbs forwarded correspondence and stories by Dorothy Guck to support Capitan's claim for first-day-of-issue rights. With all the commotion, Postmaster General William Bolger finally relented in February 1984: the stamp would be issued in Capitan.

Smokey rides in the annual July 4 parade in Capitan, New Mexico.
(Courtesy William Clifford Lawter Jr.)

So on August 13, 1984, with a barbecue and Smokey's fortieth birthday cake, the little village welcomed artist Rudy Wendelin, Smokey's old friend Ray Bell, part of New Mexico's congressional delegation and a star-studded cast of guests representing state and federal organizations. The ritual began promptly at 11:00 a.m., and after Assistant Postmaster General Harry Penttala presented an album of first-day-of-issue stamps to a costumed Smokey, for the first time in its history the Postal Service had issued a commemorative stamp to honor a bear.

Capitan's hometown animal conquered the heart of a nation. And considering Smokey's complete lack of formal education, it could be argued that he did quite well for himself. Certainly, this was no ordinary bear.

23

DEATH OF A LIVING SYMBOL

"Dear Smokey. I'm sorry that you died. I hope you are very happy in Heaven. We will all miss you and will be very careful with fires."

— Juliane and Vincent Norment, Hempstead, N.Y.

With the eventual disposition of Smokey's remains resolved, preparations for his actual demise began to crystallize.

By November 1974, packets were completed for distribution to the nation's major news and photo outlets. Each folder contained three eight-by-ten-inch black-and-white captioned photos of the bruin, a background fact sheet and Smokey's biography. Cover envelopes and contents were clearly labeled: "Hold—for release upon the death of Smokey Bear."

On December 24, 1975, zoo director Theodore Reed wrote an internal memo/work order: "Bear Crate. We will at some unspecified time be required to ship the remains of an American Black Bear from this Zoo to Capitan, New Mexico. When this project is initiated, it is going to have to move fairly fast. We will not have time to build a proper crate. It behooves us to make a shipping crate for this purpose and store it."

349

After specifying dimensions, Reed continued: "The crate should be painted an unobtrusive color. No signs identifying the NZP [National Zoological Park] or anything else is to appear on it. We will probably have to ship the remains of the bear either with ice or with dry ice so we would want to count on a heavy plastic lining inside the crate. There should be a lid on top of the crate that screws down."

Despite the crate's obvious purpose, Reed issued a word of caution. "I should like to keep this a relatively quiet operation," he insisted. "I do not want any advance publicity on this—goodness knows we will have enough flak when the crate is put into use. Any resemblance between this crate and a coffin is not to be talked about."

By March 25, 1976, an 18-by-24-inch plaque was completed and on hand at Lincoln National Forest headquarters in Alamorgordo. Its simple inscription told Smokey's history:

> SMOKEY BEAR. This is the final resting place of the first living Smokey Bear. In 1950 when Smokey was a tiny cub, wildfire burned his forest home in the nearby Capitan Mountains of the Lincoln National Forest. Firefighters found the badly burned cub clinging to a blackened tree and saved his life. In June 1950, the cub was flown to our Nation's Capital to become the living symbol of wildfire prevention and wildlife conservation. After 25 years he was replaced by another orphaned black bear from the Lincoln National Forest.

After numerous drafts, the "Information Contact Plan" for Smokey's pending death finally was issued on July 21, 1976. Unofficially dubbed the "morgue kit" among Forest Service insiders, the plan summarized in narrative and chart form (a) internal and external notification procedures, (b) issuance of press releases and TV kits to major networks and local Washington, D.C, stations, (c) the release of TV spots in New Mexico and (d) arrangements for shipment on TWA—preferably flight 217 to Albuquerque through Chicago.

Remarkably detailed, the morgue kit included office and home phone numbers of appropriate Forest Service personnel in Washington, Albuquerque and Alamogordo, and state of New Mexico contacts in Santa Fe and Capitan. The kit specified who would do what and when, and addressed actions to be taken before the bear's death, after death, transportation, burial arrangements and subsequent dedication at the Smokey Bear Historical State Park.

350

"Dear Smokey Bear. I love you and adore you. I'm sad that you died."

— Tracy Lucas, Oklahoma City

Inevitably, the end drew near for America's living legend. By human standards Smokey had reached age eighty, and his final days were not pleasant. Smokey, who received little attention from zoo visitors, certainly had fallen a long way from his place in the sun.

Almost crippled by arthritis, Smokey had to walk stiff-legged, didn't have enough energy to fight off birds claiming his food and seemed to be completely off his feed by November 5, 1976. He spent his last days sleeping in his den to avoid pain, and as his condition deteriorated, the zoo considered euthanasia to end his misery. But on Tuesday morning, November 9, zoo officials announced that finally, mercifully, the end had come. Smokey had died peacefully in his sleep at age twenty-six.

Charles Braxton, a native of Washington, D.C., and one of Smokey's keepers since 1962, apparently discovered Smokey about 8:30 a.m. on his normal rounds. "I was on the walk behind his den, looking through the iron bars," Braxton recalled. "I spotted Smokey's body and saw no movement, but Goldie was at the door standing up and looking around."

"The keepers knew Smokey was dead," Dr. Reed confirmed. "Goldie was upset; she had to be separated out. She knew something was wrong. She was standing, weaving back and forth, weaving her head, muttering and grumbling. She let us know she wasn't happy."

"So I called the vet—Dr. [Clinton] Gray, I think," Braxton explained. "Then they took him to the hospital in a crate in the back of a green, government pickup truck."

Smokey was packed into his 67 1/2 inch-long, 41-inch-wide and 29-inch-high crate that now weighed 475 pounds (125 pounds of box, 100 pounds of ice and 250 pounds of bear), then delivered to the TWA air cargo office, Allegheny Airline Hangar #11 at National Airport's North Terminal at 12:30 p.m.

"It went pretty fast," a pleased Dr. Reed admitted. "Everyone had their orders about what they were to do, and everything worked like it was supposed to."

Although TWA had insisted that the airline would not prohibit the news media from covering the story, only CFFP and other government officials were at the TWA office when the zoo truck arrived. Because no permits were required for the deceased animal, Smokey was gently loaded into the

351

cargo hold of TWA flight 217, scheduled for a 2:00 p.m. Eastern time departure. The original living symbol of Smokey Bear was going home.

"I wish you could come back to life so the children can see you again and help prevent forest fires."

— Lily Davis, Miami, Florida

Born in Denver, Colorado, Raymond H. Lutz began flying in California at age fourteen and earned his solo, private and commercial pilot's licenses at the respective minimum ages of sixteen, seventeen and eighteen. After graduating from San Diego State college and tackling a variety of flying jobs, Lutz joined the air force and flew F-80 and F-84 fighters.

In 1955, Lutz signed on with TWA to fly domestic routes out of New York on Martins, Constellations and PC-4s. After flying international commercial routes on Boeing 707s, Lutz flew military charters into Vietnam on Boeing 747s and Lockheed L-1011s.

Lutz moved to Taos, New Mexico, in 1970 and soon boasted of his "New Mexican" status. Because TWA flight 217 required a change of crews in Chicago, Lutz, then age forty-six, was assigned to return Smokey to his native state for burial.

Lutz walked into TWA's flight operations room at Chicago's O'Hare Airport at 2:30 p.m. Central time on Tuesday afternoon, November 9. "Our normal procedure was to visit the flight operations room about an hour prior to departure," Lutz explained. "As captain, I was advised of any irregularities or VIPs on board, so our operations people told me we would be carrying Smokey Bear's body in the cargo hold. They didn't make a big deal of it, but I felt that because I lived in New Mexico and that Smokey Bear was from there, that it was a nice coincidence. The crew was interested in Smokey, and we talked about him and the significance of what he stood for. We all were pleased that he was on our flight. We felt a sense of excitement. I always had a place in my heart for Smokey Bear, and I appreciated the Forest Service campaign to save forests. In this area [New Mexico], that kind of thing is a big deal."

Aboard the jet, Lutz completed his usual passenger announcements about weather, route and altitude, then added a footnote: "Sometimes we are honored to have special passengers aboard our flights and today we have a special cargo. We are privileged to be carrying the remains of Smokey Bear to be delivered to Albuquerque. It is my understanding the bear will be interred in New Mexico."

So as a sad Capitan prepared to welcome Smokey home, Ray Lutz and TWA proudly flew their precious cargo across the heart of America. "We departed Chicago O'Hare at 1547 central standard time," Lutz confirmed after consulting his log. "The flight path took us over Kirksville, Missouri, and Kansas City to Wichita, Kansas, at flight level 3100 [31,000 feet] arriving at 1734 central standard time. We departed Wichita at 1800 central standard time, flying over Dodge City, Kansas, and Las Vegas, New Mexico, at flight level 3100 for landing at 1830 mountain standard time in Albuquerque, New Mexico. It was a routine flight; nothing unusual occurred."

But the arrival of an American legend wasn't routine. TWA flight 217 taxied up to a bevy of flashing lights, TV cameras, the New Mexico Highway Patrol and an official U.S. government delegation. "A Forest Service contingent met the flight," Lutz recalled. "A lot of wheels were out there—maybe ten or twelve people. They unloaded Smokey's coffin and put it into the back of a pickup truck. It looked like a routine offloading of cargo; they were just getting the job done quickly. At that time I had not heard the rumors about the possibility of hijacking the bear."

> *"It would have been great to spend even a minute with Smokey. Sure, he wouldn't understand me if I talked to him; I probably wouldn't have gotten to pet him, either. But just by me getting to see him and him see me—just that instance, no matter how brief, would have suited me. And I've had all my 15 years to do that. And how I wanted to. Now it's too late. I can only say a prayer for him, to ask God to keep him sheltered."*

> — R. Fanella, Riverside, Rhode Island

In May 1950, fourteen-year-old Dick Cox stood in Capitan High School's doorway with Donna Cloud, his future wife. Together they watched smoke from the Capitan Gap fire billow high into the sky; later they learned of the small bear rescued from the inferno. Perhaps inspired by the dramatic fire, Cox worked summers for the Forest Service until graduating in 1958 with a degree in range management from New Mexico State University. Hired by the Forest Service, Cox learned the ropes in three national forests before his 1974 transfer to Lincoln National Forest headquarters in Alamorgordo.

"It was pure coincidence that I was back in New Mexico," Cox recalled. "Burial was assigned to the fire staff officer, and I just happened to have that job. It was clear and cold, and the phone call came about eight in the morning. We had been expecting the death, and we had planned to simply drive Smokey to Capitan for burial. But we had to change our plans. There had been a big scare that someone intended to hijack Smokey's body and cut off his claws and sell them. It didn't make any sense to me, but we treated it as a serious threat. Nothing ever developed and we never knew if there was any truth to it, but we didn't take any chances."

Lincoln Forest supervisor Jim Abbott had just transferred from Washington, D.C. "I had been in Alamogordo only a few weeks when the bear died," Abbott explained. "By coincidence, I had been in Clovis for a meeting and, while returning, the pilot gave me an overview of the Lincoln National Forest. When we flew over the area around Capitan the pilot gave me a travelogue of the Capitan Gap fire and showed me where Smokey Bear had been rescued. Then, when we landed in Alamogordo about five p.m., the dispatcher stuck his head out of his office and said, 'Hey. The bear died.' Of course, Dick Cox knew by then and the plan already was in place."

That plan included a courtesy call to Ray Bell, whose family would be most touched by the bear's death. "I felt a loss," Bell admitted. "They called to tell me about it, but I couldn't go meet the plane. I called Judy and told her the bear had died, and she felt pretty bad. Smokey was her buddy."

"Goodbye Beloved Smokey. You were the greatest guy who ever lived. I will tell my children of your unselfish gallantries. I will miss you a lot. Be happy in the great forests of Heaven."

— Jamie Soo, Albuquerque, New Mexico

"For several months, we knew the bear was going to die," explained Ray Page, district ranger at the Smokey Bear station in Ruidoso. "In preparation, I went out one afternoon with Jay Johnston, Capitan mayor, in the vicinity of where the bear had been rescued to find a boulder to mark the grave. We drove up and down the roads until we found a granite boulder that looked suitable and was close to the road. I'd guess the boulder weighs about a thousand pounds. It's weathered and looks polished. There are lots of them around there that are naturally smooth—that was part of the plan."

"We drove up into the Capitan Gap on Forest Service land," J. T. Johnston concurred, "measured some rocks and figured the weight that we could haul. Later, Ray Provine and I went up with a front-end load tractor and loaded the rock into my pickup. That rock was so big that we had to put chains around it, lift it with the loader and back the pickup under it."

"We love you very much. We hope you come back to life again."
— David Miller, Miami, Florida

"I got a call from Alamogordo," Ray Page recalled. "I was told to be in Albuquerque that evening wearing my uniform to meet the plane. We figured it would take four of us to handle the box, so we took two trucks. Paul Jones and Jim Paxon took a green Dodge four by four to carry the bear, while Bob Wagenfehr and I drove the pickup." Paxon, recreation forester in the Smokey Bear ranger district, had a new 1976 Dodge four-wheel-drive pickup with two rotating beacons on top and a bed that would accommodate the coffin."

"Dear New Mexico: Smokey the Bear died today. I wish he did not because I love him."

— Thomas Flaherty, Kenmore, New York

"We left around 3:30 or 4:00 p.m.," Page explained, "and drove to Albuquerque and met Chuck Williams at the airport. We were told to just drive out onto the tarmac and load the bear into the four-wheel-drive."

"We waited an hour on the TWA flight," Jim Paxon recalled. "I was twenty-nine years old and quite impressed. I was pretty thrilled to be a part of that; not many people got to participate. I was quite honored."

After completing his assignment in Washington, D.C., Chuck Williams had transferred to Albuquerque in 1973 as public affairs director for the Forest Service's southwestern region. "About ten Forest Service people were there to meet the plane," Williams explained. "Smokey was packed in ice but not embalmed, so there was some urgency and he had to be moved fast. It was dark, but two TV stations and the local newspaper were there. We took a low-key, low-profile approach after we got the bear in New Mexico. Although the entire plan worked like clockwork, we had some concern; we wanted to make sure it worked right."

"The airport loading only took five minutes," Paxon added. "They slid the box from the cargo door onto a hydraulic platform lift, lowered that level with the truck bed, and then we slid it onto the truck. The green box had a Forest Service shield on top and rails along each side. The lid was screwed on. We secured the box with ropes so it wouldn't slide around on the trip back, especially on the road from San Antonio to Carrizozo."

Paul Jones, an assistant fire management officer for the Smokey Bear district, had been born in Capitan in 1927, so he was pleased to see the famous animal returned to his native town. "The media showed up with video cameras," Jones recalled. "They put the story on the ten o'clock news, so my family watched it at home."

"Then we just headed out," Page added. "There was no crowd because there had been no publicity; that was intentional." The two Forest Service trucks drove off the tarmac to be greeted by a New Mexico State Police escort waiting at the gate.

> "I read in the paper where a <u>burial</u> is planned for Smokey. <u>Don't do it!</u> <u>STUFF HIM!</u> If it's good enough for the Russians to stuff Lenin and keep him on display—Americans deserve to have <u>Smokey</u> stuffed and on permanent exhibit."
>
> — Mel Miller, Albany, Oregon

"The state police decided to relay us down," Page explained. "The first patrol car did about fifty-five to Belen. The second took us to Socorro and went faster. The third took us up to seventy miles per hour to Carrizozo and the fourth was even faster into Capitan. We had a convoy—the patrol car in front, the bear in the middle and Ray and Bob in the rear."

"We had to ask one of the patrol cars to slow down," Paxon added. "He had his red lights flashing and was going about a hundred miles per hour."

Meanwhile, Ray Provine, Joe Schaeffer and Wayne Hobbs dug Smokey's grave directly west of the stone marker. "We didn't dig that grave during the day," J. T. Johnston explained. "We purposely waited until after dark—that was part of the security. Ray Provine ran the backhoe. Then we were supposed to fix the ground so it looked like he hadn't been buried; the Forest Service didn't want anyone to know the exact spot because, at the time, they were concerned someone would try to dig him up."

Jim Abbott, Dick Cox and Larry Allen, a four-year Forest Service veteran of the Lincoln National Forest, amused themselves chatting and watching firemen play cards in the Capitan fire station east of the Smokey Bear Museum. Then, about 9:00 p.m., the convoy arrived after an uneventful 150-mile-drive from Albuquerque. "We thought we had plenty of time, but they showed up at least an hour before we expected them," Abbott explained. "The media had called and I told them the bear was expected at 10:00 or later. Ray said he didn't think his truck had ever gone that fast."

356

"I am greatly saddened over Smokey's death. I really was crazy about the bear and hope his son will continue his legend."

— Lawrie Currins, Dillion, South Carolina

"But Abbott still didn't want to take any chances," Cox recalled. "It was pretty late, and we felt a certain urgency to protect Smokey and bury him as quickly as possible. We circled four or five vehicles—Abbott's car, the state police car, Larry Allen's and the pickups—around the grave and turned on their headlights so we could see what we were doing." Tim and Cyndy Livingston and state trooper Jack Johnson and his wife, Chuck (given name: Marguerite; nickname: "Chuckles"), also arrived at the site.

The Johnstons already had collected straps to use in placing Smokey in his grave. "They were heavy, nylon straps from a parachute," Dorothy Johnston explained. "Originally they had been white, but had gotten a little dirty." Uncaring of a little grime, the assemblage wrestled the nylon straps under the coffin and prepared to lower it.

They also attracted attention. Two deer hunters from Houston, Texas—one named Otto Schulte—had been enjoying themselves in a small roadhouse across Main Street. "They saw the lights and wandered over," Cox grinned. "They wanted to know what was going on. They offered to lend a hand, and we agreed. About six or seven people, including the two Texans, handled the straps as we lowered the coffin into its hole. The Texans really got a big kick out of that. They said their wives would never believe what they had been doing. Larry Allen took a few pictures to record the event, then we used the backhoe to cover the casket, parked the backhoe on the grave and took the keys. We felt the bear was pretty safe so we didn't leave a guard. No one said anything. The entire process took about thirty minutes."

"To old Smokey. Even if he is died you can hang it in his cage until you get another bear. Pore Smokey. I'm sad."

— Vincent Monn, Boise, Idaho (who enclosed a drawing for Smokey)

"There had been talk that someone wanted to steal the bear," Abbott recalled. "I didn't think there was a great deal of danger, but it was not appropriate to have a lot of fanfare about a dead bear. There had been so much media interest in the animal, so the quicker we disposed of the dead bear and got that behind us, the quicker we got rid of the media bemoaning a poor dead bear.

"We had just finished when the media showed up," Abbott continued. "A guy from a TV station—El Paso, I think—was really upset. He accused us of trying to hide something. He said, 'How do we know there was a bear in that box? How do we know you buried anything?' I told him he

Elliott Barker speaks at Smokey's memorial service in November 1976. *(Courtesy USDA Forest Service.)*

would have to accept our representations on faith. He was disgusted, but there were no skeletons. It all went very well, but in hindsight perhaps it should have been recorded. We weren't deliberately trying to keep them away—it just happened much faster than we expected."

Reflecting on the night's events, Cox wrestled with his emotions. "I saw Smokey once in Washington. He was an old, scraggy-looking bear, and I felt it was kind of a mistake to have him there till he died. I would have preferred to have the living symbol go on without bringing him back and making a big deal out of it. Yet, I had a little sense of making history. The Smokey Bear program has done a tremendous amount of good, and forest fire prevention has been outstanding, so all of us thought it was nice to be there at the end. I felt privileged to be involved."

Finally, the sometimes reluctant living symbol of Smokey Bear could rest in peace next to the boulder commemorating his life.

"Boy, I bet you were sure sorry to have Smokey die, I had some pets die and I know how you feel. Is it true that you chucked Smokey's body in a forest fire and burned him up? My Grandpa said you got him stuffed and stuck in a gift shop."

— Raggs Thornsberry, Davis, California

"We set up a dedication the following week," Abbott explained. "We had a lot of calls from people who wanted to speak, and we got concerned that we could be there for hours. We agreed to have the regional forester, the mayor, Elliott Barker, Ray Bell, state forester Ray Gallegos and Dorothy Guck speak. At the time the Smokey Bear Historical State Park was just a vacant lot with weeds and a few Chinese elm trees. Prisoners from Fort Stanton had started the rock wall, but it was only about half done and piles of dirt were spread around. It was so barren and looked so bad that we wanted to dress it up a little."

With only one "legitimate" tree on the premises, Tim Livingston helped with that effort. "We built a little fence with red pine poles around the grave on the west side of the rock," Livingston explained. "But the park was still a mess and we didn't want it to look drab, so we cut down a few small live trees and stuck them in the ground so it would look nice. But it was a windy day, and as the speakers were talking, the trees started leaning with the wind."

Unexpectedly, Capitan began to blossom from flowers sent to the deceased Smokey, as donors across the country sent condolences and funeral wreaths. "There had been a lot of press coverage," Abbott confirmed, "and flowers were pouring in, but I wouldn't let them put any flowers on the grave or at the grave site. A lot of floral wreaths were sent anyway, so we put them in the little museum until it filled up; then we put them on the porch; then they lined the sidewalk. Of course, the media and TV people were there. At the end, the TV people brought a carnation and had a little girl place it on the rock, and then they photographed her. That was the centerpiece of the media story. They were trying to make it interesting even if it wasn't exactly right.

"I was the master of ceremonies," Abbott continued. "I asked a local preacher to give the invocation, but he was concerned about presiding at a funeral for a bear. I pointed out that it wasn't a funeral; it was a rededication

Smokey's grave and stone marker at the Smokey Bear Historical State Park, Capitan, New Mexico. *(Courtesy William Clifford Lawter Jr.)*

to a cause, so he agreed. The whole thing took an hour, and about 200 to 250 people attended." So despite the dry, barren ground, the occasional brown blade of grass poking through Capitan's dirt and the hard folding chairs, Smokey's friends paid respects to their fallen hero at 1:00 p.m. on November 17. A lone microphone on a podium adorned with a Smokey Bear poster reminded visitors that "It's a grand old Forest, too."

"I love you Smokey."

— Anchorage, Alaska

360

24

AN AMERICAN LEGEND

"Smokey is more than a fire-preventing bear. He serves as the conscience of America."

— William Hurst

Suddenly, and to his displeasure, Mal Hardy was vindicated. Smokey Bear was dead, and so was his program—or so it seemed. As Hardy had feared, a significant portion of America associated the name "Smokey Bear" with the living symbol. The venerable *Washington Post* contributed to the confusion with its photos of "Poster Smokey" and "The Real Smokey." The *New York Times* proffered paired photos captioned: "Smokey Bear at the National Zoo two years ago," under the live bear, and "The image of Smokey in a Forest Ranger's hat became a symbol of the campaign against forest fires," under the poster Smokey.

Two conclusions seemed axiomatic. First, the educational portion of America's forest fire prevention effort had a major problem. Second, the rookie Smokey Bear program manager didn't have much time for on-the-job training.

Born in Bingham City, Utah, on Christmas Day, 1940, Donald T. Hansen worked summers during college as a firefighter, fire guard and fire patrolman and decided to become a forest ranger. After earning a degree in forest recreation management from Utah State University in Logan in 1966, Hansen spent ten years with the Forest Service where, among other professional duties, he told Smokey's story around campfires in Utah, Wyoming, Nevada, California and Idaho.

Then Hansen made his big decision: "I wanted to be the 'Smokey Bear' guy," he confessed. "I thought that Smokey was the heart of the Forest Service." As public information officer with the Boise National Forest, Hansen understood forest issues, and he got his wish. In 1976, Hansen was selected to replace Konrad Reinke as Smokey Bear program manager in Washington, D.C.

With Hansen steering a U-Haul truck, and his wife, Cheryl, and four kids following in the family station wagon, the caravan arrived on the East Coast in early November 1976. After moving into their suburban home, Hansen took his ten-year-old daughter, Susie, with him to return the U-Haul on November 9. "We were listening to the radio in the early afternoon as we drove on Route 50 to Fairfax, Virginia," Hansen recalled. "When the news came on, we heard Jerry Gause of the Forest Service public information office say that Smokey Bear had passed away."

Little Susie, sporting a pair of dog ears (a pony tail on each side of her head) turned to her father. "Your boss died, Daddy," she announced. "Does this mean you'll lose your job, and we'll have to move back to Idaho?"

"We thought we were going to be Smokey's first family," Hansen explained. "We took our role seriously—we were ready for this new responsibility. The kids were devastated because they did not get to see the living Smokey. We had a sad family." But Hansen had more serious concerns to confront.

"Smokey Bear as a symbol survived the death, but it wasn't easy," Hansen recalled. "I was Smokey's biggest fan, and I tended to romanticize him. But the death of the living bear was a big problem for about a year. I worked my tail off to make Smokey go, but with budget cuts, personnel changes, the 'let burn' policy, the live bear's death and other issues, Smokey certainly was under attack.

"First," Hansen explained, "we had to convince folks *internally* to continue using Smokey for the forest fire prevention program. We reminded people that the live bear actually had retired in 1975, and we encouraged them to not lose sight of the fact that the *real* Smokey Bear was a poster. The living symbol was certainly the most glorious part of the story, but it offered the least about what the public needed to know. The issue was how to prevent forest fires and be safe in the woods.

"Second," Hansen continued, "we gave a charge to the Ad Council to bring Smokey back. Foote, Cone & Belding developed three campaigns using abbreviated slogans to take Smokey back to his basic message: 'Remember, only you,' 'Smokey's Friends' and 'Repeat after me.' We just returned to the fundamental issue of preventing forest fires. It was a real challenge for Foote, Cone & Belding.

"Third," Hansen added, "we tried to beef up points of contact with the media. Kids in classrooms knew the bear had died, and visitors to national forests asked rangers about it. So we put more money into the media to emphasize that the program was working. The message was simple: 'Smokey Bear is alive and well.'"

But Goldie Bear—Smokey's surviving mate—wasn't well. On March 9, 1977, Goldie's keepers spotted blood on her right ear, and on March 22 they noticed blood dripping from her left nostril. With Goldie confined to her den for observation, her keepers again found blood on her nose on March 24 and 26, and she developed a nosebleed and diarrhea on March 28. The next day, Goldie entered the National Zoo's hospital for a checkup, and her examination revealed liver degeneration, an enlarged heart and arthritis of the neck and vertebrae. When her condition worsened and recovery seemed unlikely, the zoo's resident pathologist recommended that Goldie be euthanized.

With approval from the zoo's director, euthanasia was performed on Saturday, April 23, 1977, at 9:30 a.m. Goldie was recorded as NZP death #30544, a necropsy was performed on Monday, April 25, and her remains were sent to the Museum of Natural History for an anatomical study. Because of the damage to the forest fire prevention program after Smokey's death only five months before, Goldie's death was not publicized.

"Of course," Hansen stressed, "we promised the advertising people that there would not be another death of the living symbol. We wrote a plan to prevent it, but the second bear [Little Smokey] caught everyone by surprise and died anyway in 1990."

When Little Smokey began shaking late Saturday afternoon, August 11, 1990, and could not keep his balance, his keeper called a zoo veterinarian. The vet used a blowgun to inject steroids, but they had no effect, and because of the 250-pound bear's nasty temper, vets and keepers were unable to get close enough to examine him. Little Smokey died in his cage just after 5:30 p.m. that evening, and after a necropsy conducted the next morning disclosed advanced liver cancer, Little Smokey was quietly buried in an unidentified location in Washington, D.C.

"At one time," Hansen frowned, "there was talk of bringing in a healthy young bear from Pennsylvania every three years. How many Lassies were there—seven? But the public only needed to know one Lassie. Sam Cobb, the Pennsylvania state forester who always whittled and smoked a pipe during meetings, was on the CFFP executive committee, and he supported the idea. People listened to Sam Cobb, and he said, 'I can get you that. We can ship in new bears.'" But the plan never reached fruition.

"There are no secrets in Washington," zoo director Ted Reed explained. "If I had tried to run in a substitute, I would have been caught." So Reed suggested that, similar to other Forest Service jobs, a rotating tour of duty be established in Washington, D.C., for a "Smokey-in-residence." Under Reed's concept, a healthy, two-year-old bear would be brought in from some state for a five-year assignment, then quietly retired and replaced by a bear from a different state. The proposal, however, never was adopted.

In the end, the CFFP's efforts were successful: the caricature Smokey kept his job as America's spokesbear for forest fire prevention. And why not?

The effectiveness of America's forest fire prevention campaign has been reflected in the public's response to Smokey's message. From the time Smokey began his crusade in 1945, the area burned by human-caused forest fires decreased 90 per cent from the normal prewar level, despite a massive increase in forest visits.

Everywhere they turn, Americans see Smokey's friendly face under his wide-brimmed campaign hat. From posters, newspapers, television, billboards, magazines and radio, Smokey warns that human carelessness, stupidity or malice cause nine of every ten forest fires. Smokey's muscular chest, blue jeans and shovel tell admirers that he is a serious, hardworking bear doing his best to protect our forests.

More than 200 million Americans have grown up with Smokey; for their entire lives, Smokey has prowled the nation's forests waving his ranger's hat and reminding them of the dangers of their carelessness. Most important, kids are comfortable with the nation's foremost animal hero simply because they believe that Smokey tells the truth.

Smokey's enormously wide-ranging quest is supported by a remarkable cooperative arrangement between business, media, the Ad Council, the Forest Service and the National Association of State Foresters. In that partnership, Smokey has been a unifying force to leverage resources and help focus the commitment, energy and enthusiasm of thousands of individuals.

That partnership effort has injected Smokey into America's culture. The public refers to police officers as "Smokeys." Political cartoonists use Smokey to denote the Forest Service or the National Park Service. Smokey repeatedly is referenced in movies and on TV and radio. Thousands of civic groups campaign on Smokey's behalf. Flights for the Friends of Smokey Bear Balloon's giant hot-air balloon are scheduled two years in advance. Richard Just's Smokey Bear museum-on-wheels can barely meet demands for appearances. Large municipal museums clamor for Rudy Wendelin's Smokey Bear art. With 2,500 Smokey costumes in use, Smokey appears at sporting events, rodeos and public gatherings across the nation, giving kids a lasting impression of an imposing bear with a firm handshake and a determination to prevent forest fires. And across the country, Americans keep finding fresh, exciting ways to use Smokey in forest fire prevention promotions.

But can Smokey's triumphant half-century serve as a springboard for another fifty years? Is there a need to continue with Smokey? Must Smokey change to emulate his past achievements? Can the Smokey caricature grab attention in the next century? Is there a need for another living symbol?

American forests today present a wide array of encroachment problems and conflicting demands for usage. Power companies want to run lines through forests, loggers need to harvest trees, oil companies yearn to drill wells, and preservationists covet biodiversity habitats and ecological preservation zones. Forests are overrun by hundreds of millions of skiers, hunters, campers, anglers, hikers and picnickers, who are increasingly penetrating the back country. And many forests face the greatest menace: an invasion of homes and businesses.

A drive through the living symbol's Lincoln National Forest in New Mexico reveals hundreds of buildings reaching farther and farther into wooded areas. Firefighters on the nearby Mescalero Apache reservation fret over maps indicating increasing human intrusion into woodlands on their reservation's perimeter. The Angeles National Forest in California is essentially surrounded by urban development, and 7 million people have moved into California's forested mountains and canyons in the past twenty years. Ground fuel buildups among expensive rural homes in Colorado make controlled burns difficult. The Forest Service even tends to 3,600 lots in the city of South Lake Tahoe, California.

Because Americans don't welcome restrictions—especially those imposed by government—the jeopardy to forests is likely to grow. Despite Smokey's success, data show that each year Americans start enough fires to burn from 2 to 5 million forest acres, and most of those fires result from indifference, ignorance or bad luck. Moreover, as Americans transform land with construction, livestock management, roads and recreation, they change the amount, location and type of vegetation that affects fire hazards. By changing the fuel supplies that feed forest fires, then, people influence fires they don't actually cause.

So America's forests will continue to require professional management, and that expertise is likely to come from the Forest Service and state forest offices. With responsibility for almost 200 million acres of land covered by 156 national forests and 19 national grasslands, the Forest Service claims its share of antagonists. A disgruntled hunter, a livestock grazer, a lumberman, a wilderness guide and others may reject the Forest Service multiple-use doctrine and demand preferential treatment for their special interests. Environmental groups no longer are content with just being aware of Forest Service activities; those groups now want to influence or even direct Forest Service priorities and policies.

In every corner of the forests, battles are waged over funding levels, old-growth timber, the use of rivers, natural resource commodities, wilderness areas, clear-cutting, state claims for federal lands, spraying pesticides and herbicides, controlled fires, access to forage, protection of wildlife and dozens of other issues. Obviously, Americans no longer view themselves as having a common cause in the nation's woodlands.

"During World War II, Americans had a goal to save their forests for the war effort," Forest Service historian Terry West explained. "In that era, Americans were willing to accept authority because of their confidence that public figures would work for the common good. Today, however, the public holds a different view of government foresters that for many years enjoyed the protective status of 'we know best; we are the professionals; leave us alone and we will manage the forests.'"

Still, the Forest Service enjoys unqualified support from people across the country. In addition to its 30,000 employees, the Forest Service annually can count on more than 100,000 volunteers to build trails, repair buildings and survey forests. Headed by Don Hansen, hundreds of projects are undertaken by participants who enlist through the Forest Service Volunteers program and the Touch America Project for youth.

But because wildlands blanket almost half of the continental United States, today's fire suppression efforts are coordinated by the National

Wildfire Coordinating Group. Under this arrangement, a quintet of federal government agencies—Forest Service, Bureau of Indian Affairs, Bureau of Land Management, Fish and Wildlife Service, and National Park Service—work closely with the National Association of State Foresters. Preplanning is emphasized in each forest district. Fuel maps are developed to identify high-value resources, and in the event of fire, computers help foresters decide how to respond. But because this group can spend more than $1 million a day to fight a major forest fire, it seems cheaper and easier simply to prevent fires.

So if Americans unintentionally destroy billions of dollars' worth of property in forest fires, then Smokey Bear may be the country's most valuable citizen. In 1944, forests were far away from most Americans, but as civilization spread into woodlands, forests now are in residential backyards. In an era of increasingly urbanized forests, the two-legged denizens need reminders about fire more than ever.

"In the years to come, there may be environmental and political pressures that come to bear on how we handle our forests," Jim Felton, Smokey's former national coordinator, acknowledged, "but there will always be a place for Smokey, urging care and caution in the wilderness. There will always be lightning fires, but the fact will remain that nine of ten forest fires are man-caused. And that's where Smokey does his work—putting a brake wherever possible on man-caused forest fires."

"The forest is a special place," Cheryl Hansen maintained. "The spirit of the out-of-doors is manifested in the forest. It's a symbol of that wonderful, free, natural part of America. Smokey Bear encourages people to protect the forests, to take care of animals, to take care of water. Fire will destroy those things, and Smokey is the caretaker of all those things that cannot protect themselves."

It seems clear to many thinking citizens that America needs Smokey Bear. "Smokey is doing the right thing," Forest Service retiree Ken Bowman insisted. "There is a lot of respect for that symbol. It is heroic. It has weathered all these years. It's just like the American flag."

Undeniably, some people think that Smokey is corny or old-fashioned, but no other cartoon animal has influenced the behavior of so many millions of children and adults. In the end, there seems to be no better way to convey the forest fire prevention message than through Smokey Bear—one of the most familiar faces in America.

Attitudes toward fire, government, symbols and advertising all have changed significantly since Smokey's 1944 creation. Public attitudes about

Smokey have changed too, and because Smokey depends upon personal as well as professional support, must Smokey change to be successful for another fifty years?

"Smokey is more than a fire-preventing bear," retired Forest Service southwestern regional forester William Hurst argued. "He serves as the conscience of America. Coming on the scene long before the environmentalists, he provided this country with a new land ethic and became the symbol of a healthful and delightful environment."

As a consequence of that perception, some Smokey admirers urge that Smokey's mission be viewed as forest fire education rather than pure forest fire prevention, in which case the door should be open for change. Many people—mostly outside the Forest Service—are willing, or even eager, to expand Smokey's role to embrace concerns such as controlled burning, fire management and ecosystem management. Others have suggested that Smokey embody range fire protection, urban fire protection, wildlife, the forests themselves, the national parks, the environment or the Forest Service. Their argument has a fundamental simplicity: "change is inevitable."

But many foresters believe Smokey's narrow job description must remain inviolate. If pushed, this camp may concede that it's okay to allow Smokey to be a protector of wildlife—but only in connection with preventing forest fires. They assert that an enlarged role for Smokey will weaken his forest fire prevention message and dilute his success. They believe Smokey doesn't want to talk about those other issues—they think Smokey wants to talk about preventing forest fires started by carelessness. Further, those foresters contend that the nonthreatening, nonpartisan Smokey doesn't have to be modernized if his message continues to be interesting and relevant to the public.

"Efforts to change behavior and make Smokey a lasting success will work only if the changes are consistent with people's perceived interests," Jim Felton opined. "Smokey Bear is both a leader and a victim of the environmental movement."

Debate probably will continue because one glaring fact stands out: no other person or character has emerged to effectively represent the environment. But in the end, Smokey's single-minded advocacy seems likely to stay narrow because of another equally obvious fact: the bear has proved to be stunningly effective in his limited role.

With many worthwhile social causes in the nation, Smokey will have tough competition commanding attention from an information-saturated generation. But as an advertising vehicle, Smokey Bear is likely to survive and perhaps even thrive for a simple reason: in an increasingly multicultural nation, Smokey Bear's image can transcend language barriers and ethnic diversity. Smokey can flourish in the next century because, as a communicator, he can bridge any gap—racial, religious, cultural and perhaps even spiritual.

Because millions of dollars in free radio and TV time are contributed to Smokey each year, and the Ad Council reports that forest fire prevention still ranks among its top five campaigns, Smokey partisans believe that the public still has a hearty appetite for their bear.

"The Smokey advertising campaign is an outstanding example of a very successful marketing program that has saved the nation more than twenty billion dollars in timber that wasn't destroyed, campgrounds that weren't ravished, and recreation areas that were not eroded," Jim Felton summarized. "And it hasn't cost the taxpayers a penny.

"Smokey Bear is the perfect advertising vehicle for forest fire prevention," Felton emphasized. "Entire generations of Americans have grown up with Smokey Bear. He has become a vital part of the American culture. Kids adore him, adults respect him, and Smokey remains a consistently recognizable and accepted personality. That bear's familiar face substitutes for the personal presence of a salesman. Foote, Cone & Belding has developed a tremendously valuable and effective asset for the CFFP program.

"Smokey Bear is a real personality with a real identity to which millions of Americans closely relate," Felton insisted. "People know and understand Smokey. He is not a stranger. We recognize his looks and mannerisms, and he builds on that familiarity. We know he's a single-minded but positive fellow, so we accept immediately his admonishments as the caring direction of an old friend. We trust Smokey; he has won our confidence. So Smokey continues as the spokesman for forest fire prevention, because the approach that won so many supporters for his cause probably is the best way to win others."

Retired Foote, Cone & Belding executive Lou Scott concurred: "The symbol that has been created and the educational program that has developed is one of the great mass communication stories in the industry. Everybody has heard about Smokey Bear and everyone has a strong positive image. I can't think of another public service program that even comes close in having its depth of understanding." Perhaps the key lies in Smokey's animal magnetism.

"If you want to speak to the heart, you can do it with an animal," Nancy Budd, of Foote, Cone & Belding, asserted. "The most effective ads combine the head and the heart—one-half cerebral and one-half emotional, especially when asking people to use their conscience. You want to strike an emotional chord, which can be much more effective in affecting behavior."

So in an age of advertising overload, Smokey Bear still grabs attention—so much so that most people immediately associate Smokey's face with forest fire prevention. "In a fundamental sense," Budd continued, "an ad *has* to make a personal appeal because the salesman isn't there to answer questions, add information or correct impressions. Thus, an ad's job is complicated by time delays and the frailties of human memory. But when a personal appeal is registered, the ad may exact a mental pledge, and simple information maintains a level of awareness."

Although many Americans will be disappointed, Smokey's immediate future is unlikely to include another living symbol to represent the poster bear's familiar caricature. By the mid 1980s, in fact, the CFFP concluded that the living symbol of Smokey at the National Zoo had outlived his usefulness. Only two years after its highly publicized dedication in 1978, the National Zoo even phased out Little Smokey's new grotto.

Most foresters support the continued use of the caricature Smokey. But the possibility of another living symbol is a different story, mainly because the living bruin never was used in the Ad Council's massive national forest fire prevention campaigns.

Most Foote, Cone & Belding staffers felt that, in terms of communication, the live bear simply was insignificant. "The live bear is a strange story," Jim Felton admitted. "I have ambivalent feelings. It had absolutely nothing to do with the national Smokey Bear campaign, but it was adopted by the Forest Service anyway. To that extent, any publicity we could get was good, but the live bear never figured in the advertising campaign at all."

"Foote, Cone & Belding was not excited about the live bear," Ann King, a former FCB art director explained. "It got in the way—I think the Forest Service knew it too. They had a lot of explaining to do when he died—people wanted to know if the program was dead. We thought of Smokey as a symbol—not a real animal. Our Smokey is anthropomorphic; he has fingers and thumbs; he is not a real bear. Real bears are scary; Smokey Bear is gentle. Real bears don't wear Levi's and a hat. It's confusing."

Others harbored stronger feelings. "The biggest mistake the Forest Service ever made was the little bear," insisted a retired Foote, Cone & Belding executive. "They should have realized two things. First, anything living is going to die. How would you like to be a retailer with 10,000 dolls when the bear died? Second, kids would go to the zoo and say, 'That isn't

Smokey. Where are his pants?' It was a terrible, terrible mistake. Smokey is an image. The live bear was a dumb thing all the way around."

But others, such as Rudy Wendelin, who eschewed use of the live bear in his art, looked beyond advertising. "I believe the live bear helped America's forest fire prevention program," Wendelin said. "I think it helped considerably. It wasn't just propaganda. Kids could understand if you showed a little bear with wrapped up paws and told the story—it had a touching kind of realism. They always need stimulation, so a new bear wouldn't hurt."

Zoo director Ted Reed certainly had fond memories of the live bear. "It was great to watch small children stand in front of his cage," he recalled. "It made me feel good to hear those squealing voices singing 'Smokey the Bear.'"

So there are two schools of thought. One is that the program needs a living symbol; the other is that the Smokey Bear caricature and forest fire prevention are locked together, and there is no need for a living symbol. Current plans, in any event, do not call for another living symbol.

Could it be, some observers have suggested, that today's administrators lack the imagination of Clint Davis? Maybe, maybe not; but imagination is not the issue. Times, needs and the public have changed, but Smokey's handlers are as determined as their predecessors to prevent needless, human-caused forest fires. The only issue is how best to do that, and current thinking is that a living symbol will not help the effort. But who knows? Another dramatic event may occur, a living symbol may suddenly seem to be a good idea and America may have a living Smokey III to admire.

Hoss Stabler, a Gifford Pinchot protégé in the early days of the Forest Service, retired to his Maryland home in 1947. When asked what he considered to be his most significant contribution to forestry, Stabler reportedly leaned back in his chair, pondered the question, and then replied, "For a considerable period, I helped the American people get their money's worth."

Arguably, the same can be said for America's leading advocate of forest fire prevention. Certainly, Smokey Bear lives in the hearts of the nation's children. In their minds, Smokey is the unchallenged symbol of truth, bravery and commitment, and kids have cultivated a loving passion—perhaps even a reverence—for that furry American legend.

And that's the way it should be. America's children should always have their Smokey Bear.

Remember, only you . . .

GOLDEN SMOKEY RECIPIENTS

(By Year of Award)

1957   The Advertising Council, Inc.
American Forestry Association
American Forest Products Institute
The Children of America

1958   The Radio and Television Broadcasters of America

1959   Foote, Cone & Belding
Newspapers of America:
        National Editorial Association
        Newspaper Advertising Executives Association
        American Newspaper Publishers Association
U.S. Postal Service

1960   National Association of Transit Advertising, Inc.

1962   National Education Association
Society of American Foresters

1963   General Federation of Women's Clubs
Native Sons & Daughters of the Golden West

1964   Russell Z. Eller
National Council of State Garden Clubs, Inc.

1965   Ideal Toy Corporation
National Zoological Park, Washington, D.C.

1966   Western Forestry and Conservation Association

1967   Fire Weather Service of the U.S. Weather Bureau

1968   "The Lassie Show"

1969   Philmont Scout Ranch and Explorer Base

1970   Liller, Neal, Battle & Lindsay, Inc.

1971   Walt Disney Productions

1972   Rudolph A. Wendelin

1975   Macy's Department Stores

1976   James P. Felton
       Virginia Division of Forestry

1978   Pennsylvania Bureau of Forestry

1979   California Department of Forestry

1980   Canadian Forestry Association
       City of Torrence, California, and Torrence's Rose Float Association

1982   "Romper Room"

1984   Boy Scouts of America

1985   John Bethea
       USDA Pacific Southwest Region
       America's Outdoor Writers

1986   Joe Baker
       James R. Miller

1987   Nancy A. Budd
       William Keim
       Harry R. "Punky" McClellan

1988   Cable News Networks Weather Channel
       Del Hall

1989   John N. Graff

1990   Arthur Creelman

1991   Nelson/Weather-Rite Company
       Professional Rodeo Cowboy's Association

1994   Foote, Cone & Belding
       The Advertising Council, Inc.
       Jack Elrod

SILVER SMOKEY RECIPIENTS

(By Year of Award)

1967   Raymond M. Connarr
Clinton L. Davis
Albert K. Wiesendanger

1968   James Q. Rikard
Rudolph A. Wendelin
Barney Wozniak

1969   C.H. "Hux" Coulter
Francis Raymond
Archer Smith

1970   William W. Huber
Merle S. Lowden
Elmer S. Osterman

1971   Eugene F. McNamara
Northeastern Forest Fire Protection Commission

1972   Kenneth A. Burkholder

1973   Alan B. Beaven
Malcolm E. Hardy

1974   Richard J. Ernest
Curtis S. Nesheim

1975   Joe Delucchi
Richard Johnson

1976   W.F. "Bill" Myring

1977   Edwin Loner
Harry R. "Punky" McClellan
Don K. Porter

1978   Merlin J. Dixon
Northwest Interagency Prevention Group, Oregon and Washington

1979   David D. Devet
E. Feldman Corn
Richard T. Ford

1980   Marvin E. Newell
       Middle Atlantic Interstate Forest Fire Protection Compact

1981   Rudy A. Anderson
       Earl Meyer
       Richard F. "Dick" Thomas

1982   Luigi W. DeBarnardo
       Max L. Doolittle

1983   Jackson Weaver
       Harry Rossoll

1984   Edwin Earl Rodger
       Michael Marchese

1985   William W. Bergoffen
       John Pager

1986   Maynard Stoddard

1987   Lori Sharn

1988   Frank P. Dorchak
       Bentley Humphrey
       Arthur Sutton

1989   Loren Poore

1991   Oakland Athletics
       San Diego Padres
       California Angels
       Sierra Front Wildfire Cooperators
       Weyerhaeuser Corporation

1992   Utah Jazz Basketball Organization
       Gene Dowdy

1994   Russ Johnson

FOREST FIRE PROTECTION RESOURCES

To help protect America's forests, write or call these sources.

USDA FOREST SERVICE OFFICES AND PROGRAMS

Forest Service Volunteers Program (individuals and groups complement the work of Forest Service professionals) and **Touch America Project** (special volunteer program for youth) attract more than 100,000 volunteers annually:

Program Manager
Volunteers in the National Forests
USDA Forest Service
P.O. Box 96090, Room 1010 RPE
Washington, D.C., 20090-6090
703/235-8855

FOREST SERVICE HEADQUARTERS

Forest Service—USDA
14th & Independence, S.W.
P.O. Box 96090
Washington, D.C. 20090-6090
202/205-0957

FOREST SERVICE FIELD OFFICES

Forest Service, USDA
Alaska Region
P.O. Box 21628
Juneau, AK 99802-1628
907/586-8863

Forest Service, USDA
Eastern Region
310 West Wisconsin Avenue,
Room 500
Milwaukee, WI 53203
414/297-3693

Forest Service, USDA
Intermountain Region
Federal Building
324 25th Street
Ogden, UT 84401
801/625-5352

Forest Service, USDA
Northeastern Area—S&PF
5 Radnor Corporate Center
100 Matsonford, Rd., Suite 200
P.O. Box 6775
Radnor, PA 19087-4585
215/975-4111

Forest Service, USDA
Northern Region
Federal Building
P.O. Box 7669
Missoula, MT 59807
406-329-3511

Forest Service, USDA
Pacific Northwest Region
333 S.W. 1st Avenue
P.O. Box 3623
Portland, OR 97208
503/326-2971

Forest Service, USDA
Pacific Southwest Region
630 Sansome Street
San Francisco, CA 94111
415/705-2874

Forest Service, USDA
Rocky Mountain Region
11177 West 8th Avenue
P.O. Box 25127
Lakewood, CO 80225
303/236-9431

Forest Service, USDA
Southern Region
1720 Peachtree Road, N.W.
Atlanta, GA 30367
404/347-2384

Forest Service, USDA
Southwestern Region
Federal Building
517 Gold Avenue, S.W.
Albuquerque, NM 87102
505/842-3292

STATE FORESTERS

Alabama Forestry Commission
513 Madison Avenue
Montgomery, AL 36130
205/240-9304

Alaska Division of Forestry
State Forester's Office
P.O. Box 107005
Anchorage, AK 99510-7005
907/762-2501

Arizona State Land Department
1616 W. Adams
Phoenix, AZ 85007
602/542-4627

Arkansas Forestry Commission
P.O. Box 4523, Asher Station
Little Rock, AR 72214
501/664-2531

California Department of Forestry &
Fire Protection
P.O. Box 944246
Sacramento, CA 94244-2460
916/653-7772

Colorado State Forest Service
203 Forestry Building
Colorado State University
Fort Collins, CO 80523
303/491-6303

Connecticut Division of Forestry
165 Capitol Avenue
Hartford, CT 06106
203/566-5348

Delaware Dept. of Agriculture,
Forestry Section
2320 S. DuPont Highway
Dover, DE 19901
302/739-4811

Florida Division of Forestry
3125 Conner Blvd.
Tallahassee, FL 32399-1650
904/488-4274

Georgia Forestry Commission
P.O. Box 819
Macon, GA 31298-4599
912/751-3480

Guam Forestry & Soil Resources
Division
P.O. Box 2950
Agana, Guam 96910
671/734-3948

Hawaii Division of Forestry &
Wildlife
1151 Punchbowl Street
Honolulu, HI 96813
808/587-0166

Idaho Department of Lands
1215 West State Street
Boise, ID 83720-7000
208/334-0200

Illinois Division of Forest Resources
600 North Grand Avenue West
Springfield, IL 62706
217/782-2361

Indiana Division of Forestry
402 West Washington St., Room 296
Indianapolis, IN 46204
317/232-4107

Iowa Division of Forestry, Dept. of
Natural Resources
Wallace State Office Building
Des Moines, IA 50319
515/281-8656

Kansas Department of Forestry
2610 Claflin Road
Manhattan, KS 66502-2798
913/537-7050

Kentucky Division of Forestry
627 Commanche Trail
Frankfort, KY 40601
502/564-4496

Louisiana Dept. of Agriculture &
Forestry
P.O. Box 1628
Baton Rouge, LA 70821
504/925-4500

Maine Bureau of Forestry
State House Station #22
Augusta, ME 04333
207/287-2793

Maryland Forestry Division
Tawes State Office Bldg.
580 Taylor Ave.
Annapolis, MD 21401
410/974-3776

Massachusetts Division of Forests &
Parks
100 Cambridge Street
Boston, MA 02202
617/727-3180

Michigan Department of Natural
Resources
Forest Management Division
Stevens T. Mason Bldg., Box 30028
Lansing, MI 48909
517/373-1275

Minnesota Division of Forestry
500 Lafayette Road
St. Paul, MN 55155-4044
612/296-4484

Mississippi Forestry Commission
301 N. Lamar, Suite 300
Jackson, MS 39201
601/359-1386

Missouri Department of
Conservation
2901 West Truman Blvd.
P.O. Box 180
Jefferson City, MO 65102
314/751-4115

Montana Division of Forestry
Division of State Lands
2705 Spurgin Road
Missoula, MT 59801
406/542-4300

Nebraska Dept. of Forestry, Fish and
Wildlife
Room 101, Plant Industries Bldg.
Lincoln, NE 68583-0894
402/472-1467

Nevada Division of Forestry
123 West Nye Lane
Carson City, NV 89710
702/687-4353

New Hampshire Division of
Forests & Lands
Box 856
175 Pembroke Rd.
Concord, NH 03302-0856
603/271-2214

New Jersey State Forestry
CN 404, 501 E. State St.
Trenton, NJ 08625
609/984-3850

New Mexico Forestry Division
Conservation Division
P.O. Box 1948
Santa Fe, NM 87504-1948
505/827-5830

New York Division of Lands &
Forests
50 Wolf Road
Albany, NY 12233-4250
518/457-2475

North Carolina Division of Forest
Resources
P.O. Box 27687
Raleigh, NC 27611-7687
919/733-2162

North Dakota Forest Service
Molberg Forestry Center
First & Brander
Bottineau, ND 58318
701/228-2277

Ohio Division of Forestry
Fountain Square Building B-3
Columbus, OH 43224
614/265-6690

Oklahoma   Department   of
Agriculture
Forestry Division
2800 North Lincoln Blvd.
Oklahoma City, OK 73105-4296
405/521-3864

Oregon Department of Forestry
2600 State Street
Salem, OR 97310
503/378-2511

Pennsylvania Bureau of Forestry
P.O. Box 8552
Harrisburg, PA 17105-8552
717/787-2703

Puerto Rico Dept. of Natural Resources
P. O. Box 5887
Puerta de Tierra
San Juan, PR 00906
809/724-3647

Rhode Island Division of Forest Environment
1037 Hartford Pike
North Scituate, RI 02857
401/647-3367

South Carolina Forestry Commission
P.O. Box 21707
Columbia, SC 29221
803/737-8800

South Dakota Division of Forestry
445 East Capitol
Pierre, SD 57501
605/773-3623

Tennessee Division of Forestry
P.O. Box 40627, Melrose Station
Nashville, TN 37204
615/360-0722

Texas Forest Service
College Station, TX 77843-2136
409/845-2641

Utah Division of Forestry
3 Triad Center, Suite 400
355 West North Temple
Salt Lake City, UT 84180-1204
801/538-5508

Vermont Dept. of Forests, Parks and Recreation
103 S. Main Street, 10 South
Waterbury, VT 05671-0601
802/244-8714

Virginia Division of Forestry
P.O. Box 3758
Charlottesville, VA 29903
804/977-6555

Virgin Islands Forestry Program
King Field Post Office
St. Croix, VI 00851
809/778-0997

Washington Dept. of Natural Resources
201 John A. Cherberg Building
Mail Stop QW21
Olympia, WA 98504-7201
206/753-5331

West Virginia Forestry Division
State Capitol
Charleston, WV 25305
304/558-2788

Wisconsin Bureau of Forestry
P.O. Box 7921
Madison, WI 53707
608/266-0842

Wyoming State Forestry Division
1100 West 22nd Street
Cheyenne, WY 82002
307/777-7586

OTHER ORGANIZATIONS

Friends of Smokey
P.O. Box 545
Capitan, NM 88316
505/354-4290

Friends of Smokey Bear Balloon
P.O. Box 27800, Suite 169
Albuquerque, NM 87125
505/260-5570

Smokey Bear Historical State Park
118 First Street
Capitan, NM 88316
505/354-2748

Smokey Bear Museum
Hwy. 380—Box 730
Capitan, NM 88316-0730
505/354-4290

BIBLIOGRAPHY

Abbott, James R., "Farewell Program for the First Living Symbol of Smokey Bear," November 17, 1976.

———, February 15, 1977, letter to Otto J. Schulte.

ABC Radio, "Recycling Smokey The Bear," August 15, 1974, broadcast transcript, Radio-TV Monitoring Service, Inc.

ABC Television, "Smokey Had Own Zip Code," November 10, 1976, broadcast transcript, Radio-TV Monitoring Service, Inc.

———, "Smokey The Bear Dies Peacefully of Old Age," November 9, 1976, broadcast transcript, Radio-TV Monitoring Service, Inc.

"Action Plan, Smokey Bear Historical State Park, Burial Ceremony," undated Forest Service memorandum.

"Advertising and War Effort," *Colliers*, August 26, 1944.

"Advertising at Work," *Business Week*, June 19, 1943.

"Advertising Council: Helping Americans in the Business of Living," Advertising Council news release, 1992.

"Advertising in Wartime," *The New Republic*, February 21, 1944.

"Advertising Roster," *Business Week*, February 21, 1942.

"Airplane Helps Officers Solve Crime Problems," *Emporia Gazette*, February 24, 1956.

"Alamorgordo Beckons Noted Bear," *Albuquerque Journal*, July 27, 1961.

"Albert Staehle, 74, Creator of Smokey the Bear, Dies," *New York Times*, April 6, 1974.

Anderberg, Ken, "Smokey's Artist is Still Painting," *Atlanta Magazine*, September, 1984.

Anderson, Jack, *Washington Post*, undated and untitled commentary.

Anderson, James, "Japanese Fired on California 50 Years Ago," *Tulsa World*, February 23, 1992.

Animal Acquisition Record, Form 105, Smithsonian Institution, National Zoological Park.

"Annual Report of the Department of Game and Fish of State of New Mexico, Thirty-Eighth Fiscal Year," 1950.

"Around the Mall and beyond," *Smithsonian*, November, 1978.

Arp, Jennifer, "Smokey, Familiar face rescues Forest Service mascot," *Prescott (Arizona) Courier*, October 6, 1987.

"A wire from Smokey," *Otero Co. (New Mexico) Star*, August 3, 1961.

"Ballad of Smokey," *New York Daily News*, May 6, 1968.

Barker, Elliott S., "Ceremony Statement on Smokey Bear," November 17, 1976.

———, *Ramblings in the Field of Conservation*, Sunstone Press, 1976.

———, *Smokey Bear and the Great Wilderness*, Sunstone Press, 1982.

————, "Smokey Lives On!," *Outdoor Reporter*, December, 1976.

————, "The Whimper Heard Across the Nation," *American Forests*, September, 1961.

Batt, William L., November 15, 1941, address in Hot Springs, Virginia.

"Bear Cub Rescued From Fire To Be Presented to Zoo Today," *Evening Star* (Washington, D.C.), June 30, 1950.

"Bear That Stops Fires," *Science News Letter*, October 1, 1955.

Becker, Harry, letter to the editor, *Advertising Age*, June 5, 1972.

Belding, Don, May 29, 1942, letter to Ralph Allum.

————, September 3, 1942, letter to R. F. Hammatt.

Bell, Harold, "Merchandising Smokey Bear," address to First National Smokey Bear Workshop, Atlantic City, New Jersey, January 14, 1970.

Bell, Judy, May 9, 1958 letter to Ruth and Ray Bell.

Bell, Ray L, May 15, 1950, letter to Dorothy Guck.

————, "True Story of Smokey Bear/Zip Code 20252," unpublished manuscript dated 1970.

Bergoffen, William W., *100 Years Of Federal Forestry*, U.S. Department of Agriculture, Forest Service, December, 1976.

————, "The Legend of Smokey Bear," presentation to Izaak Walton League, March 11, 1971.

Brackebusch, Art, address to Western Forestry Conference, San Diego, California, December, 1973.

Burns, Robert, "Making Smokey Bear Work For You," address to First National Smokey Bear Workshop, Atlantic City, New Jersey, January 14, 1970.

"Business at War," unidentified source, May, 1942.

Campbell, J. Phil, July 1, 1974, letter to Congressman W. R. Poage.

"Capitan Dedication Marks Start of Smokey Bear Park," *El Paso Times*, May 16, 1976.

"Capitan Women's Club Wins Award," *Roswell Daily Record*, April 18, 1968.

Capps, Benjamin, *The Great Chiefs*, Time-Life Books, 1975.

————, *The Indians*, Time-Life Books, 1976.

Caras, Roger, *The Forest*, Holt, Rinehart and Winston, 1979.

Carroll, Franklin, address to Second National Smokey Bear Workshop, Tallahassee, Florida, January 11, 1973.

Caryle, John, "How Advertising Went to War," *Nation's Business*, November, 1944.

Casey, Phil, "Aw, Come On! Why Pick On A Good Guy Like Smokey," *Atlanta Journal-Constitution*, January 12, 1969.

————, "Girl Calls on `Smokey' She Cuddled as a Cub," *Washington Post*, May 9, 1958.

CBS Television, "Smokey the Bear Dies at 26," November 9, 1976 broadcast transcript, Radio-TV Monitoring Service, Inc.

"Celebrate National Forests 1891-1991," pamphlet, U.S. Department of Agriculture Forest Service, 1990.

Bibliography

Chapel, Bill, "The Man Who Found Smokey Bear," undated manuscript.

Charles, Mrs. Tom, "Mescalero Apache `Red Hats' Hold National Reputation For Forest Fire Control Ability," *El Paso Times*, December 7, 1952.

Charlton, Linda, "Smokey Bear Dies in Retirement," *New York Times*, November 9, 1976.

Clapp, Earle H., June 11, 1942, memorandum to Regional Foresters, Directors, and W.O. Assistant and Division Chiefs.

Clifford, William, "The real Smokey the Bear lived a fairy-tale life," *Rocky Mountain News*, February 24, 1991.

"Clint Davis," U.S. Forest Service press release, undated.

Cobb, Tom, "So Long, Smokey," *American Forests*, August, 1975.

Coleman, Charley, "Presentation of the 1973 Campaign," address to Second National Smokey Bear Workshop, Tallahassee, Florida, January 11, 1973.

Colen, B. D., "S. Bear, Fire Fighter," *Washington Post*, November 10, 1976.

"Commemorative Stamp honors Smokey," *Lincoln County News*, August 16, 1984.

"Commemorative Stamp to honor Smokey the Bear," *Lincoln County News*, August 9, 1984.

Compeau, Robert, "Has Smokey Outlived His Usefulness?", address to First National Smokey Bear Workshop, Atlantic City, New Jersey, January 14, 1970.

"Congressional Respects Paid to Aging Bear," *BioScience*, January, 1975.

Cothrun, Richard C., June 18, 1974, letter to U.S. Senator Joseph M. Montoya.

Coyle, David Cushman, "Roosevelt and Conservation," *American Forests*, June, 1958.

Creelman, Art, address to Second National Smokey Bear Workshop, Tallahassee, Florida, January 11, 1973.

Crenshaw, John, "The Smokey Bear Stamp of Approval," *New Mexico Wildlife*, undetermined date.

"Cub Saved in Fire visits City," *St. Louis Post-Dispatch*, June 28, 1950.

"Cub `Smokey' Departs June 27 For New Job," *Santa Fe New Mexican*, June 20, 1950.

Currins, Lawrie, undated letter to Smokey Bear.

Daigle, Russell D., "Smokey Bear," undated memorandum from Forest Service files.

Davis, Clint, "Smokey is Convincing a Nation: Only You Can Prevent Forest Fires," *American Forests*, April, 1951.

Davis, Lily, undated letter to Smokey Bear.

"Death of a symbol," *Albuquerque Tribune*, November 11, 1976.

DeBruin, Henry W., address to First National Smokey Bear Workshop, Atlantic City, New Jersey, January 13, 1970.

————, "How Do Others See Smokey Bear," address to Second National Smokey Bear Workshop, Tallahassee, Florida, January 10, 1973.

Dedera, Don, "Does America Still Believe in Smokey Bear?," *Virginia Forests*, Winter, 1980.

Dempsey, Mary Jane, "Smokey at Home In Zoo, Has Suite And Private Tree," *Times-Herald*, July 1, 1950.

Doolittle, M. L., "Communicating Fire Prevention Messages," address to Second National Smokey Bear Workshop, Tallahassee, Florida, January 10, 1973.

Dowdy, Gene, and Rod Kindlund, "National Special Prevention Activities: A Fire Manager's Tool," U.S. Department of Agriculture, Forest Service, Special Issue, 1992-1993.

"Duty calls, Smokey to stay in Capital," *Lincoln County News*, August 10, 1961.

Earl, Dean, handwritten instructions to Speed Simmons, May 9, 1950.

Editorial, *Salt Lake City Tribune*, July, 1974.

Edwards, Bill, "Forester Knew Smokey From Cradle To Grave," *Georgia Forestry*, Fall, 1988.

Ely, Richard, "My Job as a Fire Prevention Coordinator," comments at panel discussion, First National Smokey Bear Workshop, Atlantic City, New Jersey, January 14, 1970.

"Fabulous Bear, Famous Service Fight Annual Billion-Dollar Fire," *Newsweek*, June 2, 1992.

Fanella, R., undated letter to Smokey Bear.

Farb, Peter, *The Forest*, Time-Life Books, 1980.

Faries, Belmont, "Smokey and Rudy," *Stamp Collector*, July 9, 1984.

"Faulty Spark Arrester Can Start A Forest Fire," *Penthouse*, unidentified date.

"Elliott Barker Dies at 101 in Santa Fe," *Albuquerque Journal*, April 5, 1988.

"Fiery Capitan wins Smokey Bear Stamp issuance," *Santa Fe New Mexican*, May 6, 1984.

"Fillers--To Help Prevent Man-Made Forest Fires," 1945 Forest Service memorandum.

"Fire Occurrence Map, Fire Planning, Period 1949-1958," USDA Forest Service.

"First Smokey Bear Director Dies in California," *Press Democrat* (Santa Rosa, California), June 18, 1964.

Flaherty, Thomas, undated letter to Smokey Bear.

Flock, Kester D., "Bear that almost made me infamous; Smokey's living symbol," *American Forests*, December, 1964.

Folkman, William S., "Giving Smokey Bear a `Headstart'," address to First National Smokey Bear Workshop, Atlantic City, New Jersey, January 14, 1970.

"Forest Fire Peril," *Business Week*, April 1, 1942.

Foster, Jack, undated letter to John O'Toole.

Fox, Stephen, *The Mirror Makers*, William Morrow & Company, 1984.

Friedrich, Otto, "Day of Infamy," *Time*, December 2, 1991.

Frome, Mike, "Clint Davis," *American Forests*, April, 1968.

Frye, Dr. O. E., Jr., address to Second National Smokey Bear Workshop, Tallahassee, Florida, January 10, 1973.

Gamble, Frederic R., miscellaneous notes dated December 19, 1941.

Gause, Jerry W., "Smokey Bear--funeral plans," January 8, 1976, memorandum to Konrad Reinke.

————, "Smokey Bear--Photo Materials," November 15, 1974, memorandum to Dave Warren.

Goldie Bear Pathology Record--National Zoological Park, various dates.

Godwin, Gaylord P., "Smokey Returns Youngster's Badge," *Borger (Texas) News-Herald*, December 15, 1960.

Bibliography

Gonzalez, Christine, "This Daffy Duck Has Ribs, and They Can Really Be Broken," *Wall Street Journal*, August 3, 1993.

Gooley, Walt, address to Second National Smokey Bear Workshop, Tallahassee, Florida, January 11, 1973.

"Gov. Mechem to the Rescue: `Bring Smokey Back to Capitan,'" July 28, 1961, unidentified source.

Graft, Sam, "Remarks Regarding Smokey Bear Historical State Park," November 17, 1976.

Green, Stan, "Smokey the Bear deserves--gets medal," *Alamogordo (N.M.) Daily News*, December 14, 1975.

Grigg, William, "The Bear That Stops Fires," *Science News Letter*, October 1, 1955.

"Grouch Smokey the Bear retired," May 3, 1975, unidentified source.

Guck, Dorothy, "Apache Red Hats," *New Mexico*, September, 1951.

————, "A story of Smokey the Bear," undated and unidentified source.

————, "Capitan's Smokey Bear," undated and unidentified source.

————, "Lincoln's Worst Forest Fire Under Control; Many Narrowly Escape," *Carrizozo Outlook*, May 12, 1950.

————, "Red Hats on the Warpath," *The Denver Post, Empire Magazine*, undated.

————, "Smokey Bear," undated and unidentified source.

————, "Smokey's Museum Will Fulfill Long-Time Ambition For Capitan," unidentified date and source.

————, "Smokey 'Oscar' Presented Capitan," unidentified source and date.

————, "Whoops on the Fire Line," *American Forests*, January, 1952.

Hamlet, Sybil E. ("Billie"), "The National Zoological Park From Its Beginnings to 1973," manuscript, 1985.

Hammatt, Richard F., "Bear design for 1945," September 19, 1944, file memorandum.

————, June 13, 1953, letter to Clint Davis.

————, "Preliminary printing information needed for 1943 Wartime Forest Fire Prevention Campaign," October 29, 1942, memorandum to E. F. Gallagher.

————, September 12, 1942, letter to Don Belding.

————, "Some Highlights of the Wartime Forest Fire Prevention Campaign for 1943," undated.

————, "Special Art for Wartime Forest Fire Prevention Campaign," August 9, 1944, file memorandum.

Hanenkrat, Frank T., *Wildlife Watcher's Handbook*, Winchester Press, 1977.

"Hansen Appointed Smokey Bear Program Manager," *Forest Service News Release*, Boise National Forest, October, 1976.

Hansen, Donald T., "Death of Goldie," April 26, 1977, Forest Service file memorandum.

Hardy, Mal, "Annual Report, Cooperative Forest Fire Prevention Program," individual yearly reports, 1964 through 1975.

————, April 8, 1974 letter to J. T. Johnston.

————, "Fact Sheet--The Smokey Bear Program," February 1, 1967.

————, "History of the `Smokey Bear' Campaign," address to Second National Smokey Bear Workshop, Tallahassee, Florida, January 9, 1973.

————, January 13, 1983, letter to Joe Dooley.

————, "The Legend of Smokey Bear," *National Parks Magazine*, January, 1969.

————, "The Legend of Smokey Bear," (different article) *ACE Quarterly*, October-December, 1969.

————, "Operational Procedures (Orders, Printing, Distribution & Payment)," address to First National Smokey Bear Workshop, Atlantic City, New Jersey, January 14, 1970.

————, "Smokey Bear--A Biography," address to First National Smokey Bear Workshop, Atlantic City, New Jersey, January 13, 1970.

————, "Smokey Bear Awards," address to First National Smokey Bear Workshop, Atlantic City, New Jersey, January 14, 1970.

————, "Status report on Smokey, the living symbol," August 28, 1974, memorandum to CFFP Executive Committee, Advertising Task Force, and Key Cooperators.

Hart, Henry G., "Conservation Education in Schools Is Carefully Planned for Results," *Tennessee Conservationist*, February, 1953.

"Has Smokey Bear Stamped Out Too Many Fires in the Forest?," *National Observer*, July 14, 1973.

Haug Associates, Inc., "Highlights of the Smokey Bear Study," April 18, 1968.

Heinrichs, Jay, "The Ursine Gladhander," *Journal of Forestry*, October, 1982.

Hess, Bill, "Seeking the Best of Two Worlds," *National Geographic*, February, 1980.

Higgins, Philip, "Ere Smokey Departs, Say Foresters, He's Got Party To Attend," *Santa Fe New Mexican*, June 25, 1950.

————, "Smokey Heads For Washington," *Santa Fe New Mexican*, June 27, 1950.

"Highlights of Wartime Forest Fire Prevention Campaign," June 22, 1942, unsigned Forest Service memorandum.

"Hobbsan Who Flew Smokey To Attend Bear's Rites," *Hobbs Daily News-Sun*, November 10, 1976.

Hodges, Richard, "Smokey's Southern Accent," address to Second National Smokey Bear Workshop, Tallahassee, Florida, January 9, 1973.

Hoffman, Ellen, "Publicist Clint Davis, 62, Dies; Promoter of Smokey the Bear," *Washington Post*, February 17, 1971.

House Concurrent Resolution 564, August 6, 1974.

Hoyer, Jim C., "Where there's Smokey, there's no fire," *correspondent*, summer, 1992.

Huber, William W., May 14, 1956, letter to Paul S. Newman.

————, "The Southern Cooperative Forest Fire Prevention Program," address to First National Smokey Bear Workshop, Atlantic City, New Jersey, January 13, 1970.

Hutchinson, W. I., "Advertising Council national fire campaign program," May 16, 1942, memorandum to Dana Parkinson.

————, February 6, 1957, letter to William W. Huber.

————, May 12, 1942, telegram to Forest Service, Washington, D.C.

————, "Origin of the Wartime Forest Fire Prevention Campaign," unpublished manuscript, January 21, 1957.

"I'm A Stranger Here Myself," *Santa Fe New Mexican*, May 14, 1950.

"Information Contact Plan, `Original Smokey Bear,'" July 21, 1976, unsigned Forest Service memorandum.

"Issue of Smokey's Origins Heats Up," *AARP News Bulletin*, April, 1983.

Ivory, Reg, address to Second National Smokey Bear Workshop, Tallahassee, Florida, January 10, 1973.

Jacoby, Ed, "Smokey Turns 40," *Conservationist*, November/December, 1984.

"James," December 19, 1958, letter to Smokey Bear.

Johnson, Merlin, "Visitors Jam Capital For July 4 Fete," *Times Herald*, July 3, 1950.

Johnson, Richard F., "The Junior Forest Ranger Program," address to First National Smokey Bear Workshop, Atlantic City, New Jersey, January 14, 1970.

Johnston, J. T., March 26, 1974 letter to Mal Hardy.

Jones, Ruth Bush, March 4, 1957, letter to Mrs. Russell G. Bird.

Jones, Stuart E., and Jay Johnston, "Forest Fire: The Devil's Picnic," *National Geographic*, July, 1968.

"Joseph B. Martin, Ex-Fire Chief, Dies," *New York Times*, October 25, 1941.

Justus, Lucy, "Good-by, Smokey Bear," *Atlanta Journal and Constitution Magazine*, July 13, 1975.

Kerr, Ed, "`Life' Visits `Jelly,'" *Forests and People*, January, 1952.

Kienast, Margate S., "Smokey the Bear Goes Musical," *Christian Science Monitor*, June 21, 1952.

King, Bruce, September 20, 1974, letter to Manual Ortiz.

Kinney, Gordon, "The Advertising Council and The Volunteer Coordinator," address to First National Smokey Bear Workshop, Atlantic City, New Jersey, January 13, 1970.

Knapp, Jeanne M., *Don Belding: A Career of Advertising and Public Service*, Texas Tech University, 1983.

Lake, Robert M., July 21, 1976, memorandum to the Director, Cooperative Fire Protection.

Lalla, Alice, October 28, 1993 letter to Larry Hensen.

Lane, Dale, "Cub Bear, Smokey, Illustrates Need For Stopping Ruinous Forest Fires," *Santa Fe New Mexican*, May 21, 1950.

Larmon, Sigurd, April 28, 1942, telegram to W. C. Mendenhall.

LaRoche, Chester J., "The Need and Purposes of an Advertising Council," memorandum, January 10, 1942.

Lawler, Joseph A., "Smokey Joe, Incidents and Ancecdotes of the 47-Year Illustrious Career of Asst. Chief Martin," *W.N.Y.F.*, July, 1948.

Levey, Bob, "Sunshine in the Morning," *Washington Post*, October 21, 1992.

Lewis, Howard, "Smokey The Bear Powerful Fire Prevention Symbol," *Charleston Gazette*, November 23, 1960.

Little, Charles, "Smokey's Revenge," *American Forests*, May/June 1993.

"Little Hotfoot Welcomed by Rain," *Washington Post,* June 30, 1950.

Loeffelbein, Bob, "Smokey Hits 40!," *American Forests,* May, 1984.

Lombard, Frank L., "Conference with Mr. Allum of Advertising Council," May 19, 1942, Forest Service file memorandum.

————, "Fire Prevention Campaign," May 6, 1942, Forest Service file memorandum to P. A. Thompson.

————, "Record of meeting with Advertising Council on Forest Fire Prevention Campaign--June 3," June 3, 1942, Forest Service file memorandum.

"Los Angeles Talent Pool," undated (but apparently 1942), unsigned memorandum.

Loveridge, E. W., "Assignment to Wartime Forest Fire Prevention," June 16, 1942, memorandum to R. F. Hammatt.

Lowden, Merle S., "The CFFP Executive Committee," address to First National Smokey Bear Workshop, Atlantic City, New Jersey, January 13, 1970.

Lucas, Tracy, undated letter to Smokey Bear.

Lujan, Manuel, Jr., May 2, 1974, letter to John R. McGuire.

Lusher, Arthur A., January 28, 1954, letter to Catherine Christopher.

Lynch, F. Bradley, "A Short History of the Advertising Council," manuscript, 1991.

MacCleery, Douglas W., *American Forests, A History of Resiliency and Recovery,* U.S. Department of Agriculture Forest Service, 1993.

Martin, Judith, "He's Smokey's Brother," *Washington Post,* June 12, 1973.

McCrossen, Eric, "Elliot Barker Reacts," *Albuquerque Journal,* April 5, 1975.

cGuinn, Randi, "Smokey Bear dedication held Saturday," *Ruidoso (N.M.) News,* May 20, 1976.

McGuire, John R., April 8, 1974, letter to Senator Pete Domenici.

————, "Smokey Bear Executive Committee Meeting, Summary of Major Items," December 17, 1974 Forest Service memorandum.

McManus, Reed, "Is Smokey Sacred?," *Sierra,* January/February 1993.

McNamara, E. F., "Smokey Bear in Exhibits, Parades, Floats and Window Displays," address to First National Smokey Bear Workshop, Atlantic City, New Jersey, January 14, 1970.

Meek, Clarence E., June 3, 1969 letter to W. W. Bergoffen.

"Meet Your Game Department," *New Mexico,* March, 1952.

"Meeting with Donald Nelson and James Knowlson in Room 2520 in the Social Security Building from 11:00 a.m. to 12:30 p.m.," transcript of minutes, February 5, 1942.

"Memorial To Smokey Bear," Senate Report to accompany House Concurrent Resolution 564, August 29, 1974.

Mendenhall, William V., April 28, 1942, letter to Sigurd Larmon.

Miller, David, undated letter to Smokey Bear.

Miller, Mel, undated letter to Smokey Bear.

Miniclier, Kit, "Foster Son Smokey Pleased Poppa Bear," *Denver Post,* Denver, Colorado, March 15, 1981.

Miscellaneous articles, *Albuquerque Journal*, May 9-12, 1950.

Miscellaneous items, First National Smokey Bear Workshop, Atlantic City, New Jersey, January 15, 1970.

Monn, Vincent, undated letter to Smokey Bear.

Morgan, Ralph, "The Volunteer Advertising Agency—Southern Program," address to First National Smokey Bear Workshop, Atlantic City, New Jersey, January 13, 1970.

Morris, Joan, "Hometown bear, Postal service picks Capitan to release 1st Smokey stamps," *El Paso Times*, February 27, 1984.

Mullavey, Dick, "Fire Prevention Awards," address to Second National Smokey Bear Workshop, Tallahassee, Florida, January 10, 1973.

———, "My Job as a Fire Prevention Coordinator," comments at panel discussion, First National Smokey Bear Workshop, Atlantic City, New Jersey, January 14, 1970.

Nagle, Russell, "The Volunteer Advertising Agency—National Program," address to First National Smokey Bear Workshop, Atlantic City, New Jersey, January 13, 1970.

"Nation-wide Forest Fire Prevention in Relation to the War Effort," undated (but apparently 1942), unsigned Forest Service file memorandum.

"Natural Role of Fire," USDA Forest Service, Southern Region, and Florida Department of Agriculture & Consumer Services, Division of Forestry, October, 1989.

NBC Television, "Carson Reports Death of Smokey the Bear," November 9, 1976, broadcast transcript, Radio-TV Monitoring Service, Inc.

———, "Smokey Dies; To Be Buried In Forest Where He Was First Found," November 9, 1976, broadcast transcript, Radio-TV Monitoring Service, Inc.

Nelson, Donald M., December 9, 1941, letter to Paul B. West.

New Mexico Congressional Delegation (Pete Domenici, Jeff Bingaman, Manuel Lujan Jr., Joe Skeen and Bill Richardson), February 29, 1984, and June 9, 1984, letters to Willie Hobbs.

Newnam, Jo, "Dad Rescued Smokey The Bear," *Okmulgee Daily Times*, April 18, 1990.

Norment, Juliane and Vincent, undated letter to Smokey Bear.

"One For All And . .," *Business Week*, February 7, 1942.

"Opening of Smokey Bear Museum brings a community project to completion," unidentified date and source.

"Organization and Rules Governing the Operation of the Mescalero Apache Red Hats," undated documents from files of Mescalero Apache Tribe.

"Original Smokey Had a Baby-Sitter Who's Now an RO SCSEP," *Southwestern Region News*, January, 1990.

Ortiz, S. M., Lincoln County Sheriff's investigative report of Capitan Gap fire in May 16, 1950, letter to Dean Earl.

O'Toole, John, "Smokey Bear, The Advertising Council's Oldest Customer," from "A Retrospective of Advertising Council Campaigns, A Half Century of Public Service," The Museum of Television and Radio, 1991.

———, *From One Person To Another*, 1977.

Oxford, Edward, "One Sunday in December," *American History Illustrated*, November/December, 1991.

Parshall, Gerald, "A knight in the wilderness," *U.S. News & World Report*, July 20, 1992.

Peach, Nelson, "Is Smokey Relevant? How Does He Fit in Conservation and Environmental Quality?," address to First National Smokey Bear Workshop, Atlantic City, New Jersey, January 14, 1970.

"Pearl Harbor," *USA Today*, December 6, 1991.

"People," *Sports Illustrated*, February 15, 1971.

Phillips, Dave, "Smokey's Image," address to First National Smokey Bear Workshop, Atlantic City, New Jersey, January 14, 1970.

Pickens, Homer C., *Tracks Across New Mexico*, Bishop Publishing Company, 1980.

Pyne, Stephen J., *Fire In America*, Princeton University Press, 1982.

"Playful Cubs Cage-Mates at Zoo," *Washington Post*, September 28, 1950.

"Playmate," *Washington Daily News*, June 26, 1950.

Pratt, Mrs. J. C., address to Second National Smokey Bear Workshop, Tallahassee, Florida, January 10, 1973.

"Questionnaire, Wartime Forest Fire Prevention Campaign, South Carolina (in Region 8)," undated (but apparently late 1942 or early 1943), unsigned Forest Service memorandum.

"Record of Precipitation, Capitan Area," 1940-1970, USDA Forest Service.

Record Unit 365, Box 21, Smithsonian Institution archives.

"Red Hat Fire Record," 1950-1954, Mescalero Apache Tribe.

"Red Hats of Mescalero, New Mexico," December 1, 1954, Mescalero Apache Tribe.

Reed, Dr. Theodore H., "Bear `Crate,'" December 24, 1975, memorandum to Bob Petrella.

————, January 18, 1977, letter to Donald T. Hansen.

"Remembering Pearl Harbor," *Newsweek*, November 25, 1991.

"Reports Show Smokey Did A Good Job," *Las Cruces Sun-News*, November 17, 1976.

"Retrospective Art Exhibit of Rudolph Wendelin," (pamphlet), 1984.

Ricard, James Q., "Effective Use of the Smokey Costume," address to First National Smokey Bear Workshop, Atlantic City, New Jersey, January 14, 1970.

Richardson, Jim, September 5, 1944, memo to Forest Service Chief Lyle Watts.

Riggenbach, Eric, undated letter to Smokey Bear.

Roberts, David, "Geronimo," *National Geographic*, October, 1992.

Robertson, John, "Santa Feans attempt to set the record straight," *Santa Fe New Mexican*, November 14, 1976.

Romano, Lois, "Clothes Call at the National Park Service," *Washington Post*, July 9, 1993.

Rosecrans, May 12, 1942, night letter to American Forestry Association.

Rosemary, Kristine, "Retiree says `Smokey' was actually a grouch," *Columbia Basin Daily Herald*, July 25, 1984.

Roth, Dennis, and Frank Harmon, "The Forest Service in the Environmental Era," unpublished manuscript, U.S. Department of Agriculture Forest Service, 1989.

Rossoll, Harry, address to University of Georgia Forestry School, 1960.

————, *Little Folks Forest Friends*, U.S. Forest Service, undated.

————, *Smokey Bear's Story of the Forest*, U.S. Department of Agriculture, Forest Service-- Southern Region, undated.

"Rudolph Wendelin and the Changing Image of Smokey," U.S. Forest Service fact sheet, undated.

Runnels, Harold, May 3, 1974, letter to Jay T. Johnston.

————, Press Release, March 21, 1974.

Salcido, Proceso, undated letter to Forest Service, Washington, D.C.

Santos, Carlos, "Bear-makers bring Smokey to life," *Richmond Times-Dispatch*, January 20, 1991.

————, "Smokey Ad campaign fights bear burn-out," *Richmond Times-Dispatch*, January 20, 1991.

Schullery, Paul, "Yellowstone Grizzlies, The New Breed," *National Parks*, November/ December, 1989.

Scott, Randall W., March 23, 1993, letter to Robin Snyder.

Sheehan, Pat, "Commercial Support Program and Smokey Bear Violations," address to First National Smokey Bear Workshop, Atlantic City, New Jersey, January 14, 1970.

Shelton, Elizabeth, "Cub Scouts Here Welcome Smokey, Cub Bear, New Mexico's Gift to Washington Children," *Times-Herald*, June 30, 1950.

Shields, A. B., April 19, 1949, memorandum to Mescalero Apache Tribe.

Shollenberger, Lewis, "The Role of the Advertising Council and the Volunteer Coordinator," address to Second National Smokey Bear Workshop, Tallahassee, Florida, January 9, 1973.

Sibley, Ford, August 14, 1944, letter to R. F. Hammatt.

Sierra County Sentinel, March 27, 1974.

Simmons, L.W., fire report to Elliott Barker, June 21, 1950.

————, "This Happened To Me," *Outdoor Life*, January, 1976.

————, work report to Elliott Barker, June 5, 1950.

Singer, Patricia F., "Rudolph A. Wendelin: A Portrait," *Journal of Forestry*, December, 1979.

Skelton, Kathleen Green, "Our Life With a Bear Cub," *Saturday Evening Post*, March 26, 1949.

"Sky Writers Underwrite Smokey's Flight," *Times Herald*, June 17, 1950.

Smith, Alex, address to Second National Smokey Bear Workshop, Tallahassee, Florida, January 9, 1973.

Smith, J. Morgan, "The Story of Smokey Bear," *Forestry Chronicles*, June, 1956.

Smith, J. Y., "Radio's Jackson Weaver Dies," *Washington Post*, October 21, 1992.

"Smokey II buried in Washington, DC," unidentified date and source.

"Smokey II Dies at Zoo," *Washington Post*, August 13, 1990.

"Smokey II takes over," unidentified date and source.

"Smokey, a Cub, Helps Fight on Forest Blazes," *Chattanooga News-Free Press*, July 18, 1950.

"Smokey and Pal," *Santa Fe New Mexican*, June 14, 1950.

Bibliography

"Smokey and Sparky," *Business Week*, June 12, 1954.

"Smokey Bear," *Alamorgordo Daily News*, July 23, 1961.

"Smokey Bear II dies from cancer at age 20," *Roswell Daily Record*, August 12, 1990.

"Smokey Bear: A Living Legend," *Sun*, November 15, 1976.

"Smokey Bear birthday celebration," *Lincoln County News*, August 9, 1984.

"Smokey Bear dies; buried in own park"; unidentified source, November 20, 1976.

"Smokey Bear dies in capital," *Albuquerque Tribune*, November 9, 1976.

"Smokey Bear Disposition and Memorial," U.S. House of Representatives report from the Committee on Agriculture, July 31, 1974.

"Smokey Bear has come home," *Lincoln County News*, November 11. 1976.

"Smokey Bear Historical State Park Committee," undated Forest Service memorandum.

"Smokey Bear Park plans jell," *Lincoln County News*, April 24, 1975.

"Smokey Bear retirement near," *Chicago Tribune*, May 2, 1975.

"Smokey Bear: Sic Transit Gloria Mundi," unidentified source and date.

"Smokey Bear, the toy with a message," *American Forests*, April, 1953.

"Smokey, Fire Victim, Will Reside Here," *Washington Post*, June 17, 1950.

"Smokey gets a drink of milk after a long plane flight," *Indianapolis Star*, June 29, 1950.

"Smokey Is Safe," *Santa Fe New Mexican*, June 15, 1950.

"Smokey, Mortified by Entrancing Effect of Forester's Cap, Retires to Den at Zoo," *Washington Post*, July 1, 1950.

"Smokey Museum," dedication program, November 1, 1958.

"Smokey, Orphan Bear, Will Get Reception," *Albuquerque Tribune*, June 29, 1950.

"Smokey Portal," dedication program, 1955.

"Smokey Reaches Capital, And Sees Rain at Last," *Albuquerque Journal*, June 30, 1950.

"Smokey's Bosses Now Say Natural Fires Help the Forests," *New York Times*, September 10, 1973.

"Smokey's Creator Still Active, Enthusiastic," *AARP Bulletin*, January, 1983.

"Smokey's End Near," *Lincoln County News*, November 27, 1975.

"Smokey's Loss Strikes Deep," *Gallup Independent*, November 19, 1976.

"Smokey's Not a Pappa, Officials Are Worried," *Atlanta Journal*, July 24, 1968.

"Smokey's 20th Year," *American Forests*, March, 1961.

"Smokey Thanks Hopalong," *Washington Post*, July 16, 1950.

"Smokey the Bear Cub Joins Zoo as 500 Laugh and Cheer," *Evening Star*, June 30, 1950.

"Smokey, The Bear, Enlists Help of School Children," *Danville Register*, January 26, 1961.

"Smokey The Bear, Survivor Of NM Fire, To Become Comic Feature In Times June 16," *El Paso Times*, June 6, 1957.

"Smokey: The Billion dollar Bear," *Family Weekly*, September 5, 1965, and *Reader's Digest*, May, 1966.

Bibliography

"Smokey To Get New Quarters Plus Uniform," *Las Cruces Sun-News*, August 4, 1961.

Snyder, Robin, "Paul S. Newman, Rex," *Robin Snyder's History of the Comics*, March, 1993.

Soo, Jamie, undated letter to Smokey Bear.

Sorenson, James C., "Commercial Support," address to Second National Smokey Bear Workshop, Tallahassee, Florida, January 9, 1973.

———, "Feedback on Campaign Items," address to Second National Smokey Bear Workshop, Tallahassee, Florida, January 11, 1973.

———, "Junior Forest Rangers," address to Second National Smokey Bear Workshop, Tallahassee, Florida, January 10, 1973.

———, "What's Going on in the Field?," address to Second National Smokey Bear Workshop, Tallahassee, Florida, January 11, 1973.

"Southern California Doomed To Cycle of Build and Burn?," *Ponca City (Oklahoma) News*, November 10, 1993.

"Southern Forest Fire Prevention Program," unidentified source and date.

"Southwest Forest Fire Fighters," unidentified source and date.

"Space for War," *Business Week*, July 3, 1943.

"Staehle's Bear," 1945 Forest Service file memorandum.

Steen, Harold K., *The Beginning of The National Forest System*, Forest History Society, U.S. Department of Agriculture Forest Service, 1991.

Stout, Jared, "Smokey's New Hurrah: He's Top U.S. Symbol," *Washington Post*, April 19, 1968.

"Submarine Shells Southland Oil Field," *Los Angeles Times*, February 24, 1942.

"Summary of Cooperative Forest Fire Prevention Campaign," undated, untitled Forest Service memorandum.

Taylor, Jack, "Blue Ribbon Chairman," *blue pencil*, October 21, 1958.

"Teddy With A Hotfoot," *Santa Fe New Mexican*, May 11, 1950.

Tessier, Denise, "Smokey Bear Gets Quiet Burial," *Albuquerque Journal*, November 10, 1976.

"Third Wartime Forest Fire Prevention Campaign, California Hints and Highlights (No. 1)," San Francisco, California, July 10, 1944, unsigned Forest Service memorandum.

Thomas, Harold B., "The Background and Beginning of The Advertising Council," unpublished manuscript dated April 1, 1952.

Thornsberry, Raggs, undated letter to Smokey Bear.

"Three Lincoln National Forest Landmarks Renamed in honor of Smokey the Bear," *Lincoln County News*, December 25, 1959.

Thurston, Ken, undated and unpublished manuscript, *Belding Collection*, Southwestern Collection, Texas Tech University.

Tillis, C. Richard, address to Second National Smokey Bear Workshop, Tallahassee, Florida, January 10, 1973.

Towell, William E., address to 19th Annual Conservation Conference of the National Wildlife Federation, 1973.

"True Life Adventure Story of Forest Fire Told Kiwanians," unidentified date and source.

Turan, Kenneth, "Greatest Bear of All," *Washington Post*, undated.

———, "The Last Sad Days of Smokey the Bear," *Washington Post/Potomac*, January 13, 1974.

———, "Smokey's Enduring Appeal," *Washington Post*, November 10, 1976.

"TV Gets Results in Tulsa," *Broadcasting Magazine*, February 5, 1968.

Twain, Mark, *Roughing It*, Signet Classic, 1980.

"Unusual Visitor," *Tulsa Daily World*, June 28, 1950.

"U.S. Government Program For Wartime Forest Fire Prevention, 1944," USDA Forest Service.

"U.S. Honors Creators of Smokey Bear," *Los Angeles Times*, undated.

Walter, Harold, January 16, 1942, letter to Jimmy Liccion.

"War Baby Turns Fifty. The Advertising Council: Helping Americans in Business of Living," undated Advertising Council news release.

"Wartime Forest Fire Prevention Campaign, Forest Service--R-1, Missoula, Montana," September 23, 1942, Forest Service memorandum.

Watts, Lyle F., November 4, 1944, letter to Albert Staehle.

Wendelin, Rudolph A., "The evolving image of Smokey," unpublished manuscript (circa 1993).

———, "Smokey Says," address to Second National Smokey Bear Workshop, Tallahassee, Florida, January 10, 1973.

———, "Smokey's Visual Image," address to First National Smokey Bear Workshop, Atlantic City, New Jersey, January 14, 1970.

West, Paul, memorandum dated August 28, 1941.

West, Terry, *Centennial Mini-Histories of the Forest Service*, U.S. Department of Agriculture, Forest Service, July, 1992.

———, "The Forest Service and Fire Control," *Fire Management Notes*, U.S. Department of Agriculture, Forest Service, Volume 52, Number. 1, 1991.

———, "Reserves Redux: 100 Years of Forest Service History 1891-1991," essay, 1991.

Wharton, Don, "The Story Back of the War Ads," *Reader's Digest*, July, 1944.

Wheeler, Keith, *The Scouts*, Time-Life Books, 1980.

"Where There's Smoke," *Reader's Digest*, May, 1966.

Whitney, Stephen, *Western Forests*, Alfred A. Knopf, 1985.

Wickard, Claude, May 25, 1942, letter to Dr. Miller McClintock.

Williams, Gerald W., "Biographical Information About the USDA Forest Service Chiefs (Foresters), 1905-Present," compilation, 1991.

Williams, Richard L., *The Loggers*, Time-Life Books, 1976.

Wills, Paul C., address to Second National Smokey Bear Workshop, Tallahassee, Florida, January 10, 1973.

"Wisconsin's Smokey Costume," *Fire Management Notes*, U.S. Department of Agriculture, Forest Service, Special Issue, 1992-1993.

WMAL-TV, "Comment By Smokey's `Voice,'" November 9, 1976, broadcast transcript, Radio-TV Monitoring Service, Inc.

Wozniak, Barney, "My Job as a Fire Prevention Coordinator," comments at panel discussion, First National Smokey Bear Workshop, Atlantic City, New Jersey, January 14, 1970.

WRC Television, "Smokey the First Ecologist, Says Jackson Weaver," November 9, 1976, broadcast transcript, Radio-TV Monitoring Service, Inc.

————, "Smokey To Be Buried In New Mexico Historical Park," November 9, 1976, broadcast transcript, Radio-TV Monitoring Service, Inc.

Yaeger, Harlow A., August 4, 1991, letter to Bill Chapel.

————, January 5, 1988, letter to Robert Conrad.

————, July 9, 1990, letter to Willie Hobbs.

Young, James Webb, November 14, 1941, address at Hot Springs, Virginia.

"Zoo, Parks Lure Those Who Stayed In District, Crowds Turn Out To Watch Smokey, Famed Cub Bear; Highways Jammed," *Washington Post*, July 3, 1950.

OTHER SOURCES

Abbott, James R.; Tucson, Arizona; interview.

Allen, Larry; Tucson, Arizona; interview and photographs.

Angelos, Lew; Ojai, California; interview.

Angelos, Peter L.; San Francisco, California; interview.

Bandy, Larry; Capitan, New Mexico; general assistance.

Barker, Ethel; Santa Fe, New Mexico; interview.

Belding, Don Jr.; Escondido, California; photographs.

Bell, Don; Las Cruces, New Mexico; interviews, videotape and correspondence.

Bell, Ray L.; Las Cruces, New Mexico; interviews, correspondence, pilot log book, photographs, file materials and field trips.

Belsey, George W. Jr; Aptos, California; interview.

Bergoffen, William W.; Silver Springs, Maryland; interviews, correspondence, photographs, artwork, radio scripts and file materials.

Bitter, Richard W.; Riverside, California; interview.

Bowman, Ken; Albuquerque, New Mexico; interviews and field trip.

Braxton, Charles B.; Warrenton, Virginia; interview and photograph.

Brewster, Phil Jr; Rome, Georgia; interviews and correspondence.

Budd, Nancy; Los Angeles, California; interviews.

Cabber, Betty Pickens; Albuquerque, New Mexico; interview and videotape.

Carroll, Franklin, Jr.; Boise Idaho; interview and videotape.

Cassedy, James; Suitland, Maryland; correspondence, research assistance and material from National Archives.

Chapel, Bill; Albuquerque, New Mexico; interviews, correspondence, photographs, videotape, file materials and general assistance.

Collins, Edwin Harry; Oneco, Florida; interviews and correspondance.

Conrad, Robert; Washington, D.C.; interviews, photos, file materials and general assistance.

Cox, Dick; Capitan, New Mexico; interviews.

Cox, Donna Cloud; Capitan, New Mexico; interview.

Daines, Gladys; Arlington, Virginia; interviews and general assistance.

Davis, Roger; Oklahoma City, Oklahoma; general assistance.

Deiss, William A.; Washington, D.C.; research assistance and file materials from Smithsonian Instution Archives.

Dunlap, John; Las Cruces, New Mexico; general assistance.

Earl, Della; Sun City, Arizona; interview.

Earl, Robert D.; Houston, Texas; interviews, correspondence and field trip.

Eddy, Tom; Albuquerque, New Mexico; interviews, correspondence and file materials.

Engelking, Teresa; Capitan, New Mexico; file materials and general assistance.

Fairbairn, Susan; Los Angles, California; interview.

Felton, Jim; Irvine, California; interviews, correspondence, photographs, artwork, radio scripts, file materials and general assistance.

Fish, Elsie; Oklahoma City, Oklahoma; interview.

Flock, Kester D. ("Kay"); Boise, Idaho; interviews, correspondence, photographs and file materials.

Foster, Jack; Los Angeles, California; interviews, correspondence, photograph, file materials and general assistance.

Gallegos, Ray; Santa Fe, New Mexico; general assistance.

Gerzanich, Larry; Lakeland, Florida; interview.

Gillio, David; Albuquerque, New Mexico; correspondence and general assistance.

Glenn, Merle; Alamorgordo, New Mexico; file materials and general assistance.

Guck, Dorothy; Nogal, New Mexico; interviews, correspondence, notes, photographs, file materials and general assistance.

Guck, Tom; Nogal, New Mexico; interviews, correspondence, maps, file materials and field trip.

Guydelkon, Mason; Mescalero, New Mexico; interview.

Hansen, Cheryl; Manassas, Virginia; interview.

Hansen, Donald T.; Manassas, Virginia; interviews, correspondence, file materials and field trip.

Hardy, Mal; Anacortes, Washington; interviews, correspondence, photographs and file materials.

Harris, Bob; South Lake Tahoe, California; interview and file materials.

Heurera, Eugene; Santa Fe, New Mexico; interview.

Heurera, Juan; Santa Fe, New Mexico; interviews.

Hobbs, Willie; Capitan, New Mexico; interview.

Holmes, Sue Major; Albuquerque, New Mexico; research assistance.

Hickman, Jim L.; Albuquerque, New Mexico; interviews and general assistance.

Hurst, William D.; Bosque Farms, New Mexico; interview and correspondence.

Johnson, Jack E.; Capitan, New Mexico; interview, correspondence and Highway Patrol log book.

Johnson, Judy; Morris Plains, New Jersey; interview, correspondence, audiotape and videotape.

Johnson, Richard F.; Oceanside, California; interview.

Johnston, Dorothy; Elmer, Oklahoma; interview, correspondence, photographs and file materials.

Johnston, J. T.; Elmer, Oklahoma; interview.

Jones, Paul; Capitan, New Mexico; interviews.

Jourdan, Chuck; Albuquerque, New Mexico; interview.

Just, Richard C.; Cottonwood, California; interview.

Justice, Michele; Durham, North Carolina; Forest History Society file materials.

King, Ann; Topanga, California; interviews.

Kirgan, Ray; Mescalero, New Mexico; interview.

Klason, Richard; Salt Lake City, Utah; general assistance.

Knapp, Jeanne M., Lubbock, Texas, interview and general assistance.

Lang, Mickey; Santa Fe, New Mexico; interview.

LaPaz, Leo Jr; Mescalero, New Mexico; interview.

Lawter, Allison K.; Ponca City, Oklahoma; research assistance.

Lee, Bob; Albuquerque, New Mexico; interview.

Levy, Len; Santa Monica, California; interviews, correspondence and videotape.

Livingston, Cyndy; Capitan, New Mexico; interviews, correspondence, file materials and general assistance.

Livingston, Tim; Capitan, New Mexico; interview.

Luna, Barbara; Capitan, New Mexico; general assistance.
Luttrell, Orville; Silver City, New Mexico; interviews.
Lutz, Raymond H.; Taos, New Mexico; interviews, correspondence and flight logs.
Lynch, F. Bradley; New York, New York; interview, correspondence, file materials and general assistance.
Marchese, Michael; Williamsport, Pennsylvania; interview.
Matt, Ron; Albuquerque, New Mexico; interview and file materials.
McClellan, Harry R.; Clovis, California; interview.
McEuen, Bonnie; Capitan, New Mexico; interview.
Mendez, Aloysius; Mescalero, New Mexico; interview.
Miller, Kenneth K.; Santa Fe, New Mexico; interview.
Montonya, Francine; Espanola, New Mexico; interview.
Moore, Norma; Espanola, New Mexico; interview.
Morgan, Mike; Washington, D.C.; interview and general assistance.
Murrah, Dr. David; Lubbock, Texas; interview.
Newman, Paul S.; Columbia, Maryland; interview, correspondence and file materials.
Ortiz, S. M. ("Sally"); Carrizozo, New Mexico; interviews, correspondence and file materials from Lincoln County Sheriff's office.
O'Toole, John; New York, New York; interview, correspondence and general assistance.
Pablo, Jean; Washington, D.C.; interviews, photographs, file materials and general assistance.
Page, Ray S.; Silver City, New Mexico; interview.
Pankey, Joyce Simmons; Santa Fe, New Mexico; interviews, correspondence, photograph, file materials and general assistance.
Pankey, Reuben; Santa Fe, New Mexico; interview.
Parker, Roy; Hondo Valley, New Mexico; interview.
Paxon, James E. Jr; Truth or Consequences, New Mexico; interview.
Pellegrino, Joseph; Reston, Virginia; interview and general assistance.
Pfingsten, Fred ("Peg"); Capitan, New Mexico; interviews.
Pfingsten, Leota; Capitan, New Mexico; correspondence and file materials.
Phillips, Joe; Tularosa, New Mexico; interview.
Pickens, Homer C.; Albuquerque, New Mexico; interviews, correspondence and his "twenty-pound scrapbook."
Poole, Bob; Grants Pass, Oregon; interviews.
Provine, Angelina; Capitan, New Mexico; interview, correspondence and file materials.
Ragle, Elida; Santa Fe, New Mexico; interview.
Reed, Dr. Theodore H.; Milford, Delaware; interview.
Rossoll, Harry; Atlanta, Georgia; interviews, correspondence, photographs, file materials and general assistance.
Salcido, Proceso; Hondo, New Mexico; interview.
Samson, Jack; Santa Fe, New Mexico; interview.
Satches, Juanita; Albuquerque, New Mexico; interview.
Schoder, Elna; Lakewood, Colorado; interview, correspondence and file materials.
Scott, Lou; Port Ludlow, Washington; interview.
Servis, Sam; Silver City, New Mexico; interviews, correspondence and general assistance.
Simmons, Marcelle; Santa Fe, New Mexico; interviews.
Simmons, William; Santa Fe, New Mexico; file materials.
Smith, Dr. Edwin G.; Santa Fe, New Mexico; interviews, correspondence and file materials.
Smith, Dr. Tom; Santa Fe, New Mexico; interview.
Smith, J. Morgan; Albuquerque, New Mexico; interviews.
Smith, Pearl; Indianapolis, Indiana; interview.
Sorenson, James C.; Conyers, Georgia; interviews, correspondence, file materials and general assistance.
St. John, Chandler P.; Salt Lake City, Utah; interview.
Stow, Betty; Danville, California; interview, correspondence, photographs and file materials.

Sutton, Maud; Alamorgordo, New Mexico; interview.

Taylor, Phoebe; Lincoln, New Mexico; interview.

Taylor, Ray; Lincoln, New Mexico; interview and correspondence.

Thomas, Richard F.; Zehpyr Cove, Nevada; interview and file materials.

Thompson, Cathleen; South Lake Tahoe, California; interview and file materials.

Thurston, Ken; Pebble Beach, California; interview.

Tikkala, William; Springfield, Virginia; interview.

Tipton, Paula Fish; Beggs, Oklahoma; interview.

Vipond, David; Los Angeles, California; interviews and general assistance.

Walter, May; Santa Fe, New Mexico; interviews, correspondence, photographs and file materials.

Wehde, Craig; South Salem, New York; interview.

Wells, Buck; Capitan, New Mexico; general assistance.

Wendelin, Carrol; Arlington, Virginia; interview.

Wendelin, Rudolph A.; Arlington, Virginia; interviews, correspondence, photographs, artwork, file materials, general assistance, cover art and chapter headings art.

West, Terry; Reston, Virginia; interviews, correspondence, photographs, file materials and general assistance.

Whitcamp, Leon; Roswell, New Mexico; interview.

Wicks, Ren; Beverly Hills, California; interviews, correspondance and file materials.

Williams, Chuck; Albuquerque, New Mexico; interview.

INDEX

401

405

ABOUT THE AUTHOR

William Clifford Lawter Jr. was born in Topeka, Kansas. An avid traveler—he has visited 49 states and 53 foreign countries—his interest in Smokey Bear was sparked by a visit to the living symbol's gravesite in Capitan, New Mexico.

A benefits administrator for a large oil company, he holds a Bachelor of Science in Biology from Baker University, Baldwin, Kansas; a J.D. from Washburn University School of Law, Topeka, Kansas; and an LL.M. in Taxation from New York University School of Law in New York City.

A part-time writer, his human-interest articles have been published in magazines and newspapers in twenty states across the nation including *Newsday*, the *Miami Herald*, the *Dallas Morning News* and the *Kansas City Star*.

He and his wife, Susan, live in Ponca City, Oklahoma.